Medicine and Society
in Early Modern Europe

Second Edition

Medicine and Society in Early Modern Europe offers students a concise introduction to health and healing in Europe from 1500 to 1800. Bringing together the best recent research in the field, Mary Lindemann examines medicine from a social and cultural perspective, rather than a narrowly scientific one. Drawing on medical anthropology, sociology, and ethics, as well as cultural and social history, she focuses on the experience of illness and on patients and folk healers as much as on the rise of medical science, doctors, and hospitals. This second edition has been updated and revised throughout in content, style, and interpretations, and new material has been added, in particular, on colonialism, exploration, and women. Accessibly written and full of fascinating insights, this will be essential reading for all students of the history of medicine and will provide invaluable context for students of early modern Europe more generally.

MARY LINDEMANN is Professor of History at the University of Miami. Her publications include *Health and Healing in Eighteenth-Century Germany* (1996), which was awarded the 1998 William Welch Book Medal Prize by the American Association for the History of Medicine.

NEW APPROACHES TO EUROPEAN HISTORY

Series editors

WILLIAM BEIK *Emory University*
T. C. W. BLANNING *Sidney Sussex College, Cambridge*
BRENDAN SIMMS *Peterhouse, Cambridge*

New Approaches to European History is an important textbook series, which provides concise but authoritative surveys of major themes and problems in European history since the Renaissance. Written at a level and length accessible to advanced school students and undergraduates, each book in the series addresses topics or themes that students of European history encounter daily: the series embraces both some of the more "traditional" subjects of study and those cultural and social issues to which increasing numbers of school and college courses are devoted. A particular effort is made to consider the wider international implications of the subject under scrutiny.

To aid the student reader, scholarly apparatus and annotation is light, but each work has full supplementary bibliographies and notes for further reading; where appropriate, chronologies, maps, diagrams, and other illustrative material are also provided.

For a list of titles published in the series, please see the end of the book.

Frontispiece: The doctor's dispensary and the apothecary's shop in seventeenth-century England

Medicine and Society in Early Modern Europe

Second Edition

Mary Lindemann
University of Miami

CAMBRIDGE
UNIVERSITY PRESS

CAMBRIDGE UNIVERSITY PRESS
Cambridge, New York, Melbourne, Madrid, Cape Town, Singapore,
São Paulo, Delhi, Dubai, Tokyo

Cambridge University Press
The Edinburgh Building, Cambridge CB2 8RU, UK

Published in the United States of America by Cambridge University Press,
New York

www.cambridge.org
Information on this title: www.cambridge.org/9780521732567

© Mary Lindemann 2010

First published 2010

Printed in the United Kingdom at the University Press, Cambridge

A catalogue record for this publication is available from the British Library.

Library of Congress Cataloguing in Publication data
Lindemann, Mary.
Medicine and society in early modern Europe / Mary Lindemann. – 2nd ed.
    p.   cm. – (New approaches to European history)
Includes bibliographical references and index.
ISBN 978-0-521-42592-6 (hardback) – ISBN 978-0-521-73256-7 (pbk.)
1. Social medicine – Europe – History.   2. Medicine – Europe – History.
3. Medical care – Europe – History.   4. Public health – Europe – History.
I. Title.   II. Series: New approaches to European history.
[DNLM: 1. History of Medicine – Europe.   2. History, 16th Century –
Europe.   3. History, 17th Century – Europe.   4. History, 18th Century –
Europe.   5. Public Health – history – Europe.   6. Social Medicine – history –
Europe. WZ 70 GA1 L743m 2010]
RA418.3.E85L55   2010
306.4'61094 – dc22   2010006551

ISBN 978-0-521-42592-6 Hardback
ISBN 978-0-521-73256-7 Paperback

For Michael, again and always

Contents

List of figures

All illustrations courtesy of the Wellcome Library, London

List of tables

Acknowledgments

It has been over ten years since the first edition of *Medicine and Society* appeared. Since then, my intellectual and personal debts have accumulated. Once again I must especially thank the Wellcome Trust Centre for the History of Medicine at UCL for making me a Research Affiliate during summer 2008 when I began the process of rewriting. The Centre and the Wellcome Library were exceedingly pleasant places to work and, as always, their staffs were more than helpful. Particular debts of gratitude, however, must be paid to the Director, Hal Cook, and to my two special friends there, Sally Bragg and Tilli Tansey. In addition, a number of members of the Centre and visiting scholars provided intellectual stimulation and companionship: Roger Cooter, Bruce Moran, Constance Berman, Alisha Rankin, and Wendy Churchill. Claudia Stein (University of Warwick) is a good friend and a terrific historian and I have much benefitted from years of conversations with her. A special thank you must go to Rima Apple whose good sense was much appreciated when she reminded me "You don't have to rewrite *every* sentence, you know!" Mary Fissell's work has been particularly influential in these revisions and she will recognize where and how often. Michael Watson at Cambridge University Press was both an encouraging and a patient editor. Finally, and as always, I must thank my spouse, Michael Miller, who has lived with this book now not once but twice.

Introduction

The Kingdom of Naples, 1704. Domenica Jurlaro's mother is very worried. For a long time, her daughter has been suffering "pains in her genitals." Domenica has been treated by the city's physician and bled three times by a surgeon, yet nothing seems to help and her mother's anxiety grows day by day. While washing her clothes by a well, she confides her cares to another woman, Onofria Bufalo. Onofria is more than a mere chance acquaintance; she is a well-known "wise woman" or local healer. She promises a cure and offers her assistance, for a substantial fee. Onofria prepares a medicine sweetened with honey and administers an enema of rue and sage. Alas, Domenica's condition continues to worsen. The distraught mother and daughter now begin to suspect Onofria of having cast a spell on the young woman. They turn to a parish priest and request his blessing to lift or counteract Onofria's evil magic.[1]

This marvelous story, related in greater detail by David Gentilcore, illustrates many aspects of healing in early modern times. Some parts seem familiar to us, or appear nothing out of the ordinary. A woman suffering from a distressing complaint consults a physician (or her mother does). But then the story becomes more textured, mixing what seems commonplace (distress at the failure of a treatment to work, a search for another "opinion") with what seems considerably stranger (the decision to consult a wise woman met by chance and asking a priest to lift a curse). Yet none of this would have appeared anything out of the ordinary in early modern Europe. The temporal proximity of a succession of healers – a physician, a surgeon, a wise woman, and a priest – characterizes the range of medical choices available to early modern people.

Domenica's story was not "typical"; but it does illustrate how much has changed since then. What we today view mostly as different realms, such as medicine and religion, or how we distinguish between popular ("superstitious") and academic ("scientific") medicines, licensed and "illicit" medicines then interacted, entwined, and caused thereby no

[1] David Gentilcore, *Healers and Healing in Early Modern Italy* (Manchester, 1998), 1–2.

1

cognitive discomfort. To a large extent, these seeming polarities were by no means separate, or separated, in the minds of those seeking alleviation of their ills and cure of their ailments. In this world, legitimate medical practitioners and legitimate medicine nested in many places. Religious cures (relics, supplications to saints, blessings, and exorcisms) and the use of supernatural or folk remedies were not regarded as "alternative" forms of healing, but ran concurrently with all other sorts of medical practice. They were, moreover, not "second-best" cures, sought out only in desperation or by the ignorant and impoverished. They were the everyday face of medicine and medical practice. The wealthy Cologne city councilor Hermann Weinsberg used surgeons, empirics, and wise women and the Reverend Ralph Josselin chose a variety of healers for himself and his household, although he rarely consulted a physician. Astrological cures enjoyed immense popularity in court circles but also among the local gentry, landowners, artisans, and tradespeople in the rural parish of Great Linford, Buckinghamshire. Folk healers everywhere did a brisk trade in herbal concoctions, amulets, and common remedies such as poultices and salves.

The story that Gentilcore used to introduce his book on healing in early modern Italy also provides an excellent introduction to how medical history has come to be written over the last thirty years. Since the 1970s, it has been deeply influenced by social history and several other disciplines, especially anthropology, and more recently by the perspectives of the new cultural history and gender studies. This work reveals medicine and healing as fully imbricated in the larger contexts of the early modern world. Thus, in order to understand medicine, to comprehend healing, and to perceive what people thought about health, we must deeply immerse ourselves in the contexts of their lives. While one might want to regard the healing described above as a pattern, not everyone made the same choices as Domenica, Weinsberg, or Josselin did. Nor were the possibilities of what one might choose the same; temporal and local differences accounted for much variation.

These factors condition how this book is written and what choices were made. Two points deserve emphasis. First, this volume weights equally the two halves of its title: medicine and society. The primary goal has been to reflect the ways in which medical history has become part of a broader historical mainstream. Mainstreaming takes a historical subspeciality, like the history of medicine, lifts it out of the confining limits of a disciplinary channel and refloats it in broader historical currents. But this endeavor should not suggest that medical history is enriched merely by being contextualized. Influences flow in both directions and medical history forms an integral part of bigger histories and, perhaps even more critically, understanding medical history is essential for anyone interested in gaining a sophisticated and deep comprehension of the early modern world more generally. No longer, therefore, is it sufficient to write medical history as an epic or romantic story of spectacular breakthroughs and embattled pioneers. Medical history must rather account for all the greater social, cultural, and economic forces affecting Europeans from roughly 1500 to 1800.

The approach taken here is deliberately historiographic and argumentative. *Medicine and Society* resolutely rejects, and rejects telling, a story of progress. Instead, it presents interpretations up front and deals with scholarly controversies head on: this is the true "stuff" of history, not facts *per se* nor, for that matter, polemic. Good history never merely praises or blames. Thus, this volume sedulously avoids a version of history that postulates a single and relatively straightforward passage into the modern world leading from the dark ages of ignorance, superstition, and suffering into a brighter world of knowledge, science, and abundance. This "things-are-getting-better-all-the-time" school has been rightly condemned for its hindsight, although it would be equally foolish for us to deny the undoubted benefits of modern medicine (if we also recognize its failings).

Finally, this history reflects the revisionist stance of much medical historical writing over the last few decades. To track the variations in how medical history was written in the middle of the twentieth century to how it is written now, more than fifty years later, is to trace a major evolution. Domenica's story might have once been used to illustrate ignorance and superstition or as an example of the stubborn persistence of religious over secular or scientific explanations. Today, medical historians would take the story on its own terms, seeking to comprehend why certain decisions were made and explain what the participants in these medical encounters hoped to achieve. Yet although this "new" history of medicine differs from its older sibling in several ways and we, its practitioners, tend to assume its superiority, it is prudent to bear in mind that each age remains a prisoner of its own prejudices. If twenty-first-century scholars are less willing to accept uncritically an explanation for change based on a march-of-progress analysis, perhaps our successors will find our certainties equally dubious.

How then have historians transformed the writing of the history over the past forty to fifty years? Predictably, the influences did not always come from within the historical profession or medicine alone.[2] For a

---

[2] For some perspectives on the history of medical history, see John C. Burnham, *What is Medical History?* (Cambridge, 2005); Burnham, *How the Idea of Profession Changed*

long time, one might have termed the history of medicine *iatrocentric*. That is, physicians (*iatro-* pertains to medicine) wrote medical history as a hobby and followed well-trodden paths, concentrating on biographies, bibliographies, medical theory, and the practice of physicians. These histories were essentially what is often called *internalist*. At its worst, such writing produced exultant chronicles of medical progress, equally celebratory or even hagiographic biographies of famous medical men, and sneering condemnations of superstition and ignorance. Yet not all this history was bad; far from it. Many early studies were carefully done and meticulously researched. Moreover, they amassed a store of knowledge upon which we all still draw. Nor did all those laboring in medical history's old regime satisfy themselves with a rosy view of the present compared to a ghastly past.

Still, one can chart a sea-change beginning in the 1960s and 1970s that, not surprisingly, linked up with the tumultuous character of those decades in the western world, when much received wisdom and many venerable institutions attracted withering criticism. Those who wanted to change the world often also harnessed history to the wagon of social and political justice. New ideas as well as fresh faces entered the field and eventually reoriented it. George Rosen (an MD and a PhD) bridged the two eras. As early as the late 1940s, he began to think along new lines. In his 1967 presidential address to the annual meeting of the American Association for the History of Medicine, Rosen called upon scholars to redefine the "matter and manner of medical history." He proposed an agenda for research into the social context of medicine, into demography, into the history of emotions, and into responses to disease. Above all, he insisted that "the patient deserves a more prominent place in the history of medicine."[3] Rosen was not solely responsible for the shifts that came, of course, but his program traced out the direction in which it went.

More radical questioning attacked several pillars of modern society including science and medicine, as well as criticizing the prevalent sexism and racism of western life. Disenchantment with mid- to late twentieth-century health care profoundly affected the course of medical history. Critics of modern, technocratic medicine assailed the prerogatives of a professional, authority-claiming medical elite and likewise abhorred the

---

the *Writing of Medical History* (London, 1998); Roger Cooter, "After Death/After-'Life': The Social History of Medicine in Post-Modernity," *Social History of Medicine* 20 (2007): 441–64.

[3] George Rosen, "Levels of Integration in Medical Historiography," *Journal of the History of Medicine and Allied Sciences* (1949): 460–67; Rosen, "People, Disease, and Emotion: Some Newer Problems for Research in Medical History," *Bulletin of the History of Medicine* 41 (1967): 8.

dehumanized, and dehumanizing, authority of modern medical treatment and hospital care. As early as 1963, Ivan Illich (1926–2002) stressed
the *Limits to Medicine*. Other observers, such as the physician and eminent
sociologist, Thomas McKeown (1912–88), argued that improvements
in nutrition, rather than advances in medical science or public health,
best account for the general decline of western mortality rates since the
eighteenth century. Others suggested that people learned methods of
avoiding disease in a world where medicine had few if any cures. Doubts
about modern medicine multiplied, and many deplored the manipulative
character of a medicine physicians dominated. Psychiatry often bore the
brunt of such assaults. Thomas Szasz (b. 1920), for one, launched bitter
jeremiads against the abuses of modern psychiatry and psychiatric institutions, arguing that the diagnosis of "mental illness" was just another
way of imposing a bourgeois mentality and code of behavior on people
viewed as "deviants." The French philosopher Michel Foucault (1926–
84) battled on a broader front, presenting a basically pessimistic view of
several changes occurring in the eighteenth century that were often associated with the Enlightenment and billed as "humanitarian reforms,"
including the abolition of torture and corporal punishments. Foucault
insisted, however, that these "improvements" significantly increased
surveillance over individuals, limited their freedoms, and vastly increased
the power of regulatory mechanisms (such as the state). The "birth of the
clinic" – the rise of scientific medicine around 1800 – was one of these
pseudo-reforms.[4]

A whole generation or more of medical historians have pursued these
insights, often with excellent results. If many historians of medicine were
not quite as censorious, or polemical, as the culture critics, they certainly
doubted facile stories of scientific progress and of the "great men in
white" narrative presented earlier. They increasingly focused, moreover,
on persons and practices that older medical historiography had slighted
or scorned. In the closing decades of the twentieth century, feminist
historians, post-colonialist scholars, medical anthropologists, and queer
theorists contributed their own perspectives fructifying the field by urg-
ing historians to look again at what they "knew" about the medical past.

---

[4] Ivan Illich, *Limits to Medicine: The Expropriation of Health* (Hammondsworth, 1977);
Thomas McKeown, *The Role of Medicine: Dream, Mirage, or Nemesis?* (Princeton, N.J.,
1979); McKeown, *The Modern Rise of Population* (London, 1976); James C. Riley, *The
Eighteenth-Century Campaign to Avoid Disease* (New York, 1987); Thomas S. Szasz, *The
Myth of Mental Illness: Foundations of a Theory of Personal Conduct* (London, 1972); Szasz,
The Manufacture of Madness (New York, 1970); Michel Foucault, *Discipline and Punish:
The Birth of the Prison* (New York, 1977); Foucault, *The Birth of the Clinic: An Archaeology
of Medical Perception* (New York, 1973).

The study of women in medicine, the non-European medical experience, questions of deviance, the relationship of broader belief systems (such as religion) to medicine, and the activities of folk healers all dramatically expanded the historian's purview. Scholars began situating European experiences within global or transnational frameworks and have simultaneously eschewed a tendency to speak only in terms of the European "impact" on the rest of the world.

Still, and despite the undeniable influence of these newer perspectives, I think it is fair to say that in many ways social history (and increasingly cultural history) and professional historians continue to dominate the field, albeit with an ever-greater openness to the perspectives of other disciplines. These perspectives have won recognition in the major scholarly journals devoted to the field. (For a list of the major medical historical journals, see the list of Further reading at the end of this book.)

Despite this expansion of the field in many directions at once, some empty spots remain as well as a series of desiderata. Much medical history remains focused on the western European and, especially, the English past. That blinkeredness has diminished considerably over the last twenty years, but the tyranny of Anglo-Saxon models that once forced questionable comparisons to a paradigmatic England remain. Admittedly, for certain periods, the focus always lay elsewhere; on Italy, for instance, in discussing anatomy or early public health measures, or on Germany for the development of a more intense relationship between state and medical care, or on France for the genesis of clinical medicine. At the beginning of the twenty-first century, we find more studies of developments elsewhere in western Europe, including considerable work on the Iberian peninsula and the Scandinavian countries. Patchier remains the treatment of eastern and southern Europe, Russia, and the Ottoman world; the last, after all, controlled large parts of European lands well into the nineteenth or even twentieth century. We are still, moreover, afflicted by a western-oriented, rather traditional periodization, although newer scholarly work seeks to erase or at least blur the boundaries and deny the ruptures between the medieval, early modern, and modern worlds. This book, on "early modern Europe," pleads guilty to sustaining the artificiality of such a division at least in part, although it emphasizes many continuities between the medieval and early modern experiences on one end and, if to a lesser degree, the early modern and modern on the other. Moreover, even the "new" history of medicine is rather Eurocentric not only in its location but also in the questions it poses. Africa, Latin America, and Asia remain relatively neglected, but these areas are no longer ignored. Indeed, historians increasingly realize that the newfound lands and, later, colonies significantly shaped life in the mother country. Extremely good work on Islamic, Arabic, and Jewish medicine exists and a growing number of scholars focus on China, Japan, and India. Chronologically, coverage has concentrated on the nineteenth and twentieth centuries, reflecting a broader historical favoritism for the modern period more generally. Much of what we know about early modern Europe would never have been discovered or would have been misunderstood without the excellent work being done by the medievalists and, increasingly, by classical scholars as well.

In composing the present volume, some basic organizational and conceptual problems had to be addressed. Unquestionably the subject was "medicine," but the text was also intended to appeal to those interested in early modern history more generally. But the most basic, and basically intractable, problem was how to define "medicine" in a work that explicitly accepts that medicine by no means exists isolated from the multiple contexts in which it is embedded and which powerfully affect it. Part of the problem, therefore, lay in establishing borders and deciding what to include and what to leave out of a subject with myriad ties to other disciplines and subjects. How can, for instance, a history of medicine not deal with famine and poverty and yet also not go astray in the territory of the demographers and family historians? The solution followed in these pages has not been a very rigorous one. Like many of my historical colleagues, I have not hesitated to trespass on the "turf" of other scholars. Indeed, I have done so frequently because such encroachment seems a splendid and appropriate way to demonstrate the centrality of medicine to larger themes in European history. Likewise, I have stretched the prescribed chronological limits especially in my decision to say quite a bit about ancient and medieval developments.

A strong accent on social and cultural history characterizes *Medicine and Society*, not only because those are the fields in which I feel most comfortable, but also because that orientation reflects much of the historical work being done today. (And, even though some observers have announced the death, or at least the increasing analytic irrelevance of the social history of medicine in the wake of post-modernism, the corpse seems to have quite a bit of life still in it.)[5] These preferences, however, in no way dictate the slighting of other subjects such as medical theory and medical education. Still, the book pursues themes that most frequently attract medical historians today and which are found in many popular medical historical textbooks (see Further reading); these topics often differ from the concerns of more traditional surveys. This volume, therefore, devotes as much attention to patients as practitioners; to

---

[5] Cooter, "After Death/After-'Life'."

"general" practitioners as to physicians; to all forms of medical education and not just university instruction; to the importance of other systems, such as religion and its impact on medicine; and, finally, to the cultural and societal significance of medicine as well as to its scientific development.

A critical sub-problem in this complex of issues is how to define and understand disease. Perhaps surprisingly, disease is a very slippery concept; "feeling ill" is not equal to "having a disease" as personal experience often testifies. One can take an essentially positivist approach and argue, along with the *Oxford Concise Medical Dictionary*, that "disease is a disorder with a specific cause and recognizable signs and symptoms." That seems clear enough until we start to think about afflictions that have no discernible cause and the signs and symptoms of which fluctuate, sometimes radically. Contemporary physicians often diagnose chronic fatigue syndrome, for example, as a "real disease" (*myalgic encephalomyelitis*) and sometimes dismiss it as "yuppie flu." On the other side, even though the origins of alcoholism, obesity, hysteria, and autism remained unclear, they are increasingly labeled as "diseases" or spoken of as occurring "epidemically" as, for instance, in describing the spread of obesity in early twenty-first-century America as an "epidemic." Clearly one cannot deny that these diseases are to a large extent *socially constructed*; that is, their explanations, indeed their very reality and existence, shift with changing social and cultural expectations. A classic example is the disappearance in 1974 of homosexuality as a "disease" from the *Diagnostic and Statistical Manual of Mental Disorders* (DSM-II) after being accepted as a "disease entity" earlier. Thus, " 'disease' is an elusive entity." It is more (or perhaps less?) than a biological thing and "in some ways disease does not exist until we have agreed that it does, by perceiving, naming, and responding to it."[6]

Much recommends the view that disease is itself a historical construction; protean not fixed, and respondent to social forces and human perceptions. Most historians nowadays certainly accept that knowledge is relative: what people "knew" in the past was "true" whether we believe it or not now. Whereas we might search for the "germ" that causes syphilis, people of the sixteenth century constructed a disease in their minds and from their experiences that they recognized and perceived as the "Great Pox" or the "French Disease." Obviously, early modern peoples held attitudes toward, and drew meanings from, various afflictions, or the

---

[6] Charles E. Rosenberg, "Framing Disease: Illness, Society, and History," in Rosenberg and Janet Golden, eds., *Framing Disease: Studies in Cultural History* (New Brunswick, N.J., 1997), xiii–xv.

experience of illness altogether, that differ from ours. We shun pain, for instance, while early modern people could find meaning in it as a mark of God's favor or his displeasure. This divergent awareness, however, did not make them less intelligent or less perceptive than we are.

Yet, not everything is socially or culturally constructed and it is hard to accept a radical version that "reality does not exist"; that it is merely constructed. Much value adheres to Margaret Pelling's hard-headed observation that the social construction of disease "cannot be applied universally ... [because] some diseases are more socially constructed than others." Pelling quite astutely points out that social constructivism when carried to an extreme actually hinders a subtle understanding of others by suggesting that only people in their own time and place can have accurate perceptions of "their" illnesses.[7] This book, while avoiding a Whiggish, positivist stance that elevates current views over previous wisdom and ways of knowing, also accepts that "real things exist" and that we occasionally share the perceptions of our ancestors. Smallpox is a good case in point. Early modern peoples sometimes misdiagnosed smallpox but they generally understood it (and plague as well) as a specific disease spread by what we would term "contagion," that is, person-to-person contact. Thus, Chapter 2 speaks rather confidently of the "diseases" of smallpox and plague while it also warns of the dangers of confidently diagnosing diseases in the past – *retrospective* or *retrodiagnosis* – as if we possess some superior insight. Medical historians are divided on this issue, admittedly, so a middle path seems to reflect current approaches most accurately.

Medicine and Society concentrates on the three centuries between 1500 and 1800. The general layout is topical; each chapter addresses a group of related issues. Within chapters, chronological confines exhibit considerable elasticity. It is, for instance, absurd to discuss the early modern experience of pestilence without beginning in the mid fourteenth century. This temporal pliancy holds true for other subjects, especially for public health, medical education, and hospitals, where I pick up the story in the middle ages.

No volume of this size (or any other, for that matter) can be comprehensive or fully reflect the richness and texture of medical history. Descriptive deficiencies or analytical weaknesses generally reflect lacunae in research. Geographically, the book tries to be as evenhanded as possible, but the secondary literature available is simply more voluminous for certain periods, topics, and approaches than others. Many gaps

---

[7] Margaret Pelling, *The Common Lot: Sickness, Medical Occupations and the Urban Poor in Early Modern England* (London and New York, 1998), 6–7.

cannot be closed here, but a sincere effort is made to indicate them and suggest why they exist.

Note on the second edition

Ten years have elapsed since the first edition of *Medicine and Society* appeared. This second edition takes into account the literature published since then. I have also tried to respond to the criticisms raised by friendly commentators who suggested more coverage of certain topics or a different emphasis. I will not have, I am sure, satisfied all of them, but I have appreciated their points of view. Some chapters have been significantly rewritten and reorganized as well as expanded to devote additional coverage to topics, such as the colonial experience, that the original volume touched on only briefly. In the first edition, I tried to maintain a generally historiographical approach, emphasizing how arguments evolve, where debate lies, how opinions change, interpretations are revised, and, especially, how new perspectives influence the writing of history. I have preserved and, I hope, even enhanced that approach by directing the reader's attention to why and how historians differ and by insisting that such divergence of thought is altogether a good thing and productive of good history. Finally, the rewriting of this book has been intensely influenced by my experiences teaching "Medicine and Society" at the University of Miami. The explanations I present here are often ones I developed in teaching that course and that I found worked well with students at the undergraduate and graduate levels.

1   Sickness and health

Definition of "health" by the World Health Organization (WHO): "complete physical, mental, and social well-being and not merely the absence of disease and infirmity."[1]

[My father was] of a sanguine complexion, mix'd with a dash of choler... He was for his life so exact and temperate, that I have heard he had never in all his life been surprised by excess, being ascetic and sparing.[2]

Of each 1,000 people born, 24 die during birth itself; the business of teething disposes of another 50; in the first two years, convulsions and other illness remove another 277; smallpox... carries off another 80 or 90, and measles 10 more. Among women, about 8 perish in childbed. Inflammatory fevers cause another 150 [deaths]. Apoplexy [kills] 12, dropsy 41. Therefore, of each 1,000 born, one can expect that only 78 will die of old age, or die in old age... It is apparent enough that at least nine-tenths [of humanity] die before their time and by chance.[3]

Understanding sickness and health

Sickness and health may appear to be universal concepts, but perhaps no two terms are more difficult to grasp. The definition WHO chose for its 1946 constitution remains an unattainable goal for many people even in the most prosperous countries of the contemporary world. Certainly, such an interpretation would have perplexed early modern people whose lives were repeatedly blighted by disease, ill health, and accidents.

[1] "Constitution of the World Health Organization," *Chronicle of the World Health Organization* 1, nos. 1–2 (October 1946), quoted in Margaret Mead, ed., *Cultural Patterns and Technical Change: A Manual Prepared by the World Federation for Mental Health* (Deventer, 1953), 28.

[2] John Evelyn, quoted in Lucinda McCray Beier, *Sufferers and Healers: The Experience of Illness in Seventeenth-Century England* (London, 1987), 163.

[3] Christoph Wilhelm Hufeland, *Die Kunst des menschlichen Lebens zu verlängern* (Jena, 1797), 365–66.

Common usage tends to conflate the terms *disease* and *illness* or employs them synonymously. At least at the outset of this book, however, we should take care to differentiate between the two. One way of thinking about disease and illness is to deem both of them medical facts and ahistorical realities; that is, as having real existences and real causes (either somatic or psychological). Accordingly, one would say: "The microorganism *Yersinia pestis* causes plague." Scholars who stress the central importance of history and culture in shaping perceptions of bodies and bodily states, including disease and illness, would, however, raise strong objections. They focus instead on how social and cultural milieus determined the language used to describe illness; how different groups (elites and peasants or men and women) held disparate notions of disease and how they developed different strategies for coping with illness; and how bodies functioned as signs, symbols, and metaphors.

These varied approaches are linked to two major theoretical perspectives on disease: the *ontological* and the *functional* (or *holistic*). The ontological view regards each disease as an independently existing entity. This model carries major implications for therapy because it suggests that diseases are identical in all sufferers and that, therefore, the same methods of treatment work in all cases. The functionalist approach, however, sees disease as extant only within a specific organism. Disease results, therefore, from a dysfunction that may be attributed to an individual's personal bodily constitution or habits or to environmental effects on him or her.

The ontological view of disease gained particular favor from about the middle of the nineteenth century. Several factors contributed to its rise. Discoveries in bacteriology identified specific *pathogens*, or microorganisms, as causing particular diseases such as cholera and anthrax. Beginning with the discovery of antitoxins and serum therapy in the late nineteenth century, immunizations for diphtheria (first used in 1891) and, later, polio (Salk vaccine, 1952; Sabin oral vaccine, 1962) offered hope for the prevention and cure of diseases people once regarded with great fear and viewed as intractable. First antiseptic, then aseptic, methods in surgery began to eliminate the dangers of massive infection and deaths plummeted. In the twentieth century, the development of sulfa drugs and antibiotics seemed to offer "magic bullets" able to strike disease-causing microorganisms dead. Such successes, when combined with broader public health and educative initiatives, had a significant effect on the mortality from epidemic and infectious diseases and considerably augmented the social and cultural status of physicians, scientific medicine, and public health. Yet for thousands of years before then, functionalism dominated lay and academic medicine alike. Healers selected treatments for individuals and applied therapies gauged to restore the proper working of the organism as a whole.

The Hippocratic/Galenic tradition, dating from the works of the Hippocratic authors[4] (Hippocrates lived from c.460 to c.370 BCE) as glossed by Galen of Pergamun (129–c.199 or 216 CE), remained influential throughout the middle ages and well into the eighteenth century. This corpus of ideas tied disease to the environment (a famous Hippocratic writing addressed *Airs, Waters, and Places*) but also incorporated concepts of pollution and impurity in explaining disease causation or *etiology*. In distinction to earlier forms of medical thought, the Hippocratic writers rejected many magical or demonic causes of diseases. At least until the seventeenth century, and probably much later, a mixture of *environmentalism* and *humoralism* dominated interpretations of disease. For most people, lay and learned alike, health rested in the proper balance of the four *humors* – black bile, yellow (or red) bile, blood, and phlegm – and disease arose from humoral imbalance, that is, from a general state of disequilibrium that the environment could affect or influence. Thus, in Galenic and Hippocratic medicine, diseases were unique to individuals and *specific diseases* or *disease entities* as we normally speak of them (for example, influenza, bubonic plague, or AIDS) were unknown. Attaining and preserving a state of health, therefore, required constant attention to prevent an elusive and easily lost humoral equilibrium. Changes in the environment broadly conceived – a condition of the air or water, an especially hot or wet summer, or an unfavorable conjunction of the planets, for instance – could upset the body's internal hydraulics with pernicious results.

The Hippocratic/Galenic tradition, moreover, postulated a continuum between health and illness and located each individual somewhere on that band. Health proved, in fact, "an unattainable ideal" and most people hung "forever suspended between health and illness."[5] The presence of too much of one humor, or too little of another, could cause disease, as could the corruption or putrefaction of one or another. Any alteration in the nature of a humor or the relationship between humors spelled danger for the individual. Even minor oscillations had to be dealt with expeditiously to avert illness.

---

[4] One speaks today of the "Hippocratic corpus" rather than the writings of Hippocrates. It contains about seventy works that were probably produced by him, his students, and disciples. The collection contains a variety of writings, geared to appeal to several audiences and does not comprise an organized or comprehensive system.

[5] Georg Hildebrandt, *Taschenbuch für die Gesundheit auf das Jahr 1801* (Erlangen, 1801), preface.

Standard therapies and preventives depended on readjusting perceived imbalances by siphoning off a humor that had either grown too strong or become corrupt. The practical means of doing so were bleeding, purging, vomiting, or opening lesions in the skin to allow proper drainage. Signs, which we would call *symptoms*, indicated the body's own attempts to reestablish equilibrium. The eighteenth-century Swiss physician Samuel Tissot (1728–97) advised that there was no reason to worry about a slight looseness of the bowels or even diarrhea. This was the body's own mechanism for cleansing the whole system by "carry[ing] off a heap of matter that may have been long amassed and then putrefied in the body [and] which, if not discharged, might have produced some distemper." It made sense, therefore, to support and encourage the body's own actions. Thus, when in February 1686 Richard Salter's wife was "pained in her stomack... [and] very loose and hath bin soe sins the beginning of her sickness," John Westover, surgeon of Wedmore, England, "[s]ent her a purge of Rubarb" in hopes of further expediting the elimination of the toxic humor.[6]

In humoral medicine prevention (or *prophylaxis*) assumed as much importance as treatment (or *therapeutics*). The most reliable method of preserving health was to practice moderation in all things, especially in the use of the *six nonnaturals*: (1) air; (2) sleep and waking; (3) food and drink; (4) rest and exercise; (5) excretion and retention; and (6) the passions (including sex) and emotions. A healthy way of life (a *regimen*) depended on observing these rules of nature and avoiding exhaustion, overeating, excessive consumption of spirits, immoderate desires or unnatural appetites, including sexual excesses. Such ideas were widely accepted and informed not only medical theories but more popular conceptions of health and illness as well.

Linked ideas of equilibrium as health, disequilibrium as illness, and the individual character of each person's affliction did not alone shape people's perceptions of health and illness.

In the ancient world combinations of religion and medicine were virtually ubiquitous. The Greeks and Romans, as well as the peoples of the Near Eastern civilizations, believed that the gods could cause and cure disease. Before the middle of the fourth century BCE, Greek medicine knew few divisions between magic and medicine. Thereafter, however, religious or magical healers were increasingly marginalized. Yet, "[w]here

---

[6] Samuel August Tissot, *Advice to the People in General with Regard to Their Health*, trans. by J. Kirkpatrick (Boston, 1767), 104; William G. Hall, ed., *The Journal of John Westover of Wedmore, Surgeon 1686–1703* (typescript, December 1992), 1.

the line was to be drawn still differed from individual to individual."[7] This observation remained valid for long after the ancient world disappeared.

Throughout the medieval and early modern periods, religion played a large role in healing and continues to do so today. Most scholars have generally agreed in regarding Christianity as a healing cult and have also suggested that Christians tended to reject physicians in favor of miraculous healing. Recent scholarship, however, questions this view, arguing that early Christians were as much heirs to the cultural norms of the ancient world as their pagan contemporaries. They, too, prized physicians rather than turning their backs on them or denigrating their efforts. Certainly, it seems that most Christians, lay and clerical, viewed health as preferable to illness and accepted natural means of healing, but also believed that illness could be spiritually beneficial. Far fewer found sickness and suffering absolute goods. Many turned to divine healing in the forms of the laying on of hands, anointing with holy oil, or using the Eucharist. While virtually everyone valued the use of prayer in illness as a way to acquire providential intercession and for comfort, few refused the aid of secular healers. The idea that individual sin caused illness was not as common as one might suppose. People directly associated only a handful of diseases – leprosy was one – with individual moral flaws. Collective sin and moral decay, however, were often thought to occasion epidemics.[8]

Belief in the magical or supernatural causes of some illness was also widespread. But, once again, people did not automatically attribute every disease, affliction, or accident to spells, witchcraft, or the wrathful hand of God. Sudden, inexplicable diseases were most often thought to require magical or supernatural intervention. In these cases, sufferers and their families turned to priests and ministers for help, but also consulted cunning-folk whose white magic (that is, beneficent magic compared to the black or maleficent magic of witches, demons, and devils) could break spells or cast out demons. Few relied on either secular or spiritual healing exclusively; most people used several cures or forms of medicine concurrently or sequentially.

In effect, then, the naturalistic explanations of the Hippocratic and Galenic traditions competed and combined with religious and magical ones. Thus, while communities cast out lepers and quarantined plague patients, they simultaneously sought expiation of sins and did penance. In

---

[7] Vivian Nutton, *Ancient Medicine* (London and New York, 2004), 113.

[8] Gary B. Ferngren has mounted a significant challenge to the idea that "religious healing was normative among Christians in the New Testament" and the first two centuries CE. *Medicine and Health Care in Early Christianity* (Baltimore, 2009), 1, 140–52.

the sixteenth century, the Swiss physician Theophrastus Phillipus Bombastus von Hohenheim (or, as he is better known, Paracelsus, c.1493–1541) broke with the humoral tradition. He believed disease was caused by an entity – the *archeus* – that invaded the human body. Indeed, since classical times, arrows loosed by the gods symbolized the external cause of disease, as Apollo's shafts slew Niobe's children. Paracelsus strongly felt the influence of Luther and other Reformers and wanted to build a Christian medicine; he rejected Galenism as a pagan teaching. He likewise conceived of disease in spiritual terms and as entities (Paracelsus will be discussed more fully in Chapter 3). For Paracelsus, then, as later for Joan Baptista van Helmont (1577–1644) and Thomas Sydenham (1624–89), diseases became specific and the diseased state qualitatively differed from the healthy one.

What interests us here is the currency of all these notions. How did people regard disease (or illness) and health? To what extent did popular and academic ideas on such crucial human conditions complement each other or conflict? Scholars once confidently identified obvious contrasts between lay and academic conceptions of health and illness. Historians of medicine frequently referred slightingly to "popular errors" and superstitions, and constructed a teleological epic based on the march of scientific progress. This interpretation underpinned the equally accepted dichotomy between competent medical men, on the one hand, and pernicious "quacks" and "charlatans," on the other. By the 1970s, however, things were changing. Some observers now criticized modern medicine and stressed its *iatrogenic* character, that is, the tendency of medicine and physicians themselves to cause diseases. Many scholars rejected older interpretations about the history of medicine that focused on inevitable improvements and praised far-sighted scientific and medical giants. As a result, studies of nonelite forms of medical practice and of nonprofessional or nonacademic healers proliferated. Medical historians began to take seriously a whole range of practitioners and practices existing outside and alongside official medicine. New analytical terms arose to express these differences, such as "elite/popular," "orthodox/unorthodox," "academic/lay" medicines, practices, and personnel. Gradually, however, it became clear that the dichotomies themselves were flawed and that the overlap of "popular" and "elite" – or rather the presence of a broad substratum of common beliefs about health, illness, and therapeutics that most members of the society shared – best characterized early modern medicine. This perception informs the following discussions of sickness and health. It does not imply, however, that no conflict and no diversity existed within the world of early modern medicine (conflict was endemic and often bitter). Postulating a sharp division between popular and elite medicines, however, fails to capture the medical reality of early modern Europe. Both the lay and the learned worlds shared medical practices and concepts and accepted roughly similar views on how bodies functioned.

Experiencing the body

The science of human physiology concerns itself with the functions of the human organism and its parts. In this section, however, we will not focus on early modern physiological theories (see Chapter 3), but rather explore common patterns of belief concerning how bodies worked or failed to do so. This orientation aligns with what has over the past two decades come to be known as the "history of the body," itself closely allied to new cultural history, gender history, feminist studies, and queer theory. Scholars writing in these traditions have stressed that even what seems most *essential* (that is, unchanging and thus unaffected by history) such as sex attribution and the very fabric of the human body are, however, not immutable but historically constructed. Thus, they argue that, for example, "sex" is the product of particular times and places and that difficulties arise even in classifying people exclusively as male or female. While such perspectives obviously draw on current political agendas (such as identity politics), they nonetheless usefully sensitize us to appreciating the very different ways in which people in other cultures and earlier times thought about bodies. What is true about sex and gender is equally true about race. Moreover, not everyone experiences physicality similarly. Men and women, as well as social and ethnic groups, hold disparate attitudes; indeed, they actually experience flesh differently.

Most early modern people accepted several basic concepts about bodies, even if they did not always articulate their ideas systematically. First, the old notions of the *naturals* (including the complexions and the humors), the nonnaturals (discussed above, see p. 14), and the *contranaturals* (or diseases) prevailed almost universally. Most people understood the body as composed of a mixture of the four humors. The four ancient *elements* – water, earth, fire, and air – comprised the humors. Humors themselves had *qualities*: phlegm was cold and wet; black bile, cold and dry; blood, hot and wet; and yellow bile, hot and dry. Each individual possessed a *complexion* or *temperament* (Figure 1.1) that reflected a unique blend of qualities and that also varied according to age and sex. The young tended to be hotter and moister than the aged, who were dryer and colder. Men, as a rule, were hot and dry, while women inclined to be colder and moister. In addition, each part of the body had its peculiar quality; the heart was hot and the brain was cold. Later, when Europeans

1.1 Figures representing the four temperaments and four elements, c.1610

began to encounter other races, they worked them, too, into the existing humoral frameworks. Although Europeans generally thought women colder than men, they perceived African women as "hot constitution'd Ladies."[9]

Thus, the humors played a central role in early modern conceptions of the structure and function of the body. The human body was held to be a seething mass of fluids rather than the assemblage of discrete organs or systems (the digestive system or the excretory system, for example) as we today understand it to be. Even in the seventeenth century, as

[9] Quoted in Winthrop D. Jordan, *White Over Black: American Attitudes Toward the Negro* (Chapel Hill, N.C., 1968), 35.

ideas of the body as a machine or as a chemical distillery – *iatromechanics* and *iatrochemistry* – became more popular, older humoral physiologies and pathologies endured, especially in everyday life. People routinely spoke of humoral relationships and accepted an intimate bond between humors and temperaments. The sixteenth-century clerk Barthomäii Sastrowen remembered that his father "was rather rash" and "when the *colera* [yellow bile] got the upper hand, he could not control himself." The eighteenth-century legal scholar and publicist Johann Jakob Moser (1701–85) described his own temperament as one in which "the choleric was strongly in the ascendant," although, in his case, mixed with the sanguine. When Moser surveyed the traits of the choleric personality, he listed, among others, impatience, suspiciousness, quickness to anger, garrulity, glory-seeking, and furtiveness; in short, a person possessing both a "subtle understanding" and a tendency toward reckless and quixotic actions.[10]

The humors exhibited their own distinguishing characteristics and a preponderance of one or another fixed a person's physical and mental make-up. Phlegm was a white, clear humor and individuals with an overabundance of it tended to exhibit dull, phlegmatic temperaments. Yellow bile was produced in the liver and stored in the gall bladder; an excess resulted in a bilious and quarrelsome nature. Black bile was associated with the spleen and determined the gloomy melancholic personality. In fact, spleen was an early modern synonym for melancholy and the phrase "to vent one's spleen" indicated ill temper. Blood governed the sanguine temperament and ranked as the most necessary and elevated humor, the noblest one, so to speak. Blood was the vital juice of life and played fundamental, if poorly understood, roles in the utilization of nourishment and in reproduction. Semen as well as milk derived from blood.

The fluid humoral system underlay ideas of conception and gestation as well. Two classical theories of reproduction – the Aristotelian and the Hippocratic/Galenic – continued to mold how learned people reasoned about sexuality and reproduction in the early modern world. Aristotle believed that men and women both produced what he called *sperma*. In men, sperma was seed and, in women, menstrual blood. Women lacked seed because their quality of coldness did not permit them to generate enough warmth to excite germination. Moreover, male sperma was active, while female sperma was passive. At conception, male sperma animated menstrual blood to produce life. More influential than the

---

[10] *Deutsche Selbstzeugnisse*, Vol. V, *Aus dem Zeitalter der Reformation and der Gegenreformation* (Leipzig, 1931), 19, and Vol. VII, *Pietismus und Rationalismus* (Leipzig, 1933), 227.

Aristotelian tradition, however, was the Hippocratic/Galenic theory in which both sexes contributed in equal measure to conception. The sexes complemented one another; both produced seed. This two-seed or *semence* theory lingered through the eighteenth century. The two sexes were anatomically parallel as well in that male organs (such as testes and penis) represented external versions of the female reproductive organs (ovaries and vagina) and were so portrayed in contemporary anatomical illustrations. Ovaries were, according to the late seventeenth-century physician Friedrich Hoffmann (1660–1742), simply "female testes." Men's genitals took external forms because the hotter quality of male bodies "drove" their organs outward. It is important to note here the purposefulness he thus ascribed to human anatomy and physiology.

The prevalence of such discussions in learned literature has led some to postulate that, before the late eighteenth century, a one-sex model dominated. According to the cultural historian Thomas Laqueur, only one body existed and it was male. Males and females, therefore, peopled a spectrum. In this model, females may have been lesser males but they were not conceived as inversely related. The two-sex model that developed in the eighteenth century, however, insisted that men and women were polar opposites, radically different from one another. Laqueur did not argue that early moderns could not tell boys and girls apart. Rather, he suggested that the learned and not-learned alike did not consider men and women to be thoroughly divergent in their bodily make-up, as we supposedly do now. Historians have not fully accepted Laqueur's ideas, but acknowledge that he raised critical questions about how early modern people understood sex and sexual difference.[11]

It is, of course, difficult to judge exactly how many people accepted any of these ideas in their entirety. One can turn to the most widely published sex manual of the seventeenth and eighteenth centuries – *Aristotle's Masterpiece* – for some clues. The *Masterpiece* (not in fact authored by Aristotle) first appeared in the late seventeenth century. The *Masterpiece* recognized that "lusts" and the joys of intercourse existed in both sexes. The work stressed the significance of the clitoris and insisted that female sexual pleasure depended on adequate clitoral stimulation. Also prevalent was the belief that orgasm in woman was the *sine qua non* of conception: no orgasm, no conception.

What happened after conception – that is, how the fetus became a viable human being – proved even more enigmatic. Again, two theories

[11] Thomas Laqueur, *Making Sex: Body and Gender from the Greeks to Freud* (Cambridge, Mass., 1990).

competed. One, the *epigenetic*, postulated the sequential development of the embryo: as it matured, the fetus evolved from more primitive to more advanced forms. *Preformation*, on the other hand, maintained that minute life forms existed in the parent's (usually the father's) seed and during gestation this *homunculus*, or "little man," simply grew larger. Determining pregnancy was a tricky business and none of the signs that medical men commonly took as determinant proved infallible. In the late seventeenth century, the surgeon Cosme Viardel repeated centuries of knowledge in listing the four signs of pregnancy: "the little shiver" that accompanied fertilizing intercourse; the closure of the neck of the womb; the end of "monthly purgations"; and, finally, the swelling of the breasts with milk. Even quickening, that is, the movement of the fetus, could deceive. One needed to consider whether the content of the woman's body was really a fetus or something else entirely, such as a *mola* (a fleshy, nonliving mass).[12]

What ordinary people thought about conception, gestation, and fetal development, however, has been harder to ascertain. Yet, thanks to the work of several scholars, we now know a little more about how women discerned their pregnancies and sensed what was taking place within their bodies. Early modern women did not necessarily regard the cessation of their "monthlies" as reliable proof that they had conceived. Many signs could indicate to a woman that she was "breeding" and most of these relied on her own perceptions, her visceral feelings, and the changes she associated with previous pregnancies (Figure 1.2). The variety of possible signs was extreme. It might indeed include the end of menstruation, but also its regularity, nausea or lack of it, or because a certain vein in the neck began to beat vigorously. The seventeenth-century midwife, Jane Sharp, listed fourteen indications of pregnancy; cessation of menstruation was only sixth on that list.[13] Likewise, the concept of a fetus as an independent life was vague, at least until it quickened. Before then, neither women nor midwives worried very much about bringing their menses back in order by the use of drugs or herbs, or by letting blood in the foot to "draw the

[12] Cosme Viardel (1674), quoted in Jacques Gélis, *History of Childbirth: Fertility, Pregnancy and Birth in Early Modern Europe*, trans. by Rosemary Morris (Oxford, 1991), 46; Cathy McClive, "The Hidden Truths of the Belly: The Uncertainties of Pregnancy in Early Modern Europe," *Social History of Medicine* 15 (2002): 226.

[13] Barbara Duden, "Zwischen 'wahren Wissen' und Prophetie: Konzeption des Unge-borenen," in Barbara Duden, Jürgen Schlumbohm, and Patrice Veit, eds., *Geschichte des Ungeborenen: Zur Erfahrungs- und Wissenschaftsgeschichte der Schwangerschaft* (2nd edn. Göttingen, 2002), 45–48; Laura Gowing, *Common Bodies: Women, Touch and Power in Seventeenth-Century England* (New Haven and London, 2003), 119.

1.2 "To know if a woman is with child or noe," Boyle family recipe book, c.1675–1710

menses down"; they in no way interpreted the bloody or fleshy fluxes that resulted as abortions. The knowledge of abortion-inducing herbs was, however, fairly widespread. A range of common plants – white and black hellebore, savory, and pennyroyal – could successfully induce abortions. Female wisdom on contraception, the *Secreta mulierum*, included the use of suppositories and pessaries as well as contraceptive herbs such as willow tree leaves and maidenhair fern.[14]

Understanding how the body worked offered clues about how to preserve health. Much depended on a good regimen; that is, the rules to be followed in everyday life especially in regard to the six nonnaturals. Besides general regimens, special ones pertained to the sick, the elderly, infants, and convalescents. Moderation in all things hallmarked early modern advice on regimen, and contemporaries took that counsel to heart. The indefatigable civil servant we met above, Johann Jakob Moser, observed that because he made no unreasonable demands on either mind or body, neither had ever failed him. By modifying lifestyle, especially in the realm of diet, a person could hope to retain or regain health. Common instructions warned people to avoid draughts, exhaustion, too much strong drink, and a sedentary life as well as rich and fatty foods. On a trip from Delft to The Hague in 1641, John Evelyn (1620–1706) was told, for example, that lepers "contract their diseases from their too much eating of fish."[15] Health was predicated on adhering to the rules of nature; every abuse of nature had to be requited and the sins of culinary overindulgence, intemperance, and lasciviousness brought on bodily pains. Some writers on regimen attributed almost all illness to dietary indiscretions, while others joined disease to "hampered evacuations." For the latter, the appropriate and regular expulsion of feces, sweat, and urine were essential to health.

Ideas on regimen dovetailed with those about *constitution*. Accordingly, each person possessed an individualized constitution that exceeded the sum of bodily parts, humors, and habits. Both learned and lay opinion saw a person's predisposition to certain afflictions and diseases as closely allied to his or her unique physical nature. In Hippocratic and Galenic medicines, and throughout the early modern period, people stressed the criticality of knowing an individual's constitutional idiosyncrasies if health was to be preserved or restored. Thus, cures must be carefully attuned to the individual in question. Constitutional differences could also, however, explain why some persons contracted a disease (and even ones generally viewed as highly contagious like plague or smallpox), while others living in close proximity, or even in intimate contact, remained unaffected. Contemporaries commonly labeled constitutions as "strong," "weak," "robust," or "delicate." The frequent notations in parish registers on the

---

[14] Robert Jütte, *Contraception: A History*, trans. Vicky Russell (Cambridge, 2008), 45–46, 62–75.
[15] Moser in *Pietismus und Rationalismus*, 227; John Evelyn, *The Diary of John Evelyn*, ed. by William Bray (London, 1973), 16.

deaths of children "delicate since birth" (or some similar phrase) indicate how prevalent the concept of constitution was. Bodies feeble at birth never righted and accounted for deaths even in late adulthood. But bad habits, horrible accidents, or frightening experiences could shatter even rugged frames. The "slings and arrows of outrageous fortune," like the terrors of wars and the insidious effect of chronic overwork and unrelenting worry, imperiled all minds and bodies no matter how inherently sound.

What went on inside the shell of the body's outer surface was hard to discern and people tended to refer to bodily processes metaphorically. The language of anatomy and constitution was always heavily laden with broader meanings and the body provided rich imagery for political commentators, novelists, and playwrights. In Shakespeare's *Macbeth*, Malcolm describes how Scotland "weeps, it bleeds, each day a new gash is added to her wounds."[16] People thought more concretely as well, frequently referring to organs and especially to the heart, liver, brain, and womb. Just as often, however, they spoke of balances and sympathies, assessed the relationship of one humor to the others, focused on a specific organ as almost alive, and conceived of the entire human organism as a *microcosm* of the larger universe or *macrocosm*.[17]

To grasp the internal state of the human body, people relied on the signs inscribed on the body's exterior: the color of the skin, the set of the limbs, and especially the testimony of the visage. Complexion, for example, showed on the facial features. A red or florid color revealed the sanguine personality, yellow a bilious one. Likewise, the "black looks" of the melancholic and the phlegmatic soul's "dull eye" were immediately recognizable. According to the Elizabethan gentlewoman and medical practitioner, Lady Grace Mildmay, defects of countenance, like "foul pimples or warts," betokened "the stopping and inflammation of the liver." Character traits, whether good or bad, also appeared on the face and the physiognomist's skill allowed one to deduce the body's inner state from the external marks that made hidden intentions manifest. Physicians, too, closely noted details of constitution and complexion. Typical were the observations Dr. William Brownrigg set down in his casebook: for Mr. Carlisle Spedding, "robust and of keen wit and sanguine temperament"; for "the famous artist," Mr. Rhead, "thin and of a melancholic temperament, living a very temperate lifestyle, of a keen wit and utterly wrapped up in his work"; for Mrs. Holmes, a widow "much given to

---

[16] Act 5, scene 3, line 153.
[17] Dorothy and Roy Porter, *In Sickness and in Health: The British Experience, 1650–1850* (Oxford, 1988), 46.

hysterical affections, 45 years old with a spotty complexion, slow, and also suffering from some complaint or other"; and, finally, for Mr. Lamplugh Simpson "an obese and leucophlegmatic disposition."[18]

Physicality and the terms used to describe it are historically determined, and it is exceedingly difficult, as Barbara Duden observes, for us to transcend our own medicalized modern perceptions and think back into our ancestors' minds and bodies. Duden's close examination of the casebooks an early eighteenth-century German physician, Johann Storch (1681–1751), kept on his female patients, allows us a fascinating glimpse into how people, and especially women, sensed the workings of their bodies. Storch and his female patients accepted the basic opacity of the body; its interior remained inaccessible. His patients spoke most frequently of the osmotic and fluid processes they felt viscerally. They tied femaleness, for instance, to no particular organ, neither to womb nor breasts. Rather, rhythms and periodicity – menstruation, for instance – defined the female. For them, the mental and physical permeated each other, and they viewed the body as easy prey to outside influences that could permanently alter it. Whereas we think of our bodies as separate from others and closed off from the outside world, early modern people believed in a far more porous relationship between flesh and its surroundings. Mikhail Bakhtin, in discussing the world of the late Renaissance physician and author, Rabelais (1494–1553), portrayed a world that emphasized the "parts of the body that are open to the outside world, the parts through which the world enters the body or emerges from it, or through which the body goes out to meet the world." The influence of humoral thinking is here immediately obvious.[19] Likewise, of course, the much larger environment, including the stars and planets, deeply affected bodily states.

Understanding illness and seeking cures

Understanding early modern views on health and illness allows us to grasp more easily the logic of cures that might at first appear ineffective, superstitious, counterproductive, or just plain silly. The methods of recovering health in the humoral system, however, made perfect sense. If

---

[18] Generally on "reading the face," see Mary E. Fissell, *Patients, Power, and the Poor in Eighteenth-Century Bristol* (Cambridge, 1991), 29–33; Linda Pollock, *With Faith and Physic: The Life of a Tudor Gentlewoman, Lady Grace Mildmay, 1552–1620* (London, 1993), 125; *The Medical Casebook of William Brownrigg, M.D., F.R.S. (1712–1800) of the Town of Whitehaven in Cumberland*, ed. and trans. by Jean F. Ward and Joan Yell (London, 1993), 50, 53, 58–59.

[19] Barbara Duden, *The Woman Beneath the Skin: A Doctor's Patients in Eighteenth-Century Germany*, trans. by Thomas Dunlap (Cambridge, Mass., 1991); Mikhail Bakhtin, *Rabelais and His World*, trans. by Helen Iswolsky (Bloomington, Ind., 1984), 26.

illness was caused by an imbalance, a cure could be worked by restoring that balance or removing a humor gone bad. The reasoning behind a spring cure – a seasonal purging, sweating, or bleeding – rested on just this premise. In addition, oppositions such as hot/cold and wet/dry could both explain the occurrence of disease and point to means for its alleviation. People also sought to expel their diseases by loading them onto other objects. The principle of *transference* taught, for instance, that if one rubbed a wart with the cut side of an onion and then buried the onion, the wart would shrivel as the onion rotted. As late as the eighteenth century, stories circulated about peasants who brought sheep into the bedroom of fever patients so as to induce the fever to pass from the human to the beast. Sympathetic healing worked both by likes and antagonisms. For example, yellow herbs, such as saffron, yellow broomseed, and radish, cured jaundice and evoked strong diuretic reactions. Likewise red plants and roots, such as bloodroot, dealt successfully with bloody discharges, much as the "red cure" (wearing red clothes, consuming red foods, and drinking red wine) combated smallpox (a red rash). Shapes and textures indicated proper applications: lungwort for all lung ailments; spotted and scaly plants against skin eruptions; and maidenhair for baldness.

Early modern people believed that the road to health flowed through the bowels, bladder, skin, and veins. The stoppage or unnaturally meager or heavy flow of sweat, urine, stools, and blood (menstruation, hemorrhoidal flows, and nosebleeds) surely caused illness and, in severe or unremedied cases, death. John Evelyn prevented a recurrence of piles (hemorrhoids) that had tortured him each spring by ensuring "greater evacuations" than normal. When habitual excretions failed and waste-products accumulated in the body, their foulness was thought to attack internal organs with damaging or even fatal results. Accordingly, a whole array of serious or milder diseases could emanate from the same cause. Catarrh was, therefore, not merely the cough and cold we might think it to be, but a far more general condition where the watery and phlegmy humors thickened beyond their normal state and then clogged up the areas where they naturally accumulated: the bowels, lungs, and nose. Such noxious build-ups produced not only sniffles, but "wet coughs," "slimy diarrheas," and the "whites" (a nonvenereal vaginal discharge). A very different affliction, apoplexy (stroke or brain aneurysm), resulted from abuses of the nonnaturals: too cold, too warm, too humid air; too sedentary or too active a life; violent passions; gluttony; or the omission of a customary purging or blood-letting. Even using a strong sulphur salve to soothe a skin eruption, like scabies (itself thought caused by corrupted humors), could drive it back into the body where it might work malignantly on the brain. In a like manner, obstructed perspiration produced rheumatism. Even melancholy was caused by something going on, not in the brain but in the abdomen, stomach, or spleen.

Such ideas conditioned treatments. The sixteenth-century Italian physician and natural philosopher Girolamo Cardano (1501–76) handled a case of paralysis with a bleeding "not only on account of the magnitude of the disease, but also because of the consideration of his lifestyle and the disease itself. I conjectured that the whole mass of blood was putrid. Nor did the judgment made about this thing fail me in any part. Indeed all the blood that went out was putrid." Laxatives, emetics, and phlebotomy remained common therapies even two hundred years after Cardano. For William Lees, a blacksmith who suffered from rheumatism and a "pulmonary abscess," Dr. Brownrigg (1712–1800) first prescribed a bleeding, then tried a laxative, had blisters set to the neck and chest, and used poultices of bread, milk, and butter to open the hard swellings on Lees's sternum. Nothing worked, however, and after a month's treatment, Lees was coughing up "whole pieces of lung mixed with blood." Two days later he died, "asphyxiated by purulent material."[20]

Equally important forms of early modern healing drew on supernatural forces. Scholars generally accept that magic and the heavenly bodies exerted a potent influence on the early modern mind (although one must be cautious not to draw divisions too sharply between "natural" and "supernatural" cures because, for instance, the actions of the planets were regarded as "natural"). While much of this story belongs to a later chapter on healers, it is important to understand how disease was cast in magical and astrological terms. Under magical healing, we usually understand a form of supernatural aid for curing diseases. In this sense, another supernatural intervention is religious healing. It is not necessary that the disease itself be magically caused, although the use of white or beneficent magic was employed to counter magical harming or black magic. Those believed bewitched might be sent to cunning-men or women to have the curse lifted or "deafened." A person affected by evil demons or possessed could be exorcized by a priest or minister. The Ambrosian monk Francesco Maria Guazzo (?–c.1640) exorcized the members of several ducal and princely families, including the bewitched Cardinal Charles of Lorraine and his relative, Eric, bishop of Verdun.[21] Rarely were physicians involved in such cases. Other magical cures involved amulets and the recitation of prayers or incantations. But resort to

---

[20] Nancy Siraisi, *The Clock and the Mirror: Girolamo Cardano and Renaissance Medicine* (Princeton, N.J., 1997), 171; *Medical Casebook of William Brownrigg*, 26–27.
[21] Wolfgang Behringer, *Witches and Witch-Hunts: A Global History* (Cambridge, 2004), 106.

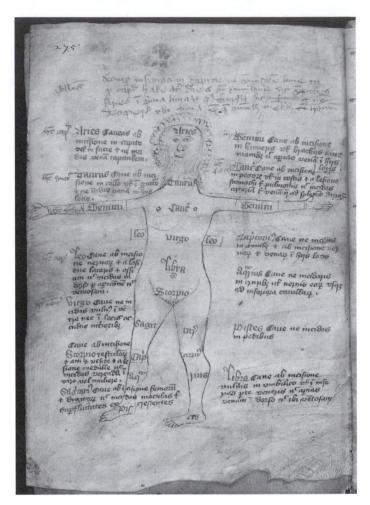

1.3 Astrological man, fourteenth century

supernatural aid did not preclude the simultaneous, prior, or subsequent employment of natural medicines. For a persistent toothache, for example, one might procure an amulet but also rub aching gums with oil of cloves.

In astrological medicine, "man is said to be a Microcosm (or little World) and in him the Almighty has imprinted his own Image"[22] (Figure 1.3). Sympathetic cures worked because they accorded with

---

[22] Quoted in Fissell, *Patients, Power, and the Poor*, 22.

the prevalent belief that intimately associated the universe with human beings. Whereas magic healing was generally neither well articulated nor systematic and consisted of bits and pieces of folklore and customs, astrology in the sixteenth and seventeenth centuries drew on the *Neoplatonist* tradition of the Renaissance that regarded all nature as animate and alive and on beliefs concerning the movements of the heavenly spheres. Put simply, astrology accepted that celestial motions could and did influence the human body; could and did cause illness. During the sixteenth and seventeenth centuries, astrology was a thoroughly reputable intellectual pursuit that fascinated Europe's best minds and became very fashionable among elevated social groups, especially princes and courtiers. Like the naturalistic means discussed above, astrological healing involved restoring the harmony between the macrocosm and the microcosm. While diagnosis depended on casting a horoscope, therapies usually looked very much like those other practitioners employed: attempts were made to adjust a humoral derangement by purging, sweating, and bleeding.

Unfortunately, much of the evidence we possess on supernatural curing comes from hostile witnesses: from those who were interested in one way or another in its extirpation and who were quick to brand such interventions superstitious practices or even heretical ones. Moreover, and especially in the realm of supernatural healing, one must take special care to recognize change over time, the importance of religious differences, and the interplay of political and social factors. As Michael MacDonald brilliantly demonstrated in his work on the healer Richard Napier (1559–1634), faith in magical and astrological cures, with their affinities to religious enthusiasm in seventeenth-century England, lost their appeal because of their associations with fanaticism.[23]

As the Napier example suggests, it would be wrong to think that nothing changed in perceptions of the origins of disease or their treatment over the course of the early modern period. Beginning in the eighteenth century, for instance, a *new Hippocratism* or environmentalism arose and alloyed itself to older beliefs, thus strengthening the effect climatic and environmental conditions were believed to have on human health and illness. The new environmentalism did not necessarily downplay the workings of the humors or supplant them. Rather, it maintained that factors of climate and environment, and especially weather patterns, water levels, and the presence or absence of *miasmas* (or bad air), profoundly

---

[23] Michael MacDonald, *Mystical Bedlam: Madness, Anxiety, and Healing in Seventeenth-Century England* (Cambridge, 1981), 229–31.

influenced the solid and liquid parts of the body.[24] One eighteenth-century authority argued that external factors, such as the weather, explained numerous afflictions, especially in persons whose constitutions were already predisposed or who were infirm or elderly:

> external cold affects such people [strongly], making their pores contract [so much] that the discharge of harmful sera is inhibited. [This purulent matter] then finds its way into the already weakened lungs, where its sharpness irritates them [and causes] a persistent cough and expectorations . . . and [it] also strikes other parts, for example, the stomach, inducing vomiting, or the glandular parts of the head, resulting in a cold, or the bowels, provoking diarrhea.[25]

What ailed people?

The apparently simple question "what ailed people in the past?" is perhaps one of the trickiest the medical historian faces. Scholars who study the early modern period have spent a great deal of time and energy examining the impact of what we today would call epidemics and infectious diseases and which contemporaries more frequently regarded as *pestilences*. There exists, certainly, much justification for this orientation: in demographic terms, epidemic and infectious diseases were the greatest killers. Nonetheless, plagues and pestilences were, by definition, unusual or extraordinary occurrences, not everyday events. Thus, before examining early modern pestilences in detail (Chapter 2), we want to survey the more mundane but nonetheless critically important everyday diseases, afflictions, and accidents that early modern people suffered.

One way to do so is to think in terms of the life course: what diseases were people likely to suffer at what points in their lives? Obviously, some afflictions and accidents were strung out equally along the life-line; others commonly affected the young, the old, or those of child-bearing age. What did people expect? How did they think about disease in terms of their own lifespan?

A long tradition of dividing life into stages continued throughout the period. Most people calculated points in life not, or not exclusively, by numbers but by assigning attributes that they only vaguely and imprecisely equated with years. The ages of man, in French the *degrés des âges*, broke down into some familiar-sounding categories, such as infancy, adolescence, youth, and maturity, but also into some more colorfully

[24] James C. Riley, *The Eighteenth-Century Campaign to Avoid Disease* (New York, 1987), x.
[25] Gottfried Samuel Bäumler, *Mitleidiger Arzt, welcher überhaupt Alles Arme Krancke . . . lehret/ wie Sie mit Gemeinen Hauß-Mitteln und anderen nicht allzukostbaren Artzeneyen sich selbst curiren können* (3rd edn., Strasbourg, 1743), 54–55.

descriptive ones such as (for old age) "never-wise," "children's joke," and "child-again." Divisions varied according to social groups: a peasant woman might seem ancient at thirty, while a noblewoman was viewed as still youthful at fifty.[26]

Beyond these qualitative or literary tropes lies a vast area of quantitative uncertainty. In efforts to gauge rates of *mortality* (death) and *morbidity* (sickness), historians have mined numerous types of documents: parish registers, funeral sermons, medical treatises, government records, diaries and memoirs, censuses (where such exist), chronicles, and mortality tables. All these furnish abundant information about health and illness in the past, but all of them present certain problems for the researcher. Parish records, for instance, are usually incomplete. Moreover, they note burials and baptisms rather than deaths and births. They provide even sketchier insights into morbidity. Diaries and memoirs, while often affording to the historian a colorful slice of life, best relay insights on the experiences of individuals and families, although journals kept during epidemics – such as that of the Barcelona tanner Miquel Parets in 1651 – are more instructive, if not necessarily more accurate. Daniel Defoe's wonderfully evocative, fictional account of plague in London, *A Journal of the Plague Year* (1722), conveys a picture of unmatched immediacy and vibrancy, but offers no help to those interested in death rates, for instance. Yet Defoe significantly increases our understanding of what his contemporaries thought about plague.

Equally fraught are attempts to diagnose diseases in the past. Most medical historians remain exceedingly cautious in venturing opinions about what a disease "really" was. Retrospective diagnosis, or retro-diagnosis, is filled with perils and often leads to serious and sometimes laughable misreadings. Contemporary terms for disease can baffle us. Even those we recognize easily – for example, dropsy, plague, or small-pox – are deceptive; they do not invariably correspond to modern disease entities. Dropsy, for instance, in early modern times was a disease; today we would understand the watery swellings of dropsy as a symptom, some-thing like edema, caused, however, by a variety of ailments. The word "plague" as employed in early modern times is similarly complex and cannot be facilely equated with bubonic plague; plague or pestilence was rather a catch-all term for a number of ailments, quite different afflic-tions (even nonmedical ones as the phrase "a plague of locusts" illus-trates), or generally awful circumstances. Under the rubric of smallpox lie concealed cases of measles, rubella, scarlatina, and scarlet fever. Early

[26] David G. Troyansky, *Old Age in the Old Regime: Image and Experience in Eighteenth-Century France* (Ithaca, N.Y., 1989), 15–26.

modern "syphilis" is better understood under its contemporary name "the Great Pox."

The convention of classifying diseases as disease entities, moreover, arose only in the late seventeenth century when medical writers began proposing *nosologies* (categories of related diseases, such as fevers). Because these nosologies depended on conceptions of cause that substantially diverge from modern ones, we find it almost impossible to determine what early modern people meant by cynanche, dyspnea, phthisis or consumption (which was not necessarily pulmonary tuberculosis), catarrh, costiveness, marasmus, hypochondriasis, lethargy, and melancholy. Even such familiar-sounding ailments as vertigo, dyspepsia, dysentery, jaundice, or asthma were not the same as what we today understand under these names. In dealing with non-English sources, the problem only becomes greater.

Must we then relinquish all hope of determining what ailments afflicted people in the past or, for that matter, in different cultures? Some historians argue that it is best to take people on their own terms and resist entirely the temptation to make retrospective diagnoses. Others find that we should use the language of the times but remain sensitive to the peculiar historical context and the contemporary diagnostic conventions. For instance, we must bear in mind that the old woman listed in a parish register as succumbing to jaundice may well have died from something else entirely. If we must be cautious in identifying and interpreting illnesses in the past, that circumspection does not mean that we should abandon all attempts to understand illnesses and how people once coped with them. Nor does it seem fruitful to deny the understanding of certain diseases as epidemics (smallpox, for example) when early modern peoples understood them in just those ways. Not everyone is convinced that a social constructivist perspective – one that largely avoids using modern labels to describe past events – is useful. The geographer and demographer Robert Woods has recently observed that such approaches are at once "strangely liberating and restrictive, realistic and idealistic in what they propose." For him, they limit the ability to compare disease and illness experiences as well as fail to address questions of mortality and morbidity across time and space. The on-going intense debate on whether the pestilence of the fourteenth century was indeed bubonic plague demonstrates that many historians see great value in pursuing comparisons others believe rest on dubious principles.[27]

---

[27] Robert Woods, "Medical and Demographic History: Inseparable?" *Social History of Medicine* 20 (2007): 486. On the intensity of the plague debate, see Vivian Nutton, ed., *Pestilential Complexities: Understanding Medieval Plague* (London, 2008).

Demographic studies have made it plain that the mortality curve for the early modern period differs in several ways from that of modern times. Most striking are the enormous variations in rates of death during the first years of life. Today, infant death is considered highly unusual, even tragic, at least in the affluent areas of the world. One expects a tiny number of stillbirths and a very high survival rate from birth to age twenty.[28] Twenty-first-century children, of course, suffer many childhood diseases, such as measles, chickenpox, colds, influenza, and the like, but normally these prove more nuisance than serious threat and many have virtually disappeared due to widespread immunization. Typically, good health and vigor characterize the middle years of life and persist well into one's sixth or seventh decade. For women, childbearing (with an average of two to three births) results in very few maternal deaths and serious complications (trauma, hemorrhage, or childbed fever) are rare. Women enter menopause in their fifties. By their seventies, many men and women still enjoy quite good health but incidents of degenerative diseases or diseases linked to smoking or obesity, like heart disease, osteoporosis, arteriosclerosis, diabetes, stroke, and cancer, begin to increase. A number of pesky problems plague older people more frequently: weakening eyesight, glaucoma, cataracts, deafness, poor digestion, arthritis, and rheumatism. These troubles often combine with a general decline in physical capacity and mental acuity; the latter includes various forms of dementia, such as Alzheimer's. Illnesses, such as pneumonia, influenza, and other viral diseases, staphylococcal and streptococcal infections, and food poisoning may strike at any time, but are usually fatal only to the very young, the elderly, the frail, or those with impaired immune systems. Automobile accidents and other forms of violent death (in the United States, especially from handguns) claim a significant number of lives, although mostly among certain age groups (adolescents and young adults) and particular classes (the poor). The impact of deaths from infectious diseases of all kinds is generally not great. Sophisticated drug "cocktails" have even made AIDS, once the leading cause of death in the United States for people aged twenty-five to forty-four, into a chronic condition. Recent events, such as the worldwide concern over SARS (Severe Acute Respiratory Syndrome) and the H1N1 virus, should remind us, however, that our conquest of infectious diseases is at best partial and perhaps only temporary. Today, most people eventually die of heart disease or other degenerative ailments, such as cancer. Expanded lifespans and more years of old age have, of course, created

---

[28] The mean stillbirth rate in the United States is approximately 1 in 115 births; in Australia, England, Wales, and Northern Ireland, about 1 in 200; in Scotland, 1 in 167.

Table 1.1. *Infant mortality, pre-1750*

	Number of deaths/1,000 live births
England	187
France	252
Germany	154
Scandinavia	224
Spain	281
Switzerland	283

Source: Michael W. Flinn, *The European Demographic System, 1500–1820* (Brighton, 1981), 16–17.

problems of their own, psychological and medical as well as social and financial.

In early modern Europe, structures of mortality and morbidity diverged dramatically from this modern pattern.[29] Neonatal mortality was high, indeed sometimes enormous. In general terms, and even after the middle of the eighteenth century when infant and child mortality began to decline, the most dangerous ages of life were infancy and early childhood. In early modern times, one out of every four or five people failed to survive the first year of life. Child mortality in the ages one to five also remained substantial and about 50 percent of it occurred before age ten (see Tables 1.1 and 1.2). Overall infant mortality rates varied between 150 and almost 300 per 1,000 live births, although substantial geographical and occupational gradations were typical. In Geneva, for example, infant mortality for the upper and middle groups stood at about 208/1,000 live births, while for the working classes it was 358/1,000. Culture also played a role in determining mortality. In places where mothers breast-fed their own children, mortality was often appreciably less.[30]

Childbirth could be fatal for infant and mother alike. Logically, the more pregnancies a woman experienced the greater was her chance of dying in childbed or soon after. But childbirth was not inevitably fatal. Early modern rates may seem surprisingly low; maternal mortality wavered between 1 and 2 percent. In a careful study of midwifery in late seventeenth- and eighteenth-century England, Adrian Wilson found that about 20 stillbirths occurred per 1,000 live births. Deformed or abnormally narrow pelvises frequently caused fatally difficult pregnancies. In

---

[29] On the "demographic transition," see Anders Branström and Lars-Göran Tedebrand, eds., *Society, Health and Population During the Demographic Transition* (Umeå, 1988).

[30] Michael W. Flinn, *The European Demographic System, 1500–1820* (Brighton, 1981), 17–18.

Table 1.2. *Rates of infant mortality and of survival to age 10 (per 1,000)*

	Less than 1 year	1–5 years	5–10 years	Survival to 10 years
France				
1740–49	296	253	107	469
1780–89	278	239	90	501
Germany				
1740–49	182	156	58	650
1780–89	177	161	58	650
England				
1580–89	168	88	38	730
1620–29	153	81	33	752
1680–89	202	130	59	654
1780–89	163	109	33	721

Source: David Kertzer and Marzio Barbagli, eds., *The History of the European Family*, Vol. I: *Family Life in Early Modern Times, 1500–1789* (New Haven, Conn., 2001), 165.

fact, however, most births were normal and the majority of deliveries relatively straightforward. Major complications, including hemorrhage and *eclampsia* (convulsions that occur late in pregnancy), were rare, although fatal unless an immediate delivery was effected. The incidence of *puerperal* or *childbed fever* increased in the nineteenth century when more women began to give birth in hospitals. Most women recovered quickly from minor complications – trauma, torn perinea, and postpartum weakness – although prolapsed uteruses, vaginal tearing and scarring often became more serious problems later in life.[31]

Wilson's study, of course, pertains only to England. It is certainly possible that unique social, cultural, and economic factors favorably skewed the statistics there. Yet evidence from the continent suggests a similar situation. An investigation of eighteenth-century mortality in the small town of Belm (in the Germany duchy of Osnabrück) found a maternal death rate of about 1 percent. In France, before 1700, maternal mortality likewise hovered around 10 per 1,000 (1 percent). The casebooks of the eighteenth-century Frisian midwife Catharina Schrader reveal that she lost only 14 mothers in 3,017 deliveries.[32]

---

[31] Adrian Wilson, *The Making of Man – Midwifery: Childbirth in England, 1660–1770* (Cambridge, Mass., 1995).

[32] Jürgen Schlumbohm, "Micro-History and the Macro-Models of the European Demographic System in Pre-Industrial Times: Life Course Patterns in the Parish of Belm

Not all scholars, however, accept this relatively favorable picture of early modern childbirth. It was once typically argued that childbirth formed an extremely hazardous event in a woman's life, one which many women approached with great fear and trepidation. Comfort in such trying circumstances came less from physicians or even midwives than from religion, female relatives, and close friends.[33] Married women experienced more pregnancies (and miscarriages) than women do today. Contraception or birth control, while by no means unknown, had only limited effect and was best suited to space out rather than prevent births. Obviously, the more pregnancies, the greater the risk of dying in childbirth. Furthermore, little doubt exists that difficult circumstances – especially the abnormal *in utero* presentations that required the fetus to be turned to facilitate delivery – could prove fatal to mother and child alike. The widespread introduction of forceps in the eighteenth century allowed some otherwise undeliverable children to be born safely. But, because these problems were seldom, such mechanical innovations probably contributed little to improving overall maternal and infant mortality rates. Obstetrical instruments, however, could tear membranes and introduce infection, even if they saved some lives. Caesarean sections were seldom performed and almost always resulted in the death of the mother.

What frequent childbirth and high infant mortality rates meant for individual lives and families can be portrayed using a variety of historical documents. The diary of the seventeenth-century Englishman Ralph Josselin (1616–83) recounts that he and his wife, Jane, had ten children, of whom five lived to marry and five died before they wed. Of the five deaths, two children perished soon after birth, one in early infancy, one at eight years of age, and one as a young adult of nineteen. For Germany, Arthur Imhof used a computer-assisted program to construct a fascinating set of family histories that move from demographic facts to a realization of what patterns of mortality, fertility, and nuptiality meant in real lives. One couple who married in 1680 had seven children of whom three were still alive when the wife was forty-five. But another pair who bore nine children saw none of them live beyond its seventh month.

(Northwest Germany), Seventeenth to the Nineteenth Centuries," *History of the Family* 1, no. 1 (1996): 81–95; *Mother and Child were Saved: The Memoirs (1693–1740) of the Frisian Midwife Catharina Schrader*, trans. and ed. by Hilary Marland (Amsterdam, 1996); Laurence Brockliss and Colin Jones, *The Medical World of Early Modern France* (Oxford, 1997), 62.

[33] See the articles by Patrice Veit and Ulrike Gleixner in Barbara Duden, Jürgen Schlumbohm, and Patrice Veit, eds., *Geschichte des Ungeborenen: Zur Erfahrungs- und Wissenschaftsgeschichte der Schwangerschaft, 17.-20. Jahrhundert* (Göttingen, 2002).

Theirs was hardly ever a family in the demographic sense of parents and children living together.[34]

Nuisance ailments, but also killing ones such as smallpox, whooping cough, and infantile diarrheas, punctuated the years of childhood. A host of other diseases, like plague, tuberculosis, and typhus (which were not, of course, uniquely fatal to infants) increased the mortality of this age cohort. Injuries suffered while young, such as fractures, often crippled children and rendered them unable to participate fully in life thereafter. Birth defects ranged from the merely unsightly or odd (birthmarks, extra fingers or toes, ambiguous genitals) to the deforming and life-threatening, including cleft lips and palates, multiple limbs, and conjoined twinism. Children born deaf or blind often suffered the added stigma of being thought idiots as well. Many ailments were almost ubiquitous. Worm infestations weakened youngsters and made them more vulnerable to other illness. Eye infections diminished sight or blinded and the accidents of the farmyard, workshop, city street, and castle – falls, wounds, and burns – killed or maimed. Frequently, children died while teething which contemporaries attributed to the process of teething itself. Rotten teeth had to be extracted, but the incidence of tooth decay was probably less in early modern Europe then later, at least until the widespread introduction of sugar as a sweetener in the eighteenth century. Bleeding gums resulted from nutritional disorders, such as scurvy, that had more general bodily effects.

What we might roughly define as environmental factors – diet, sanitation, housing, and war – played major roles in determining disease incidence. All ages suffered from insufficient or improper diets, as well as from the illnesses produced by consuming adulterated or rotten foods. Although diet varied greatly with time and place, a *subsistence crisis* or famine struck about one year in six almost everywhere in Europe until about the middle of the eighteenth century. Inadequate amounts of food left people prey to pathogens (any agent able to cause disease). Still, and although we know that some correlation exists between dietary deficiencies and morbidity and mortality, the exact relationship has evaded easy assessment. The poor tended to consume too little protein and too few vitamins. The rich often ate too much meat and too little roughage and the high consumption of animal protein accounts for the heightened

---

[34] Alan Macfarlane, *The Family Life of Ralph Josselin, A Seventeenth-Century Clergyman: An Essay in Historical Anthropology* (Cambridge, 1970); Arthur E. Imhof, *Die gewonnenen Jahre: Von der Zunahme unserer Lebensspanne seit dreihundert Jahren, oder von der Notwendigkeit einer neuen Einstellung zu Leben und Sterben, ein historischer Essay* (Munich, 1981).

incidence of gout among them.[35] Constipation and looseness (slight diarrhea) caused by eating too little bulk or too much indigestible fiber were both common. Paradoxically, some diseases tended to bypass the weak or ill and seek out the strong as do plague and some forms of influenza. Lepers, for example, appeared to enjoy a certain immunity to tuberculosis. Although it seems sensible to argue that poorly fed people suffer more disease than the well nourished, the connection between nutritional levels and disease has proved less straightforward than one might expect. Moreover, although famines and epidemics are linked, the causal relationship eludes easy definition.

Yet some relationships are clear. Faulty sanitation facilitated the spread of intestinal parasites and diseases caused by water-borne bacilli, while poorly ventilated and overcrowded lodgings increased the rate of droplet infections, including tuberculosis and influenza. Inadequate shelter and exposure to wind, rain, or cold reduced individual resistance and opened the body to more serious infections. Infrequently washed woolen clothing (wool was the commonest fabric until cotton became widely available later in the eighteenth century) harbored body vermin that spread diseases, as well as producing numerous skin ailments such as scabies (caused by mites) and known as "the itch."

Dangers lurked almost everywhere in the home and workplace. The caustic substances employed in many trades – dyeing, bleaching, tanning, and etching, to name just some – were serious hazards to health, as were the molten metals of the silver and gold trades, the flames of the smithy, and the sharp knives of butchers. The open hearths and boiling cauldrons found in almost every home and kitchen proved especially dangerous for small children, but adults were hardly immune from scalds and burns. Close proximity to horses and other livestock generated its share of broken limbs, contusions, and concussions, although falls from horseback and tumbles from coaches and carts must have been less hazardous than automobile smash-ups.

Wars, civil disorders, and revolts may also be viewed as environmental conditions with profound influences on health. The disturbances of the sixteenth and seventeenth centuries and, in particular, the Dutch Revolt and the Thirty Years War, tended to be more disruptive and more generalized in their violence than the conflicts of the eighteenth century. The degree of suffering depended much on location. The Thirty Years War (1618–48) ravaged some areas of Germany while leaving others virtually untouched. English civilians, however, escaped the immediate death and destruction of the continental religious wars of the sixteenth century

[35] Roy Porter and G. S. Rousseau, *Gout: The Patrician Malady* (New Haven, Conn., 1998).

and of the imperial conflicts of the eighteenth, but suffered grievously during the English civil upheavals in the middle of the seventeenth century. Northern Italy served as the battleground of all Europe in the late Renaissance and declined accordingly, but then became less centrally involved at least until the outbreak of the revolutionary struggles of the late eighteenth century. Marauding soldiers destroyed crops and rustled livestock. Armies, whether friend or foe, quartered soldiers on the population. Overcrowding and makeshift sanitary facilities encouraged the spread of typhosoid fevers, dysentery, body vermin, and syphilis, to say nothing of the harm inflicted on the populace in the form of rape and casual violence. Every government knew that troop movements meant a higher incidence of disease and necessitated more concern for public health. Epidemic diseases and food shortages due to war, however, always killed more combatants and civilians than did force of arms.

And mortality charts hardly tell the whole story. Just as important as the diseases that killed were those that incapacitated or made life burdensome and painful. Any quick perusal of poor relief rolls or parish registers reveals a whole series of ailments that plagued our ancestors and which, to some extent, still bother us today. Complaints we today consider minor – bladder infections, skin eruptions, and dental problems – were infirmities that became chronic for early modern people: kidney stones bothered Samuel Pepys, bad teeth tortured Queen Elizabeth, and gout crippled Samuel Johnson, to name a few famous English patients. A list of such disorders is practically unending. Skin ailments like "scald" or "the itch," circulatory impairments like "running sores" and ulcerated varicose veins, persistent complaints such as "weepy-eyes" or "wry-neck" were common. Accidents and injuries ran up the score. The seventeenth-century surgeon Gerhard Eichhorn, for example, regularly treated gangrene, ulcers, tumors, all sorts of wounds (including gunshots), blows, mutilating injuries, contusions, dislocations, skull fractures, and burns.[36]

Still, while it is commonly argued that early modern people experienced lives of intermittent, sometimes constant, pain and were thus more inured to it than we moderns are, we should regard such statements with some skepticism. Although early modern people did not enjoy better health than we do, those who survived the perils of infancy and childhood were pretty hardy specimens whose immunological systems probably coped well with future diseases and infections. Furthermore, no good reason exists to assume that our ancestors stoically or fatalistically resigned themselves to suffering or necessarily regarded all afflictions as

---

[36] Robert Jütte, "A Seventeenth-Century Barber-Surgeon and His Patients," *Medical History* 33 (1989): 184–98.

spiritually beneficial. They recognized that the angel of death hovered about at all times and they might well have understood that this world was a vale of sorrows compared to the riches of everlasting life, but they seldom nonchalantly accepted either pain or ill health as inevitable or even positive. Rather, they did all they could – and that was considerable – to alleviate their miseries and banish their illnesses. Moreover, attitudes changed over the course of the centuries. A religiously conditioned acceptance of pain or deformity as a mark of God's grace was more common in the sixteenth and early seventeenth centuries than later. Yet, individuals also varied enormously in their outlook on the providential cause or spiritual benefit of disease. Not all sixteenth-century sufferers folded their hands and bowed to God's will gracefully. Some persons in the eighteenth century were necessarians who deemed attempts to combat illness and to use medicine, or to submit themselves or members of their families to inoculation or vaccination, as blasphemy and hubris. Moreover, the relationship between medicine and religion was a far more complicated and subtle affair that left room for much collaboration and cooperation.

Mental illness

We know less about the incidence of mental illness in the past than that of other afflictions, despite a great deal of historical interest in the subject. Mental illness is notoriously hard to specify, partly because its definition heavily depends on cultural factors. One society's madness is another's sanity. Clearly behaviors that the contemporary western world describes as "mad" or "insane" were not always deemed such nor do all cultures judge them so today. Trance or fugue states that westerners today regard as symptomatic of mental distress or malfunction were, for example, common elements of religious expression in medieval and early modern Europe as they remain in many parts of our twenty-first-century world. In early modern Russia, for instance, the mad sometimes fell into an undifferentiated group of "unfortunates" but could also be viewed as "blessed ones."[37]

Particularly since the appearance in the 1960s of the provocative works of Michel Foucault, many historians have tended to speak about the "manufacture" or even the "myth" of mental illness. In its most extreme form, this line of argumentation insists that mental illness does not in

---

[37] Kenneth S. Dix, "Madness in Russia, 1775–1864: Official Attitudes and Institutions for Its Care," PhD diss. (UCLA, 1977), 8.

truth exist (as does a somatic illness like leprosy or tuberculosis) and that ideas about madness and insanity developed historically as a form of social control; that is, as a way to inculcate proper behaviors by designating more and more actions, once considered acceptable, merely odd, or even reflecting a special religious status, such as saintliness, as radically unacceptable or "mad." Erik Midelfort, in his study of the *Mad Princes of Renaissance Germany*, observes that until well into the sixteenth century many behavioral traits fit easily within the range of the allowable and "one could be strange, eccentric, irresponsible, dangerous, willful, or just plain nutty without being judged crazy." But this relative acceptance of difference would not prevail much longer.[38]

Foucault argued that, beginning in the middle of the seventeenth century, Europeans embarked on a "great confinement": the wholesale incarceration of all those society viewed as deviant; criminals, the poor, and the insane. The wish to rehabilitate the prodigal and make the poor industrious drove the great confinement; neither humanitarianism or medical improvements provided the real motivation. One of the faults the mad shared with the poor was their apparent refusal to work. In various institutions – the prison, the almshouse, and the insane asylum – "the mad, the bad, and the sad" could be better controlled and disciplined. Here, within four stout walls, desirable behaviors, and especially a bourgeois work ethic, could be implanted, by force if necessary. Later, even when freed from their chains at the end of the eighteenth century, the insane remained "moral prisoners" as the softer bonds of close supervision, moral suasion, guilt, and conscience replaced iron fetters.[39]

According to the critics of psychiatry, the age of reason formed a turning point in the treatment of the insane in Europe and was a disaster for them: stigmatized and shunned, they were sequestered behind the walls of asylums and madhouses and, in Foucault's words, "silenced." Whereas madmen and madwomen supposedly once roamed free, were restrained only if violent, and were regarded as "voyagers both in reality and in imagination, fools whose hermetic wisdom signified to the sane the animality of the human and the humanity of vice,"[40] the mad were now banished and ridiculed.

---

[38] Thomas S. Szasz, *The Manufacture of Madness: A Comparative Study of the Inquisition and the Mental Health Movement* (New York, 1970); H. C. Erik Midelfort, *Mad Princes of Renaissance Germany* (Charlottesville, 1994), 20.

[39] Michel Foucault, *Madness and Civilization: A History of Insanity in the Age of Reason* (New York, 1965) and *Discipline and Punish: The Birth of the Prison* (London, 1977).

[40] MacDonald, *Mystical Bedlam*, xi.

The great strength of these perspectives, and especially the Foucauldian interpretation, is that they highlight the importance of historical context and historical change in shaping concepts of diseases. Moreover, they vigorously question the cogency of a narrative predicated on humanitarian improvements. Few scholars now doubt that definitions of madness and sanity are culturally and historically determined. Still, critics have also raised substantial objections to this argument. First, Foucault and his disciples insist that authorities – governmental and medical – defined madness and then foisted that definition on a populace that previously had little conception of it and felt little fear of the mad. Second, those who believe in the "manufacture of madness" tend to deny that the mad themselves felt pain or anxiety about their condition. In short, the mad did not know their affliction. Over the past twenty years, numerous studies have demonstrated that neither premise is entirely valid. Ordinary people indeed possessed a conception of madness. As Michael MacDonald shows, English villagers of the seventeenth century feared the mad for what they might do. Onlookers deemed mad those who tore their clothing, disobeyed their natural masters (whether parents, employers, or social betters), or wandered around unclothed. The casebooks of the Anglican divine and astrological physician Richard Napier show that a goodly number of those who consulted him did so for mental problems that deeply disturbed them, their relatives, their friends, and their neighbors. While there is no denying that the meanings of madness have shifted over time (and that the ways in which definitions evolved can tell us much about the values of any society), there seems little reason to embrace the view that the early modern world was somehow a heaven for the insane. They were often defined as ill, sometimes shut away, sometimes beaten, sometimes treated, but their peculiarity was neither unremarked nor ignored. Finally, the timing of Foucault's Great Confinement seems all wrong; far more people were confined after 1800 than before.[41]

How, then, did people recognize madness and interpret the underlying cause of the affliction? People generally identified madness by the way the mad behaved. Madness could be read in the face, in rolling, unfocused eyes, twisted features, vacant stares, but also on the body more generally. Jerks and twitches, an impaired or unusual gait, strange motions of the body, obsessive actions, such as a frantic, ceaseless wringing or washing of hands, could mark the disturbed in mind. Doing bodily harm to oneself or others, threatening members of one's family (and especially one's

---

[41] Colin Jones and Roy Porter, eds., *Reassessing Foucault: Power, Medicine, and the Body* (London, 1994).

own children), flouting authority, going naked, or rending one's clothes were clear signs that all was not right. Sitting idle, sighing, showing indifference to one's surroundings also indicated a troubled mind. Unusual or unseemly actions were also suspect. The seventeenth-century Dutch diplomat and burgomaster Coenraad van Beuningen (1622–93) first manifested his illness by offering a valuable set of porcelain to casual acquaintances who came for tea.[42]

Everyone agreed that madness was fickle in its objects and protean in its manifestations. Popular and academic names for addled wits abounded and many terms described a vast array of mental disorders. One might speak, colloquially, of the mad, the lunatic, the distracted, the troubled in mind, the giddy, and the anxious, or, more learnedly, of those suffering from *animi infirmitas*, *eroticos*, petrified malice, and *furor uterinus*. Symptoms were equally prolix and ranged from childishness, confusion, and mopishness, to irrationality, wild behavior, hallucinations, and suicide. Academic practitioners and the laity alike took all these things, and many more besides, as evidence of mental distress.

The causes of madness were legion: a crack on the head, a fever, a long illness, religious enthusiasm, disappointment in love, and childbirth. Emotional excesses, such as jealousy, hatred, and anger, could scramble the wits. Because the roots of madness were so multiple and could spring from physical, intellectual, moral, or religious factors, mad-doctors came from many walks of life. Physicians enjoyed no monopoly over the right to diagnose and treat insanity or to care for the afflicted. Ministers, priests, divines, surgeons, family members, and others who did not necessarily have medical training were as likely to care for the mad as university-trained physicians. In the 1620s, the Dutch Calvinist minister Henricus Alutarius practiced bodily and moral "physick" in treating the mad and the melancholic. Especially at the beginning of this period, people did not always perceive madness as either a disease or a curse; it could betoken special insight or Providence's favor. The fifteenth-century mystic Margery Kempe (c.1373–after 1438) periodically saw visions and had hallucinations with religious overtones. She even "rived the skin on her body against her heart with her nails spitefully" without being adjudged mad.[43]

---

[42] Entry of November 8, 1689 from Constantijn Huygens, *Journaal van Constantijn Huygens, den zoon, van 21 October 1688 tot 2 Sept. 1696 (Handschrift van de Koninklijke Akademie van Wetenschappen te Amsterdam)* (3 vols., Utrecht, 1876–88).

[43] Willem Frijhoff, *Wegen van Evert Willemsz.: een Hollands weeskind op zoek naar zichzelf 1607–1647* (Nijmegen, 1995); *The Book of Margery Kempe* (1436), quoted in Dale Peterson, ed., *A Mad People's History of Madness* (Pittsburgh, 1982), 9.

In early modern Europe one particular type of healing in the realm of mental health fell to the care of the clergy: spiritual physic. Spiritual physic aimed at restoring a good mental balance to those plagued by many sorts of problems, ranging from simple and temporary, to suicidal depressions and demonic possession. Spiritual physicians healed with a range of tools: prayer, exorcism, confession, communion, laying on of hands, and the use of relics.

In the sixteenth and seventeenth centuries, if less frequently in the eighteenth, people accepted that a spirit or Satan himself could possess persons and drive them out of their minds. Likewise a witch's *maleficium* (harm) could destroy reason. Contemporaries acknowledged that divine madness and religious melancholy caused troubles in mind, and fears of salvation lost, religious doubts, or a sin unshriven could provoke mental breakdowns. George Trosse (1631–1713) described the religious terrors that drove him mad:

From this Perswasion, that I had been guilty of the Sin against the Holy Ghost, I was fill'd with grievous Horrour and Anguish, with great Anxiety and sinking Despair . . .
I strongly fancy'd that GOD watch'd opportunities to destroy me; but I also presum'd that GOD must get in by the Door, or he would not be able to come at me; and I foolishly conceited, that if I did but tie the Door with a particular sort of a Knot, He would be effectually shut out; which I attempted to do, that I might be secur'd from his Wrath.[44]

Throughout the early modern period there existed a strong tendency to link afflictions of mind with bodily disturbances such as a perceived humoral imbalance or indigestion. Thus, the body moved mind as easily as the mind affected the flesh. Lady Mildmay felt frenzy and madness to be "near of kin" and "proceed of the inflammation of the phlegms of the brain." The Württemberg pastor Philipp Matthäus Hahn blamed an episode of melancholy on flatulence.[45]

Melancholy is the form of madness that had the most venerable pedigree. "Melancholy" derived from the Latin and Greek words for black bile, choler; melancholics were thought to suffer from an excess of that humor. Today's definition of melancholy – sadness or depression of the spirits, gloom, pensive reflection, or contemplation – by

---

[44] Quoted in Richard Hunter and Ida Macalpine, *Three Hundred Years of Psychiatry, 1535–1860: A History Presented in Selected English Texts* (Hartsdale, N.Y., 1982), 155.

[45] Quoted in Carol Thomas Neely, *Distracted Subjects: Madness and Gender in Shakespeare and Early Modern Culture* (Ithaca, N.Y., 2004), 72; Sabine Sander, "'. . . Gantz toll im Kopf und voller Blähungen . . .': Körper, Gesundheit und Krankheit in den Tagebüchern Philipp Matthäus Hahns," in *Philipp Matthäus Hahn 1739–1790: Aufsatzband* (Stuttgart, 1989), 104.

no means includes the many characteristics subsumed under the label in early modern times. Moreover, we do not recognize it as a disease today but rather assign it to the category of moods or dispositions. Early modern melancholy was mutable and could be represented by a variety of attitudes and behaviors. The most famous work on melancholy, Robert Burton's (1577–1640) *Anatomy of Melancholy* published in 1621, displays on the title page the many attitudes of the afflicted: "Jealousye," "Solitarinesse," "Inamorato," "Hypochondriacus," "Superstitious," and "Maniacus." Near the end of the sixteenth century, Philip Barrough (fl. 1590), the Elizabethan physician who is often credited with publishing the first English book on medicine, wrote:

Melancholie is an alienation of the mind troubling reason, and waxing foolish, so that one is almost beside him self . . . The most common signes be fearfulness, sadnes, hatred, and also that they be melancholius, have straunge imaginations, for some think them selves brute beastes, & do counterfaite the voice and noise, some think themselves vessels of earth, or earthen pottes, therfore they withdrawe them selves from them that they meet, lest they should knocke together [and break]. Moreover they desire death, and do verie often behight and determine to kill them selves, and some feare that they should be killed. Many of them do alwayes laugh, and many do weep, some think them selves inspired with the holie Ghost, and do prophecy uppon thinges to come.[46]

Madness could take different forms in different social groups and also bore political implications. Melancholy, already fashionable in Elizabethan England, became especially modish as a disease of courtiers after the appearance of Burton's work. Where nobles, princesses, and intellectuals sighed in melancholy's somber throes, their more common kinsmen and women went about "mopish" or distracted and giddy. When rulers went mad, kingdoms trembled. Madness probably struck royal, imperial, or noble families no more frequently than others, but it was more remarked and became a matter of state. The daughter of Ferdinand of Aragon and Isabella of Castile and the mother of the emperor Charles V, Doña Juana (1479–1555), was kept under lock and key for almost fifty years. The behavior of the Holy Roman Emperor Rudolf II (1552–1612) – he hallucinated, had paranoid delusions, and suffered bouts of melancholy – led to the fear that he, too, had taken leave of his senses. Periodic bouts of madness beset George III (1738–1820) of England and led to a constitutional emergency that eventually resulted in a regency. The dynastic crises and power vacuums that could result from the lunacy

---

[46] Philip Barrough, *The Methode of Physicke, Conteyning the Causes, Signes, and Cures of Inward Diseases in Mans Body from the Head to the Foote* (London, 1583), quoted in Hunter and Macalpine, *Three Hundred Years*, 27–28.

of rulers meant that the mad business could disrupt or immobilize courts and governments.

Social position affected the mad diagnosis, but so, too, did gender. In modern society, it appears that more women than men suffer from mental illness or at least women seek help more frequently. This situation evidently held true in the European past as well. Observers have often interpreted the disproportion as a result of the inferior status of women in almost all cultures and this subordination, of course, also pertained in the early modern period. We know less about the madness of women than men because fewer writings – medical, biographical, or autobiographical – deal with them. Most autobiographical accounts of madness come from the pens of men (reflecting, of course, their generally greater literacy as well as their fuller access to the world of learning and publishing). And this is as true for queens as for scullery maids. Nonetheless, early modern people felt that the very same mental infirmities affected men and women equally. As Erik Midelfort found for the late Renaissance in central Europe, the "medical language of melancholy and madness was not yet highly gendered, and except for hysteria . . . physicians expected to find roughly the same maladies among men and women."[47]

The existing evidence, however thin, strongly indicates that the incidence of mental troubles was greater among women than among men. The casebooks of Richard Napier are again a good guide. He listed substantially more women than men among his mentally distressed patients. Physical infirmities – menstrual difficulties, gynecological disorders, traumatic childbirth, and infertility – could ravage the mind as well as afflict the body. The disasters of normal life – miscarriages, the death of children or other close relatives, infertility, pressures to receive undesired suitors (or being forbidden to marry a preferred lover), or marital infidelities – all sent women (and men, too, although in smaller numbers) to Napier. Deaths and illnesses perhaps preyed more on women's minds because they were the primary healers, caretakers, and nurses not only for children but for families, neighbors, and friends.

Much contemporary learned opinion concurred that women were more susceptible to such disturbances than men because of their physical and humoral make-up. The early seventeenth-century physician Edward Jorden (1569–1632) observed that "the passive condition of womankind is subject unto more diseases and of other sorts and natures than men are" and he especially identified the womb and its afflictions, such as the "suffocation of the mother" or hysteria, as principally

---

[47] Midelfort, *Mad Princes*, 17.

responsible.[48] A counterargument suggests, however, that women's periodic "cleansings" – their menstrual cycles – made them mentally and physically healthier than men.

Some historians have argued that women persecuted as witches, or those who felt themselves the victims of witchcraft, suffered from mental illness. Early modern writers often agreed. The French skeptic and philosopher Pierre Bayle (1647–1706) felt that "an imagination that is alarmed by the fear of a witch's spell can overthrow the animal constitution, and produce... extravagant symptoms." He also thought it "very possible for a woman to persuade herself that someone has put the Devil into her body," causing her to believe herself possessed and act so by screaming and convulsing. The court-physician Johannes Weyer (1515–88) diagnosed witches, and especially those who confessed, as "indeed poor women – usually old women – melancholic by nature, feeble-minded, easily given to despondency."[49]

Attempts to explain, or explain away, witchcraft as the product of a sick mind, however laudatory their purposes, are basically inadequate. It is historically naive to seek simple rational explanations for cultural phenomena of great complexity, like the witch-crazes and witchcraft of the early modern period. Likewise, other instances or manifestations of insanity in women (or men, for that matter) in early modern Europe must be dissected with great caution. There is, no doubt, a temptation to believe that women who fled marriage, hallucinated, and had vivid sexual fantasies – such as Margery Kempe – were sexually repressed. In an examination of many late medieval and early modern female saints, Rudolph Bell concluded that many female saints, including famous ones such as Catherine of Siena (1347–80), were in truth anorectic and suffered for many of the same reasons that twenty-first-century pubescent women do: sexual frustrations or confusions. Caroline Bynum has amply demonstrated, however, that Bell's retrospective diagnosis of *anorexia nervosa* proves quite inadequate. The reasons for behaviors that seem to us pathological arose from deep religious motivations and were not sexual in origin. Since then, anorexia nervosa has been variously diagnosed and explanations have ranged from the somatic to the psychosocial to the cultural.[50]

[48] Edward Jorden, *A Brief Discourse of a Disease Called the Suffocation of the Mother* (London, 1603), quoted in Hunter and Macalpine, *Three Hundred Years*, 71.

[49] Pierre Bayle, "Superstition and Imagination" (1703), in Alan C. Kors and Edward Peters, eds., *Witchcraft in Europe, 1100–1700: A Documentary History* (Philadelphia, 1972), 361; Weyer, quoted in Behringer, *Witches and Witch-Hunts*, 171.

[50] Rudolph Bell, *Holy Anorexia* (Chicago, 1985); Caroline Bynum, *Holy Feast and Holy Fast: The Religious Significance of Food to Medieval Women* (Berkeley and Los Angeles,

Histories of the mental illnesses of children are practically nonexistent. Napier treated very few people under the age of twenty and even fewer aged less than ten. The question is why. Historians once simply assumed that parents did not value young children as they were so likely to be swept away by disease or accident before they developed any real identity. The argument that early modern families wasted little affection on their children has been seriously undermined by a range of work in family and demographic history. Even if family life did not revolve around children as it came to the late nineteenth century, parents nonetheless were deeply concerned about their offsprings' health and went to much trouble to preserve or restore it. Mental distress or distraction in children was often understood in religious terms. People frequently thought that youngsters who suddenly exhibited bizarre or aberrant behavior were possessed or bewitched; they might be turned over to priests, ministers, or cunning-folk to be exorcized. Children who did not walk or talk at the appropriate age might be considered "slow," or, worse, idiots, but one rarely sought assistance of any kind for them, unless a clear physical problem existed. Children born deaf (or those who showed symptoms of what we today might regard as autism) could be treated as weak in mind or under the devil's control and were sometimes abandoned. Yet many parents devoted themselves to teaching their deaf children to communicate using signs. Most people regarded children as relatively happy creatures. Their basically animalistic and unreflective nature was thought to protect them from worldly concerns and they thus seemed immune to mental distress as well.

Old age, however, was generally regarded as a time of life especially prone to melancholy (Burton regarded senescence as one of its primary causes), as well as to forgetfulness and childishness. Again it is very difficult to ascertain how much of this behavior people attributed to mental disorder and how much they considered unremarkable in the final stage of life. Unquestionably, contemporaries joined the physical infirmities of age to crabbiness and misanthropy, as the old person contemplated death, family woes, and declining powers. Yet, such grumpiness was not necessarily thought tantamount to mental illness. At this point in life few hoped for cures or worried about treatment because death would soon put an end to the problem. Thus, the physical afflictions of old age were not necessarily assessed as medical problems that required the care of a healer, but neither did people abandon the elderly to their fate.

1987); Joan J. Brumberg, *Fasting Girls: The Emergence of Anorexia Nervosa as a Modern Disease* (Cambridge, Mass., 1988); David Lederer, *Madness, Religion and the State in Early Modern Europe* (Cambridge, 2006), 1–21.

In sum, early modern peoples perceived sickness and health, understood the workings of their bodies, and anticipated their mortality in ways that diverged meaningfully from our own. Yet if they differed from us, they were not unconcerned with health; nor were they inured to pain and suffering. If they fought disease and afflictions with other means than those we employ today, they fought them no less fiercely, as the following chapters will show.

2   Plagues and peoples

In the same year [1348] there were immense upheavals in many parts of the world, as the result of a cruel pestilence which first broke out in countries across the sea and killed everyone in various horrifying ways. First, through the malignant influence of the planets and the corruption of the air, men and animals in those countries were struck motionless while going about their business, as if turned to stone . . . Those who escaped carried the pestilence with them, and infected all the places to which they brought their merchandise . . . and the neighboring regions through which they traveled.[1]

[The rash] extended over all parts of their bodies. Over the forehead, head, chest . . . Many died of it. They could no longer walk, they could do no more than lie down, stretched out on their beds. They couldn't bestir their bodies, neither to lie face down, nor on their backs, nor to turn from one side to the other. And when they did move, they cried out. In death, many [bodies] were like sticky, compacted, hard grain . . . many [survivors] were pockmarked . . . some were blind . . . this pestilence lasted sixty days, sixty lamentable days.[2]

In recent times I have seen scourges, horrible sicknesses, and many infirmities afflict mankind from all corners of the earth. Amongst them has crept in, from the western shores of Gaul, a disease which is so cruel, so distressing, so appalling that until now nothing so horrifying, nothing more terrible or disgusting, has ever been known on this earth.[3]

One of the most striking and frequently reproduced early modern images is the "Four Horsemen of the Apocalypse." Mentioned in the Book of Revelation, they are traditionally named after four omnipresent evils:

I have borrowed the title of this chapter from William H. McNeill's influential and eminently readable work: *Plagues and Peoples* (New York, 1976).

[1] From "Continuatio Novimontensis," quoted in *The Black Death*, ed. Rosemary Horrox (Manchester, 1994), 55.

[2] Fray Toribio Montolinia, *History of the Indians of New Spain* (1541), quoted in Donald R. Hopkins, *The Greatest Killer: Smallpox in History* (Chicago, 2002), 206.

[3] *Libellus Josephi Grunpeckii de mentalagra, alias morbo gallico*, quoted in Claude Quétel, *History of Syphilis*, trans. by Judith Braddock and Brian Pike (Baltimore, 1990), 17.

war, famine, death, and pestilence. The last of these, pestilence, forms
the subject of this chapter. While today we would probably associate
pestilence with "plague" (and mean the plague that swept across Europe
in the mid fourteenth century) or with an outbreak of epidemic disease
more comprehensively conceived, for early modern people, pestilence
bore broader associations. They yoked disease with more general misery, "heavy afflictions," and "perilous times." Early modern peoples had
several names for these outbreaks such as "the catching disease," "the
prevailing disease," and "the dangerous disease." Diseases that killed
huge numbers of people would fall into the category of pestilence or
plague, but so, too, would a "plague of locusts." Today we use the label
epidemic disease to describe such pestilences, but this term, indeed the
entire concept of epidemic, is itself a retrospective diagnosis. The science
of *epidemiology* itself is only about 150 years old. The modern definition of
epidemic – "a prevalence of a particular type of infection which appears
to be highly concentrated in time and space"[4] – was one early modern
people did not share. Yet, early modern people were perfectly capable of
identifying diseases (using their own concepts and words, of course) and
of understanding how they spread, even if, of course, they were unable
to identify the disease-causing and -spreading vectors and mechanisms
we recognize as relevant today. Epidemics are, therefore, always named
and, in some real sense, always fashioned retrospectively.

Epidemics, like diseases more generally, are of themselves empty of
sense and substance. Any disease and any epidemic "only acquires meaning and significance from its human context, from the ways in which it
infiltrates the lives of the people, from the reactions it provokes, and from
the manner in which it gives expression to cultural and political values."[5]
Giving relevance to large-scale disease outbreaks has long occupied the
historian in two ways: in discussing how people in the past understood
these diseases and in evaluating their attendant social, economic, demographic, and cultural consequences.

Historians have created categories to organize how people in the past
explained the occurrence and spread of pestilences: either (1) diseases
were thought to be communicated from person-to-person directly or indi-
rectly or (2) diseases were believed to arise and be transmitted through
water and air; thus, particular locations breed certain sicknesses. Scholars
have frequently labeled these explanations respectively *contagionist* and

---

[4] Macfarlane Burnet and David O. White, *Natural History of Infectious Disease* (4th edn.,
Cambridge, 1982), 127.
[5] David Arnold, "Cholera and Colonialism in British India," *Past and Present* 113 (1986):
151.

anti-contagionist (or *miasmatic*). Ideas about individual predispositions (themselves often predicated on humoral compositions) and contingent causes accounted for why some people remained unaffected even during the most virulent occurrences and for why the same environmental circumstances sometimes did, and sometimes did not, precipitate outbreaks.

The concept of contagion played little role in either Hippocratic or Galenic medicines. The Hippocratic work *On Airs, Waters, and Places* postulated that environmental factors bred and spread disease. The Bible offered more support for the idea of contagion, especially, for example, in respect to leprosy. In 1546, Girolamo Fracastoro (c.1478–1553) formulated the classic tract *On Contagion*, in which he argued that "seeds" or "fomites" propagated diseases. Thus, rigorously enforced quarantines, fumigation, and isolation of individual cases could check the transmission of disease. The microscopic work of the Jesuit natural historian and collector Athanasius Kircher (1602–80) and of the Dutch lens-grinder Antonj van Leeuwenhoek (1632–1723) bolstered the contagionist position: both men observed *animalcules* ("little animals") through their instruments.

Despite the discovery of microscopic entities, many people believed that most pestilences arose from factors that one can roughly categorize as environmental. Such environmental causes included impropitious meteorological and cosmic events, such as severe heat or a peculiar conjunction of the heavenly bodies, and miasmas or "bad air." Medical historians have often attributed the heyday of this explanatory mode to the late eighteenth and early nineteenth centuries and, in particular, link its rise to several yellow fever epidemics in North and South America (in Havana in 1761–62, Jamaica in 1655, Charleston in 1706, 1728, 1732 and intermittently between 1792 and 1799, and, especially, that of 1793 in Philadelphia) and to the waves of cholera that swept through European and American cities in the middle of the nineteenth century. In fact, however, both notions coexisted in early modern Europe and both ideas conditioned responses to epidemics. As the eminent medical historian Charles Rosenberg observes, "much of the epidemiological thought between classical antiquity and the present can be usefully understood as a series of shifting rearrangements of these thematic building blocks. In the great majority of instances, both styles of explanation were employed in combination, with one element or another figuring more prominently."[6]

---

[6] Charles Rosenberg, *Explaining Epidemics and Other Studies in the History of Medicine* (Cambridge, 1992), 295.

What ordinary people caught in the throes of a frightening biological experience thought is less clear. It appears, however, that a basic reaction was to consider dangerous outbreaks of disease as most often spread by contact and to shun if possible those who were ill. Even if learned opinion favored explanations relying on miasmas, popular reactions were generally based on avoidance. Thus, it seems probable that most people viewed epidemic diseases as somehow or other "contagious."

Clearly, academic and lay thinking on the underlying causes of disease outbreaks demonstrates greater complexities than the simple dichotomy postulating a conflict between the contagionist and anti-contagionist positions implies. Responses to disease emergencies mixed precautions derived from both theories, although, admittedly, governments and physicians usually favored quarantine and isolation as the most effective means of handling the problem. Thus, it was not the sanitarians of the nineteenth century who first began to combat environmental ills in order to stave off or curtail the ravages of epidemic disease. Early modern cities in the grip of plague worked to purify the air by shooting off cannon or building fires and to correct the corrupt atmosphere of diseased houses with applications of vinegar or aromatic oils. Large-scale projects to drain swamps began quite early in the middle ages and sought, on the one hand, to win more arable land but, on the other, to eradicate dangerous disease-brewing miasmas. Efforts to deal with dysentery focused primarily on trying to modify behaviors: advice to adjust diet and to avoid drafts and chills were prominent parts of prophylaxis. Even in the sixteenth and seventeenth centuries when anti-contagionist theories seemed to hold the upper hand among the learned, contagionist-conditioned responses to disease remained part of the package. Of course, religious and pious endeavors, such as prayers and processions, always formed a critically important weapon in any city's armory against disease and one of the first implemented.

A short natural history of disease

One might wonder where diseases came from in the first place. When did large-scale outbreaks become a problem for human beings? A trip far back in time answers some of these questions.

The history of human disease properly begins in the Paleolithic period (c.2,000,000 BCE to c.10,000 BCE) when human hunters and gatherers lived in small nomadic groups of fewer than one hundred individuals. Their mobility and the very low density of population prevented the rise of infectious or catching diseases or at least of those diseases that no other animal carried. Thus, the earliest humans enjoyed relative security from these diseases and from parasitic infestations. All this changed with the greatest event in human history: the Neolithic agricultural revolution (c.8,000 to c.3,500 BCE).

In simple terms, the settling down of populations and, in particular, the introduction of irrigated agriculture created the preconditions for the rise of infectious diseases. These diseases require a pool of susceptible victims that only a population of sufficient density can generate. With the domestication of animals, some *zoonoses* (animal diseases) passed to humans. For example, it is now thought that measles originally came from dogs, syphilis from monkeys, and leprosy from water buffalos. The growing number of people that agricultural labor demanded and made possible also produced poorer hygienic conditions. Living in close proximity to domesticated animals made the rapid spread of infectious diseases possible. From that point, and until well into the twentieth century, infectious diseases occasioned most human mortality.

Before examining the impact of large-scale disease outbreaks in early modern Europe, it is useful to review briefly the biology and ecology of infectious diseases in order to realize how multifarious disease-causing mechanisms are. While macroparasites like worms can certainly effect illness, microparasites – that is, bacteria, protozoa, or viruses – cause most human diseases and these diseases are propagated in several ways: through the air, by water or food, and through nonhuman vectors, such as mosquitoes, ticks, fleas, and lice (these include the arboviruses, or those spread by arthropods/insects). Major infectious diseases include bubonic plague (caused by a bacillus; bacilli are rod-shaped bacteria); dysentery (bacillus); typhus (bacterium); syphilis (bacterium); malaria (protozoan parasites); yellow fever (virus); and diphtheria (bacillus). Genetic predispositions and nutritional factors, of course, influence individual susceptibility. A correlation exists between famine or malnutrition and disease, although it is not a simple one. A *Malthusian theory* postulating that dramatic and rapid population increases intensified the effects of crop failures in the early fourteenth century (when the weather was unusually cold) and accounted, in some part at least, for the virulence of plague, has been shown to be unsatisfactory. In other words, while famines sometimes precede epidemics, they by no means inevitably do so. There is no direct causal connection because the disease cannot develop in the absence of the responsible microorganism. Malnutrition can reduce resistance to disease or at least to some diseases. However, well-nourished people with a fairly high standard of living do not enjoy complete protection from infections either; especially in the case of airborne viral diseases, such as smallpox, they are fully susceptible (as long, of course, as they have not had a previous case of smallpox or have not been inoculated or vaccinated). Moreover, the bacillus that causes bubonic plague requires a certain level of iron in the blood to multiply in the human body, and thus people with anemia prove poor hosts.

"Plague" in early modern Europe

When the "great dying" began in Siena in May 1348, Agnolo di Tura took up his pen to "recount the awful truth." His words reflect the feeling of many that "it was the end of the world."

[O]ne who did not see such horribleness can be called blessed. And the victims died almost immediately. They would swell beneath the armpits and in their groins, and fall over while talking. Father abandoned child, wife husband, one brother another; for this illness seemed to strike through breath and sight. And so they died. And none could be found to bury the dead for money or friendship. Members of a household brought their dead to a ditch as best they could, without priest, without divine offices. Nor did the death bell sound. And in many places in Siena great pits were dug and piled deep with the multitude of dead. And they died by the hundreds, both day and night, and all were thrown in those ditches and covered with earth. And as soon as those ditches were filled, more were dug.[7]

What di Tura described was a disease that despoiled Europe in the middle of the fourteenth century and which frequently reappeared with greater or lesser killing force until it rather mysteriously vanished from the European continent almost 400 years later. Many historians still accept that this disease was *bubonic* plague or a mixture of bubonic and *pneumonic* plagues. The most popular name for the disease outbreak of 1348–50 is the Black Death, although this name did not arise until the sixteenth century and was not commonly used before the nineteenth. Early modern Europeans would have spoken of pestilence or plague and meant thereby not a specific disease but any one occasioning frightening mortality. Still, the frequency with which the disease reappeared – in virtually every generation after 1348 – allowed people to recognize it as something particular and specific.

The causative agent of bubonic plague remained unknown until the end of the nineteenth century when researchers in China in 1893–94 discovered the responsible bacillus, *Yersinia pestis* (now less frequently known by its older name, *Pasteurella pestis*). Subsequent work uncovered the mode of transmission. Basically, the story is one of an *epizootic* (an epidemic of animal populations). In this case, a disease of the European black rat (*Rattus rattus*) transferred to humans through the bite of the rat flea (*Xenopsylla cheopis*). When the flea's preferred host (the rat) dies,

---

[7] Chronicle of Agnolo di Tura, quoted in *The Black Death*, ed. by William Bowsky (New York, 1971), 13–14.

the flea seeks another home, often biting a human and transmitting the disease to a new victim. For the disease to become epidemic, a suitable environment must exist to support this mechanism. Fleas, rats, and humans must live in close proximity and the populations of each must be dense enough to sustain the epidemic.

Once infected, a person develops alarming symptoms within about six days. A very high temperature of 103 to 104 F (39.5 to 40 C) soon follows initial feelings of discomfort, nausea, and pains in the limbs and lower back. *Buboes*, or swellings in the lymph nodes, typically appear in groin or armpit, and are extremely painful. Individual *case mortality* (that is, the chance an infected individual has of dying from the disease without treatment) is about 60 percent. A more severe form of plague, pneumonic plague, evolves when plague bacilli settle in the lungs and are then expelled with every cough. It is virtually always lethal.

It is important to recognize, however, that the disease mechanism described in the last two paragraphs is that observed in modern cases of plague. Epidemiologists have cautiously identified one form of plague, *Medievalis*, with what they also label the second *pandemic* (an epidemic spread over a wide geographical area) of bubonic plague. The modern medical and biological evidence on plague, concerning cause and transmission, however, has proved difficult to reconcile with the historical record. Indeed, a recent article concludes that "[w]hatever the precise nature of the disease that hides behind *pestilence* and *pest* in premodern Europe, it cannot be identified with modern bubonic plague."[8] Almost every point in the simple, rather elegantly constructed story of rats and fleas has come under fire. Historians and demographers have raised doubts about the suitability of various vectors to spread the disease in the manner described, about the requisite density of fleas and rodents, and about whether the disease we today diagnose as bubonic/pneumonic plague was the "plague" of the fourteenth century.

These problems know no easy solutions and raise crucial questions about how we deal with diseases historically. As we have seen, many medical historians are wary about the whole enterprise of trying to diagnose diseases in the past. Those who are less reticent to do so (among these, one must count the historical demographers) still have come to question whether the epidemic of early modern times that has been facilely labeled "plague" was indeed bubonic plague, pointing out that many facts do not correspond well to modern manifestations. Critics have argued that perhaps another disease entirely was responsible (one scholar has, for

---

[8] Peter Christiansen, "'In These Perilous Times': Plague and Plague Policies in Early Modern Denmark," *Medical History* 47 (2003): 416.

example, proposed anthrax), while others wonder if perhaps the "plague," considering its great lethality, did not combine several diseases, including smallpox, typhus, and dysentery. Recently, the DNA from medieval corpses that died from other causes has tested positive for *Y. pestis* which seems to suggest that it was at the very least a contributing factor in the "great dying" di Tura knew.[9]

Whatever the plague of the mid fourteenth century truly was, its course is historically traceable. It apparently began in China and moved along the trade routes to Tashkent, Astrakhan, and cities in southern Russia. By 1346, it had reached the Crimean peninsula and spread to Genoese merchants in Caffa then under siege by the Mongol army. Fleeing merchants carried the plague all along the Mediterranean littoral, to the islands of Sicily, Sardinia, and Corsica and thence to Spain, Italy, and north Africa. Plague edged its way up the Rhône river valley and into France, traversed Italy into central Europe, and penetrated southern Germany. By 1348, France, Sweden, south England, Germany, Switzerland, and Poland had all been affected. Plague's initial attack has generally been viewed as curiously uneven; some areas, such as Italy, suffered cruelly, while other parts of Europe, especially the Low Countries and Bohemia, escaped virtually unscathed. Still, some recent research strongly suggests that even these supposedly untouched areas were also hit and, furthermore, that the greatest impact of plague was in rural not urban areas.[10]

After the middle of the fourteenth century, plague did not disappear but rather recurred in almost every generation from 1350 to 1721 in western Europe (and there was a great epidemic in Moscow in 1770–72). For instance, in the United Provinces from 1450 to 1668, plague appeared in one or more places in 107 individual years. The longest reprieve lasted from 1539 to 1550. Major epidemics in several places at once occurred in 1557–58, 1573–74, 1595–1605, 1624–25, 1635–37, 1652–57, and, finally, 1664–67; thereafter plague disappeared from the Low Countries for good. In addition, after 1557–58, and especially after 1599, plague tended to affect larger areas with each subsequent incursion.[11] Later plagues, however, were more scattered and, while they could be quite disruptive, such as in Florence and Pisa in 1631, in Barcelona in 1651, and in London in 1665, lethality began to abate. Still, plague recurred

[9] Vivian Nutton, ed., *Pestilential Complexities: Understanding Medieval Plague* (London, 2008) offers up-to-date assessments of these difficulties.

[10] Ole J. Benedictow, *The Black Death, 1346–1353: The Complete History* (Woodbridge, 2004).

[11] L. Noordegraaf und G. Valk, *De gave gods: de pest in Holland vanaf de late Middeleeuwen* (Bergen, 1988), 225–28.

frequently enough to constitute a very real threat and to remain a vivid and frightening image in the minds of Europeans.

Historians have made a veritable industry out of plague; both the mid-fourteenth-century incursion and subsequent ones have attracted hundreds, even thousands, of researchers. For generations, scholars rated plague, along with the Renaissance, the Reformation, the Thirty Years War, and the Enlightenment, as major factors in the subsequent evolution of European society. Over the past two decades, however, skepticism has grown as to whether plague, and especially the plague of the mid fourteenth century, really represented a turning point in European history. Admittedly, it seems counterintuitive to argue that an outbreak of disease that caused so much death – and estimates range from one third to two thirds of the entire European population – might not be as disruptive as once asserted. Yet the progressive dismantling of the "plague-as-unequaled-crisis" theory has come to downplay the global dimensions of plague's effects, while stressing its unique social and cultural implications for specific places and groups. Certainly, an assessment of plague's impact is neither easy nor self-evident. Many of the ways in which scholars interpreted the consequences of plague, products of a consensus that crystallized in the 1940s and 1950s, have shown themselves to be less convincing. Plague now appears to be a considerably more complex phenomenon than once believed.

Above all, the debate still rages about the impact of plague-caused mortality on broader historical trends. We are now, for instance, much less sure about the economic consequences of plague than we once were. Did real wages climb in response to a shortage of workers? Did fertility bounce back? Did areas recover quickly or only slowly from the plague? Did it contribute to the rise or decline of serfdom? None of these questions has received a fully satisfactory answer. Historians have found it extremely difficult as well to disentangle the effects of plague from the other factors that made the 1300s, and especially the second half of that century, so "disastrous." Endemic warfare, famine, and declining population even before plague hit characterized those decades. Moreover, aggregated economic and population data are simply too crude to allow us to draw sustainable conclusions, except for very restricted areas, certain occupational groups, or isolated religious communities.

In short, although there is no reason to deny that plague was a great blow for the European population, it is no longer obvious exactly how to measure and appraise the totality of its effects. Moreover, despite the horror an incursion of plague produced, there was always a reasoned response. The methods of preventing and controlling plague, of course, depended heavily on contemporary understandings of its causes and

2.1 Christ throwing down arrows of plague, 1424

course. Everyone accepted that the ultimate source of all disease was God and many interpreted "great dyings" as a mark of divine disfavor, as a punishment for collective wickedness, or as a harbinger of Armageddon. Under such circumstances, one typical reaction to plague involved attempts to expiate sin or placate God's wrath. The remedy the priest Dom Theophilus of Milan prescribed for plague advised that

> Whenever one is struck down by the plague they should immediately provide themselves with a medicine like this. First let him gather as much as he can of bitter loathing towards the sins committed by him, and the same quantity of true contrition of heart, and mix the two into an ointment with the water of tears. Then let him make a vomit of frank and honest confession, by which he shall be purged of the pestilential poison of sin, and the boil of his vice shall be totally liquefied and melt away. Then the spirit, formerly weighed down by the plague of sin, will be left all light and full of blessed joy.[12]

Cities organized processions and religious services in hopes of checking plague's spread. Catholics and Protestants alike prayed and fasted either

---

[12] Quoted in *The Black Death* (ed. by Horrox), 55.

to prevent or to alleviate plague. In Anglican England, for instance, in 1636, the government ordered copies of *A Forme of Common Prayer, Together with an order of Fasting: For the Averting of God's heavie Visitation upon Many places of this Kingdome* to be printed and distributed and four years later proclaimed "a generall fast to be kept thorowout the realm." In Amsterdam in 1655, the Reformed church council, following a week when 750 people died, convened a prayer meeting each Wednesday evening. Flagellation cults, which had began earlier, reappeared during the late medieval plague in central and northern Europe. Their members sought to do penance and thus ward off the plague. In 1349, Pope Clement VI condemned them as heretical. Jews, too, often suffered persecution during plague outbreaks and were sometimes accused of spreading the plague by poisoning wells. Christian mobs attacked Jewish settlements and by 1351, sixty large and some 150 smaller Jewish communities had been destroyed. Migrants and aliens of all kinds, and especially vagrants and beggars, ran the danger of being accused of carrying the plague with them. In some places, tales of plague-spreading conspiracies made the rounds. Women perceived as licentious also came in for criticism and were even thought to be trying to do away with their menfolk and rivals by poisoning them.[13] Curiously, the scapegoating of witches or cunningfolk as the propagators of plague was rare and healers in general were seldom blamed.

But religious responses, while ubiquitous, served as only one reaction to plague, albeit a very important one. Ordinary people, as well as those in positions of authority (secular, intellectual, and religious), did not reject the idea that plague could have natural *and* supernatural origins. Both faith and reason conditioned responses to plague and the solutions chosen did not prove antagonistic to one another. The two systems of belief worked together, usually harmoniously. Neither did physicians and the clergy, or secular and religious authorities more generally, engage in an obvious tussle for power (although individual instances of conflict occurred). Even if most people accepted the ultimate divine origin of plague, they also acknowledged the role of other factors, including odd weather patterns (scorching summers or frigid winters), famines, troop movements, wars, "fetid miasmas," stagnant pools of water, prodigies, monstrous births, and other premonitions. The French chronicler Guillaume de Nangis (d. 1300) observed a "great star" which "sent out many separate beams of light," which he felt "presaged the incredible

---

[13] William G. Naphy, *Plagues, Poisons, and Potions: Plague-Spreading Conspiracies in the Western Alps* (Manchester, 2002); Suzanne E. Hatty and James Hatty, *The Disordered Body: Epidemic Disease and Cultural Transformation* (Albany, N.Y., 1998).

pestilence which soon followed." De Nangis lived and died before the great plague of the mid fourteenth century, but faith in the predictive qualities of celestial phenomena was still strong fifty years later.

Acknowledging the divine fount of all disease did not prevent people from seeking assistance from mortal healers nor governments from enacting public health ordinances, however. Besides the religious restoratives of penance, prayer, and submission, one deployed natural remedies and dietary prescriptives. Galenic principles continued to determine most physical treatments. Physicians and surgeons bled patients and lanced buboes hoping to eliminate corrupted humors and restore health. Healers prescribed medicines of numerous kinds in great profusion including, for those who could afford them, the famous *theriac*, which contained a vast number of ingredients. One formula, called Venetian treacle, specified as many as sixty-four components, including viper flesh, opium, and cinnamon, all mixed with honey to make it palatable. Plague preventives also emphasized moderate diets, the burning of aromatic herbs, and the use of essence of myrrh or vinegar to purify clothing, goods, and papers. Writing during the plague of 1631 in Pistoia, the physician Stefano Arrighi advised patients to take "meals of good meat and eggs," apply "cupping glasses morning and evening," and swallow a daily dose of eight drops of *olio contravelem* (anti-venomous oil).[14]

Prevention and control mixed old rules and more recently evolved practices. When confronted with plague, individuals sought help in many forms. Prayer and repentance formed perhaps the initial recourse, but so, too, did avoidance. People stayed home, shunned the ill, and sometimes abandoned family members. Perhaps the most common reaction (and one that formed the basis for the *Decameron* of Giovanni Boccaccio) was flight, which physicians, municipal officials, and religious authorities all sanctioned. Martin Luther, for example, vindicated magistrates who fled their jurisdictions in times of plague as long as they appointed appropriate substitutes to carry out essential duties in their absence. Failure to flee could even constitute a mortal sin as a form of suicide. During the plague of 1651 in Barcelona, the tanner Miquel Parets remarked that

it is quite right to flee in order not to suffer from this disease, for it is most cruel, but it is just as right to flee in order not to witness the travails and misfortunes and privations that are suffered wherever the plague is found, which are more than any person can stand.

---

[14] Quoted in Carlo Cipolla, *Fighting the Plague in Seventeenth-Century Italy* (Madison, Wisc., 1976), 64.

And flee people did. During the Great Plague of 1665 in London, Samuel Pepys lamented in his diary, "But Lord, how empty the streets are, and melancholy."[15]

Governments set up quarantines, arranged for the fumigation of goods and persons, forbade public assemblies (and even church-going), established special hospitals for the isolation of victims, closed houses, provided medical and nursing care to sufferers, and hired more grave-diggers. Although authorities instituted these measures almost every-where, cities enforced them more vigorously than did territories or villages. After the invention of printing in the mid fifteenth century, municipalities and territorial states began issuing short pamphlets deal-ing with "preservation and cure." These so-called plague tracts advised on rules of diet and regimen and proposed treatments, such as lancing buboes and then cauterizing the wounds. A virtual flood of such advice, often in the form of self-help literature, poured off the presses in the sev-enteenth and eighteenth centuries and, over the years, came to address not only plague but other sorts of "folk-diseases" including smallpox and dysentery.

The city-physician of Ulm, Germany, Heinrich Steinhöwel (1420–82), laid out typical rules in his *Büchlein der Ordnung der Pestilenz* (Little Book of Rules for Plague, 1473). One should, he wrote, pay close attention to purifying houses and should throw open windows and doors to allow light and air to enter. Bonfires should be lighted to expel feculence from the atmosphere. Rooms should be thoroughly scrubbed with water and vinegar and strewn with "sour and cooling" as well as fragrant plants. One should, if possible, avoid living near slaughterhouses and cemeter-ies and shun contacts with beggars and vagrants. In general, one should eat lightly, and consume nothing when not hungry or until the previ-ous meal had been well digested and evacuated. In winter, one should choose warm foods; in summer cool but not cold or chilled ones. Mod-erate exercise after meals was good; strenuous exercise, however, quite injurious.

Intricate dietary rules touched on almost all foods. Steinhöwel advised that black and blue plums were good, but one must peel them and dust them with sugar before eating. Meat from pastured animals was far bet-ter than from those kept in stalls. One should abstain from all organ meats with the exception of chicken livers, cock testicles, sheep and goat brains; all should be prepared with liberal quantities of pepper and

---

[15] James S. Amelang, trans. and ed., *A Journal of the Plague Year: The Diary of the Barcelona Tanner Miquel Parets 1651* (New York, 1991), 59; Samuel Pepys, *The Diary of Samuel Pepys: A New and Complete Transcription*, edited by William A. Armstrong, *et al.*, (11 vols., Berkeley, 1970–83), entry for October 16, 1665.

ginger. Moreover, one should quell strong emotions of all kinds and seek out "harmless pleasures." He recommended a moderate enjoyment of sexual intercourse, but warned that venereal excesses were perilous.

If someone in the household fell ill, others nearby must take great care to purge the air of the sickroom. Steinhöwel advised the use of smelling salts and witch hazel or "good old wine" with which one should rinse the mouth and nasal passages, wash hands and face. Sprinkling some behind the ears and rubbing it on arms and the genitals, as well as drinking some, was beneficial. He advised the use of "pest tablets," boluses, and suppositories.

Steinhöwel cautioned that those who took ill must be treated rapidly if they were to survive: the first day was absolutely critical. Besides cleaning and airing the sickroom, the patient should have a light diet of gruel, chicken broth, vinegar, delicate meats, and lemon juice in water. Singing and good conversation would keep the patient in good spirits. On the first day, one should not permit the patient to sleep because during sleep the "poisonous material" could move to the heart and kill. Mild vegetable laxatives (plums and tamarind) would keep bowels open and the patient should also be bled in moderation. Once the characteristic buboes formed, an application of "drawing" poultices would encourage them to burst. If necessary, they might be lanced, then dressed with egg white and a healing salve. These directives were by no means unique to Steinhöwel; all could be found elsewhere.[16]

Many historians have seen in the pestilence of the mid fourteenth century the initial stimulus for humankind's first effective disease-preventing interventions. Others are less sure, suggesting that many public health practices were actually much older or derived from other sources and concerns. One argument maintains that only the repeated experience with several epidemics generated the first real public health measures which took shape, therefore, in the late fifteenth rather than the mid fourteenth century. Factors other than disease also appear to have played a substantial role. Ann Carmichael, for example, concludes that plague legislation had more to do with long-term shifts in attitudes toward the poor than with an immediate experience of plague. Brian Pullan points out that some hoped to assuage the anger of God by directing acts of charity toward the destitute, although the endowment and construction of plague hospitals could just as easily be motivated by practical considerations as by religious and charitable motives.[17]

---

[16] Karl Sudhoff, *Der Ulmer Stadtarzt Dr. Heinrich Steinhöwel (1429–1482) als Pestauthor* (Munich, 1926), 196–204.

[17] Ann G. Carmichael, *Plague and the Poor in Renaissance Florence* (Cambridge, 1986); Brian Pullan, *Rich and Poor in Renaissance Venice: The Social Institutions of a Catholic State, to 1620* (Oxford, 1971).

This pestilence, whether it was bubonic plague or whether it represented a confluence of afflictions conveniently gathered under the umbrella term of "plague," dominated European mortality and the European psyche from the fourteenth to the middle of the seventeenth century or longer. It gripped the imagination and sent shivers of fear down the spines of everyone when its presence was documented or when it approached. Then its grip on Europe began to loosen, and it fell away entirely (at least for western Europe) after 1720–21; Marseilles was the last major city to suffer a serious epidemic. Already by the end of the sixteenth century, however, plague had ceased to cause major reversals in general population growth, despite the two great waves of plague that broke over Europe in 1630–31 and 1665–70. The question that continues to perplex historians is why.

The mystery surrounding the end of plague in Europe has defied the combined efforts of historians, epidemiologists, and demographers to dispel it completely. Whereas it was once thought that the replacement of the black rat by the brown rat was responsible, few today accept this as a convincing explanation. Current thinking on the disappearance of plague from western Europe usually turns in one of two directions. Some scholars insist that, quite simply, quarantine and other *cordon sanitaire* measures worked, or at least significantly helped. Thus, by interdicting travel early modern governments contributed substantially to the disappearance of plague from the European landscape.[18] One problem with this interpretation is that it is by no means clear that states and cities were capable of enforcing restrictions rigorously; much anecdotal evidence testifies to the contrary.[19] Moreover, the network of public health arrangements typical of early modern Europe – including rules about quarantines, the founding of pesthouses, and measures for sanitary reform – developed as regular parts of urban policies only later and were largely absent even in rudimentary forms until the middle of the sixteenth century or after. In a world that lacked effective means of policing, it is perhaps not very likely that quarantines could effect such a change. Furthermore, this argument turns on the idea that plague was always imported into Europe and that no foci of infection existed there. It now seems clear that reservoirs of the disease (probably among burrowing rodents) had developed in Europe and the Middle East by the sixteenth century.

---

[18] Christiansen, "'In These Perilous Times'," 450.

[19] Carlo Cipolla, *Faith, Reason, and the Plague in Seventeenth-Century Tuscany* (New York, 1979); Alexandra Parma Cook and Noble David Cook, *The Plague Files: Crisis Management in Sixteenth-Century Seville* (Baton Rouge, 2009), 168–75, 190–99.

Other observers have suggested that shifts in the Eurasian trade routes disrupted the movement of diseases from east to west. Another explanation emphasizes climate change. The last great plague epidemics in northern and southern Europe (respectively in the 1660s and in 1720) coincided with what climatologists call the Little Ice Age when mean temperatures averaged lower than usual, reducing crop yields and subsequently resulting in economic dislocations that swelled the numbers of migrants on the roads. New building materials and sanitation measures could have played a role as well, but it is difficult to document what these were and when, where, or even if they took hold. Also possible is that the disease organism responsible mutated to a less virulent strain as other microparasites are known to do in a biologically "seasoned" population, that is, in a population with a long experience of a particular disease.

Even though plague vanished, its memory remained vivid and daily vocabulary retained the word as a synonym for misery and evil. Plague had a profound effect on the consciousness of Europeans and on their art and literature, even if one can no longer accept that plague alone wrought great tidal changes in European mentalities. The famous Dutch historian Johan Huizinga set the tone in 1919. In *The Autumn of the Middle Ages*, he argued that the disasters of the fourteenth century, and especially plague, marked the end of the flourishing culture of the high middle ages and ushered in a period of despair, cultural exhaustion, and lack of innovation. Art became morbid and people less creative; the rich learning of the high middle ages evaporated and was replaced by arid and unimaginative scholarship. More recently, scholars have come to suspect this picture of gloom and doom. Clearly the plague influenced art and literature; Boccaccio's magnificent *Decameron* is only one celebrated example. We realize now, however, that many of the themes, topics, religious practices, and attitudes that seem to have emerged from the horrors of plague were actually in place well before the mid fourteenth century. Yet, there is little doubt that plague helped shape the trajectory of Italian painting, for example, even if it may have only accelerated tendencies already under way. The general popularity of themes associated with death was not new in the middle of the fourteenth century, but they did become more common, appearing in the motifs of *momento mori* and the many splendidly rendered Dances of Death. More recently, Samuel Cohn has argued that plague stimulated an artistic revival. Survivors did not slip into religious pessimism and civic inactivity, but rather became even more active patrons of the arts.[20]

---

[20] Samuel K. Cohn, Jr., *The Cult of Remembrance and the Black Death: Six Renaissance Cities in Central Italy* (Baltimore, 1992).

2.2 Dance of Death, 1493

Plague could also serve political purposes. Consider, for example, the canonization of Domenica Nardini da Paradiso during the outbreak of 1630–31 in Florence. In a close study of the events, Giulia Calvi reveals how the ecclesiastical proceedings that began at the very height of the outbreak formed a "political theater" in which the Medici rulers of the city used "the drama of votive masses, of the exhumed body and relics [of Domenica] . . . [as] a deliberate attempt to proclaim the legitimacy of the embattled regime through an appeal to 'its' plague saint."[21]

The Great Pox

It is unclear whether the plague of the mid fourteenth century represented a disease new to Europe, but the one that broke out during the French king's Italian campaign of 1494–95 almost certainly did. A frightful and

---

[21] Giulia Calvi, *Histories of a Plague Year: The Social and the Imaginary in Baroque Florence* (Berkeley and Los Angeles, 1989), xiii–xiv.

Table 2.1. *Plague mortality in some Italian cities*

	City	Pre-plague Population	Deaths	Deaths/population (%)
1576–77	Venice	180,000	50,000	28
1630–31	Bologna	62,000	15,000	24
	Cremona	37,000	17,000	46
	Florence	76,000	9,000	12
	Milan	130,000	60,000	46
	Padua	32,000	19,000	59
	Pistoia	8,000	1,200	15
	Venice	140,000	46,000	33
	Verona	54,000	33,000	61
1656–57	Genoa	75,000	45,000	60
	Naples	300,000	150,000	50
	Rome	123,000	23,000	19

Source: Carlo Cipolla, *Fighting Plague in Seventeenth-Century Italy* (Madison, Wisc., 1976), 64.

previously unknown affliction with quite horrifying symptoms first struck Venetian troops:

several men-at-arms or footsoldiers who, owing to the ferment of the humours, had "pustules" on their faces and all over their bodies. These looked rather like grains of millet, and usually appeared on the outer surface of the foreskin, or on the glans [of the penis], accompanied by a mild pruritus [itching]. Sometimes the first sign would be a single "pustule" looking like a painless cyst, but the scratching provoked by the pruritus subsequently produced a gnawing ulceration. Some days later, the sufferers were driven to distraction by the pains they experienced in their arms, legs, and feet, and by an eruption of large "pustules" [which] lasted . . . for a year or more, if left untreated.[22]

This physician's observations formed one of the first clinical descriptions of the "Great Pox" or the "French disease," a malady that would within a decade sweep over Europe and subsequently destroy the bodies and haunt the imaginations of Europeans for centuries. It has generally been identified as syphilis, but, like all such identifications, it is a historically problematic one.

Syphilis (if the "Great Pox" or "French disease" was in truth the same as modern syphilis) in the sixteenth century assumed an alarmingly

[22] Quoted in Quétel, *History of Syphilis*, 10.

virulent form. Today we know syphilis as a chronic disease, contracted either by venereal infection or blood transfusion, and one that normally exhibits long periods of asymptomatic latency. Even untreated, two thirds of those infected will suffer little or no impairment, although more severe symptoms such as motor dysfunctions, paresis (muscular weakness caused by disease of the nervous system), and serious cardiovascular problems appear in the rest. The sixteenth-century Great Pox seemed to exhibit another disease profile entirely. The first epidemics were especially malignant, and the disease – atypically for modern chronic syphilis – often killed in its initial stages. Fracastoro composed a lengthy poem that gave the disease its now-familiar name (but one that was not used commonly until the eighteenth century). In it, he described disgusting pustules filled with purulent matter and even "joints stripped of their very flesh, bones rotting, and foully gaping mouths gnawed away." Joseph Grünpeck (c.1473–1532), whose infection dated from 1498, narrated how "the disease loosed its first arrow into my Priapic gland which, on account of the wound, became so swollen that both hands could scarcely circle it."[23] Contemporaries feared that even casual contact could pass the malady on to others and thus avoided or sequestered its victims in "pox" hospitals (see Chapter 5).

The apparent novelty of the disease led many in the sixteenth century, and since, to speculate as to its origins and to suggest that syphilis had arrived in Europe from the recently discovered New World hidden deep within the bodies of Columbus's returning sailors. If this is true (and there are dissenting views), then syphilis illustrates the consequences of contact and exchange between two worlds that had for millennia been isolated from each other.[24] (Smallpox is another excellent illustration, although in that case the worst consequences affected the Native American populations.) Later on, the establishment of colonial empires, the new regularity of traffic between Europe, America, and Africa, and a burgeoning triangular commerce, transported disease pathogens across oceanic expanses and altered the world's biological and demographic history. Malaria, long present in Europe, may have become more prevalent due to reinfection from the Americas and Africa. Yellow fever was probably carried from Africa to America in the sixteenth century, where it dealt a devastating blow to many colonial settlements, and then from

---

[23] Girolamo Fracastoro, *Syphilis sive morbus Gallicus* (1546), quoted in Roderick E. McGrew, *Encyclopedia of Medical History* (New York, 1985), 331; Joseph Grünpeck, *Libellus Josephi Grunpeckii*, quoted in Quétel, *History of Syphilis*, 17.

[24] Alfred W. Crosby, Jr. is the best-known advocate of the Columbian theory. *The Columbian Exchange: Biological and Cultural Consequences of 1492* (Westport, Conn., 1972).

America to Europe where appalling (if ultimately very limited) outbreaks occurred in the seventeenth and eighteenth centuries.

But *did* this new disease come from the New World? Soon after its first appearance, some observers crafted what is now known as the Columbian theory. Gonzalo Fernandez de Oviedo (1478–1557) singled out Columbus's crews as the point of origin and in 1539 Rodrigo Ruy Diaz de Isla (1462–1542) ventured a similar assertion in his *A Treatise on the Serpentine Malady*. For Oviedo and de Isla, syphilis was an American disease brought back to Europe. Paleopathologists have compared Old World and New World bones for hundreds of years before the 1493 return of Columbus's flotilla and have spotted evidence of syphilitic-like lesions in skeletons from the New World, but not from the Old. Bone evidence, however, offers no unequivocal proof because other diseases produce similar pathological traces.

Another position is the *unitarian theory*. According to this point of view, syphilis had always been present in the Old World. Some sixteenth-century observers maintained that the writers of the ancient world had described all diseases and that descriptions of leprosy or elephantiasis also included syphilis. More modern versions argue that several types of related infections, such as contemporary bejel (endemic syphilis in a nonvenereal form whose causative microorganisms are similar to those of syphilis), have always been present in the Old World and are frequently found on the African continent. Bejel and similar diseases, like yaws and pinta, typically thrive in hot, dry climates. The unitarian theory further postulates that, in more temperate and wetter zones like Europe, the spirochetes that cause syphilis recede deeper into the body and find a congenial habitat in the human genitals. To explain the virulence of the sixteenth-century epidemic, then, the unitarian theory stresses sociomilitary factors, especially those accompanying the almost constant warfare of the sixteenth century. A good deal of heated historical debate, therefore, continues to boil over the origins of syphilis. Neither theory is fully convincing, although it does seem that the Columbians have made the stronger case to date.

Whatever its origins, the Great Pox placed new demands on the healing arts. To treat it, physicians and surgeons first tried traditional therapies. They often turned to a long-favored way to correct humoral imbalances: bleeding. When that failed, the search for other remedies began and a whole array of them quickly became popular. One of these was guaiacum, a decoction from the resin of a New World tree imported from Hispaniola (the island that Haiti and the Dominican Republic today share). Its advocates argued that because the source of the disease lay in the New World, so, too, had God placed its cure there. Paracelsus popularized another treatment that quickly gained many adherents: mercury. Mercury apparently exerted at least some retardant effect on the progress of the disease; but it was a dangerous therapy. The saying "a night with Venus, a lifetime with Mercury" described a sad reality for the syphilis sufferer. In the sixteenth century, mercury was applied externally as a salve, ointment, plaster, or rub; it was later taken internally. According to many who underwent mercury treatments, the cure proved as bad as, or worse than, the ailment. Mercury corroded the membranes of the mouth, loosened teeth in their sockets, and even ate away jawbones, often turning the mouth and throat into one large stinking ulcer. Patients salivated profusely. By the eighteenth century, the preferred substance for the treatment of venereal disease was sublimate of mercury (know as "Van Swieten's liquor" after its most famous physician-proponent). Not until the twentieth century did more effective and safer medicines (first the arsenic compound Salvarsan and then penicillin) become available. In addition, because of the ghastliness of both the disease and the mercury cure, and because of the well-known sexual nature of its transmission, there arose a huge market for alternative remedies and ways for sufferers to obtain them discreetly. In the eighteenth century, newspapers printed numerous advertisements for proprietary medicines for syphilis, often sold under euphemistic names such as Kennedy's Lisbon Diet Drink.

The impact of the Great Pox was, however, in the end more cultural and social than demographic. Because of the nature of the disease, its mortality rate remained low, far less than for plague or the other common pestilences that afflicted early modern Europe. The pox was often viewed as an incurable disease much like leprosy; its sufferers were what the Italians called *incurabili*. Like plague, syphilis stimulated a harsher attitude to beggars and vagrants whose sores appeared to be syphilitic lesions. Governments closed down traditional social institutions, such as bathhouses and brothels, to prevent infection and took stronger measures to control prostitutes. Harsher attitudes toward licentiousness and sexuality grew out of the fear of spreading the disease and many believed that men who had sex with "morally ruined women" – a category which apparently included not only professional prostitutes and courtesans but also flirts and those who dressed above their station – would contract the disease. Some historians have documented attempts (in Venice, for example) to lock up beautiful young women to prevent them from becoming infected and then infecting others.[25]

---

[25] Jon Arrizabalaga, John Henderson, and Roger French, *The Great Pox: The French Disease in Renaissance Europe* (New Haven and London, 1997), 51; Laura J. McGough,

The speckled monster

If plague and syphilis were new diseases in early modern Europe, a disease familiar since antiquity – smallpox – was another great killer. Smallpox scared and scarred as well as slew. In 1715, the twenty-six-year-old Lady Mary Wortley Montagu (1689–1762) was a great beauty. Then she got smallpox. Although she survived, she was badly disfigured. "How I am changed!" she moaned in verse, "alas! how I am grown/ A frightful spectre to myself unknown."[26] Nonetheless, she was lucky; she lived. One quarter of those who contracted smallpox in early modern Europe were less fortunate. Many more were, like Lady Mary, severely pox-marked or even blinded by the disease. Millions of Europeans and millions more in the New World were affected.

Smallpox is no longer an active infection. Beginning in 1967, the World Health Organization embarked on a campaign to eradicate smallpox that succeeded ten years later. Today, smallpox virus exists only in laboratories. Because smallpox only infected human beings (other mammals have their own forms of the disease: cowpox and monkeypox, for example), the disease could not hide away in animal reservoirs, as plague does in rodent populations, to reactivate among humans later. Smallpox was an acute viral disease transmitted by droplet infection. There were two important types, *variola major*, which exhibited a mortality rate of about 25–30 percent, and a less virulent form, *variola minor*, with far milder symptoms and a death rate of no more than 1 percent. Variola minor seems to have appeared in Europe only in the nineteenth century and thus the far more deadly variola major prevailed in earlier centuries.

The first symptoms often did not seem alarming. High fever, severe pains in limbs and back, splitting headaches, and sometimes convulsions, however, soon followed the vague aches and soreness that heralded the onset of the infection. The typical red rash manifested itself within two to five days and could be mild, with just a few, discrete pustules on face, hands, or legs; or more severe, with the pox covering the limbs and torso, and producing scarring, blindness, or impotence (in men); or confluent, which caused the skin of the victim to become necrotic and peel away in large sheets. This last form frequently resulted in death when the virus attacked major internal organs such as the liver, lungs, or intestines. Populations previously unexposed to the virus, such as the indigenous

"Quarantining Beauty in Early Modern Venice," in Kevin Siena, ed., *Sins of the Flesh: Responding to Sexual Disease in Early Modern Europe* (Toronto, 2005), 210–36.

[26] Quoted in J. R. Smith, *The Speckled Monster: Smallpox in England, 1670–1970, with Particular Reference to Essex* (Chelmsford, 1987), 19.

peoples of North and South America, suffered terribly. A Portuguese man in Bahia, Brazil, described the 1563 outbreak there:

This was a form of smallpox or pox so loathsome and evil-smelling that none could stand the great stench that emerged from [the victims]. For this reason many died untended, consumed by the worms that grew in the wounds of the pox and were engendered in their bodies in such abundance and of such great size that they caused horror and shock to any who saw them.[27]

Surviving an episode, however, conferred a perfect lifelong immunity.

Smallpox is a very old disease that probably beset even the aggregating Neolithic populations. Many epidemics apparently ravaged the ancient world and perhaps smallpox was responsible for the famous "Antonine plague" (briefly described by Galen in his *Methodus Medendi*) which struck the Roman Empire in the second century CE. Smallpox probably became permanently established in western Europe by the twelfth century, although it did not have a major impact on European populations until the sixteenth and seventeenth centuries when it became, in the words of the nineteenth-century historian Thomas Macaulay "the most terrible of all the ministers of death." Despite the tendency to confuse smallpox with other diseases that produced similar rashes, such as measles, Europeans understood smallpox to be a specific, contagious disease. As early as the late ninth century, the Persian physician Muhammad ibn Zakarīya Rāzi (865–925 CE), often known in the West as Rhazes or Rasis, identified smallpox and measles as two distinct contagious diseases.

At the beginning of the 1520s, smallpox crossed the Atlantic Ocean to strike the unseasoned and disease-inexperienced populations of the New World, which it decimated. For decades, scholars were pretty much unanimous in accepting that the great die-off among the indigenous peoples of the New World, and especially of the Aztecs and the Incas who perished during the first century following conquest, was due to the biological weapons, especially smallpox, the Europeans unwittingly deployed. Indeed, a fairly lively debate continues over the possibility that European settlers deliberately waged bio-warfare by giving Indians blankets from smallpox victims.[28] Recently as well, historians have reevaluated the effects of social and economic dislocation, war, racism, and genocide to suggest that smallpox's role may have been less influential, or at least less dominant, than once thought. Smallpox certainly killed far more effectively than the swords and firearms of the conquistadors and

---

[27] Quoted in Hopkins, *Greatest Killer*, 214.
[28] See, for instance, Harold B. Gill Jr., "Colonial Germ Warfare," at www.history.org/Foundation/journal/Spring04/warfare.cfm accessed August 6, 2009.

it, in combination with other European diseases, was probably mostly responsible for the great decline in the numbers of indigenous peoples in the first two centuries after contact.[29]

In Europe, by the sixteenth century, smallpox had become mostly a disease of childhood, and young children in urban areas ran the greatest risk. Epidemiologists have frequently noted the tendency of diseases to strike with fearful results at both adults and children during their first incursions. (Consider, for example, the extensive mortality among adults and children when measles first reached the Hawaiian islands in 1848.) Gradually, however, populations and diseases accommodate to one another. Diseases tend to become less virulent and more likely to affect only specific groups, usually children. Over time, ever fewer adults are susceptible because of exposure in their youth (even if their cases are so mild that they show no symptoms, that is, their experience is subclinical). This is apparently what happened with smallpox. In early modern Europe, smallpox was almost a biological rite of passage. It was "the river that all must cross." Smallpox accounted for about 10–15 percent of all deaths, and most of its victims (up to 80 percent) had not yet reached their tenth year.

Smallpox assumed increasing demographic impact in Europe, therefore, in the sixteenth and seventeenth centuries and continued to be one of the chief biological killers of the 1700s. Epidemics were common throughout these years and often had calamitous histories. Northern Italy was hit hard in the 1560s and 1570s, smallpox raged Europe-wide in 1614, and England suffered frightfully in the second half of the seventeenth century, recording widespread outbreaks in 1667 and 1668. The eighteenth century brought little respite; in 1707 an epidemic in Iceland seems to have affected almost every one of its 50,000 inhabitants and as late as 1733–34 smallpox almost extinguished the Greenland colony. The great European cities experienced major flare-ups as well: in London in 1719, 1723, 1725, 1736, and 1746; in Rome in 1746 and 1754; in Paris in 1734–35; and in Geneva in 1750. Even sparsely settled areas, such as Scandinavia, suffered several outbreaks from 1736–39. Smallpox respected neither status nor wealth, striking rich and poor, high and low alike. Numerous members of several royal lines – the English/Scottish Stuarts in the seventeenth century, the Austrian Habsburgs, the Spanish Bourbons, and the Russian Romanovs in the eighteenth century – died of smallpox. Willem II, stadhouder of Holland, perished in 1650 at

---

[29] See David E. Stannard, *American Holocaust: Columbus and the Conquest of the New World* (New York, 1992); Russell Thornton, *American Indian Holocaust and Survival: A Population History Since 1492* (Norman, Okla., 1987).

the zenith of his political career (and just twenty-four years old) leaving a posthumously born heir; the promising young king of Spain, Louis-Philippe (Louis I), succumbed in 1724 just eight months after ascending the throne; and the old monarch, Louis XV of France, died a horrible rotting death in 1774.

Once a person contracted smallpox, survival depended mostly on whether one had been infected with a mild form – "a good-natured pox" in the parlance of the times – or a severe one, and upon the strength of one's own body. No one understood just how the disease circulated, but contemporaries widely believed smallpox, like plague, to be contagious. Treatments had little positive effect. Healers often tried bleeding and heat or sweating regimens. Bleeding from a vein was supposed to drain off the impurities causing the disease. Or one might prescribe a purgative for the same effect. The sweat therapy became known in Europe through the writings of Rhazes who in his *Treatise on the Small-pox and Measles* recommended that patients be wrapped up and kept as warm as possible to induce a copious perspiration that would carry the corrupted humors out of the body through the pores. This therapy, along with the "red cure" (which had patients dress in red clothing, sleep in a bed hung with red curtains, and even drink red liquids), represented a fairly common procedure and both together formed normal ways of dealing with smallpox patients at least until the seventeenth century. Then the English physician Thomas Sydenham, in his 1682 *Dissertatio Epistolaris* (Dissertation on the Letters), proposed a radically new way to handle smallpox cases. Instead of enclosing patients in hot, stuffy rooms, Sydenham recommended a "cooling treatment." Patients were to be cared for in airy bedrooms, covered only by light blankets, kept clean, and given chilled drinks.

In the eighteenth century, Europeans began an experiment that focused on prevention, not cure, and that innovation is known as *inoculation* or *variolation*. To inoculate a person, one made small, rather deep incisions in the flesh of the arm or leg (the most usual sites), inserted a scab and some pustulous matter from an active smallpox case in the gash, and then bound the wound. The inoculee would develop a true case of smallpox, although typically a far milder one than he or she might have contracted "naturally." In the eighteenth century, no one knew why less dangerous cases resulted from inoculation, although inoculators knew to select donors with mild symptoms. The process of "ingrafting" described above – that is, introducing the virus through the skin rather than inhaling it into the lungs (the normal means of transmission) – might itself have been most responsible for the attenuation of the disease in inoculees.

Legend has it that Lady Montagu learned of inoculation while in Turkey with her husband, the British ambassador, and had her young son undergo the procedure there. She then introduced the method into Europe. Writing to a friend in England, she spoke of a practice which rendered smallpox "entirely harmless." "There is," she continued, "a set of old women [here], who make it their business to perform the operation, every autumn ... when the great heat is abated ... thousands undergo this operation ... [and there] is not example of anyone that has died in it."[30] After returning to England, Lady Montagu had her daughter inoculated in 1721. Inoculations among the royal family soon followed and thereafter smallpox inoculation became firmly established in England. Similarly, after Catherine the Great (r.1762–96) of Russia had herself and her son, the future Tsar Paul, inoculated in 1768, support grew among medical practitioners in Russia, while a similar decision of the French Regent, Philippe, duc d'Orléans (1674–1723), helped turn the tide in France.

While there is undoubtedly truth to this appealing tale and good reason to appreciate the roles Lady Montagu and the royals played, other factors proved equally important. First, "buying the pox" seems to have been a folk practice in several parts of Europe (and throughout the world) long before 1721. Healthy children would be sent to play with those who had mild manifestations of the disease. Inoculation itself had been practiced not only in Turkey, but also, for example, in India and parts of Africa for hundreds of years. Second, the introduction and eventual success of smallpox inoculation in England must be attributed to a confluence of forces, of which Lady Montagu and royal example were only two. Reports on native practices had already reached England before Lady Montagu's return. The *Transactions of the Royal Society* printed letters from Dr. Emanuel Timonius, who observed the method in Constantinople, and Jacobus Pylarinus, who was an eye-witness to it in Smryna, in 1714 and 1716. Important and influential men, such as the physician Hans Sloane (1660–1753) and the surgeon Charles Maitland (1668–1748), who had inoculated Lady Montagu's daughter, worked tirelessly to popularize inoculation and to improve its technique. The realization slowly took hold that one had a better chance of surviving inoculation than "natural" smallpox and this became a more compelling argument over time as a general statistical sense began to permeate more levels of the European population.[31]

The continued fury of smallpox, especially during the middle decades of the eighteenth century, surely accounted for popular acceptance of

---

[30] Quoted in Hopkins, *Greatest Killer*, 47–48.
[31] Andreas-Holger Maehle, "The Ethics of Prevention: German Philosophers of the Late Enlightenment on the Morality of Smallpox Inoculation," in John Woodward and Robert Jütte, eds., *Coping with Sickness* (Sheffield, 1995), 91–114.

inoculation, but other elements also promoted the practice. Most significant of these were substantial improvements in inoculation techniques and meaningful reductions in expense. In the 1760s, an English family of physicians and inoculators introduced what came to be known as the "Suttonian method" that shortened the preparatory process and simultaneously cut costs. The Suttons (Robert and Daniel) also instructed inoculators to make superficial, rather than deep, incisions, thus lowering the number of complications and minimizing scarring. Famous propagandists for smallpox inoculation sought to elucidate the process by simple explanations. Voltaire, in his *Lettres philosophiques ou lettres anglais* (Philosophical or English letters, 1734), compared the action of inoculation to the ferment of yeast in dough, thus simultaneously familiarizing and taming the process. Governments promoted inoculation by offering it free to impoverished families and by requiring orphans and military conscripts to undergo the procedure. Finally, enthusiasm for inoculation became a touchstone of fashionable, up-to-date, European life and a marker of one's membership in an enlightened society.

Smallpox inoculation, of course, also provoked opposition. Religious concerns about whether inoculation represented an arrogant human interference into the working of Providence and sheer pigheaded superstition have often been highlighted as primary reasons for popular antipathy to the process. Voltaire had pilloried parents who "sacrificed" their children to smallpox because they clung to foolish and anachronistic beliefs. Still, predicting who could be found in the ranks of pro- and anti-inoculation was never easy, and numerous factors determined individual positions. In New England, for example, the Puritan minister Cotton Mather (1663–1728) championed inoculation during a smallpox outbreak in 1721 and he was vigorously opposed by the Edinburgh-educated and extremely reputable physician, Dr. William Douglass (c.1700–52). Douglass's opposition can be explained in at least two ways, one based on medical objections, the other resting on ideas of who was properly entitled to practice medicine. According to the first, Douglass felt that the process was dangerous and charged that Mather and the physician Zabdiel Boylston (1676?–1766), who had inoculated almost 250 people, were acting irresponsibly. The second, more recent, interpretation points out that Douglass was not opposed to inoculation but rather to "clerical meddling" in medicine. Mather, on the other hand, and despite his role in the Salem witch trials, represented a clerical movement toward "enlightened positions . . . with respect to scientific pursuits and the causes of human suffering" that reflected older ties between religion and medicine as well as changes in those relationships. Mather, moreover, subscribed to the *Philosophical Transactions* of the Royal Society and had perhaps read

Timonius's and Pylarinus's communications, although he had probably acquired hearsay information on African inoculation practices from his black Sudanese slave, Onesimus, as early as 1706–07. This example illustrates that opposition to inoculation was not, or not exclusively, the result of ignorance or misplaced religious zeal.[32]

Increasingly it has become clear that many objections – and hardly irrational ones – bore weight. Inoculation was *not* a totally safe process. The inoculee developed a real case of smallpox and could infect others or trigger an epidemic among the unprotected. Medical men, too, as the Boston debate suggests, could divide on the benefits and dangers of the operation. While some medical men fervently advocated inoculation, others, just as learned and respectable, worried about disseminating smallpox or spreading other diseases, and doubted whether the immunity accorded by inoculation was permanent (it was). Inoculation did result in a small number of deaths, and complications, including serious infections and unsightly scarring, occurred more frequently. Nonetheless, only six (2.4%) of the 244 people Boylston inoculated died. Of the other 5,980 Bostonians who took sick with smallpox in 1721–22, 844 or 14% succumbed. In any case, and these very real objections notwithstanding, inoculation tended to take hold fairly rapidly in England during the late 1720s and 1730s, if somewhat more slowly on the continent where medical faculties tended to be more conservative and medicine more strictly regulated. In France, the opposition to inoculation was strong, despite the best efforts of Voltaire and the mathematician and geographer Charles Marie de La Condamine (1701–74) to promote the practice. Not until the mid-1750s did isolated inoculations begin. Slowly, however, in the middle of the century, inoculation dispersed throughout the continent and by 1770 had become a common, if not quite routine, and often still contested, method of combating smallpox.

Inoculation or variolation proved a short-lived medical phenomenon, however. Early in the nineteenth century, the far safer technique of *vaccination* supplanted it. In 1796, the English naturalist, physician, and inoculator Edward Jenner (1749–1823) engrafted lymph taken from a pustule of cowpox on the hand of a milkmaid into the arm of a young boy, James Phipps. When Jenner subsequently inoculated Phipps with smallpox, no reaction resulted, leading Jenner to conclude that inoculation with cowpox bestowed immunity against smallpox. Over the next few years, Jenner experimented with his newfangled process (which he called

---

[32] John Blake, "The Inoculation Controversy in Boston: 1721–22," *The New England Quarterly* 25 (1952): 489–506; Maxine Van De Wetering, "A Reconsideration of the Inoculation Controversy," *The New England Quarterly* 58 (1985): 46–67, quote 47.

vaccination, from the Latin for cow, *vacca*), finally publishing his results in a 1798 pamphlet: *An Inquiry into the Causes and Effects of Variolae Vaccinae, a Disease, Discovered in some of the Western Counties of England, particularly Gloucestershire, and known by the Name of Cow Pox*. Although objections to smallpox inoculation had been widespread, if by no means universal, people more rapidly accepted vaccination and evinced only little of the opposition that had greeted the older practice. Concerns about the rectitude of infecting humans with animal diseases occasioned flurries of opposition (and hilarious cartoons showing vaccinated patients growing miniature cows from their vaccination sites), but these soon died down. Vaccination conferred protection against smallpox, although not for life as was later discovered. A program of regular revaccinations at specific intervals solved this problem. Vaccination was, therefore, safer and less expensive than inoculation; those vaccinated could not spread smallpox and did not have to be isolated.[33]

Jenner was not the only, or even the first, person to notice that people who caught cowpox did not fall prey to smallpox; the fact was well known in dairy areas. Jenner did, however, demonstrate that cowpox could be transferred from human to human without the intermediary of the cow. As vaccination gained favor, governments began to forbid inoculation as dangerous to public health. Still, the earlier experiences gained in intro-ducing inoculation, such as offering free inoculations to the poor, won its acceptance among many and smoothed the path to a widespread and (relatively) swift adoption of vaccination.[34] Its success also contributed to the growing authority of medicine and possibly stimulated the sense that human intervention could have a significant impact on diseases once thought inescapable.

With the introduction of inoculation and vaccination, for the first time Europeans had at their disposal effective prophylaxes against a fearsome disease. Both procedures – inoculation and vaccination – can be seen as forming initial steps in the process of the worldwide eradication of smallpox achieved in the second half of the twentieth century. Moreover, it may well be, as Peter Razzell has argued, that smallpox inoculation had a significant and positive effect on population growth in the eigh-teenth century, both in terms of reducing deaths from the disease and in preventing male impotence (a frequent complication of smallpox in adults), although a close study on Finland found that "inoculation did

---

[33] See the special issue on "Reassessing Smallpox Vaccination, 1789–1900," of the *Bulletin of the Social History of Medicine* 83, no. 1 (Spring, 2009).

[34] Peter Sköld, "The Key to Success: The Role of Local Government in the Organization of Smallpox Vaccination in Sweden," *Bulletin of Medical History* 45 (2000): 201–26.

not explain why population in the eighteenth century began to increase so quickly."[35]

Other "plagues"

Plague, smallpox, and syphilis were not, of course, the only pestilences of early modern times. Contemporaries, however, seemed to understand them as specific diseases and generally considered them contagious, that is, able to be spread from person to person, even if they also believed that environmental conditions could generate, disseminate, or exacerbate them. People also possessed a fairly clear sense of each disease and even laypeople identified them readily. Of course, there must have been many misdiagnoses, measles for smallpox, for instance. An inclination to identify all deaths during an outbreak as due to, for instance, plague, surely augmented recorded mortality; it did nothing to lessen the prevailing sense of being in the grip of a particular pestilence.

Other common diseases, and ones we know well today, almost certainly were also important in early modern times. Yet a prolixity of labels and symptoms make them difficult for us to perceive, let alone name. Sometimes we think we can identify them as, for instance, measles or malaria or diphtheria, and at other times we are as bewildered as our ancestors. Measles and scarlet fever probably always accounted for a portion of deaths attributed to smallpox although measles was by no means as deadly as the other two. People commonly identified epidemics of the "bloody flux" or diarrhea (although diarrhea could also indicate a milder, temporary, or fairly innocuous condition). True dysentery was a harrowing and often fatal disease that struck hardest at large groups, like armies. Patients suffered massive bloody diarrhea accompanied by fever, and perished from extreme dehydration and progressive debilitation. Many pathogens could have caused such symptoms. Dysentery in somewhat milder forms surfaced in late summer and early fall and seemed somehow connected to the fullness of the harvest season. Popular and learned opinion alike blamed overeating, or consuming too much fruit, especially that not fully ripe, for the disease.

Dysentery affected the bowels, but consumption and wasting attacked other vital organs. Consumption is today commonly equated with

---

[35] Peter Razzell, *The Conquest of Smallpox: The Impact of Inoculation on Smallpox Mortality in Eighteenth-Century Britain* (Firle, 1977); Razzell, "The Conundrum of Eighteenth-Century Population Growth: Essay Review," *Social History of Medicine* 11, no. 3 (December 1998): 469–500; Oiva Turpeinen, "Die Sterblichkeit an Pocken, Masern und Keuschhusten in Finnland in den Jahren 1751 bis 1865," in Arthur E. Imhof, ed., *Mensch und Gesundheit in der Geschichte* (Husum, 1978), 135–61.

tuberculosis, although pneumonia must also have played a substantial role in making up the early modern category. Tuberculosis is an ancient disease that probably dates from the earliest civilizations. Early modern people usually spoke of *phthisis*, consumption, or wasting because the disease "consumed" its victims leaving only husks behind. Demographers and historical epidemiologists have argued that tuberculosis was probably very common in sixteenth- and seventeenth-century Europe and accounted for a substantial percentage (perhaps 20 percent) of all deaths. Unquestionably the accelerating urbanization of the sixteenth century contributed in no small measure to the burgeoning incidence of tuberculosis, but it was not until the eighteenth century that "the world's greatest epidemic of tuberculosis" began; it continued well into the late nineteenth or early twentieth century. Indeed, it is now believed that almost everyone in major cities such as Paris or London had developed some form of tuberculosis if often only in a subclinical manifestation. Tuberculosis, however, evoked little of the fear and none of the public health measures that smallpox, plague, or syphilis did, because the symptoms it manifested were thought to arise from humoral imbalances or derive from individual constitutional flaws.

Despite the invisibility of tuberculosis to early modern people (at least as we understand it), its cultural impact was pronounced. If early modern Europeans did not understand consumption as a specific disease, they were quite familiar with one of its manifestations: tubercular infections of the lymph nodes of the neck that they termed *scrofula*. For reasons that are somewhat unclear, it was believed that scrofulous swellings could be reduced by the touch of a monarch's hand (and thus it was known as the *King's Evil*). From the twelfth to the end of the seventeenth century, the sacrality of royalty was believed curative; thus the monarchs of France and England "touched" scrofula sufferers to heal them. Thousands with scrofula, including the young Samuel Johnson, went through an elaborate ceremony that included the "touch" itself followed by the presentation of a medal or "cramp-ring" to the recipient. Subjects high and low might judge the legitimacy of monarchs by their ability to work such miracles. Moreover, faith in such ceremonies proved quite tenacious. Marc Bloch (1886–1944), in his pioneering work on the royal touch, suggests that a complex set of effects that he called "the psychology of the miraculous" explains the persistence of this ritual. Because scrofula often goes into remission by itself, touching might appear to cure. Moreover, the whole legacy of a sacred royalty was ancient and was consistently strengthened by monarchs who needed to raise their prestige and assert their legitimacy. Publicists and politicians believed in the ritual themselves even while they exploited its political potential. Toward the end of the eighteenth century, and far more often in the nineteenth century, writers linked consumption to genius and it acquired other metaphoric meanings; but that story belongs to another book.[36]

Two other diseases – malaria and influenza – do not, as such, appear in early modern records, although it seems certain both had a significant impact on mortality and morbidity. Malaria, like tuberculosis, is quite an old disease. As "intermittent fever," it was described already in fourth-century (BCE) Greece and also by Roman authors such as Galen and Celsus. Apparently, the ancient forms of malaria were less virulent than those prevalent in the early modern and modern worlds. Still, some historians and historical epidemiologists associate Rome's decline with the growing prevalence of malaria in the Mediterranean basin. The modern name, malaria, is derived from the Italian for "mala" (bad) and "aria" (air). Marco Cornaro (fl. 1440s) first used the term *mal aero* in a 1440 publication, *Scritture delle laguna* (Writings of the lagoons). People believed that miasmas arising from marshes and swamps caused a disease characterized by periodic or intermittent fevers, chills, and sweating.

We know malaria today as a disease caused by protozoan parasites and transferred from human to human through the bite of the female *Anopheles* mosquito. In early modern times, people associated these fevers with specific places and seasons. Lodovico Castelvetro (1505–71) warned a friend in 1552 that "Pisa is not a place you should stay in May if you value your life."[37] The pronounced cold conditions brought on by the Little Ice Age in the late sixteenth and early seventeenth centuries probably reduced the impact of malaria in Europe, but the gradual warming that followed allowed the disease to resurge; it eventually reached as far north as southern Scandinavia, Poland, and Russia.

The burden of malaria bore heavily upon Europeans living in Africa and the Americas and surely accelerated the already pronounced decline of the indigenous peoples of the New World. Malaria-carrying mosquitoes had probably traveled with ships sailing from Africa to the Americas ever since contact and these transoceanic disease migrations represent yet another biological result of a developing globalization. First striking coastal areas, malaria then moved inland to affect large sections of North, Central, and South America. The Mississippi River Valley as far north as modern St. Louis and Illinois, for example, became

---

[36] Marc Bloch, *The Royal Touch: Sacred Monarchy and Kingship in England and France*, trans. by J. E. Anderson (London, 1973 [1924]); Susan Sontag, *Illness as Metaphor* (New York, 1978).

[37] Quoted in Carlo Cipolla, *Miasmas and Disease: Public Health and the Environment in the Pre-Industrial Age* (New Haven, Conn., 1992), 79.

a reservoir of malarial infestation and these areas proved death traps for early settlers. The first effective treatment for malaria – Peruvian bark or *cinchona*, which contains quinine – came from the New World in about 1632 and healers dosed patients liberally with these "Jesuit powders."

Influenza is another disease that must have been exceedingly common. An acute viral disease that is transferred by droplet infection, it was at home for millennia on all three Old World continents – Africa, Asia, and Europe – but was probably only introduced into the Americas in the sixteenth century. Epidemiologists now believe that widespread outbreaks of influenza first occurred in Europe at the end of the fourteenth century. The disease then recurred on a large scale several times in the sixteenth century, including a massive manifestation in England from 1557–59. The incidence of influenza seems to have receded in the seventeenth century, but affected large areas in almost every decade of the eighteenth century. In most cases, influenza caused many people to fall sick, but relatively few to die, and these deaths, as they are today, were scattered mainly among the elderly, the already ill, or the malnourished. Still, sometimes influenza was just as lethal to the young and strong. Outbreaks snaked along commercial routes and one can track the progress of the disease from city to city and from towns into the countryside. Influenza is a particularly mutable virus (if modern experience pertains) and thus mortality rates and symptoms, as well as target populations, probably varied greatly. These factors, of course, make its identification in the past extremely difficult.

If historians, demographers, and epidemiologists are fairly comfortable in identifying certain outbreaks as resulting from particular diseases or combinations of diseases, some diseases came and went and remain as mysterious to us today as they did to contemporaries. We have seen how often people were able to link disease occurrences over time and confidently name them as "smallpox" or "plague." But all too often the diseases that struck and killed seemed totally unfamiliar. A classic example here is the sweating sickness or English sweat (*sudor anglicus*). Victims suffered sudden high fevers accompanied by profuse perspiration. They fell into comas and died within a day or two. A physician writing during the first outbreak described "a grete swetying and stynking, with redness of the face and of all the body, and a contynual thirst, with a grete hete and hedache because of the fumes and venoms." The eminent English physician John Caius (1510–73) believed the disease to be caused by impure spirits and corrupted humors and "by the nature and site of the soil and region." He recommended familiar dietary remedies to correct the humoral imbalances.[38] Cases initially appeared in London in 1485 or 1486 and the disease then reappeared several times during the first half of the sixteenth century. It has never been identified; it was almost certainly not influenza. It may have been a totally new and lethal virus that struck and then disappeared, perhaps because it killed so effectively and thus rapidly depleted the pool of susceptibles.

Sweating sickness continues to be what many call an "unsolved puzzle" in the history of disease. But perhaps it is wise to end a chapter on pestilence with a mystery as a cautionary tale about the perils of diagnosing diseases in the past and a warning against smugly assigning contemporary names to early modern epidemics. While we do not have to accept a position that wishes only to deal with diseases as people in the past saw them, described them, defined them, and dealt with them, we need to stay mindful of the limits of speculation. Yet we must also be willing to speculate cautiously; otherwise attempts at comparing diseases in the past, ascertaining patterns of mortality, or understanding why some people initiated certain responses and others sought different ones remain futile and frustrating tasks.

The richness of historical writing on epidemics is sometimes almost overwhelming. Perhaps no other subject in medical history has attracted so much interest. Social and cultural historians have been extremely successful in exploiting the vast documentation that widespread outbreaks of disease and great mortalities produced and have plumbed these mountains of evidence not only to determine the number of deaths and the kinds of public health measures introduced, but also to open windows on worlds we have lost, to understand the ways in which early modern peoples thought and acted and not only in times of pestilence. Still, many gaps and unanswered questions remain and, as the still-lively debate over the actual identity of plague testifies, there is much to be won from revisiting and reevaluating received wisdoms.

---

[38] Quoted in George Childs Krohn, ed., *Encyclopedia of Plague and Pestilence: From Ancient Times to the Present* (rev. edn., New York, 2001), 92.

3 Learned medicine

[Medicine is] the most obscure of all [the arts].[1]

Like all of nature, medicine must be mechanical.[2]

Open up a few corpses; you will dissipate at once
the darkness that observation alone could not dispel.[3]

Western medicine inherited its theoretical framework from the Greeks
and the Romans and especially from Hippocrates and Galen. *Galenism*
dominated medical thinking until the seventeenth century and Galenic
therapeutics remained resilient for at least another hundred years. Thus,
the story of early modern learned medicine begins in the ancient world.

Older historiography often pictured the decline of Galenism and
the rise of "modern medicine" as results of medical progress and scientific breakthroughs. Accordingly, a series of momentous discoveries
dealt repeated blows, eventually fatal ones, to the whole wheezing edifice of Galenism. Scholars have identified several crucial points in this
process. Andreas Vesalius's innovations in anatomy and William Harvey's discovery of the circulation of the blood were the most obvious ones. Supposedly, these original thinkers corrected the misconceptions bequeathed to the early modern world from antiquity, ones that a
Church-supported Aristotlean natural philosophy and the Galenic conservatism of medieval university studies further validated. Eventually,
a medicine based on experiential knowledge, observation, and experimentation came to replace the medicine of texts and authorities. In
this interpretation, the Flemish anatomist Andreas Vesalius, the English
physician William Harvey, and poor Michael Servetus who was burned

---

[1] Laurent Joubert, 1578, quoted in Laurence Brockliss and Colin Jones, *The Medical World
of Early Modern France* (Oxford, 1997), 115.
[2] Friedrich Hoffmann, *Fundamenta medicinae*, trans. and ed. Lester S. King (London,
1971), 6.
[3] Quoted in Irvine Loudon, "Medical Education and Medical Reform," in Vivian Nutton
and Roy Porter, eds., *The History of Medical Education in Britain* (Amsterdam and Atlanta,
1995), 232.

in Geneva for his heretical teachings, become pioneers, or even martyrs, in the cause of science and valiant opponents of religious obscurantism.

Not too surprisingly, the truth of the matter is rather different, less simple, and far more intriguing. The story presented here takes into account the events of what has generally been termed the Scientific Revolution, but stresses that by no means all (or maybe even most?) of the men posterity has celebrated as its heroes themselves accepted its projects or methods. Harvey, for instance, explicitly distanced himself from the "new science." Others, like Isaac Newton (1643–1727), remained deeply influenced by older magical and alchemical traditions; he has often been referred to as the "last of the *magi*." Recent work in the history of science has even sometimes insisted that the Scientific Revolution never existed and regards as myth the idea of unilinear scientific progress. The authoritative *Cambridge History of Science* in summing up the last generation of scholarship on the subject points out that "[i]t is no longer clear that there was any coherent enterprise in the early modern period that can be identified with modern science, or that the transformations in question were as explosive and discontinuous as the analogy with political revolution implies, or that those transformations were unique in intellectual magnitude and cultural significance."[4] In short, the once clear track toward modernity seen as emanating from a cohesive "scientific project" in the late sixteenth and seventeenth centuries is now more often pictured as a branching road with several alternative routes and multiple ways of traveling them. There were, moreover, many dead ends. Indeed, the guides on the road were themselves often unsure of their direction or even their eventual destination.

"Science" in our modern understanding did not exist in the early modern world. It makes considerably more sense in the context of the times to speak instead of *natural philosophy*. Natural philosophy was a comprehensive intellectual endeavor that reached back into antiquity. Natural philosophers sought to read the "book of nature" and they accepted as valid occult or "secret" ways of knowing, ways that seem antithetical to modern scientific methods.

Because those who identified themselves with the "new science" of the sixteenth and seventeenth centuries did not necessarily agree on means and purpose and often lacked intellectual acceptance, it was difficult – indeed impossible – for medicine and medical practitioners to base their authority on science. Rather, and until the very end of our period, people

---

[4] Steven Shapin, *The Scientific Revolution* (Chicago, 1996), 3–5; Katherine Park and Lorraine Daston, eds., *The Cambridge History of Science*, vol. III, *Early Modern Science* (Cambridge, 2006), 13.

regarded "learnedness" as the most reliable way of judging the value of a practitioner. Learned practitioners came in different shapes and while physicians (university-trained) had an edge, surgeons and apothecaries also often qualified as learned. Different ideas competed for dominance within the learned world, and much of the history of medicine deals with controversies over specific ideas and concepts, as well as more general approaches.

Medical theory did not change through an uncomplicated process of uncovering errors and rectifying them, nor were shifts in learned medicine determined internally, that is, in an environment isolated from other influences. Scholars today generally stress the contexts to which medical thinking was anchored. Some were intellectual pillars, such as humanism, others were religious (the impact, for instance, of the Reformation) or institutional (the establishment of scientific societies, for example). In addition, as historians have come to expand their purview of the many "sites" where science was done, moving beyond the universities or even scientific societies to include the household and the workshop, the contribution of artisans and women has loomed larger.[5] Furthermore, scholars no longer view the boundary between the medieval and early modern worlds as rigid or impermeable. Much flowed from one to the other and many early modern innovations rested firmly on medieval precedents. Finally, it is necessary to jettison a tendency to dismiss older forms of medical thinking and practice as "ignorant," "superstitious," or "benighted." Rather, we must try to accept these medical systems and explanations on their own terms rather than just rejecting them as "wrong." This thought experiment permits us to develop more sophisticated ways of discussing and comprehending these metamorphoses instead of merely relying on the simplistic mechanism of "correcting errors" or judging them on the "progress" they made toward specific goals.

Medicine in the Galenic mold

Galenism bound the ancient, medieval, and early modern medical worlds together. During the middle ages, Arabic sources had transmitted some writings of the second-century Greco-Roman physician Galen to the West. By the thirteenth century, a limited corpus of Galenic writings

[5] See the section on "Personae and the Sites of Natural Knowledge," in Park and Daston, eds., *Early Modern Science*, 179–362; Pamela H. Smith, *The Body of the Artisan: Art and Experience in the Scientific Revolution* (Chicago, 2004); Deborah E. Harkness, *The Jewel House: Elizabethan London and the Scientific Revolution* (New Haven, 2007).

provided the basis for university medical training. Only in the sixteenth century did scholars recover a fuller range of Galenic texts; these became widely available when the Aldine Press in Venice published comprehensive Greek editions in 1525. This "new Galen" became the "modern" standard and engendered a revival of Galenism that animated, for instance, the Renaissance anatomy project (discussed below). Many humanists involved in translating Greek medical writings viewed Galen as the ultimate authority. The physician John Caius insisted that "[e]xcept in trivial matters, nothing was overlooked by [Galen]."[6] "New Galenism" proved extremely durable; it shaped medical theory and university education at least until the middle of the seventeenth century. "Indeed," as one noted medievalist has observed, "certain basic physiological concepts and associated therapeutic methods – notably humoral theory and the practice of blood-letting to get rid of bad humors – had a continuous life extending from Greek antiquity into the nineteenth century."[7]

Galenism endured because it was pliant and because its adherents were clever in weaving seemingly contradictory ideas and discoveries into its fabric. Far from being a rigid and immutable system, Galenism responded adroitly to challenges and even absorbed them, sometimes emerging stronger from its confrontation with critics. No single discovery was able to undermine the whole edifice, and the decline of Galenism in academic medicine was a long, slow process just barely completed by 1800. Many of its canonic parts, such as the criticality of the humors, held on much longer in everyday medical practice and popular belief and in widely dispersed and attenuated forms.

What was Galenism then and why was it such a hardy intellectual construct? First, "Galenism" must be distinguished from the teachings and writings of Galen the man. Galen wrote prolifically. His complete oeuvre remained unknown, however, in the middle ages. The medieval "Galen" lacked his materials on anatomy, most importantly *On the Use of the Parts* and *Anatomical Procedures*. What medieval Europeans knew about Galen was filtered through Arabic sources and had been transformed by Arabic additions. The learned medicine of the middle ages, nonetheless, accepted a series of fairly standard ideas that can be legitimately termed "Galenic." Still, these concepts were not the sole property of professors and learned physicians; learned and lay medicine overlapped and many Galenic precepts were almost universally held.

---

[6] Quoted in Charles D. O'Malley, "Medical Education During the Renaissance," in O'Malley, ed., *The History of Medical Education* (Berkeley and Los Angeles, 1970), 73.

[7] Nancy Siraisi, *Medieval and Renaissance Medicine: An Introduction to Knowledge and Practice* (Chicago, 1990), 70–71, 97 (quote).

Like other ancient physicians, Galen focused not only on medical theory but also on practice. In tune with the Hippocratic authors, he believed in natural causes of disease and recommended nonsupernatural cures, although he, like Aristotle, also believed in teleology and purpose. Galen ascribed intent to anatomical organs, for instance, in their relationship to a divinely ordered universe. Galenic medicine was additionally learned and rational. Galen had stressed in equal measure the detailed knowledge of the human body and a love of philosophy as the prerequisites of the good physician. His contention that "the best doctor is also a philosopher" allowed for the linkage of medicine and philosophy that characterized the "good" physician of the medieval and early modern world, at least until near the end of our period.[8]

During the middle ages, a Galenic system developed out of the teachings that had reached the West in several waves. This system worked on the basis of the nonnaturals (listed by Galen but named by Johannitius in his ninth-century translation of *The Art of Medicine*; these were discussed in Chapter 1; see p. 14); the contra-naturals, which were pathological conditions, that is, diseases; and the naturals. The last of these – the naturals – described the make-up of the human body and explained how it functioned. The naturals comprised seven things: (1) the four classical elements of earth, air, fire, and water; (2) the four humors (phlegm, blood, black bile, and red or yellow bile); (3) the complexions or temperaments, which reflected an individual's unique blend of hot, cold, wet, and dry qualities; (4) the parts of the body, including major organs such as the liver, heart, and brain; (5) an animating spiritus, which was a sort of air or pneuma produced in the heart and carried throughout the body by the arteries; (6) the virtues, which were the activities of systems; and (7) the operations, which were the functions of individual organs. While all this may seem a tremendously complicated, bizarrely artificial, and extremely peculiar construct (at least to modern eyes), a combination of the seven naturals effectively accounted for the workings of the human body.

Three organs, known as principal members, anchored Galenic anatomy and physiology: these were the heart, liver, and brain. Each governed a specific bodily system, although the Galenic meaning of "system" differs from what we mean when we speak of, for example, the circulatory system or the reproductive system or the central nervous system. (The modern meaning of system in anatomy is a group of organs and tissues

---

[8] On the importance of the "good physician" as a learned man with a "good story," see Michael McVaugh, *Medicine Before the Plague: Practitioners and Their Patients in the Crown of Aragon, 1285–1345* (Cambridge, 1993).

associated with a particular physiological function.) The heart, liver, and brain in Galenic anatomy governed – that is, held the highest position hierarchically – in a group of organs with discrete functions. The heart, for instance, formed the principal member of the organs of the chest. The arteries served as spiritual members because they distributed a mixture of blood and spiritus (pneuma) throughout the body. This pneuma was the source of life; it animated the body and was a central part of the purposeful anatomy of Galenic medicine. The brain was the principal member of a collection of organs that included the spinal cord and the nerves. This system controlled thought, motion, and sensation: the animal virtues. The liver bore responsibility for the natural virtues: nutrition, growth, and reproduction. Other organs in this group included those associated with digestion, such as the stomach, but also the veins, which carried venous blood as nourishment to all parts. For Galen, therefore, there existed two vascular systems but not a circulatory system in the sense that it would later come to be defined (see below, pp. 96–97). The stomach transformed food into chyle that the vena cava conveyed to the liver. The liver concocted (cooked or blended) chyle into the four humors. A part of blood further distilled into semen, but the vast majority of blood coursed through the veins carrying nutrients throughout the body. The Galenic physiological system proved marvelously resilient, able to adapt to newer ideas yet still survive. Even at the end of the seventeenth century, and despite robust challenges to its integrity, respected physicians continued to speak in basically Galenic terms. Friedrich Hoffmann, writing for a scholarly audience in Latin, explained, for instance, that chyle "poured into the blood, by whose motion it is broken up and rendered finer, passes in part into the blood itself . . . partly into nutritive juices, and . . . partly into lymph." François du Port (d. 1624) wrote in Latin, but a French translation made his work accessible to a broader audience. Du Port praised the liver as the fountainhead of health "by making the good blood which nourishes all parts."[9]

   These groups of organs ordered the body and accounted for its functions, albeit in ways that may appear strange to modern eyes. Consider the disparities between the Galenic principal systems and current thought on the circulatory or cardiovascular system. Twenty-first-century definitions of the cardiovascular system typically include a discussion of "the heart together with two networks of blood vessels – the systemic circulation and the pulmonary circulation." The cardiovascular system

---

[9] Hoffmann, *Fundamenta medicinae*, 21; François du Port, *The Decade of Medicine or the Physician of the Rich and the Poor in which all the Signs, Causes and Remedies of Disease Are Clearly Explained* (reprint edn., Berlin, 1988, from French original, 1694), 8.

thus "effects the circulation of blood around the body, which brings about transport of nutrients and oxygen to the tissues and the removal of waste products."[10]

The Galenic understanding differed strikingly. For instance, Galen believed that the human body was supplied with the several fluids and the spirits that made it live and these fluids and spirits flowed through veins, arteries, and nerves. The veins, for example, carried venous blood that had been produced in the liver. This venous blood provided nutrients to the body, while the arteries bore pneuma or living-giving spirits. Thus, Galen postulated two systems: the arterial system carried spiritus and blood and remained fully separate from the venous system, except when blood seeped through small, invisible (and, in fact, nonexistent) pores in the septum dividing the ventricles to permit blood to mix with spiritus. The heart was not a pump which sent blood coursing through the vessels of the body. Blood rather ebbed and flowed and was attracted to organs by their need for nourishment; the flow of blood was thus purposeful. Galen had no conception of the circulation of the blood in the sense that blood moved in an unending circuit throughout the body. There was no need for such a perception because the Galenic system perfectly explained how necessary life-processes worked. Thus, if the Galenic idea of blood flows was "wrong," it was nevertheless rational and logical. Still, even before William Harvey's famous demonstration of the circulation of the blood in 1628 took place, numerous anatomists noticed quirks and problems with the Galenic model. How, for instance, did one explain the action of the heart, the pressure difference in veins and arteries (much higher in the latter), and the way in which blood was used up?

Beginning in the Renaissance and accelerating in the sixteenth century, a series of challenges began to undermine the old Galenic order, albeit gradually. Real breaks with the Galenic system took centuries to occur. Curiously, significant opposition arose from the "new Galenism" of the sixteenth century. Certainly, Galen's cardinal rule on anatomy – "to see for one's self," which is the meaning of *autopsy* – did much to foster a new era in anatomy. More serious subsequently were the Paracelsian attack on medical (Galenic) orthodoxy and the "medicine of the schools"; the rise of chemical and mechanical systems; the Hippocratic revival of the late seventeenth and, especially, eighteenth centuries; a renewed emphasis on purpose in life; the development of a medicine of nerves; and, finally, the unfolding of a school of pathological anatomy or clinical medicine.

---

[10] *Oxford Concise Medical Dictionary* (7th edn., Oxford, 2003).

Renaissance anatomy

One of the oldest misconceptions in the history of medicine is that no one dissected human beings in the middle ages. Dissection had, it is true, fallen into desuetude since Hellenistic times, but the dissection of animals revived at Salerno in the twelfth century and human dissection in the next. Thus, in anatomy, as in other branches of knowledge, the Renaissance represented a less abrupt break with the middle ages than once portrayed. Renaissance anatomy built on the accomplishments of late medieval anatomy as well as addressing questions posed earlier. Admittedly, however, anatomy had failed to develop as a standard part of the medical curriculum at medieval universities. In the early sixteenth century, however, with the rediscovery of Galen's texts on anatomy and with the teachings of the Flemish physician Andreas Vesalius (1514–64) at the University of Padua in the 1530s, anatomy became increasingly central to medicine and medical education. This "new anatomy" built, however, on the precepts of Galen.

The impact of the Renaissance on medicine (like that of the Reformation later) was nonetheless profound. During the closing decades of the fifteenth and opening years of the sixteenth century, humanist scholars were busily engaged in reviving classical learning that, at this point, consisted of the recovery of ancient Greek texts, their publication, and their translation into Latin. Many texts, of course, had been preserved in Arabic or Hebrew translations. Only after 1525, however, was Galen's full anatomical corpus available.[11] At the same time, Renaissance artists studied anatomy in order to portray the human body with greater accuracy. Most famous of these virtuosos were Michelangelo Buonarroti (1475–1564) and Leonardo da Vinci (1452–1519), but almost all the great artists of the time familiarized themselves with the human form. Influence flowed in the other direction as well. Drawings assumed more space in anatomical texts and their quality greatly improved as printing techniques became more sophisticated. The most famous anatomical work ever written (surpassing even *Gray's Anatomy*) is Vesalius's magnificent *De Humani Corporis Fabrica* (On the fabric of the human body, 1534, see Figure 3.1) and it is renowned as much for its splendid prints as for its verbal descriptions. Peter Paul Rubens (1577–1640) created equally beautiful anatomical studies at the beginning of the seventeenth century, although his *Théorie de la figure humaine* (Theory of the Human Figure) was not published until 1773.

---

[11] Vivian Nutton, "The Rise of Medical Humanism: Ferrara, 1464–1555," *Renaissance Studies* 11 (1997): 2–19.

Generations of scholars have cast Vesalius in the mold of the intrepid trailblazer who broke with Galenic and medieval traditions and led medicine into a brave new world of "seeing is believing"; that is, he made observation the key to knowledge. This bifurcation of the history of anatomy into "pre-Vesalian" and "post-Vesalian" periods perpetuates several fallacies, however. First, it suggests that Vesalius and his followers were "better" than their predecessors and were engaged in a radically new project. Second, it ignores the fact that Vesalius and many of the Renaissance anatomists who followed him saw themselves as treading in the footsteps of Galen rather than rejecting him. Finally, not all anatomists accepted Vesalius's findings; many disputed and amended them. Admittedly, Vesalius had available much more human material for his dissections than anyone before him (courtesy of an obliging magistrate who allowed him the bodies of many executed criminals) and could therefore conduct more methodical and detailed investigations into the substance of the human body.[12]

In fact, the anatomy of the late medieval world often looks very similar to that of the Renaissance innovators. It is, for instance, false that pre-Vesalian professors kept their hands clean, lecturing while assistants (or surgeons) performed the actual cutting. In 1315, Mondino de' Liuzzi (1270–1326) performed the first human dissection recorded for western Europe. Dissections then became more common, but by no means either frequent or regular, in the fifteenth century, fueled by the Galenic texts then in circulation and true to Galen's ideas of how to practice anatomy. At the same time, an intense interest with the sheer physicality of the body became central to religious sensibility. Artistic representations of Jesus' sufferings on the cross or the martyrdom of saints became more graphic. Early anatomical practices often had ecclesiastical roots as well; saints' bodies were often "opened" to locate physical signs of holiness.[13] Still, corpses remained in short supply and were hard to preserve (especially in hot weather). Anatomy itself often evoked disgust. Moreover, in a pre-print era pictures were expensive. The anatomical illustrations that existed did not – and were not supposed to – accurately represent human forms, but rather served as teaching aids. The frequent image of the "wound man" (Figure 3.2) was, for instance, not to be taken as a graphic representation of all possible injuries but used as a mnemonic device for students.

---

[12] Andrew Cunningham, *The Anatomical Renaissance: The Resurrection of the Anatomical Projects of the Ancients* (Aldershot, 1997).

[13] Katherine Park, *Secrets of Women: Gender, Generation, and the Origins of Human Dissection* (New York, 2006).

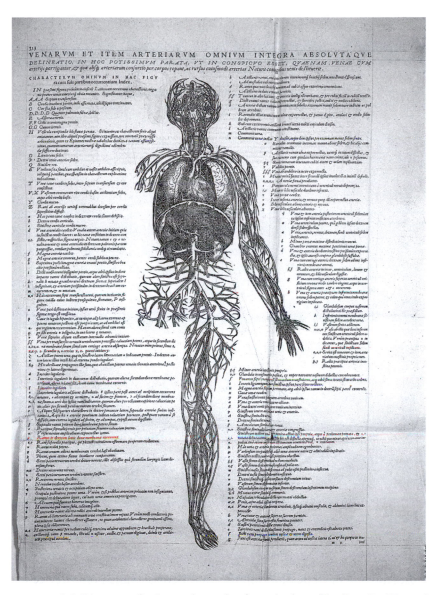

3.1 Diagram of veins and arteries from Andreas Vesalius, *De Humani Corporis Fabrica* (1543)

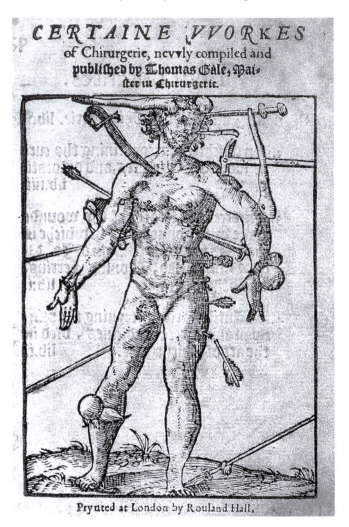

CERTAINE VVORKES
of Chirurgerie, nevvly compiled and
publiſhed by Thomas Gale, Maiſter in Chirurgerie.

Pryated at London by Rouland Hall.

3.2 Wound man, c.1563

Anatomy in the sixteenth century was, therefore, an enterprise involving many men, including Vesalius, and all their endeavors rested on the Galenic precept of seeing for oneself. Before Vesalius, Jacopo Berengario da Carpi (1460–c.1530) at the University of Bologna argued in his 1522 *Isagoge Breves Prelucide ac Uberime in Anatomiam Humani Corporis* (A Short Introduction to Anatomy) that observation was the sole path to truth. Guinther von Andernach's (1505–1574) publication in Latin of Galen's *On Anatomical Procedures* kept the ball rolling. Many anatomists who published or worked before Vesalius also privileged observation and had raised doubts about some Galenic assertions. They also came to suspect that Galen had not dissected humans but only animals. The Venetian Niccolo Massa (c.1485–1569) and the Marburg (Germany) professor Johannes Dryander (1500–60) were merely two of these.

Inherent in Galen's own vision of how to do anatomy lay the seeds of its own destruction. Better observations, more observations, and more refined methods could always overturn – as they eventually did – Galen's knowledge. By faithfully following Galen's motto, many anatomists went beyond their master. What Vesalius did was to carry out Galen's own anatomical program and in so doing he demonstrated Galenic mistakes, which had often resulted from Galen's too facile assumptions about the comparability of human and animal structures. Yet Vesalius dissected according to Galen's model, starting with the bones, moving on to the muscles, and then turning to the internal organs. His *Fabrica* reflected this method. Vesalius indeed corrected several of Galen's misconceptions. He noted, for instance, that the *rete mirabile*, that "marvelous network" of blood vessels found at the base of the brain in many animals, did not exist in humans. He showed that the human liver was not five-lobed as Galen had maintained and that the human breastbone had three not seven segments. Furthermore, he doubted the existence of Galen's invisible pores between the ventricles of the heart. This was, as we shall see, an important step in conceiving of a systemic blood circulation. Vesalius's meticulousness and his reliance on seeing for oneself were critical steps in the development of anatomy. Yet, observation was not as transparent a process as it might seem. Prior beliefs could cause people, and even astute anatomists, to "see what they believed" rather than vice versa. Moreover, while Vesalius challenged Galen on some points of anatomy, he never rejected Galenic physiology and accepted unquestioningly the central tenets of that system.

Vesalius paved the way for further anatomical studies with his careful plan of dissections and with his success in raising the status of anatomy. Anatomy became the "queen of the medical sciences" and gross anatomy an indispensable part of university medical education in the late sixteenth and seventeenth centuries; it has remained so. Nonetheless, there never existed a single unified program of Renaissance anatomy, but rather, as Andrew Cunningham has argued, many strands coexisted.[14] Not much later several other whole-body anatomies appeared which criticized Vesalius, such as the *Historia de la Composción de la Cuerpo Humano* (The Account of the Composition of the Human Body) of the Spaniard Joán de Valverde de Hamusco (c.1525–88) that appeared in 1566 and the

---

[14] Cunningham, *Anatomical Renaissance*.

Observationes Anatomicae (Anatomical Observations) of Gabriele Falloppio (1523–62) in 1561. Others concentrated on certain parts of the body. Bartolomeo Eustachi (c.1500–74) worked on the kidney, the venous systems, and the ear (the Eustachian tube in the middle ear is named for him). Comparative anatomy, pioneered by the Dutchman Volcher Coiter (1534–1600?), also burgeoned and made critical contributions. In addition, many anatomists took an interest not only in structures, but also in how parts worked. The noted comparativist, Hieronymous Fabricius ad Aquapendente (1533–1619), was one of these and his writings on the "little doors" (the valves of the veins) proved an important step toward Harvey's demonstration of the pulmonary circulation of the blood.

When William Harvey (1578–1657) published *De Motu Cordis* (On the Motion of the Heart) in 1628, he was fulfilling the anatomical program of the Renaissance and can therefore be seen as the last of the great Renaissance anatomists. Harvey's "discovery" of the systemic circulation was not a great "aha" moment, but rather built on earlier findings. Vesalius, as we know, denied that the septum dividing the ventricles of the heart was permeable and had also shown that the vena cava which, according to Galenic anatomy, originated in the liver and carried nutritious blood throughout the body, did not. Realdo Colombo (1516–59) vivisected animals and observed that blood moved from the right to the left ventricles of the heart not through invisible pores but rather through the lungs (Michael Servetus in the middle of the sixteenth century, and the Arab Ibn al-Nafis in the thirteenth century, had advanced similar ideas). These observations, along with Aquapendante's "little doors," provided the essential building blocks for Harvey's perception.

Harvey had been trained in anatomy at Padua and was heir to that tradition. In postulating how the blood circulated through the body, Harvey thought critically about the Galenic model, employed the methods of Renaissance anatomy, and worked out clever ways to demonstrate important principles. He also made an inspired guess. "I meditated," Harvey says in *De Motu Cordis*,

on the amount, i.e., of transmitted blood, and the very short time it took for its transfer, and I also noticed the juice of the ingested food could not supply this amount without our having the veins, on the one hand, completely emptied and the arteries, on the other hand, brought to bursting through excessive inthrust of blood, unless the blood somehow flowed back again from the arteries into the veins and returned to the right ventricle of the heart; I then began to wonder whether it had a movement, as it were, in a circle.[15]

---

[15] William Harvey, *The Circulation of the Blood and Other Writings*, trans. by Kenneth J. Franklin and with an introduction by Andrew Wear (London, 1990), 45–46.

Harvey dissected human corpses and vivisected cold-blooded animals to observe the less rapid motion of their hearts. He noticed that if one sliced into veins and arteries one found blood in both but no air or spiritus in the arteries as Galenic physiology had predicted. A whole series of other demonstrations validated his great perception. One of these was his calculation of the quantity of blood in the human body. But most famously he showed the direct linkage between the veins and the arteries, and thus between two circulatory systems. Taking a cord (a *ligature*), Harvey tied it very tightly around an arm to prevent arterial blood from moving in the limb. Harvey then loosened the tourniquet somewhat, allowed arterial blood to flow down the arm, which caused the veins to swell because the pressure in the veins was lower and because the arteries lay deeper; thus venous blood could not move past the ligature. Thus, Harvey made visible the attachment between arteries and veins and postulated that blood must pass from one to the other through tiny intermediary vessels, even though these connections remained invisible to the naked eye. The existence of capillaries, literally the missing link in this picture, was proven by Marcello Malpighi (1628–94) who, using a microscope, identified these minute blood vessels in the lung tissue of a frog. Almost as important was Malpighi's discovery that the trachea terminated in tiny bronchial filaments where, as it would eventually be shown, oxygen entered the blood. Indisputably, then, blood streamed through the body in two great circles: one systemic (through the entire body) and the other pulmonary (to and through the lungs).

Harvey's use of observation and even a form of experimentation seems to set him squarely on the side of modern science. Yet Harvey explicitly, even vehemently, distanced himself from those later tagged "practitioners of the new science." Like Aristotle, he believed in providential design and purpose, and he thought the soul responsible for the workings of the body. When he spoke of the pulmonary circulation, he argued that when "Nature wished the blood to be filtered through the lungs, she was forced to make the extra provision of a right ventricle." Unlike those who later would postulate the separation of body and soul, like the philosopher René Descartes (1596–1650), or those conceived of the body as a machine, Harvey did not regard the human body as purely mechanical. If Harvey was not a scientific pioneer as usually understood, what was the relationship of the "new science" to medicine in the sixteenth and seventeenth centuries?

The "new science"

As we have already seen, contemporary historians of science are wary of the whole concept of "The Scientific Revolution" and of any well-articulated program labeled "scientific" endeavor. Likewise, modern scientists have themselves become skeptical about the reality of a scientific method in the sense of "a coherent, universal, and efficacious set of procedures for making scientific knowledge" that arose in the seventeenth century and which succeeding generations received as orthodoxy.

Popular writers on science and medicine, however, still often convey simpler images of the victory of truth over obscurantism and experiment over belief to create a narrative of medical progress. For example, a 1993 publication outlining the history of science admits that "few scientists pretend anymore" that they are strictly "detached" and "objective." Nevertheless, it insists that Vesalius "threw down the gauntlet . . . to challenge the intellectual hold of the ancients" and describes Harvey's work as "the last major blow to Galen and the stranglehold that the ancients held upon medicine." Men such as Harvey and Vesalius are valorized as far-sighted individuals, who struggled often alone, misunderstood, and against huge odds, to shine the light of truth on the darkness of error. Vesalius was, we learn, a precocious genius who dissected animals on his mother's kitchen table; the seventeenth century was the "age of individual scientific endeavor," which spawned the fathers or founders of this, that, or the other; such as Malpighi as the founder of *histology* (the study of tissues by microscopy) or Wilhelm Fabricius (1560–1634) as "the father of German surgery."[16]

Such judgments are fraught with difficulties. Vesalius worked completely in the Galenic mode of anatomy and Harvey accepted Aristotelian philosophy. These positions prevent us from setting them up as right-thinking moderns against wrong-thinking ancients. To be sure, a contemporary conflict raged between those who venerated classical learning and those who believed that the teachings of the past were flawed and must be jettisoned to facilitate the quest for knowledge. Yet the line dividing the "Ancients" and the "Moderns" often blurred in complex ways, as the examples of Vesalius and Harvey indicate. Indeed, it often seems best to see Modern projects as "attempts to give birth (re-naissance) to the Ancient projects, not to reject them." Renaissance anatomy presents a clear case in point.[17]

Can we then speak about a "new science" in any meaningful way? Instead of a "single coherent cultural entity called 'science'," Steven Shapin finds "a diverse array of cultural practices aimed at

---

[16] Ray Spangenburg and Diana K. Moser, *The History of Science: From the Ancient Greeks to the Scientific Revolution* (New York, 1993), viii, 81, 84, 89, 110.

[17] Cunningham, *Anatomical Renaissance*, 7; more generally on the "Ancients" and the "Moderns" in medicine, see Joseph Levine, *Dr. Woodward's Shield: History, Science, and Satire in Augustan England* (Berkeley, 1977).

understanding, explaining, and controlling the natural world, each with different characteristics and each experiencing different modes of change."[18] Even if these men (and some women) believed that they were involved in change, their ideas of how that transition would occur and of what constituted proper method often diverged from one another and differed substantially from our twenty-first-century perceptions. Nowhere were these differences more evident than in the theories on what life was and how the body functioned.

Challenging Galen

Vesalian anatomy and even Harvey's discoveries opened few cracks in the Galenic system. Over the next century and a half, however, the number of challenges to Galenism multiplied and, by the eighteenth century, it had lost its hold as the basis of learned medicine; new ideas flooded in to fill the gap. One of the first, and one of the most forthright attacks on Galenism, came from Paracelsus. Born in Einsiedeln (in today's Switzerland) in 1493, Paracelsus's place in the history of medicine has occasioned enormous debate. Charles Singer and E. A. Underwood's well-known *A Short History of Medicine* (2nd edn., 1962) concluded that "it is not easy to assess the importance of Paracelsus to medicine. Some of his ideas were in advance of his time, but their expression is so clouded in mystical language that it is hard to separate the gold from the dross."[19] Work since the 1960s, and especially that of the last decade, has, however, significantly reevaluated and elevated Paracelsus's place in medical theory and practice, traced his profound influence on both, and come to appreciate him as a systematic thinker rather than a muddle-headed mystic.[20]

Paracelsus lived a restless life and one filled with controversy in a controversy-filled century. He almost certainly studied medicine at a university. He became the city doctor for Basel in 1527, feuded with the medical faculty there, and left. Paracelsus's opposition to Galenism was extreme: he explicitly rejected school medicine and lashed out at the university system as a whole. But he did not stop there. He strongly

---

[18] Shapin, *Scientific Revolution*, 3.
[19] Charles Singer and E. Ashworth Underwood, *A Short History of Medicine* (2nd edn., Oxford, 1962), 100.
[20] Walter Pagel, *Paracelsus* (Basel, 1958) remains extremely valuable for understanding Paracelsus's influence. Charles Webster, *Paracelsus, Magic and Mission at the End of Time* (New Haven, 2008) offers a major reinterpretation of Paracelsus as a systematic thinker and a medical practitioner set within the context of the radical social movements and religious reforms of the early to mid sixteenth century.

disapproved of anatomy as "dead knowledge" and proposed a new system of natural philosophy linked to older alchemical traditions and based on chemical principles very different from Galenic ones. He argued that "there are three things [his *tria prima*] which give every single thing its body. The names of these three things are Sulphur, Mercury, and Salt." He also believed that the world was alive with spiritual forces. These *archei* controlled internal bodily processes. Infections originated in "star-poisons . . . concealed beneath the goodness in everything" or arose from minerals (and especially salts) hidden in the earth. Such precepts announced a radical departure from Galenic principles. Whereas in the Galenic system, an imbalance of humors within the body caused diseases that were unique to each individual, Paracelsus denied the effect of the humors and taught that diseases were specific. He thus laid the basis for an ontological understanding of disease (a view of each disease as a real entity with an independent existence). If this seems to be a more modern concept of disease than the Galenists offered, it is not necessarily so; Paracelsus also envisioned a world full of occult energies. Other parts of his teachings reflected his bent toward mystical and magical explanations. He firmly believed in the relationship between the macrocosm and the microcosm and the influence of the celestial bodies on the human form: "The stars compel and cause the animal man, so that where they lead he must follow." He accepted the alchemical *doctrine of signatures* that "like cured liked" (again in direct contravention of Galenic teachings) and believed that objects with shapes or colors similar to particular organs could cure their ills, applying maidenhair for baldness or lungwort for pulmonary afflictions. (Much later, and admittedly in a different form, the idea of "like cures like" would be revived by Samuel Hahnemann [1755–1843] and forged into a homeopathic system that continues to attract adherents.) Paracelsus also advocated chemical remedies, relying on poisons like mercury, antimony, and arsenic for drastic cases.[21]

Paracelsus's assault on Galenism may seem rabid, but his ideas mirrored the times in which he lived. Although he remained a nominal Catholic, his medicine followed many contemporary developments in religion and intellectual life. Luther's insistence on the sole authority of scripture and his call for a priesthood of all believers (the Reformer's claim that priests were unnecessary and perhaps even counterproductive to securing salvation) paralleled Paracelsus's conviction that anyone could practice medicine by reading the book of Nature and that one should turn to artisans and ordinary people for instruction. Knowledge

---

21 Quotations from *Paracelsus: Essential Readings*, selected and trans. by Nicholas Goodrick-Clarke (Wellingborough, 1990), 51, 78, 185.

was not found in weighty tomes or at universities but could only be gained through personal experience. While academic medicine fixated on the scholastic dissection of texts, Paracelsus consulted the people, perused the book of Nature, and disdained all other authorities. In addition, the religious reformers were prolific pamphleteers who wrote in the vernacular. Paracelsus first gained public recognition with his short German *Prognosikation auf 24 zukünftige jahre* (Prophecy for the next twenty-four years) in 1536. It was one of the handful of writings published in his lifetime. Few people were actually acquainted with his medical works; he was far better known as an interpreter of portents, such as comets.

The teachings of Paracelsus attracted few members of medical faculties or among academically trained physicians. Not too surprisingly, Catholic universities excoriated both Paracelsus and Paracelsianism. His violent repudiation of the theory and practice of Galenic medicine did little to endear him to the medical establishment. When denounced by his opponents, he responded fervently:

You are serpents and I expect poison from you. With what scorn have you proclaimed that I am a heretic. I am Theophrastus . . . and a monarch of physicians as well, and can prove what you are not able to prove.[22]

Paracelsus did not limit his radicalism to medicine; his religious views, his social revolutionism, and his millenarianism made him suspect. The Catholic Counter-Reformation later condemned his works as heretical, as dangerous for their crypto-Protestantism as for their magical content.

Nonetheless, Paracelsus attracted many supporters and disciples after his death, and especially after the publication of several works in the 1570s. During the last quarter of the sixteenth century, Paracelsianism spread rapidly. It served as the fount from which additional challenges to Galenism sprang. Despite the inherent populism of Paracelsus's message, it also appealed to Renaissance rulers and courts that had previously been interested in magic, astrology, alchemy, and neoplatonism. Princes intrigued by Paracelsianism and chemical medicine were often Calvinist, frequently Protestant, but also Catholic. The Holy Roman Emperor Rudolf II supported several Paracelsian doctors, as well as alchemists, astrologers, and astronomers at his court in Prague. An early enthusiast was Otto Heinrich (r.1556–59), the elector of the Palatinate, while Moritz of Hesse (r.1592–1627) was supporter and practitioner alike; he established a *Collegium chymicum* in Marburg in 1609. Royal and princely patronage of Paracelsian physicians was ample and generous in the late

---

[22] *Ibid.*, 73.

sixteenth and early seventeenth centuries. No less a personage than Henri IV (r. 1589–1610) of France preferred Paracelsian physicians.

Gradually, as Paracelsians sought to gain greater acceptance, or to avoid charges of religious heterodoxy, they moved away from the full Paracelsian program that included the master's philosophical and cosmological thought and principally promoted chemical remedies. Eventually, the more orthodox medical world began to incorporate some Paracelsian elements, such as the use of chemicals (themselves, of course, not solely Paracelsian in origin). The endorsement of chemical remedies by several varieties of practitioners (including Galenists) proceeded with some rapidity and these medicines soon found their way into standard medical armamentaria. If, for instance, one surveys the pharmacopoeias published after the late sixteenth century, it is immediately apparent how many contained chemical medicines in the form of minerals, salts, and metals. The second edition of the *Pharmacopoeia Londinensis* (1612), for instance, listed 122 chemical preparations, including mercuric sulphate, calomel, and several amalgams of antimony.

Moreover, Paracelsian medicine itself was changing. Gradually, many physicians came to accept Paracelsian remedies if not Paracelsian philosophy. They later introduced chemical medicine in the form of what is often known as iatrochemistry. ("Iatro" as a prefix means "medicine" or "doctors.") Iatrochemistry, like iatromechanism and iatromathematics, was a system of medical explanation and practice that arose in the seventeenth century and contested Galenic physiology and held on, albeit somewhat altered, until almost 1700.

Popular during this time was the iatrochemistry the Flemish natural philosopher Joan Baptista van Helmont formulated. Van Helmont, much like Paracelsus, embedded his medicine in a broader social program and philosophical framework. He argued that processes such as digestion and respiration were essentially chemical in nature and that a special ferment or gas produced each. Iatrochemists, in general, stressed the chemical reactions of *effervescence, fermentation,* and *putrefaction* as the basis of all physiology. Van Helmont believed as well that chemical analysis provided the passkey to a profounder understanding of God and nature alike. Similar to Paracelsus, van Helmont regarded disease as an individual entity. Whereas Paracelsus had spoken of a "religion of medicine," van Helmont proposed a physiology that denied the teachings of the ancients as non-Christians; this blanket exclusion included Galen, of course. Thus, a strong thread of reformism ran through van Helmont's teachings, and through iatrochemistry more generally, as it had through Paracelsianism. As a Catholic, van Helmont evoked the ire of the Counter-Reformation Church. But soon chemical physicians gained a reputation as more charitable and accessible than the purportedly haughty and avaricious Galenists. Much like Paracelsus, van Helmont believed that one could treat diseases with cheap, simple chemical remedies. Another chemical physician, Théophraste Renaudot (1586–1653), organized a facility in Paris for the sick-poor. His and similar endeavors contributed considerably to the growing popularity of the chemicalists. While van Helmont's teachings and method won adherents and advocates throughout northern Europe, they may have had the greatest influence in England, where serious attempts were made in 1665 (albeit in vain) to establish a Society of Chemical Physicians to supplant the authority of the College of Physicians in London.

Van Helmont's ideas proved as about as unpalatable to university faculties of medicine as Paracelsian ones. Nonetheless, with time, both the faculties and the Galenic system found ways to accommodate themselves to this challenge as well, in part by assimilating some iatrochemical notions and practices. In doing so, Galenism extended its lifespan by decades. Although some historians argue that Galenism was "in tatters" by 1600, others see a Galenism modified by iatrochemistry (and also influenced by iatromechanics; see below, p. 105) that retained vitality at least until the 1680s.

Iatrochemistry as a Christian philosophy is not what conquered the medical faculties; rather it was iatrochemistry in the version that developed during the early eighteenth century in France, England, and Italy that won the day. François de le Boë Sylvius (1614–72), for instance, rejected the philosophical and theological bases of van Helmont's system. He and others constructed a theory more congenial to academic medicine and more compatible with Galenism. The iatrochemists did, after all, offer what seemed sensible explanations for several bodily functions. Sylvius, for example, described digestion as a chemical reaction, that is, as the result of acid–alkali fermentation occurring in the stomach. He also recognized the importance of saliva and pancreatic secretions for digestion. Neither idea, it should be noted, seemed fundamentally incompatible with older humoral doctrines and explanations.

Chemical medicine answered more questions about bodily processes than did either Galen or gross anatomy. Renaissance anatomical investigations had revealed the precise structure of the organs of respiration, for example, but had little useful to say about their functions or purpose. The seventeenth-century diarist Samuel Pepys (1633–1703) observed "that it is not to this day known or concluded among physicians . . . how the action [of respiration] is managed by nature, or for what use it is."[23] Galen believed that the lungs acted like great organic fans to cool the "fiery heart." Only in the seventeenth and early eighteenth centuries did investigations into air help solve the riddle of respiration. Using a vacuum jar, the gentleman natural philosopher, Robert Boyle (1627–91), demonstrated in 1660 that animals could not live in the absence of air nor could flames be sustained, thus correctly associating the processes of respiration and combustion. Seven years later, the microscopist Robert Hooke (1635–1703) kept a dog alive by using bellows to pump air through its opened trachea, suggesting that some chemical change in blood involving air maintained life. This finding allowed Hooke and another Englishman, Richard Lower (1631–91), to account for the difference between the bright red blood in arteries and the darker venous blood; the first was full of air. They noted that blood going to the lungs was bluish but, when it returned, it was scarlet, having been "transformed." Later researchers, such as the Frenchman Antoine Lavoisier (1743–94) and the Englishman Joseph Priestley (1733–1804) discovered that atmospheric oxygen supported life and that the oxygenation of the blood was the vital respiratory process.

Equally perplexing in function was reproduction. As we know (see Chapter 1, pp. 20–21), opinion divided almost equally between ovists and spermists. Some physicians, such as Friedrich Hoffmann, understood fertilization and early embryonic growth in terms of vital motions:

For reproduction, the ovum must be suitable for fertilization. This is accomplished by the extremely subtle spirituous effluvia of the masculine seed, introducing a new internal vital motion into the fluid parts contained within the egg.[24]

Despite the criticality of the "male seed," it was the "female ovule" that contained "the material principle of the offspring." Hoffmann offered, however, no good idea of how the fetus matured after fertilization. Major advances in the understanding of reproduction and fetal growth had to wait until nineteenth-century work in embryology and for the discovery of hormones at the very beginning of the twentieth century.

Respiration and digestion formed parts of what we now call human metabolism, the sum of all the chemical and physical changes that take place within the body and enable its growth and survival. Rather early in our period, interest in measuring such processes and probing their unseen motions led to the invention of new instruments and new forms of comprehending these findings. The Paduan professor Sanctorio Sanctorio

---

[23] Quoted in Fielding Garrison, *An Introduction to the History of Medicine* (4th edn., Philadelphia and London, 1929), 267n4.
[24] Hoffmann, *Fundamenta medicinae*, 35.

(1561–1636) collected data on what he called "insensible perspiration." Sanctorio devised a chair-balance to weigh himself to determine the exact mathematical relationship between food intake and excretions. He was also the first to describe a clinical thermometer and a pulse-clock (the pulse-watch was introduced by John Floyer [1649–1734] in 1707).

Among the new instruments, none could compete with the microscope, however. The work of the early microscopists rendered visible what the naked eye failed to discern. The polymath Jesuit priest Athanasius Kircher examined under his lenses putrefying matter as well as the blood of plague victims in which he identified "little worms." The ingenious Robert Hooke scrutinized as much of the living world as would fit between the plates of his microscope. His magnificent *Micrographia*, published in 1665, portrayed a vast range of life, plant and animal, including what he referred to as "little boxes, or cells." Zoology fascinated Jan Swammerdam (1637–80) and he, like Hooke, published bewitching prints revealing the tiniest sections of animal anatomy. Particularly relevant for medicine were his observations of what we now know as red corpuscles, which the great Dutch microscopist Antonj van Leeuwenhoek fully depicted somewhat later. Leeuwenhoek observed spermatozoa as well as grinding his own exceptionally fine lenses. We have already seen how Malpighi revealed the capillaries that coupled the arterial and venous systems.

The precise mathematical and mechanical nature of the work of Sanctorio and the microscopists reflects the rise of another strand of medical explanation known as iatromechanism. Although histories of medicine often present iatromechanism and iatrochemistry as opposing systems, the truth of the relationship is more complex. In fact, they interacted and influenced one another to the extent that an easy sorting of physicians and natural philosophers into one or another of the two schools proves difficult. Iatromechanists argued that the body obeyed the same laws of physics as did the larger terrestrial and celestial bodies. Thus, the human body, like the heavens, followed precise mathematical rules (a perception sometimes referred to as iatromathematics). Thus, whereas an iatrochemist might explain digestion as a process of fermentation taking place in the stomach, iatromechanists believed it was more the result of a pulverizing and churning action. For the Armenian physician Giorgio Baglivi (1668–1707), the human edifice "operate[d] by number, weight, and measure." Significantly, early work on a quantitative description of the body was done by an astronomer and mathematician, Giovanni Borelli (1608–79). Borelli, in writing on animal motion, described the workings of the limbs in terms of simple machines, such as levers and pulleys.

The French mathematician and philosopher René Descartes exerted an enormous influence on iatromechanical theories. In his *Traité de l'homme* (Treatise of Man, 1664), Descartes separated the soul, which he viewed as incorporeal, immortal, and infinite, from the body, which was corporeal, mortal, and finite; the latter was measurable, the former not. As nature was a giant clock set into motion by the Creator, so, too, was the human body a mechanism. This way of thinking, of course, seemed to negate the purposefulness that Galen and Aristotle, but also Harvey and many others, attributed to nature and to workings of the human body.

The great Dutch physician and teacher Herman Boerhaave (1668–1738) applied Cartesianism to human physiology. Students flocked to Leiden, where Boerhaave taught, and they disseminated his ideas throughout Europe. Boerhaave proposed a hydraulic model of the human body, which he saw as composed of "membranous pipes or vessels." Like Borelli, he compared parts of the body to simple tools and mechanisms. For Boerhaave, health was a balancing act of maintaining a proper fluid pressure in the receptacles of the human body. Boerhaave insisted that knowledge derived from sense experience alone and he would have no truck with discussions of purpose or first causes as such "are neither possible, useful, or necessary to be investigated by a physician."[25] A German contemporary of Boerhaave, Friedrich Hoffmann, likewise argued in his *Fundamenta Medicinae* (Fundamentals of medicine, 1695) that "Medicine is the art of properly utilizing physico-mechanical principles, in order to conserve the health of man or to restore it if lost." Both Hoffmann and Boerhaave avoided the ascription of purpose (which they denigrated as "occultism") to specific organs or processes in the body. This "refusal to speculate" and the adamant denial of purpose characterized important trends in late seventeenth- and early eighteenth-century medicine and in science more generally.[26]

Sense experience and scientific experimentation, rather than texts, gradually became the new authorities. "In the course of the seventeenth century, natural philosophers increasingly appealed to the results of specific experiments rather than, as previously, to a philosophical consensus about what happens 'all or most of the time.'" This shift eventually had an impact on physiology. Of considerable importance was the work done

---

[25] Harold Cook, *Matters of Exchange: Commerce, Medicine, and Science in the Dutch Golden Age* (New Haven, 2007), 393.

[26] Hoffmann, quoted in Thomas H. Broman, "The Medical Sciences," in *The Cambridge History of Science*, vol. IV, *The Eighteenth Century*, ed. by Roy Porter (Cambridge, 2003), 469. The phrase "refusal to speculate" is a chapter title in Cook, *Matters of Exchange*.

by one of Boerhaave's students, the Swiss physician Albrecht von Haller (1708–77) at the new university of Göttingen founded in 1737 in the Duchy of Hanover. In 1757, Haller supervised 567 experiments which clarified the difference between nerve impulse (which he termed *sensibility*) and muscular contraction (*irritability*). These findings greatly influenced medical theory and laid the basis for yet another new departure in medicine, one focusing on the nerves. Nerve theories fed, and fed on, the concurrent cult of sensibility expressed in the best-selling sentimental novels: Abbé Prévost's *Manon Lescaut* (1731), Samuel Richardson's *Pamela: Or, Virtue Rewarded* (1740), and Jean-Jacques Rousseau's *Julie, ou la Nouvelle Héloïse* (1761).

The Scottish professor of medicine at Edinburgh, William Cullen (1710–90), and the German physician Johann Blumenbach (1752–1840) elaborated innovative systems of medicine based on nerves. While Boerhaave had viewed the body as a hydraulic machine, Cullen emphasized the nervous system. Cullen argued that a pathological action of "spasm" caused all disease. To treat fevers, therefore, he recommended a series of therapies: removal of the source of irritation; sedation with opiates; bloodletting; and bed rest. From here it was but a short step to the theories of John Brown (1735–88) that maintained life resulted merely from the action of external stimuli or excitement. Brown divided diseases into two groups, either *sthenic*, those arising from too much systemic stimulation, or *asthenic*, of too little. Brown also proposed quantitative measures for each. He suggested that excitement could be mathematically calibrated on a scale, like a thermometer measured degrees of fever. Brown's system, called *Brunonianism*, never became very popular in France or England, but gained a large number of converts in Italy, central Europe (including Johann Peter Frank), and in the young United States where one of his disciples was Benjamin Rush (1745–1813), a signer of the Declaration of Independence and the most famous North American physician of his day.

Not everyone subscribed to either iatrochemistry or iatromechanism. Nor should we be too quick to make these systems more complete, solid, and exclusive than they were. For some, men like Thomas Sydenham, all theory was irrelevant or even harmful. For others, neither the iatrochemists nor the iatromechanists could adequately explain life because both seemed to deny (as Boerhaave did explicitly) what the Galenists had always found central: purpose. Thus, those sometimes classified as *vitalists* or *animists* (and this term is no more or less valid than iatrochemistry or iatromechanism) argued that neither chemistry nor physics could convincingly account for physiological processes. Neither persuaded the Halle professor of medicine Georg Stahl (1659–1734). For Stahl, the body was more than an animate machine or a chemical cooker; it was a God-driven and soul-directed organism.[27] The Montpellier professor François Boissier de Sauvages (1706–67) postulated something similar: each organ had a unique vital force that maintained it and ensured its proper functioning. By the end of the eighteenth century, what came to be known as *vital phenomena* attracted the interest of many natural philosophers including Luigi Galvani (1737–98), best known for his experiments with the effects of electricity on frogs' legs that had been severed from their bodies; Antoine Lavoisier for his work on oxygen; and the German natural historian and explorer Alexander von Humboldt (1769–1859). Blumenbach, who is today most famous for his work on craniology and is often considered a founder of physical anthropology (and, more negatively, as an early constructor of concepts of racial differences), identified a life-force driving toward regeneration that was akin to the ideas of the animists and vitalists. Similarly, the renowned surgeon and anatomist John Hunter (1728–93) affirmed the presence of a life-principle to distinguish between living and nonliving things. At virtually the same time, however, Julien La Mettrie (1709–51) declared in his *L'Homme machine* (Man a Machine, 1747) that organized matter alone produced thought and constituted the soul.

Historians have often associated each of these particular theories with political and larger philosophical systems. "Iatromechanism could be represented as very much an 'absolutist' medical theory, where the body was largely controlled by a single centre, the brain; vitalism was the more 'democratic' ideology in that the bodily parts governed themselves." Or one might suggest, as Harold Cook has done, that the commercial practicality of Dutch merchants fostered a down-to-earth pragmatism that privileged sense experience and stuck to "simple things," eschewing grand interpretations, as Boerhaave did.[28] Such attempts to map intellectual process on larger social, economic, and political contexts have become prevalent in medical history and reflect widespread recognition that intellectual life, like medical theories, does not proceed in a vacuum but is significantly influenced or even generated by broader contexts.

When we consider individuals, however, the lines separating the iatrochemist from the iatromechanist from the vitalist often smudge. Friedrich Hoffmann, for example, has most often been characterized as an important iatromechanist, but this label may pigeonhole him too neatly.

---

[27] On Stahl, see Johann Geyer-Kordesch, *Pietismus, Medizin und Aufklärung in Preussen im 18. Jahrhundert: Das Leben und Werk Georg Ernst Stahl* (Tübingen, 2000); Peter Hanns Reill, *Vitalizing Nature in the Enlightenment* (Berkeley, 2005).

[28] Brockliss and Jones, *Medical World*, 429, 431–32; Cook, *Matters of Exchange*, 378–409.

Hoffmann also employed the language of chemistry in speaking, for example, of blood as "volatile, fixed, alkali, or sulphurous." Thus Hoffmann and others might be better called eclectics.[29]

One must also bear in mind that the categories sketched out here have no real life of their own and these systems always proved far less than fully systematic. All classifications are mere historical shorthand and ways of organizing and interpreting information. For the iatrochemists, iatromechanists, and vitalists, we are at least using terms many contemporaries themselves employed. No school or program was rigidly defined or constructed. Yet, no unique set of beliefs glued them together. There was no iatrochemical bible, for instance, that all iatrochemists swore on nor a rulebook that guided their actions. Reality was messier and more beguiling than even well-substantiated generalizations can convey.

Medicine and the Enlightenment

The medical theorizing of the eighteenth century largely dedicated itself to unraveling the complexities of life. Debate revolved around whether life was purely mechanical or chemical – what the eighteenth century referred to as *material* – or whether some vitalistic principle made the body and human life add up to more than the sum of mathematical equations, mechanical movements, or chemical reactions. The discussions of Stahl, Haller, Cullen, and Brown above have moved us well into the eighteenth century. As always, such medical theories were embedded in broader contexts. Thus, we need to explore in greater depth the relationship between medicine and the cultural movement generally referred to as the Enlightenment.

Defining what "enlightenment" meant is not easy. One must bear in mind that "the" Enlightenment was a composite phenomenon that frequently assumed distinctly different forms in different places. People who included themselves in that movement could be statist or anti-statist, conservative or radical, pious believers or atheists. Scholars have recently come to doubt the once widely accepted notion of the progressive nature of the Enlightenment.[30] Similar questions bedeviled those in the eighteenth century who thought that they lived not in an enlightened age perhaps, but in an age of enlightenment. One common thread was the tenet that the world could be made a better place. The *philosophes* (the French word for those who promoted enlightenment), despite

[29] Broman, "Medical Sciences," 469–71.
[30] Thomas Munck, "Enlightened Thought, Its Critics and Competitors," in Peter H. Wilson, ed., *A Companion to Eighteenth-Century Europe* (Oxford, 2008), 141–57.

representing a wild plurality of stances on important issues such as the role of religion, sought secular improvements. They generally agreed that rational planning and an unceasing vigilance against obscurantism and folly could perfect man and society. While the growth of a public sphere separate from the state proper provided the venue for the creation and expression of many enlightened ideas (in the forms of print, conversations in private clubs and coffeehouses, and in novels), many looked to the state for the realization of significant beneficial changes. In this sense, the Enlightenment in many places was hardly revolutionary but rather dovetailed neatly with mercantilist schemes to augment the productivity of the state through meticulous forms of socioeconomic planning. Moreover, most philosophes retained a belief in God, although not all remained orthodox Christians. Only a handful, such as Jean-Adrien Helvétius (1662–1727) or the medical materialist La Mettrie, chucked God out and embraced fully secular and material explanations. Yet, the general orientation of the philosophes was this-worldly and thus they promoted "a radically different conception of health, which was now figured as the key to terrestrial happiness."[31] This profound transformation in mentality manifested itself best in efforts to correct deficiencies in environmental conditions, to augment the size of population (a program known as populationism), and to cultivate the better health of the people as a whole. (For more on these subjects, see Chapter 6.)

But one should bear in mind that the interaction of religion and medicine during the Enlightenment remained strong. There was, moreover, no inescapable conflict between religion, on the one hand, and science and medicine, on the other. Anti-Christian philosophes/physicians formed only a small subgroup and Enlightenment and Christianity cross-fertilized in interesting ways. Religious groups could, for instance, shape medical thinking to substantiate their belief in witches and the devil. The ideas of the Enlightenment in medicine were, therefore, extraordinarily complex and subject to numerous influences; religion played a great role in stirring up the mixture.[32]

Older medical historiography tended to represent most of the eighteenth century (the Enlightenment included) as a lull before the clinical storm of the late 1790s broke. Like Enlightenment more globally, no single item or belief defines the Enlightenment in medicine. Yet, as Roy Porter has pointed out, the eighteenth century "produced extensive and innovative medical discourses," and, just as evidently, "medical

[31] Brockliss and Jones, *Medical World*, 378.
[32] Ole Peter Grell and Andrew Cunningham, eds., *Medicine and Religion in Enlightenment Europe* (Aldershot, 2007).

images . . . were central to the sociopolitical visions of the philosophes."[33] Certainly, many initiatives launched in the Renaissance and the seventeenth century continued. Anatomy progressed steadily from the time of Vesalius through the eighteenth century becoming ever more established as a mainstay of medical knowledge and education. A more abundant supply of corpses, as governments delivered the bodies of criminals, lunatics, and paupers to the dissection table, fostered anatomical investigations on a large scale. At the same time, protests against dissection, as well as against the vivisection of animals, swelled, crescendoing in the mid nineteenth century. Everyone came to fear the "resurrection men" (body snatchers) who robbed graves or even murdered the unsuspecting and sold the corpses to those starved for dead flesh. Not only ghouls and shady characters plied the trade. Fully respectable men, like the Hunter brothers, John and William, purchased anatomical raw materials.[34]

The greater availability of bodies generated a keener interest in *morbid* or *pathological anatomy*, a new discipline that made anatomy more immediately relevant to medical theory and practice. Giambattista Morgagni (1682–1771) sought signs in specific organs that he believed revealed the seats of disease. Morgagni, for instance, documented lesions of tuberculosis in the kidney and identified the clinical features of pneumonia. Distinguished successors to Morgagni were the Scot Matthew Baillie (1761–1823) and the Frenchman Xavier Bichat (1771–1802). Baillie first accurately described cirrhosis of the liver. Bichat shifted the focus of morbid anatomy to the tissues that make up organs rather than the organs themselves. All three men moved toward thinking in the opposed categories of normal and abnormal (rather than, as the Galenists had done, locating individuals on a spectrum, each more or less closely connected to the others). All believed with Bichat that "opening up corpses" would supply the solutions to medical puzzles.

The spatial location of morbid anatomy migrated as well. Many scholars now believe the hospital to be the fountainhead of "Paris medicine" and the birthplace of the clinic. According to this interpretation, in the clinic of the late eighteenth century, medicine became truly "objective" and truly "scientific" in the sense of being derived from quantifiable results. The rows of patients in hospital beds supplied the material for the case histories that could be approached numerically or statistically

---

[33] Roy Porter, "Introduction," to Porter, ed., *Medicine in the Enlightenment* (Amsterdam and Atlanta, 1995), 3.
[34] Ruth Richardson, *Death, Dissection and the Destitute* (London, 1987); Lisa Rosner, *The Anatomy Murders: Being the True yet Spectacular History of Edinburgh's Notorious Burke and Hare and of the Man of Science who Abetted Them in the Commission of Their Most Heinous Crimes* (Philadelphia, 2009).

for the first time. Case histories themselves were not newly initiated on the wards of the Paris hospitals (where this development is often seen as originating), of course. Earlier records, however, were generally disjunctive; that is, they were not composed in a standard form. Instead, they were idiosyncratic narratives (to reflect the individualized medicine of Galenism, for example) that defied easy quantification and frustrated comparisons. Physicians walking the Paris wards, however, standardized case-taking. These practices, including pathological anatomy, laid the basis for a clinical pathology that applied the knowledge obtained from "opening up corpses" and quantifying illnesses to treatments. The second step took considerably longer to accomplish than the first. Much of this story, however, belongs to the history of medical education (see Chapter 4) and to the development of hospitals (see Chapter 5).

Theories and therapeutics

The *clinico-anatomical method* aimed at locating the precise site of disease in the body. But to what extent did the discoveries in anatomy, physiology, and pathology described above contribute in any substantial way to therapeutics, that is, to methods of treatment? Throughout early modern times, therapeutics had remained mostly Galenic in character, as did most medications, albeit with a significant addition of chemical remedies beginning in the late sixteenth century. Few theoretical changes made very much difference to how medical practitioners treated illnesses; none, by itself, contributed to cures. Rather, the discovery and introduction of previously unused or unknown substances – some of which originated in the New World or Asia – promised advances in drug therapies.

Galenic therapeutics was highly individualized. Because the Galenists viewed disease as the effect of a particular and peculiar imbalance of humors unique to every human being, Galenic physicians had to exercise great care in selecting proper regimens and prescribing appropriate drugs. Galenic therapy was, moreover, allopathic: a system of medicine in which the use of drugs is directed to producing effects in the body that directly oppose and so alleviate the symptoms of disease. The French seventeenth-century country doctor, François du Port, succinctly noted that "every disease is expelled by its opposite."

Etna's heat is nullified by glacial cold, dryness and moisture interact, fire absorbs fluid and renders it dry, the thin sunders the thick, hard iron resists what is soft, the rough opposes the smooth, the porous the solid, what is closed or joined is contrary to the open, the sticky to the polished.

In medical terms, thus, "when a purple humor distends the vessels, opening a vein is helpful," while in fever "a healing draught will cool and water give relief, countering the body's drought." These Galenic precepts relied as well on polypharmacy: the prescription of *composita* containing many different ingredients carefully chosen, blended, and refined to fit an individual's singular condition, body type, complexion, and humoral imbalance. The Galenist du Port, for instance, would first tap a vein in a case of diarrhea accompanied by "fever and flow of bile" and then order that

three sandalwoods and rhubarb be swallowed; or infuse these with water of barberry, endive, plantain, drunk with liquour of pomegranate, myrtle or rose. Prepare an enema of roses and red dragon's blood [a New World plant], Armenian bole with scalded milk. And let the diet be light . . . [and] the water should contain iron, and one part of wine diluted with two parts of water.[35]

Herbal remedies remained a mainstay of the early modern pharmacopoeia, albeit supplemented ever more frequently with chemical ones. Patients' and physicians' reactions to the actions of drugs varied enormously. Some feared harsh purgatives and preferred medicines with milder actions; others felt that only a strong response indicated effectiveness.

The efficacy of these methods is terribly difficult to judge and most modern medical historians advance opinions on "what worked" as cautiously as they approach retrodiagnosis. Obviously, the feeling of having done "something," like the extremely well-documented placebo effect, loomed large in any personal assessment of efficacy. Some herbal remedies undoubtedly alleviated symptoms. Willow bark tea, for instance, is a good *febrifuge*; it reduces fever. In the nineteenth century, chemists discovered that willow contains salicylates, the active ingredient in aspirin. The ancient world also recognized the pain-stilling actions of wine, opium, hemlock, and mandragora. By the middle ages, belladonna was being used to still cramps (and also as a cosmetic to dilate pupils and give eyes a special sparkle). Ergot was known to cause abortions, although it could also be administered to induce labor or expel a retained afterbirth.

Unlike Galenic treatments that prescribed opposites, Paracelsian remedies relied on the motto of "like cures like" and were, as we know, often chemical in origin. Many chemical remedies, especially the often-prescribed mercury, antimony, and calomel, had dramatic effects. Mercury when used to treat syphilis seems to have been somewhat useful, but the therapy also produced distressing salivation, loosened teeth, and

---

[35] Du Port, *Decade of Medicine*, 84–85, 159, 204–05.

progressively poisoned the patient. Calomel (mercurous chloride) was an effective, but harsh, laxative.

Besides the new chemical remedies, the widening world offered a cornucopia of new drug possibilities and even new ideas about therapeutics. This knowledge flowed to Europe from both east and west, from the "New Found Lands" of the Americas as well as from China, India, and the Spice Islands. Soon after first contact with the Americas, reports of medicinal herbs and medical practices began to filter back to Europe. At Tenochtitlán, soldiers accompanying Cortés were amazed by the many herb sellers in the city; one wrote that "in this street they lay out the peppers, in that medicinal roots and herbs." Observers almost invariably noted the use of chocolate and tobacco for health and pleasure.

The impact of the medicinal plants and the medicine of the New World on the Old is a topic of considerable debate. Some have argued that these eye-witness accounts made little impression in Europe because they were not published and often lay unread on dusty library shelves. An account of Aztec medicine from 1552, the *Codex Barberini*, for example, was translated into Latin and sent back to Europe as a gift for the Holy Roman Emperor; it lay unnoticed in the Vatican Library until rediscovered in 1929. Still, even if the material in the Codex was never printed, that does not mean its content remained unknown. The manuscript itself, copies of it, or excerpts from it, may have been passed around privately among friends and fellow scholars as was customary in natural philosophical circles. Teresa Huguet-Termes, in investigating the impact of the Pomar codex which recorded the 1570 expedition of Francisco Hernández (1514–87) to study plants and animals in the New World, takes exception to the generally accepted argument that his observations had little impact on scholarly medicine in the sixteenth century. She notes that "information from the manuscripts and reports of the expedition circulated widely ... and many important physicians ... had a look at them." Thus, the question of how much impact knowledge of New World plants had on European medicine remains an open one.[36]

Clearly important was the work of a Spanish physician, Nicolás Monardes (c.1512–88), who never visited the New World; he practiced medicine in Seville. In 1574, he published a book on American medicines, based on second-hand evidence. The several editions and

---

[36] J. Worth Estes, "The European Reception of the First Drugs from the New World," *Pharmacy in History* 37, no. 1 (1995): 3–23, tends to think there was little early impact of New World medicines and little knowledge of them. Teresa Huguet-Termes questions that interpretation in "New World Materia Medica in Spanish Renaissance Medicine: From Scholarly Reception to Practical Impact," *Medical History* 45 (2001): 359–76, quote 366.

translations of this work exerted more influence on Europe than any earlier writings. He argued that materials from the New World would cure
many diseases for which European drugs did not exist. Moreover, and
just as importantly, Monardes recognized the possibility of great commercial gain from the importation and sale of New World medicines.[37]

Europeans in the New World recognized – or thought they recognized –
there indigenous plants identical to, or very like, those they already knew,
such as peppers, resinous balsams, or what they called "dragon's blood,"
a plant believed identical to an East Indian palm. From the New World,
the Europeans took several plants and herbal remedies, such as guaiac,
sarsaparilla, jalap or the "rhubarb of the Indies," sassafras bark, coca,
tobacco, and cacao, as well as bezoars (stone-like substances found in the
digestive tracts of ruminants, known and prized in Europe since ancient
times). The most profitable drugs imported from the New World in the
sixteenth century were guaiac (used to treat syphilis), sarsaparilla, sassafras, and tobacco. Physicians originally lauded cacao and tobacco from
the western hemisphere (like tea and coffee from the eastern hemisphere)
for their health benefits. Hoffmann recommended that "the smoking of
tobacco should be permitted more as a medicine than for pleasure."
Peruvian or Jesuits' bark came from the New World in the 1630s; it
contained quinine and proved effective against intermittent fevers (like
malaria). Another seventeenth-century import was ipecacuanha, a useful
emetic (vomitive) that also loosed thick congestion in the chest. Initial
enthusiasm for the drugs of the "New Found Lands" was strong, but
waned when physicians recognized that many proved less effective, or
at least no more effective, than the cheaper, easily available European
varieties.

But what did colonists who lived in these New Worlds do for medicines
and medical care? Life in a recently planted colony was extremely
hard. George Percy wrote in 1606 from Jamestown that "our men were
destroyed with cruell diseases." Colonists frequently sought cures for
the ills they suffered from products nearby. Richard Ligon in Barbados
expressed a common belief when he argued that "certainly every Climate
produces Simples more proper to cure the diseases that are bred there,
than those that are transported from any other part of the world." Thus,
colonists often preferred local drugs to European ones even if they evoked
the same effects. But, here, too, another side of the story needs to be told;
there was also a sense that native medicines and indigenous plants did
not suit European constitutions. Many colonists remained wary of the

[37] Estes, "European Reception"; Londa Schiebinger, *Plants and Empire: Colonial Bioprospecting in the Atlantic World* (Cambridge, Mass., 2007), 73–81.

medical practices of indigenous peoples, which they regarded as abhorrent or heretical. Others acknowledged that the natives possessed much useful knowledge.[38]

Europeans regarded the medicine of Asia, especially of China, Japan, India, and the Spice Islands, differently from the cures of the Americas. First, the "orient" was not a sixteenth-century discovery; China or Seres ("the land of silk") was known to the Romans. Still, greater exploration and colonization produced considerably more knowledge about drugs and practices, and simulated lively European debates about them. Perplexing were the apparent congruities. Europeans, Chinese, and Japanese, for example, all gauged the pulse but the Japanese and Chinese systems of pulse evaluation differed drastically from the European one.[39] Likewise the Japanese displayed a fascination with carbuncles while these excrescences concerned European practitioners hardly at all. Two Dutch natural philosophers, in particular, spent years in Asia investigating medicine. Willem ten Rhijne (1647–1700) studied Japanese medicine and expressed admiration for Japanese practitioners. Jacobus Bontius (1592–1631) harvested a trove of medical and botanical information from the East Indies. A Dutch Reformed minister in Batavia composed a short treatment on moxibustion (which involves burning mugwort herb on the skin of a patient) that triggered lively interest back in Europe; the same was later true for acupuncture.[40]

How much influence this knowledge exerted on European theory and practice of medicine remains hard to gauge. The European educated world (and the commercial world, too) entertained a lively curiosity about the useful plants of Asia and some – coffee, tea, camphor, and opium – crossed the ocean to be put to use as medications. These and many others were transplanted to botanical and medicinal gardens, such as the famous botanical garden of the University of Leiden laid out in 1595 or the Chelsea Physic Garden set up by the Society of Apothecaries in 1673.[41] Herbaria formed integral parts of medical instruction. But "abstract concepts crossed much less readily." Nonetheless, if "[c]ulture

---

[38] George Percy, "Observations Gathered out of a Discourse of the Plantation of the Southerne Colonie in Virginia," in P. L. Barbour, ed., *The Jamestown Voyages Under the First Charter, 1606–1609* (Cambridge, 1969), 144; Karen Ordahl Kupperman, "Fear of Hot Climates in the Anglo-American Colonial Experience," *William and Mary Quarterly*, 3rd. ser. 41, no. 2 (April 1984): 226–27, Ligon quote 226.

[39] Shigehisa Kuriyama, *The Expressiveness of the Body and the Divergence of Greek and Chinese Medicine* (New York, 1999), 75–91.

[40] Cook, *Matters of Exchange*, 349–61.

[41] *Ibid.*, 304–48; M. N. Pearson, ed., *Spices in the Indian Ocean World* (Aldershot, 1996).

certainly made translating the whys and wherefores ... extraordinarily difficult ... it was no barrier to useful goods."[42]

New therapies could also involve novel devices or inventions, such as the magnetic tractors developed by Elisa Perkins (1741–99) in New England and used to cure by "stroking." The physician Franz Anton Mesmer (1734–1815) took Paris by storm with his demonstrations of the curative properties animal magnetism or hypnosis possessed. Although an investigation ordered by Louis XVI declared his claims valueless, that decision hardly dampened fashionable enthusiasm. Perhaps the most enterprising of the medical magnetists was James Graham (1745–94) whose "celestial bed" promised to relieve impotency in a thrice. All these therapies, as well as many others, indicate the growing importance of consumer demand on the evolution of medicines and medical care. Judgments on what worked passed to a great extent from the hands of physicians and societies of medicine into those of an affluent consuming public.

But a greater choice did not inevitably betoken greater confidence in the efficacy of medicine. Beginning in the late seventeenth century and increasingly throughout the eighteenth century, skepticism about existing drug therapies grew. These critiques went in two directions. First, as Galenism itself lost adherents, the polypharmacy that accompanied it fell into disrepute. The newly prevalent tendency to regard diseases as entities and to reduce their number and complexity played an important role. Cullen and Brown, for instance, pared down a broad spectrum of diseases to just two, or two types anyway. Brown's schema of sthenic and asthenic diseases allowed for an extreme simplification of medications and treatments. For Brown, medicines needed to do merely one of two things: stimulate if the disease was asthenic in nature or calm if it was sthenic. He turned to alcohol in the first case and opiates in the second. Sometimes changes proved even more radical. The French physician François Joseph Victor Broussais (1772–1838) believed that disturbances (he called them "irritations") in the gut underlay all disease. Thus, he reasoned, mild blood-letting would cure every ailment. Brown's American disciple, Benjamin Rush, recommended blood-letting combined with extreme purgations as a remedy for virtually everything, including madness. To combat yellow fever in 1793 in Philadelphia, Rush advised depleting up to 80 percent of the body's blood. While such cures seem completely wrongheaded and even barbaric to us today, it is necessary to realize that Rush was not some wild-eyed radical or ignorant "quack," but an extremely respected physician, citizen, and political figure. Proprietary remedies, too, proliferated in the medical marketplace

---

[42] Cook, *Matters of Exchange*, 377.

of a growing consumer society. Jean Ailhaud (1684–1756) and his son built up a huge, and hugely profitable, commercial enterprise on the sale of their "purgative powders" which worked on the simple theory that all disease arose from retained feces; thus a thorough purging corrected whatever was wrong.

The other major strand of skepticism about the existing drug therapies arose from the new empiricism of the seventeenth and eighteenth centuries. Some physicians, like Thomas Sydenham, came to doubt the purpose of medical theorizing altogether and cast a jaundiced eye on heroic interventions, the complex and outlandish polypharmacy of the Galenists, and the harsh therapies of the chemicalists alike. Sydenham has earned the name the "English Hippocrates" because of his emphasis on an empiricism thought typical of the Greek "father of medicine." Although interest in Hippocrates was quite old, as Galen's star waned in the seventeenth and eighteenth centuries, Hippocrates's burned brighter. Sydenham valued Hippocrates for his clinical (bedside) observations and for his stress on the physician's duty to "do no harm." Sydenham's therapeutics, although they did not radically differ from those of his contemporaries, were more restrained. He advised the use of cinchona, vegetable simples, and "cooling treatments." He did not eschew blood-letting, although he preferred to let a little blood often rather than much once.

Sydenham expressed great impatience with what he considered the "sophistry" of elaborate systems. Instead he advocated close clinical observation and the gradual assemblage of meticulous case studies. He believed that such investigations could be used to classify diseases like plants. "It is necessary," he wrote, "that all diseases be reduced to definite and certain species." He held diseases to be real things and thus continued the move toward an ontological view of disease along the lines that both Paracelsus and Helmont had set into motion. His own descriptions of diseases exhibited clinical genius. He is best known for his masterpiece on gout (1683) as well for his commentary on epidemic diseases, which he connected to climatic conditions in speaking of "epidemic constitutions."[43]

Sydenham's influence was profound but so, too, were the broader intellectual currents that led to a reevaluation of "facts." The older Aristotelian tradition endowed facts with a "rather low standing" in issues of persuasion, because they only referred to "temporally and spatially specific particulars" and "could not [therefore] easily be incorporated into universal causal demonstrations." In the seventeenth century, however,

[43] W. F. Bynum, "Nosology," in W. F. Bynum and Roy Porter, eds., *Companion Encyclopedia of the History of Medicine* (London, 1993), 340–43.

the fact was becoming "the most important conceptual link between the natural and human sciences."[44] Boerhaave was deeply influenced by Sydenham and by Baglivi who argued that in medicine the only "solid knowledge" was "derived from Experience." The practical, commercial hard-headedness of the Dutch Republic in which Boerhaave lived may have been equally influential. He attacked anything that posed as "science" if it were "based on theoretical speculation without any reference to practical experience." He, too, praised the Hippocratic method (as he understood it) and argued that only by taking nature "as the sole guide" could medicine be perfected.[45]

In some cases doubt led to *therapeutic nihilism*, the idea that no medicines or therapies then in use really worked. During the last half of the eighteenth century, many physicians expressed caution about most medications. The vitalist professor Paul-Joseph Barthez (1734–1806) at Montpellier taught that no one could adequately explain how drugs worked in the body; thus the only reasonable course of action lay in proceeding with great prudence. After thousands of cases had been successfully collated it might be possible, he opined, to (re)establish therapeutics on a sound basis. Another Frenchman, Esprit Calvet (1728–1810), admitted limited value to a small handful of remedies. The French *Encyclopédie* (published between 1751 and 1772) was, typically, much blunter: "[E]verything that medical theory has established in this regard is absolutely null and void; it is only mere jargon." Pursuing a series of early clinical trials, Pierre Louis (1787–1872) tested the efficacy of blood-letting in treating pneumonia and concluded that it did no good whatsoever.[46]

Such determined skepticism about received therapeutic wisdoms led to a shift in how physicians perceived the practice of medicine. Many eighteenth-century physicians, following in Sydenham's steps, prided themselves on their empiricism. "Empiricism" as a word had a long and checkered career. Academic physicians had once sneered "empiric" at practitioners who were not university-trained. The eighteenth century, however, endowed the term with a new and far more positive valuation: knowledge "based on experience and observation." Eighteenth-century physicians tended to become less interventionist. (There was, of course, another side to the story, especially among the adherents of Brown and Cullen.) These men repeatedly invoked the healing power of nature and

---

[44] Park and Daston, eds., *Early Modern Science*, 158–59.
[45] Boerhaave, quoted in Cook, *Matters of Exchange*, 390; Baglivi quote, 409.
[46] Article on "medicament" quoted in Brockliss and Jones, *Medical World*, 437; Laurence Brockliss, *Calvet's Web: Enlightenment and the Republic of Letters in Eighteenth-Century France* (Oxford, 2002), 151–53.

thought it better to do nothing than to act too quickly or too vigorously. An emphasis on nature's healing power had never been absent from Galenic medicine, but it got a new lease of life in the wake of the Enlightenment's enthusiasm for nature and all things natural. These forces combined to make the medical world of the late eighteenth century look very different from that of a hundred or even fifty years earlier. These changes in turn profoundly affected medical education.

4   Learning to heal

I admit that not everything [I have written] adheres to the rules of academic style . . . Where I have erred, I will be grateful to the one who corrects me with good reasons.[1]

[N]othing is more certain than demonstration from experience.[2]

[Hospitals are] the principal pillars of a rational system of instruction in the healing art.[3]

Multiple roads led to the practice of "physic" in early modern Europe: apprenticeship, self-tutelage, oral transmission, experience, and academic study. This chapter travels all these pathways, but begins with the observation that the majority of medical practitioners in the early modern world were women and the most frequent sites of medical education (broadly understood) were families, households, and neighborhoods. For this reason, the chapter title is not "medical education" but rather "learning to heal," in order to emphasize how varied were the teachers of the healing arts and how different their schoolrooms.

Learning begins at home

When early modern Europeans became sick, they almost always first turned to self-help or the assistance of family members, often women. Women's role in day-to-day healing assumed particularly large dimensions. Hannah Woolley's (fl. 1670) *The Accomplisht Ladys Delight: In Preserving, Physick, Beautifying and Cookery* (1675) demonstrates that

---

[1] Justine Siegemund, *Die Chur-Brandenburgische Hoff-Wehe-Mutter* (1690), quoted in Waltraud Pulz, *"Nicht alles nach der Gelahrten Sinn geschrieben": Das Hebammenanleitungsbuch von Justina Siegemund* (Munich, 1994), 65.
[2] Herman Boerhaave, quoted in Lawrence I. Conrad, Michael Neve, Vivian Nutton, Roy Porter, and Andrew Wear, *The Western Medical Tradition 800 B.C. to A.D. 1800* (Cambridge, 1995), 361.
[3] William Blizzard, *Suggestions for the Improvement of Hospitals and Other Charitable Institutions* (London, 1796), 34.

medical care was as much a part of a woman's household duties as cooking and equally reveals how that valuable medical knowledge was conveyed from person to person, generation to generation.[4]

What, then, did people learn and where exactly did they learn it? Medical lore circulated orally and in writing. The greater literacy of noble and middle-class men, and especially women, meant that in such households one might find more written information in the forms of laboriously assembled medical recipe books and treasured collections of tried-and-true cures. Correspondence between family members near and far or between them and other practitioners also produced goldmines of advice. Oral and informal transmission remained exceedingly important and not only, of course, in nonliterate households. Men and women of all social standings possessed a far more intimate and extensive knowledge of herbs and common remedies than most of us do today. Noblewomen and others of gentle birth acted as healers not only for their relatives and household members but for wider groups. Women's prominent roles in charity, too, moved them to the forefront of medical care as integral parts of their Christian duty. Neighbors swapped remedies and advice and provided nursing care for one another. Moreover, the barriers dividing the family from the larger milieu of the community or, in the case of the nobility, gentlefolk from all members of the court high and low, were very porous.

Although records revealing how such informal conduits of information worked are less easily found than evidence in printed curricula at universities or embedded in articles of apprenticeship, it is nonetheless there. We must, however, delve deeply into varied sources and learn to read documents in different ways. Diaries and correspondence abundantly testify to how and how often recipes and remedies traveled and changed hands. Mothers passed advice to daughters, aunts to nieces, and friends to other friends. Virtually everyone knew how to make and use soothing unguents for burns and cuts and how to still a headache with willow bark decoctions. In the area of reproductive knowledge, the exchange of "women's little secrets" moved quickly among the literate and the illiterate alike.[5] Almost as widespread as common cures was the awareness that ergot relieved the pains of labor and herbs like pennyroyal or savin (the latter known as "the bastard killer") could "[force] the courses," that is,

---

[4] Hannah Woolley, *The Accomplisht Ladys Delight: In Preserving, Physick, Beautifying and Cookery* (London?, 1675); Monica Green, "Women's Medical Practice and Health Care in Medieval Europe," *Signs: Journal of Women in Culture and Society* 14 (1989): 434–73; Susan Broomhill, *Women's Medical World in Early Modern France* (Manchester, 2004).

[5] Susan Broomhill, "'Women's Little Secrets': Defining the Boundaries of Reproductive Knowledge in Sixteenth-century France," *Social History of Medicine* 15 (2002): 1–15.

restore a woman's menses or cause an abortion. In writing about agriculture, Olivier de Serres (1539–1619) acknowledged the prevalence of this knowledge: "Several ladies and young ladies, earning much praise, have knowledge of the virtues of herbs and simple plants, with which they aid their families and the poor in times of need."[6] Nursing orders of nuns also were repositories of medical information; organizations such as the Daughters of Charity not only provided medical and nursing care, they also created and distributed it.

While, of course, women passed on much know-how informally, one should not be too quick to gender informal knowledge and oral transmission as exclusively or even primarily female. These networks by no means excluded men. Nor does the extant evidence suggest that men disdained feminine medical learning or pushed away the healing hands of women. While it is true that family medicine, and especially nursing care, usually fell to the women of a household, fathers, sons, uncles, and brothers also treated and tended the ill.

It is equally mistaken to assume that women's wisdom was solely informal and "nonacademic." In fact, women patronized scientific and medical study and not a few engaged in it themselves. Many women kept medical recipe or "medical cookbooks," but a goodly number also experimented with medicines and distilled or prepared remedies on a fairly large scale, as did the Elizabethan gentlewoman Grace Mildmay and the Electress Anna of Saxony (1532–85). Men and women shared a fascination with Paracelsian medicine. Alchemy attracted disciples and adepts of both sexes at many seventeenth-century courts. The literate often consulted the same medical books that physicians wrote and referenced. As more popularly written materials and those composed in the vernacular became increasingly available (by the end of the sixteenth century at least), more people, women and men alike, read them. Thus, they acquired medical knowledge from a variety of sources: written and oral, formal and informal. One should also not be too quick to believe that the learned medical occupations closed out women entirely. Apparently, for example, at least a few women obtained surgeons' licenses in England in the seventeenth century; the records of the archbishop of Canterbury list seven. Some, like Elizabeth Francis, licensed in London in 1690, restricted their practice to women, that is, to midwifery; but others did what might be called general surgery.[7]

---

[6] Robert Jütte, *Contraception: A History*, trans. by Vicky Russell (Cambridge, 2002), 62–75; Serres, quoted in Broomhill, *Women's Medical Work*, 98.

[7] Doreen A. Evenden, "Gender Differences in the Licensing and Practice of Female and Male Surgeons in Early Modern England," *Medical History* 42 (1998): 207.

Other lay-healers assembled their store of knowledge in a mixture of formal and informal ways. Some forms of healing required little or no learning whatsoever. Astrological healing, based as it was on an elaborate intellectual system, was conveyed through books but its "secrets" often passed directly from a master to his followers. The means of magical healing moved along even more informally. Cunning-folk learned their trade from older healers. Those whose healing powers came as providential gifts, such as the healing abilities possessed by the seventh son of a seventh son, or those able to cure by the laying on of hands, such as Valentine Greatrakes whose "stroking" was thought to banish scrofula, required no training at all. But these were the exceptions.

Despite the usefulness of a heuristic distinction between informal and formal training, the combination of formal and informal, oral and written instruction characterized the education of virtually every early modern healer, even academically trained physicians.

Midwifery and man-midwifery

Throughout the early modern period, and virtually everywhere in Europe until well into the twentieth century, midwives delivered the vast majority of infants. Virtually no spot in Europe, however small or remote, lacked a midwife, a wise woman (a *sage-femme*, also the French word for midwife), or a capable neighbor. Only in larger cities did midwives find enough regular employment to earn their living solely by delivering babies. Even then, most combined midwifery with other occupations, sometimes, but not inevitably, health or care related. The skills of midwifery were generally imparted by word of mouth or acquired by working at the side of an older, more experienced practitioner. Older midwives thus communicated their expertise to younger women; not infrequently, to their daughters, nieces, or other female relatives. (For more on the practice of midwifery, see Chapter 7.) Sometimes teaching occurred within a more structured, guild-like system with apprentice midwives being assigned to licensed midwives for their training. Nowhere, however, did midwifery constitute a guild like that of surgeons or apothecaries.

Experience was highly desired in a midwife and frequently formed the sole form of instruction even in the late eighteenth century. In one rural area in northern Germany, for instance, many women explained their qualifications in just these terms. Elisabeth Heine had no formal training, her knowledge having come from her own background of bearing eleven children and "having learned this and that from the other midwives." She had, however, also obtained books from the local physician, studied them, and "the rest came with time." By 1757, Catherina Gackens had been a midwife for seventeen years. Her proficiency had been acquired in her own practice. "If something happened that I felt unable to handle," she turned to "the famous midwife, Mother Elisabeth" for assistance. The education of the famous French midwife Louise Bourgeois (1563–1636) who delivered six children of Marie de Medici, the queen of France, probably did not differ all that much from these simple village midwives. She may have received some instruction from her husband, the barber-surgeon, Martin Bousier, and probably spent some time working with an experienced midwife. But she herself reported that, once she decided to become a midwife, "I started to study the works of Paré, and [then] offered my services to our porter's wife."[8] Not everyone felt that such "training" sufficed. One eighteenth-century observer believed midwives to be "the very death and destruction of the human race."[9] Yet, despite such frequent criticisms of midwives (especially in rural areas) as almost irredeemably ignorant, most communities seemed quite happy with their midwives and local physicians by no means expressed universal dissatisfaction with them as individuals.

Clearly, as these examples indicate, the skills of midwifery were not only acquired at the bedside. As early as the sixteenth century, some cities required midwives to attend public dissections or courses given by the city-surgeon or city-physician. In early seventeenth-century Paris, at least for a time, the Office des Accouchées at the Hôtel-Dieu provided for the instruction of midwives by other midwives within the framework of the French medical establishment.[10] Influenced by concerns for population growth and worried about infant mortality rates, many municipal and territorial authorities began to institute more rigorous midwifery courses in the seventeenth century. In attempts to improve their skills, midwives might be, for instance, required to attend lectures on female anatomy and learn the methods of version (turning the child within the womb so that a safe delivery could be effected). If special academies for surgeons existed, they sometimes admitted midwives. The German duchy of Braunschweig-Lüneburg established the first school exclusively for midwives in Hanover in 1751. Several similar ones appeared in Italian cities: in 1732 in Turin, 1757 in Bologna, 1767 in Milan, and 1774 in Padua. In the middle of the eighteenth century, under the protection of the king and with a royal privilege in her pocket, the talented midwife

---

[8] Quoted in Mary Lindemann, *Health and Healing in Eighteenth-Century Germany* (Baltimore, 1996), 213; Wendy Perkins, *Midwifery and Medicine in Early Modern France* (Exeter, 1996), 17.

[9] Quoted in Lindemann, *Health and Healing*, 205.

[10] Laurence Brockliss and Colin Jones, *The Medical World of Early Modern France* (Oxford, 1997), 263, 265.

and charismatic teacher Madame du Coudray (1712–89) traveled the length and breadth of France giving instruction in the art and craft of midwifery. Her "road-show" and mission lasted over twenty years and in that time she and her entourage (which included her daughter) trained more than 5,000 women and about 500 physicians and surgeons. If her story is extraordinary, she did not stand alone as the only woman who made a great educational impact. Several midwives produced instructional manuals. Most famous were those written by Louise Bourgeois in France, Sarah Stone in England (fl. mid eighteenth century) and Justine Siegemund (1636–1705) in Brandenburg-Prussia. Others of lesser fame enjoyed more limited, but by no means insignificant, reputations. The manual the practically forgotten Anne Horenburg published in 1700 was used for decades throughout northern Germany.

The number of courses to prepare men and women in midwifery proliferated especially rapidly in the eighteenth century. Despite much modern opinion to the contrary, early efforts at improving midwifery did not have as their primary goal the suppression of women healers. While no doubt exists that midwifery was to some extent masculinized during the eighteenth century (and more rapidly over the next hundred years), that trend dated back to the middle ages.[11] Most physicians and surgeons wanted to control midwives not replace them.

Midwives had, after all, never completely monopolized the birthing of children. Surgeons often assisted at difficult births. When fetuses proved undeliverable, for instance, a surgeon might use an instrument, called a crochet, to perforate the infant's skull, collapse it, and then extract the dead infant piecemeal from the mother's womb. Surgeons also performed caesarean sections. But if this procedure saved children, it almost invariably proved fatal for the mother. Unfortunately, in many cases, the appearance of a surgeon at a lying-in produced terror, portended pain, and often presaged a death. Beginning in the eighteenth century, however, men became more regularly involved in the business of childbirth and more *accoucheurs* or *man-midwives* began to practice. The men not only assisted in dangerous cases. Even before 1700, men gained some entry into the chambers of women in labor. In 1663, Louis XIV ordered a male midwife to the bed of his mistress in order to deliver his child; the same surgeon later attended the *dauphine* during her confinement.

The rise of man-midwifery coincided with the development of new surgical and gynecological instruments. The Englishman Peter Chamberlen the Elder (1560–1631) developed obstetrical forceps in the early

[11] Monica H. Green, *Making Women's Medicine Masculine: The Rise of Male Authority in Pre-Modern Gynaecology* (Oxford, 2008).

seventeenth century. He, his brother, Peter Chamberlen the Younger (1572–1626), and their descendants successfully kept the forceps a secret. Not until the end of the life of the younger Peter's grandson, Hugh (1664–1728), did the secret become public. Nonetheless, by then, other practitioners had sniffed out the "secret" and were also using forceps, often designing their own. Obstetrical forceps allowed man-midwives to deliver children otherwise doomed. The forceps-wielding Chamberlens enjoyed a fashionable and lucrative practice. Enthusiasm was, however, not universal and many physicians, surgeons, and especially midwives, sharply opposed the use of such instruments altogether as dangerous for mother and child alike. Such forceps, often padded with leather and impossible to keep clean, surely spread infection. The story of the Chamberlens is a perfect example of how important family connections and trade secrets handed down through generations were in the creation and transmission of medical knowledge. Technically, rules forbade midwives the use of instruments, but much evidence indicates that, while most midwives preferred their hands, they did not shy away from instruments entirely.

Thus, while it was unusual to have a man deliver a child before 1700, fifty years later it was by no means uncommon. If royalty and the aristocracy were the first to accept accoucheurs, the custom soon spread and by the late eighteenth century, at least in the northern, western, and urbanized parts of Europe, members of the bourgeoisie, and even those outside the middling layers of society, frequently called on men to deliver their children. Once lying-in hospitals connected with teaching wards or charitable endeavors became common, the poor women who usually delivered there were attended by both midwives and man-midwives in training, as well as by medical professors. These developments allowed some men (usually surgeons) to specialize in obstetrics. In the French town of Reims, Pierre Robin was delivering about 200 infants a year in the 1780s. William Hunter (1718–83) built up an extensive obstetrical practice in London in the middle of the eighteenth century. More relevant in terms of medical education, he also established a private school for anatomy in Great Windmill Street. Schools like Hunter's in London and that of François Solayrès de Renhac (1737–72) in Paris offered special training for surgeons in midwifery. A midwife or a man-midwife learned the skills she or he needed in ways that combined oral transmission, practical experience, formal anatomical instruction, and medical theory. While it is certainly true that man-midwives had more book-learning and formalized anatomical instruction than did most midwives, many midwives, too, attended lectures, perused books, and acquired theoretical sophistication in obstetrics. Nor did midwives necessarily champion women's "instincts" or value natural sympathy for birthing over "male learning." Madame du Coudray, for example, saw herself as fully representative of the best medical and theoretical practice and harshly criticized the ignorance of common midwives.[12]

Training surgeons and apothecaries

If the education of midwives mixed practice and theory and was only partly anchored in a rigorous formal course of study, the training of apothecaries and surgeons took place within a guild structure. The education of surgeons differed from that of apothecaries, but the guild system encompassed them both. Indeed, surgeons, barber-surgeons, and apothecaries often belonged to one guild (which sometimes, as in Italy, included physicians) or were combined with other related trades. In London, the apothecaries were incorporated with the grocers in 1606 and did not have their own guild, the Society of Apothecaries, until 1617. Venice had a College of Surgeons in addition to one for physicians and another for barber-surgeons.

One way to distinguish between physicians, on the one hand, and surgeons and apothecaries, on the other, is to argue that until almost the very end of the eighteenth century apothecaries and surgeons received training, while physicians became educated. That is, the instruction of apothecaries and surgeons occurred within guilds, while physicians studied at universities; the first was practical and hands-on, the second theoretical and learned. While this statement is not false, it also privileges physicians over apothecaries and surgeons in historically unjustified ways. For instance, many people who acted as "doctors" trained as apprentices and never enrolled in university courses. Many more received instruction at universities but never took a degree. John Clavell (1601–43), who conducted a medical practice in Ireland, had certainly attended university (Brasenose, Oxford), but left without a degree. Little information exists on his medical training or his qualifications "which may be explained by the high probability he had neither, and was entirely self-taught." Clavell was also an author, lawyer, and highwayman.[13] Apothecary and surgical training was neither inherently simpler nor less rigorous than medical education. While, for instance, even in the eighteenth century a dichotomy existed between surgical and medical schooling, we should

---

[12] Nina Rattner Gelbart, *The King's Midwife: A History and Mystery of Madame du Coudray* (Berkeley, 1998), 74, 76, 100.

[13] John H. P. Pafford, *John Clavell, 1601–43: Highwayman, Author, Lawyer, Doctor* (Oxford, 1993), 222.

not convert this dichotomy into a hierarchy; we must not assume that medical education was somehow better than surgical, merely because medical men – as members of a learned profession – enjoyed more cultural authority.

Guilds, like universities, were a great medieval institution intimately connected to the urban revival of the middle ages. Masters, journeymen, and apprentices comprised their membership. Guilds were polyfunctional and not merely economic organizations. Each possessed a "comprehensive, binding lifestyle that encompassed everything."[14] They offered sociability and social security; guilds had their own saints, their own chapels, their own pension – and sick-insurance schemes, and other charitable arrangements. Yet one of their most important functions was always education.

Education formed part of the guilds' responsibility for quality control. Anyone who worked with the authorization of the guild was assumed to possess a certain degree of skill. Apprentices and journeymen had to fulfill the demands of the assembled guild masters to become masters themselves. In medicine, increasingly in the sixteenth and seventeenth centuries, governments began to insist on a second step and appointed councils or specific individuals to examine and license candidates (for a fee) before allowing them to practice.

To become a surgeon or barber-surgeon, a (male) child would be bound over in apprenticeship to a master for a period of time (in the Germany duchy of Württemberg, for example, for a term of three years). The apprentice or his family paid a fee to the master and in return he received room, board, and instruction in surgery. The apprenticeship contract signed by John Beale of Woolscot (Warwick, England) in 1705, for example, specified the length of his surgical apprenticeship at four years. During that time,

the apprentice shall faithfully serve his master, his secrets keep, his lawful commandments gladly obey; the apprentice neither to do damage to his master nor see it done . . . The apprentice not to commit fornication nor contract matrimony during the term; the apprentice not to play cards or dice or any unlawful games that may cause his master loss. The apprentice not to haunt taverns nor alehouses nor be absent unlawfully day or night from his master's service but in all things behave as a good and faithful apprentice.

For a fee of £53 16s, William Edwards promised in return to teach Beale "all the art he uses by the best means he can." He also agreed to

---

[14] Hans-Ulrich Wehler, *Deutsche Gesellschaftsgeschichte*, vol. I, *Vom Feudalismus des alten Reiches bis zur defensiven Modernisierung der Reformära, 1700–1815* (Munich, 1987), 191–92.

provide "meat, drink, washing and lodging."[15] Typically, an apprentice surgeon learned how to bandage a wound, set a broken limb, lance a boil, let blood, and so on. He might also be taught the rudiments of legal medicine in order to be able to distinguish between lethal and nonlethal injuries.

After successfully completing his apprenticeship, the young man became a journeyman for another, usually longer term. During this time, he was expected to "wander" (hence, the German term: *Wanderzeit*) from place to place, laboring for other masters and sharpening his skills. Journeymen were not permitted to work independently as surgeons and generally were forbidden to wed. After completing his Wanderzeit, the journeyman returned to his home or place of apprenticeship and stood for his mastership. Early in our period, the guild itself, or rather a group of masters, administered the test. As time passed, however, it became customary to involve others – physicians and members of the city magistracy – in the examination process. Thus local *collegia medica* (boards of health) would examine surgeons and then distribute licenses to candidates judged qualified. Increasingly, therefore, becoming a surgeon meant that one must become a member of a guild and satisfy a medical executive organ. After successfully passing his examination and paying a set fee, the newly minted master-surgeon could open his own practice and take on his own apprentices and journeymen. Thus the process reproduced itself.

The mastership examination itself blended demonstrations of practical and theoretical knowledge. Although the examiners placed much emphasis on the prospective surgeon's ability to prepare, for example, a poultice, or prove his facility in bandaging, applying a truss, or opening a vein, he was also expected to demonstrate command of theoretical knowledge. The *viva voce* was often, if not invariably, conducted in Latin. (The procedure for barber-surgeons and bathmasters proceeded along similar lines, although it generally concentrated more on practical matters and was conducted in the vernacular.) In eighteenth-century Württemberg, for instance, the requisite theoretical knowledge covered anatomy, osteology (bones), myology (muscles), splanchnology (internal organs of the abdomen), and the circulation.[16] Especially in the eighteenth century, surgeon-candidates might also be questioned about obstetrical practice. But even two hundred years earlier and within the confines of the guild

---

[15] Joan Lane, "The Role of Apprenticeship in Eighteenth-Century Medical Education in England," in W. F. Bynum and Roy Porter, eds., *William Hunter and the Eighteenth-Century Medical World* (Cambridge, 1985), 100.

[16] Sabine Sander, *Handwerkschirurgen: Sozialgeschichte einer verdrängten Berufsgruppe* (Göttingen, 1989), 174.

system, surgeons often provided and received considerable "scientific" training, especially in anatomy.

Heterogeneity characterized the training of surgeons as well as the skills they attained. While most barber-surgeons might have only a mechanically oriented education, many surgeons possessed a far greater trove of knowledge. Already in the sixteenth century, surgeons emphasized the need for theoretical and practical knowledge of anatomy. The French surgeon Aloïs Carséna (1517–1611) learned his trade from his father, who was barber-surgeon to the duke of Savoy. When Carséna was fifteen, his father told him that although he had acquired adequate skill in purging, bleeding, and administering emetics, nonetheless, "a barber[-surgeon] was not able to pretend to have science if he did not possess [a knowledge of] anatomy!" His father then procured parts of hanged criminals to use in instructing his son.[17] Certainly, in many places, the time spent becoming a surgeon could well exceed that for a physician. Numerous students, before they were apprenticed, had already enjoyed a reasonably good education, and sometimes an outstanding one. Many had learned Latin and attended secondary schools.

Limited work has been done on the social origins of surgeons, and much of what there is pertains to the eighteenth century. In Württemberg, from 1742 to 1792, the percentage of surgeons' sons who also became surgeons exceeded half.[18] (Surgical dynasties were common and some of them, like the Chamberlens, became extremely famous and influential.) Other fathers were artisans, a few were pastors, and, perhaps somewhat surprisingly, an equally small handful were apothecaries. Few children of prosperous parents chose surgery, and those from inferior backgrounds lacked the preparatory education or the wherewithal to apprentice themselves. The education given surgeons and barber-surgeons varied, but the need to pass a mastership test and, increasingly, the demand for licensing and examination by territorial health administrations meant that most surgeons were by no means ill prepared for their subsequent careers.[19]

The quality of surgical education and the overall status of surgeons rose perceptibly during the early modern period. New and improved surgical methods expedited this development. The move toward more active and extensive surgical interventions can be traced to the fifteenth century with the introduction of gunpowder and small firearms. Warfare itself required, or at least fostered, innovative surgical techniques.

[17] [Aloïs Carséna], *Alohim, chirugien au XVI siècle* (Paris, 1969), 15–16.
[18] Sander, *Handwerkschirurgen*, 136–43.
[19] Lindemann, *Health and Healing*, 191–92.

Ambroise Paré (1510–90) was the most illustrious of all early modern surgeons and his career illustrates the mixture of learnedness and practical knowledge characterizing them. Trained as a barber-surgeon in the French provinces, Paré became an army surgeon in the wars between the Habsburgs and the Valoises. Military service was for him, as for many medical practitioners, a great if grisly school. He wrote extensively on surgery and published a massive tome on the subject in 1564. His work on the treatment of gunshot wounds and on the use of vascular ligature (tying off veins and arteries with cotton thread) rather than cauterization to halt bleeding from amputated limbs was especially valuable. In another writing, he discredited the use of ancient treatments such as mumie and unicorn's horn and taught podalic version, that is, how to turn a fetus to present its feet. He also penned works on birth defects or what the sixteenth century referred to as "monsters."

Military surgeons found their war service invaluable and, like Paré, worked out better ways to treat wounds; these procedures had immediate civilian applications. Several people seconded Paré's stress on the simple treatment (non-cauterization) of gunshot wounds, as Thomas Gale (1507–87) described in *An Excellent Treatise of Wounds made by Gonneshot* (1563). Elaborate surgical procedures supplemented battlefield treatments, such as those which Hans von Gersdorff (d. 1529) advocated in his *Feldbuch der Wundartzney* (Field Guide to Surgery, 1517). Gaspare Tagliacozzi (1549–99), in an early work on the use of skin and flesh grafts to rectify mutilations, delineated methods of *rhinoplasty* (surgery to alter the shape of the nose, see Figure 4.1). Interestingly, these procedures were not Tagliacozzi's invention, but rather his publication of the "secret" held by a Sicilian family of itinerant operators, the Brancas. Exposés, like publications on the Chamberlens' forceps, spread widely knowledge of once carefully concealed methods. The implementation of these raised the status of surgeons and gave surgery its increasingly good repute.

The protection of secrets passed down through families illustrates how one branch of surgery could still be considered a specialized skill which its practitioners devoted themselves to perfecting and monopolizing. Some of these men were itinerants; others settled in towns large enough to make their skills frequently needed. A French family of lithotomists named Colot worked out a new way of cutting for the stone (the *grand appareil*), and this procedure, too, remained undisclosed to outsiders from the middle of the sixteenth century until early in the 1700s. The Colot method reduced tissue damage and complications as well as death from infection and shock. By the 1720s, grand appareil surgery was widespread and viewed as relatively safe.

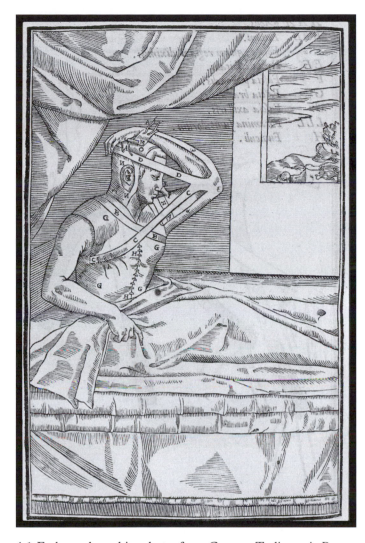

4.1 Early modern rhinoplasty, from Gaspare Tagliacozzi, *De curtorum chirurgia per insitionem* (1597)

Many such "specialists," like those who did cataract surgery or dentists, did not organize in guilds. Their valuable knowledge moved by word of mouth and was frequently taken up by the assistants and helpers who accompanied them on the road. In spite of the casualness with which they acquired their learning and their peripatetic ways, these healers were by no means unskilled. Cataract operations always counted among the

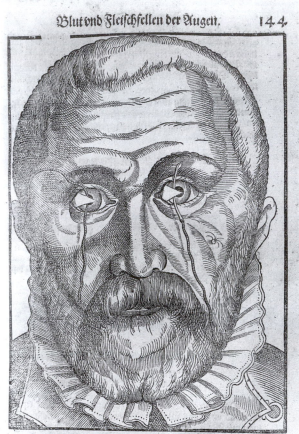

4.2 Operation for pterygium (benign growth), from Georg Bartisch, *Ophthalmodouleia* (1583)

most successful procedures specialists and itinerants performed. "Couching" a cataract, which consisted in depressing the lens of the eye, had achieved good results as early as the sixteenth century. Several operators and surgeons, including the famous German oculist Georg Bartisch (1535–1607) dedicated themselves to eye operations (Figure 4.2). Some oculists, like Jacques Guillemeau (1550–1613), were learned men and wrote important works, such as his *Traité des maladies de l'oeil* (Treatise on the Diseases of the Eye, 1585). The level of skill necessary for such operations was often achieved by performing hundreds of them; that experience, too, evolved new methods. But ophthalmology could cross the boundaries that putatively divided itinerant practitioners, surgeons, and physicians. In the middle of the eighteenth century, Jacques Daviel (1693–1762), who had earned his medical degree from Rouen, developed a means of extracting rather than depressing the lens of the eye and this procedure remained the basis for cataract surgery until lasers came into common use in the late twentieth century.

Surgery was considerably transformed over the course of the early modern period and so, too, were its instructional methods. Although apprenticeships and guilds persisted, surgeons – often backed by royal or ducal governments – began to cut their ties with barbers and barber-surgeons. In eighteenth-century France, for example, surgery broke free of the guild system. Lectures and practical demonstrations, combined with walking the wards of hospitals, comprised the education of "modern" surgeons. Surgeons increasingly entered the academy and, as early as 1672, the surgeon Pierre Dionis (1643–1718) lectured on anatomy and surgery in Paris. In Italy even earlier chairs of surgery as well as of anatomy existed. In Naples, Marco Aurelio Severino (1580–1656) held such a post and worked at the Incurables Hospital.[20] In trying to provide better medical care for all their people, governments quickly moved to establish a whole series of surgical colleges or academies that combined theoretical and practical knowledge and that were in no way inferior to medical faculties. Especially after the mid eighteenth century, many European states established surgical schools, such as the Royal College of Surgery in Madrid or the Royal Surgical Academy in Denmark. Surgeons were, moreover, more frequently appointed to hospitals and offered instruction there as well. Hospitals developed in-house lecture courses on surgery and students paid fees directly to teachers. Private surgical colleges sprang up in many places but were especially thick on the ground – and fiercely competitive – in metropolitan hubs like London and Paris.

These developments paralleled and paired with ones in the education of physicians that we will examine below. Changes in surgical education helped eradicate the still-existing divisions between medicine and surgery. The French Revolution disestablished medical schools. The laws that refounded them in the early nineteenth century combined the education of surgeons and physicians. Even before then, dual surgical/medical degrees were coming into vogue. As early as 1728, Montpellier offered

[20] David Gentilcore, *Healers and Healing in Early Modern Italy* (Manchester, 1998), 78.

a degree in surgical medicine for physicians who sought greater qualifications in surgery and in the second half of the century more students chose this option. By 1794, Montpellier had graduated 627 surgeon-physicians.[21]

These and other successes contributed to the growing reputation of French surgery as the best in the world, or at least in Europe. Surgical learning, once held tightly under wraps in families as secrets, now became more widespread and surgeons' education more theoretical. Yet even in the ivory tower of the university, family connections could mean a lot. Generations of medical practitioners were quite common. One needs only mention the hold that Alexander Monro primus (1697–1767), Alexander secundus (1733–1817), and Alexander tertius (1773–1859) had on the professorship of anatomy at the highly respected University of Edinburgh.

The education of apothecaries, too, fell within the framework of the guild system. Many apothecaries possessed extensive medical knowledge reaching well beyond an understanding of pharmacy and chemistry. Learned apothecaries contributed much to early modern science and actively engaged in the European Republic of Letters. Although they seldom published general or broad works on natural history, they were valued for their broad knowledge of "chymistry" and medicinal plants. Jesuit apothecaries, for example, greatly increased European familiarity with extra-European flora. Johannes Steinhöfer (Juan de Esteyneffer, 1664–1716) catalogued and described the vegetation of Mexico in his *Florilegio medicinal de todas las enfermedades* (The Medical Bouquet of All Illness, 1712), while Georg Joseph Camel (1661–1706) did the same for the Philippines in 1703.[22]

Apothecaries, too, trained within a guild system. While we today tend to think of apothecaries as pharmacists, their role in early modern medicine was far more extensive and they often served as general medical practitioners (see Chapter 7). Their education, too, was not merely mechanical. Almost everywhere in Europe, apothecaries followed similar, although by no means identical, life courses. Apothecaries were almost never itinerants (although traveling medicine peddlers and oil-sellers existed by the hundreds), but resided in cities and towns and owned or leased an often valuable piece of local property: the apothecary shop. Indeed, the word itself comes from the Latin for storehouse: *apothēca.*

---

[21] Brockliss and Jones, *Medical World*, 602–03.

[22] The role of apothecaries in the intellectual life of Europe was extensively examined in a symposium on "The Knowledgeable Apothecary" held at the Wellcome Trust Centre for the History of Medicine at UCL (London) on June 13, 2008.

While over the course of time, requirements for training as an apothecary and entry into the relevant guild or corporation became more
demanding, the basic system was simple. In France, for instance, in the
sixteenth and seventeenth centuries, candidates for admittance to the
guild as masters had to have reached their mid-twenties and to have been
apprenticed for a minimum of three years. The length and conditions of
the subsequent journeymanship differed, but, for example, in Montpellier at the very end of the sixteenth century, no one could become a master
until he had served a full decade as an apprentice and journeyman and, of
course, passed both theoretical and practical examinations. Candidates
were frequently expected to demonstrate competency in making several
complex preparations; electuaries (a drug mixed with sugar or honey
for oral ingestion), syrups, plasters, and poultices made up of numerous
ingredients. Montpellier required the production of four such master-
pieces. But the examination of apothecaries could be even more rigorous. In the kingdom of Naples, for example, a hopeful apothecary had
to document where he served his apprenticeship and be quizzed on the
Latin pharmacological text of the Assyrian physician Mesuë (or Yuhanna
ibn Masawaih, 777–857 CE) in addition to preparing medicines.[23]

What did apothecaries learn to do during these years of apprenticeship?
Most apothecaries knew Latin, or at least its rudiments, before embark-
ing on their apprenticeships. Ordinances regulating apothecary guilds
set terms of instruction and fees, very much like those pertaining to surgeons. One such contract from 1760 specified that the master would
provide instruction "in arte Pharmacaephtica as well as in chemistry
and Gallenici [Galenic preparations]."[24] Like many other apprentices,
student apothecaries did not necessarily retain fond memories of their
education. Ernst Wilhelm Martius (1756–1849) reminisced that

My duties at first only required the most mechanical work, such as pulverizing
[materials using a mortar and pestle], slicing roots [into tiny pieces], and the
like. I learned the academic part of the business less from personal instruction
[given by the master] than by paying attention to what others did ... [Still] the
apprentice had much to do in order to make himself familiar with the German
and Latin nomenclature and the very numerous raw materials and compounded
medicines.

In addition, Martius also studied a series of texts, including Johann Got-
tlieb Gleditsch's (1714–86) compendium on medicinal plants, Louis
Lémery's (1677–1743) "universal pharmacopeia," and several books

---

[23] Brockliss and Jones, *Medical World*, 190–91; Gentilcore, *Healers and Healing*, 35.
[24] Quoted in Andreas Winkler, *Aspekte bürgerlichen Lebens: Am Beispiel einer Innsbrucker
Apothekerfamilie zwischen 1750 und 1850* (Innsbruck, 2001), 79–80.

on *materia medica*. Absolutely invaluable to him was the *Dispensatorium Württembergicum*.[25] In the seventeenth century, some universities began to schedule regular lectures on chemistry and botany. Although these were primarily intended for medical students, apothecaries also attended them. Thus, although much apothecary training occurred within a more or less formal guild structure with more or less formally defined apprenticeship conditions, education far exceeded the mere artisanal.

Apothecaries frequently possessed considerable learning, as the educational experiences of Johann Wilhelm Neubauer (1663–1731) testify. His family intended to educate him at a university and so sent him to a Latin school as a youngster. When altered family circumstances punctured that dream, he found a place as a tutor in Hamburg. His connections there facilitated his apprenticeship to the Royal Privileged Apothecary "King Solomon" in Copenhagen. He then worked in several apothecaries in northern German and Danish lands. He was influential in developing a "field apothecary" for the Danish army. When he died he (and a partner) were running the "The Golden Ball" apothecary in Nuremberg.[26] Neubauer was perhaps not typical, but he was not odd either.

Educating physicians: the medieval background

For hundreds of years, the education of physicians was exclusively based in the universities. This education was far more theoretical than practical, although one should not overstate the level of theoretical instruction or underestimate the amount of hands-on experience among physicians with medical degrees. On the other hand, many practicing doctors who lacked university credentials had vast training and experience.

The story of university-based medical education begins in the middle ages. For generations, historians of medicine regarded medieval medical education as "scholastic," text-based, and antiquated.[27] The overwhelming emphasis on textual analysis and authorities, it was argued, continued to stultify medical education long after the middle ages ended. Accordingly, medical education remained "untouched" by the Renaissance and lay "like some antiquated fossil buried beneath layers of tradition and an

[25] Ernst Wilhlem Martius, *Erinnerungen aus meinem neunzigjährigen Leben* (Leipzig, 1847), 18–19.

[26] Christoph Friedrich, "Autobiographischer Lebensbericht eines Apothekers aus dem 17./18. Jh.," *Geschichte der Pharmazie* 49 (1997): 55–58.

[27] My discussion of medieval medical education relies heavily on the work of Nancy Siraisi and especially her *Medieval and Early Renaissance Medicine: An Introduction to Knowledge and Practice* (Chicago, 1990).

inert mass of indifference."[28] The "backwardness" of medieval medical education, however, has been – as here – vastly overstated.

Even after the middle ages, universities continued to produce the academically trained physicians of Europe. As we have seen, however, the vast majority of people who were healers had little or no formal training, while others gained considerable knowledge through apprenticeships, received secrets passed down through families, or educated themselves. Here, however, we want to follow the story of the education of physicians as it evolved from the late middle ages until the eighteenth century when nonuniversity institutions – such as private schools and hospital wards – supplemented university-based teaching.

The oldest universities in Europe appeared in Italy, France, England, and on the Iberian peninsula in the twelfth and thirteenth centuries, to be followed by another wave of foundings in central Europe beginning in 1348 when the Holy Roman Emperor Charles IV chartered a university at Prague. This second stage lasted through the sixteenth century; Martin Luther's Wittenberg was, therefore, a new university in the sixteenth century. The first university in Sweden was established in 1477 in Uppsala and in Denmark at Copenhagen in 1479; Finnish universities came much later, not until the seventeenth century.

One major medieval center of medical learning was Salerno in southern Italy which existed as early as the tenth century; its prestige had, however, waned by the 1200s. It was replaced successively by Bologna, Montpellier, and Paris, and, in the fifteenth century, by Padua, which remained important through the eighteenth century, and Ferrara which enjoyed only a brief popularity. Areas on the periphery, such as Russia and the Scandinavian countries, had no universities at all in the middle ages. The first Russian university opened in 1755 and a medical faculty was established in 1764 but it did not receive the right to award doctorates until 1791. The number of physicians in Russia grew very slowly (in 1690–1730, somewhere between 125 and 150 and perhaps only as many as 236 in 1800); until late in the eighteenth century, all were foreigners. Most were recruited from Germany or had been trained at Uppsala.

University medical education began in the New World with the establishment of chairs of medicine at, for instance, the Royal and Pontifical University of Mexico in 1578 and with the endowment of two medical professorships at the University of San Marcos in Lima in 1571. Medical schools in North America came considerably later; Harvard's famous

---

[28] C. H. Talbot, "Medical Education in the Middle Ages," in Charles D. O'Malley, ed., *The History of Medical Education: An International Symposium Held February 5–9, 1968* (Berkeley, 1970), 85.

medical school, the third-oldest in the north American colonies (behind King's College, now Columbia, in 1754 and the University of Pennsylvania in 1765), was not endowed until 1782 and did not graduate physicians until 1788. Even then, most practicing physicians in the north American colonies and the infant United States learned in an apprenticeship or preceptor system. Full-blown medical curricula took longer to develop but were firmly in place throughout the colonies by the beginning of the nineteenth century.

In Europe by the 1200s, medical education was well established in the medieval universities. It rested on the body of ancient knowledge filtered through Arabic texts and Latin translations. In a pre-print age, the number of medical manuscripts remained very limited and most professors owned only a tiny portion of the then-available medical literature. How, then, did medical students learn? Professors explicated topics such as regimen, therapeutics, diseases, and symptoms orally. Instructors also lectured from three major sources (and some students must have had their own copies): the *articella*, the *commentaries*, and the *consilia*.

The articella was the most important and long-lived of these texts; the final version appeared in 1534. A compendium created at Salerno in the thirteenth century, the articella covered basic Hippocratic and Galenic teachings. The commentaries, first presented verbally, but sometimes subsequently written down, conveyed the professors' own interpretations or explanations of standard works. The consilia described individual cases. Texts were studied scholastically, which meant that "questions on which opinions differed were isolated, the views of authorities were listed and distinguished, objections to each were raised and solved in turn."[29]

Yet lecturing comprised only part, if admittedly the major part, of medieval medical education. Before students could obtain their doctorates, they were supposed to acquire practical experience under the watchful eye of an older mentor. Students also attended public dissections (begun in Bologna in 1316). Thus, many of the "evils" and "insufficiencies" scholars have attributed to medieval medical education and, for that matter, to its early modern successors, prove less damning than its critics would have us believe. Still, one cannot deny that "the centerpiece of medical education remained the spoken and written word."[30] If one compares fairly typical curricula from the middle ages and the eighteenth century – the beginning and end of our period – one immediately

[29] Siraisi, *Medieval and Early Renaissance Medicine*, 76.
[30] Thomas H. Broman, *The Transformation of German Academic Medicine, 1750–1820* (Cambridge, 1996), 30.

notices a considerable degree of overlap, although the texts presented and the character of the knowledge conveyed differed. Both had come to reflect, for example, the introduction of chemical and mechanical concepts in the seventeenth and eighteenth centuries and the relative decline of Galenism.

In the middle ages, medical students mastered a precise body of material. Learning was primarily aural. Professors delivered information through lectures, although Socratic querying and illustrations enriched the lecture format. Texts were few and expensive, and students were expected to memorize extensively. The structure of the texts and of the curriculum as a whole assisted this process of assimilation and recollection. Professors taught students how to apply the subtle tools of scholastic inquiry and to think analytically. Texts often assumed the question-and-answer form common to religious catechisms. A professor might query: "What is phlebotomy?" or "What is an aphorism?" He then expected the student to supply the authoritative answer (in Latin, of course).

Lectures, too, relied on repetition. At Bologna, for instance, four lectures took place each day. The two in the morning covered theory; the remaining two, in the afternoon, took up practice. Lectures, therefore, addressed the practical as well as the theoretical side of medicine. The spoken word was frequently supplemented by a series of pictures that were intended less as accurate representations of anatomical structures than as mnemonic devices. In addition, the instructors employed a highly stylized form of lecturing. Mannered movements of the professor's body, and especially his arms and hands, emphasized particular items, indicated avowal or disapproval, and generally signposted points of special value. Instruction, therefore, approximated interpretive dance.[31]

Over four years, students heard several reiterations of essential subjects, for example, explanations of the Hippocratic *Aphorisms*, Galen's work on critical days, and the like. During the second year, afternoon lectures introduced no additional materials, but merely repeated and amplified the first year's courses. Moreover, the entire fourth year recapitulated what had already been offered in the previous three. At the end of this sequence, the student would publicly defend his thesis on a medical topic. At such disputations, professors set questions and raised objections. The student's rhetorical skill in responding to inquiries and exceptions determined whether or not he would be awarded a baccalaureate. The

---

[31] Cornelius O'Boyle, *The Art of Medicine: Medical Teaching at the University of Paris, 1250–1400* (Leiden, 1998); O'Boyle, "Gesturing in the Early Universities," *Dynamis* 20 (2000): 249–81.

newly minted bachelor then went on to acquire the advanced degrees of licentiate and doctorate after further study and the presentation of additional theses. By no means all (or perhaps even most) students took these higher degrees. They were more expensive and did not necessarily result in a larger or more lucrative practice. While the universities themselves provided no clinical teaching, students could – and did – accompany practicing physicians on patient visits for more direct training.

Continuity and change, 1500–1800

Universities remained the locus of academic medical training for the next several centuries. Continuity was marked, yet change was inevitable and not insignificant. If we compare, for example, medieval medical curricula to those followed at early modern universities, we note a large number of similarities in the character of education as well as several modifications in substance: little changed in how medicine was taught, but much in what was taught. The curriculum indicated as preparation for the baccalaureate in Paris in the early seventeenth century differed in content, if not form, from medieval precedents, for example. Galenism retained its strength, but had changed with the passage of time. As Galenism absorbed new ideas (such as chemical medicine), teaching, too, shifted its emphasis. In addition to the substance of the medieval curriculum – hygiene, pathology, physiology, semiotics, and therapeutics – other materials had worked their way into the curriculum since the sixteenth century. These included, among others, practical anatomy, surgery, botany, and pharmacy. But one should not overestimate the centrality of these "newer" subjects. For example, few universities had proper anatomical theaters; not until 1749 was one constructed in Paris. The lesson plan, moreover, continued to rely on the repetition of topics to inculcate knowledge.

One striking feature of post-fifteenth-century medical education was the far greater availability of texts for students. With the advent of printing and with the subsequent decline in the cost of books, medical students no longer had to depend exclusively (or almost so) on the spoken word. Students and professors alike enjoyed greater access to more elaborate and detailed anatomical prints. Early ones, known as *fugitive sheets* (Figure 4.3), were cleverly designed with lift-up flaps to reveal deeper structures. These appeared in the late Renaissance as guides to dissections and publishers ran them off especially for students. How many students owned books and how many books they owned is not clear, but we know that physicians had been assembling libraries ever since printing began in Europe. As early as the 1500s, medical bibliophilic collections could be quite extensive. John Hatcher (d. 1587) of Cambridge

4.3 Anatomical fugitive sheet, c.1545

owned 350–400 medical titles and Thomas Lorkyn (d. 1591), also of
Cambridge, had a library of 588 books: 400 were medical texts.[32]

[32] Peter Murray Jones, "Reading Medicine in Tudor Cambridge," in Vivian Nutton and
Roy Porter, eds., *The History of Medical Education in Britain* (Amsterdam and Atlanta,
1995), 163; Brockliss and Jones, *Medical World*, 96.

Eventually, the introduction of practical medical courses would replace textual commentary, but even in the early eighteenth century, texts remained central to medical instruction. Professors still read out passages and then offered supplementary information in the oral form of explanations and extended commentaries. Two widely used texts were the *Fundamenta medicinae* (Fundamentals of Medicine, 1695) of Friedrich Hoffmann and the *Institutiones medicae* (Institutions of Medicine, 1708) of Herman Boerhaave. Courses in the "institutes of medicine" (a concept dating at least to the middle ages) included the five subjects mentioned above (physiology, pathology, semiotics, therapeutics, and dietetics or hygiene) and Hoffmann, like others, divided his book into chapters with these titles. Medical education lasted either three or four years. Topics introduced in some places in the sixteenth and seventeenth centuries – botany, anatomy, and chemistry – became routine parts of medical curricula. This "lesson plan," however, provides only a sketch and individual medical faculties varied it. Little instruction at universities was practical in the sense we would understand it, at least not until the early-to-mid eighteenth century. Even anatomy remained mostly theoretical because of the general shortage of cadavers. Before we criticize the "obvious insufficiencies" of such abstract training and book-learning, however, we should consider that the definition of a physician (rather than a "doctor" or "healer") turned as much or more on his erudition as it did on his performance at the bedside. The increasing emphasis on "medicine at the bedside" was, however, already modifying the structure of medical education by the mid- to late seventeenth century and would transform it in the eighteenth century.[33]

Clinical instruction

A vast sea of ink has been spilled in arguing about when and where clinical teaching – often viewed as the cornerstone of modern medical education – became dominant. One can maintain that the "birth of the clinic" represented a sudden shift that occurred in France in the 1790s, or, to be even more precise, on the wards of the Paris hospitals in 1794–95. One scholar did not doubt that "[t]he modern period began in 1795 [with the opening of the new school of health]. The long hibernation that had prevailed since the middle ages gave place to a sudden and radical change." Antoine François Fourcroy (1755–1809) said something similar in his report to the French revolutionary government in 1794.

---

[33] Thomas H. Broman, "The Medical Sciences," in *The Cambridge History of Science,* vol. IV, *The Eighteenth Century,* ed. by Roy Porter (Cambridge, 2003), 465–66.

He emphasized that what "has up to now been lacking in schools of medicine, the practice of the art and observation at the patient's bedside, would become one of the main parts of teaching."[34] Others, however, insist that the "rise" of the clinic was far less precipitous and, for that matter, less conclusive than has been suggested. Let us examine each of these possibilities in turn, beginning with the description of the "birth of the clinic" as a radical shift.

The standard story can be quickly summarized. According to it, the "birth of the clinic" and the concomitant rise of "hospital medicine" formed "the critical epoch" in modern medical history and marked the watershed from premodern to modern medical science and education.

[The clinic's] consequences for medical knowledge unified medicine and surgery, taught doctors to think in terms of local lesions, to use the techniques of careful, systematic physical diagnosis, to correlate whenever possible the signs and symptoms observed during the patient's life with the changes in his body discoverable at post-mortem examination, and to make use of the large medical experience available through hospitals in more accurate disease descriptions and more careful therapeutic evaluations.[35]

Even those scholars who maintain that the birth of the clinic was a critical turning point recognize its precursors in what have been termed *proto-clinics*. The question then becomes: to what extent did these protoclinics differ from the clinic of the 1790s?

Lines of continuity thread from the elementary protoclinics of the middle of the seventeenth century to the full-blown clinics of the late eighteenth and early nineteenth centuries. While it is, of course, impossible to identify all the professors who invited one or more favored students to accompany them on their rounds of patients, the numbers were probably not trifling. Although bedside teaching made up only part of the clinic's supposedly revolutionary program, it is indeed important. Organized bedside instruction apparently began in Padua in the 1540s with Giovanni Battista da Monte (1498–1551), who taught practical medicine at the Hospital of St. Francis. One of his Paduan students, the Dutchman Jan van Heurne (1543–1601), carried these ideas with him to Leiden when he become professor of medicine there. Although it is not clear

---

[34] Charles Coury, "The Teaching of Medicine in France from the Beginning of the Seventeenth Century," in Charles D. O'Malley, ed., *The History of Medical Education: An International Symposium held February 5–9, 1968* (Berkeley, 1970), 168; Caroline Hannaway and Ann La Berge, eds., *Constructing Paris Medicine* (Amsterdam, 1998); Dora Weiner, *The Citizen-Patient in Revolutionary and Imperial Paris* (Baltimore and London, 1993), 30–31, 92–99, 127–29.

[35] W. F. Bynum, "Physicians, Hospitals and Career Structures in Eighteenth-Century London," in Bynum and Porter, eds., *William Hunter*, 107.

whether Jan van Heurne actually introduced bedside teaching in Leiden, his son Otto (1577–1652) certainly did. In 1636, the university set up a *collegium medico-practicum*: a three-month course of systematic practical training at the Caecilia Hospital. Eventually, two special wards of six beds each were designated for the collegium's use.

Yet bedside teaching at Leiden – generally regarded as the first protoclinic – happened only sporadically throughout the seventeenth and eighteenth centuries. François de le Boë Sylvius, professor of medicine from 1658, taught at the bedside, but it was Herman Boerhaave whose name has been most frequently associated with this sea-change in medical education. Boerhaave enjoyed the reputation of "the teacher of all Europe." For more than a quarter-century, he offered clinical teaching at Leiden and his course regularly appeared as part of the standard curriculum. Boerhaave apparently presented a single patient at a time to a group of students. He explained why he had recommended particular drugs, diet, and regimens, and students recorded the master's words. This was, therefore, a revamping of the traditional lecturing procedure; students did not get "hands-on" training.

Bedside or clinical teaching was hardly unique to Leiden. In 1717, Johann Juncker (1679–1759) established his *Collegium clinicum* in Halle. Here, as elsewhere, the goal was not solely, or perhaps even primarily, the betterment of medical education. Rather the Collegium clinicum was closely joined to poor relief. From Halle, the system spread to Berlin, and later to Göttingen, Jena, and Erfurt. Ernst Baldinger's (1738–1804) *Institutum clinicum* in Göttingen extended the clinic established earlier by Rudolf Augustin Vogel (1724–74). It, too, had a double purpose: medical education and charity. (For more on the charitable functions of clinics, see Chapter 6.[36]) In France, clinical or bedside teaching had existed in Strasbourg since at least 1729. By the middle of the eighteenth century, students could find clinical training at hospitals in Aix-en-Provence and Avignon. Similarly Anton de Haën (1704–76) ran a clinic in Vienna from 1754 which sought to unify theory and practice. Pavia replicated the Viennese model in 1770; Freiburg im Breisgau in 1780; and Prague and Pest in 1786.

In Edinburgh, clinical teaching began at the Royal Infirmary in 1748 with John Rutherford (1695–1779), a pupil of Boerhaave's. In the preface

---

[36] Wolfram Kaiser, "Theorie und Praxis in der Boerhaave-Ära und in nachboerhaavianischen Ausbildungssystemen an deutschen Hochschulen des 18. Jahrhunderts," in *Clinical Teaching, Past and Present* (special issue of *Clio Medica*, 1989), 71–94; Isabella von Bueltzingloewen, *Machines à instruire, machines à guérir: Les hôpitaux universitaires et la médicalisation de la société allemande, 1730–1850* (Lyon, 1997).

to his first clinical lecture, Rutherford clarified his objectives. Addressing his students, he promised that

> I shall examine every Patient capabel of appearing before you, that no circumstance may escape you, and proceed in the following manner: 1ˢᵗ, Give you a history of the disease. 2ndly, Enquire into the Cause. 3rdly, Give you my Opinion how it will terminate. 4thly, Lay down the indications of cure yt [that] arise, and if any new Symptoms happen acquaint you them, that you may see how I vary my prescriptions. And 5thly, Point out the different Method of Cure. If at any time, you find me deceived in giving my Judgment, you'll be soo good as to excuse me, for neither do I pretend to be, nor is the Art of Physic infallible, what you can in Justice expect from me is, some accurate observations and remarks upon Diseases.[37]

These examples demonstrate that at least some form of clinical teaching was downright common, if not universal, in eighteenth-century medical schools. Two questions, however, need to be considered in greater detail. First, was the "Boerhaavian tradition" indeed the direct forerunner of the Paris clinic? And, second, what impact did such teaching have on students?

Many scholars (including the philosopher Michel Foucault who coined the term protoclinic) readily concede that clinical teaching predated the Paris school and was available to those students who sought it. Nonetheless, these observers also note major qualitative and quantitative gaps between those clinics and the "real" clinic spawned in the late eighteenth century. Simply put, the numerical dimensions of the protoclinics were too small to effect a major shift in medical education or, for that matter, medical knowledge. The protoclinics drew on very few cases. University towns often had no hospitals or only very modest ones, and these demographic realities restricted, sometimes severely, the number and types of cases available for clinical evaluation. Only great cities, like Paris, could deliver pedagogic raw material in bulk. A close analysis of the Leiden clinic, for instance, shows that between 1699 and 1753 the number of patients fluctuated strikingly. The total was 832 or an average of just 15 or 16 a year. Moreover, the general trend was downwards. Between 1700 and 1710, some 43 or 44 patients were admitted annually, then the numbers dropped off dramatically (albeit with another short-lived peak from 1737 to 1742). The 87 patients admitted in 1704 marked the absolute zenith.[38]

---

[37] Quoted in H. P. Tait, "Medical Education at the Scottish Universities to the Close of the Eighteenth Century," in F. N. L. Poynter, ed., *The Evolution of Medical Education in Britain* (London, 1966), 64.

[38] Harm Beukers, "Clinical Teaching in Leiden from its Beginning until the End of the Eighteenth Century," in *Clinical Teaching*, 146.

This line of argumentation insists, therefore, that what happened in Paris in the 1790s was quantitatively different and that this quantitative difference engendered a critical qualitative one. Theoretically, Paris's public hospitals offered a vast number of patients, about 20,000, for teaching purposes. Students who attended at the bedside encountered an incomparable range of cases. But that was not the clinic's only advantage. Investigative postmortems that emphasized pathological anatomy and the isolation of lesions as the cause of disease followed close examination of patients. Thus, the "Paris clinic" not only disseminated existing knowledge – as the protoclinics had done – but actually also produced knowledge. Accordingly, in Paris, attributes considered central to modern medicine, including objectification and standardization, were first fully expressed.

While these arguments seem quite cogent, the story presented above has failed to gain universal acceptance. Some scholars, for instance, point out that, rather than there being one dominant clinical tone, many variations existed. It has been argued, for instance, that enough pedagogic material existed in several places outside Paris and before the 1790s to begin generating the kind of knowledge generally associated with the Parisian model. Moreover, there were other ways "to improve the evidence of medicine" and educate medical students.[39]

Private medical education

If university training dominated the education of physicians in most (if not all) European countries, it became less important in eighteenth-century England and, to a lesser extent, elsewhere. Well into the eighteenth century, two English universities – Cambridge and Oxford – alone granted medical degrees. Englishmen who studied medicine at a university increasingly preferred other European venues, such as Padua, Leiden, and, later, Edinburgh. Increasingly, in England, or rather in London, by the middle of the eighteenth century, private or commercial teaching and medical education outside universities had come to dominate medical training. Students frequented a number of private schools or "walked the wards" of the city's hospitals with attending physicians and surgeons.

The great city of London, of course, had no university at the time so it was not possible to link university teaching with metropolitan hospitals or with any of the new voluntary (charitable) hospitals established in the eighteenth century. Still, the separation between universities and

---

[39] Ulrich Tröhler, *"To Improve the Evidence of Medicine": The 18th Century British Origins of a Critical Approach* (Edinburgh, 2000).

hospitals was never total. Cambridge students, for example, attended at St. Thomas's Hospital in London to study with the best-known practitioner of his day, Richard Mead (1673–1754). Soon private teaching in hospitals and in commercially run schools became widespread in the capital. A leading surgeon, William Cheselden (1688–1752), known for his skill in removing bladder stones, regularly lectured on anatomy and physiology at St. Thomas's. Richard Kay (1716–51) attended the London lectures of Samuel Sharp (1700?–78) and John Girle (fl. 1740s) in 1743–44. From August to December 1743, Girle presented on "Anatomy, Aliment through body, Slink calf [aborted fetus], Eye, Ear, Amputation of a leg, Cranium, [and] Teeth and bones of lower cranium."[40]

In the eighteenth century, a bevy of private teachers offered training, especially in surgery and anatomy, in the form of fee-for-services. The most famous was the Great Windmill Street School, founded by the Scot William Hunter in 1746. Hunter gave instruction in anatomy and midwifery (he was a famous man-midwife and wrote a foundational study of the pregnant uterus). A series of talented collaborators, including his own brother, the great surgeon John Hunter, William Hewson (1739–74), and William Cruikshank (1745–1800), more than ably collaborated. Between 1710 and 1810 at least twenty-seven schools provided lectures in anatomy and opportunities for dissection. Some survived the competition for only a year or so. Others were hardy perennials. Joshua Brookes (1761–1833) opened the Blenheim Street School of Anatomy in 1787; it was still functioning in 1820. Private medical teaching, however, seems to have been monopolized by George Fordyce (1736–1802) from 1764 through 1802. Almost all these medical entrepreneurs advertised in the capital's newspapers.

Finally, whereas in many continental countries a hospital post became the *sine qua non* for achieving medical prestige and was an excellent means of launching a career, the conjunction proved less relevant in England. Even there, however, an appointment at a voluntary hospital could be of great importance for a physician because it opened doors to affluent middle- and upper-class benefactors and endowed him with the cultural good of appearing in the humanitarian and benevolent role that characterized an elite group. In addition, the opportunity to teach from a hospital generated a welcome source of income for a physician. Nonetheless, "British hospital physicians and surgeons almost always had at least one eye on their private consulting rooms, for it was here that the wealth that spelled professional success was to be had." Moreover,

---

[40] F. N. L. Poynter, "Medical Education in England," in O'Malley, *History of Medical Education*, 238; Lane, "Role of Apprenticeship," 101.

medical research that conferred professional respectability on French physicians, for instance, determined one's future less in England. Historians have often maintained, therefore, that modern medicine developed differently in England than on the continent and that the difference did not merely derive from the relative weakness of English medical faculties but from the very structure of medical careers. Likewise, it has been argued that there existed in England more than elsewhere a consumer-oriented, free-wheeling society that fostered a "more piecemeal, informal and individualistic development of the medical profession."[41]

But are the differences between England and the rest of Europe meaningful or, in fact, real enough to speak of "English exceptionalism"? The answer is: probably not. Private medical teaching, after all, by no means exclusively distinguished England and older historiography has frequently overplayed English singularity. In France, for example, private medical tutelage began in the early eighteenth century and was, effectively, the only feasible way for students to receive clinical training. Private anatomy schools in Paris existed some twenty-five years before Hunter founded his. Everyone knew that Paris's private teachers provided the best surgical instruction. By the middle of the century, medical students in Paris just as typically as in England, it seems, attended private courses. Antoine Petit (1718 or 1722–94), for example, lectured on anatomy, surgery, and obstetrics, and attracted leading physicians to his private amphitheater. By the final decades of the century, many professors and members of the Academy of Surgery gave such courses. This was also true at the Royal Academy of Surgery in Denmark. In order to gain clinical experience, therefore, before the clinical "revolution," most students paid a physician or surgeon to allow them to accompany him on his hospital rounds. By the 1780s, a rather informal system of walking the wards was undergoing a transformation into a more elaborate system of medical tuition in hospitals. This setup pertained not only in Paris but in other university cities as well. The sites of medical education in France were scattered and medical lecturing of high quality could be found not only at universities but at a range of other public and private institutions, such as provincial *académies*, military and civilian hospitals, and even among clubs with intellectual pretensions, such as the Paris Lycée de Monsieur, founded in 1781. Amsterdam's "illustrious school" (Athenaeum Illustre), although not quite a university, was a civic and municipal project that opened in 1632. It acquired its first professor of medicine in 1660 and he covered all the subjects thought

---

[41] Bynum, "Physicians, Hospitals and Career Structures," 107–09, 119, 122.

necessary.[42] Indeed, one might confidently venture the opinion that most western European countries possessed forms of private medical instruction, although these do not appear to have been as popular or widespread in central or eastern Europe.

Medical students

The purpose of academic medical education no matter where it occurred centered on producing physicians. As the definition of physician changed, and the expectations of what he should be shifted, so, too, did educational objectives and methods. Yet, for most of the period learnedness continued to be the key attribute expected of "medical men." Physicians used "their credentials as learned gentlemen" to separate themselves from "others lower down the social hierarchy."[43] Still, the image of the physician had undergone some significant modifications apparent even before the eighteenth-century clinical revolution. First, greater emphasis came to be placed on practice and on therapeutics. Second, the public now expected the physician to assume more multifaceted responsibilities. He was to "embrace the novel and crucial function of a medical administrator; he was to become the leader and supervisor of a team of trained subordinates," including surgeons, apothecaries, and midwives, although this vision had hardly been realized by the end of the Old Regime.[44]

Where did medical students come from and what were their ambitions? While it is hard to generalize about medical students over the course of some three hundred years, we can hazard a few informed guesses about their origins. Medicine recruited most students from the ranks of the middle classes and from families of clerics, physicians, and lawyers. In France, for instance, we find the children of magistrates, physicians, merchants, and lawyers in about equal numbers. Only very rarely did nobles enter the field of medicine and, if they did, the aspiring physician usually sprang from the lower ranks of the titled. Poor students might study medicine, but this happened rather seldom, because medicine was one of the more expensive degrees and there were fewer bursaries for them. In Germany, for example, the majority of needy students supported by private benefactions tended to prefer theology to medicine. A number of countries and territories (Spain, some German and Italian states, for example) forbade their subjects to matriculate at foreign universities,

---

[42] Brockliss and Jones, *Medical World*, 504; Annet Mooij, *Doctors of Amsterdam: Patient Care, Medical Training and Research (1659–2000)* (Amsterdam, 2002), 71–76.

[43] Broman, "Medical Sciences," 468.

[44] Brockliss and Jones, *Medical World*, 476.

often for religious reasons. Some, like Russia, had no universities until the mid-to-late eighteenth century; perforce their students went elsewhere, often to German universities or Uppsala in Sweden. In Protestant countries, Catholics might have difficulty obtaining a university place while the same barrier constrained Protestants in Catholic areas. Jews were restricted almost everywhere. In some places, universities denied admission to illegitimate sons and the children of hangmen, or those whose fathers belonged to other "dishonorable" occupations. Women generally did not study at universities (although there were some rare exceptions) and so, at least until the late nineteenth century, they were also excluded from obtaining medical degrees.

The domestic popularity of universities ebbed and flowed, as did their ability to attract foreign matriculations. Padua, for instance, was fashionable in the fifteenth century, as was Paris in the sixteenth and seventeenth, and Leiden at the beginning of the eighteenth. Thereafter, the torch passed successively to Göttingen, Vienna, Erfurt, Erlangen, and – most important of all – Edinburgh. Edinburgh was very well attended in the second half of the eighteenth century, boasting a truly international student body. From 1726 to 1799, 1,143 men took the MD degree there. Of these, 639 came from Scotland, England or Wales; 280 from Ireland; 195 from the West Indies and North America; 2 from Brazil; 1 from the East Indies; and 26 from Europe.[45] By the end of the eighteenth century, Paris was once again in vogue.

Student life at early modern universities was not all work and no play and students exhibited the high spirits that one might expect in a relatively young group of men (typically between seventeen and twenty-three years old), often living away from home for the first time. One celebrated example is that of Felix Platter (1536–1614) of Basel (Figure 4.4).[46] Felix Platter rose from a rather humble background. His father, Thomas, was born in very low circumstances, although by the time Felix was growing up Thomas had established himself as the director of a boarding school and proprietor of a publishing house. He never became rich, but he was ambitious enough, and affluent enough, to send his son to France to study medicine. At the age of sixteen Felix arrived in Montpellier to "begin without delay to follow the curriculum of the school." Felix's diary, which covers the next five years of his life, records much of what living in a sixteenth-century town was like in an age of upheaval: religious controversy and violence were rife. The entries on his studies

[45] Tait, "Medical Education at the Scottish Universities," 65.
[46] All quotes in the following section are from *Beloved Son Felix: The Journal of Felix Platter, a Medical Student in Montpellier in the Sixteenth Century* (London, 1961), 46–47, 54–55, 75, 88–89, 115, 124–25.

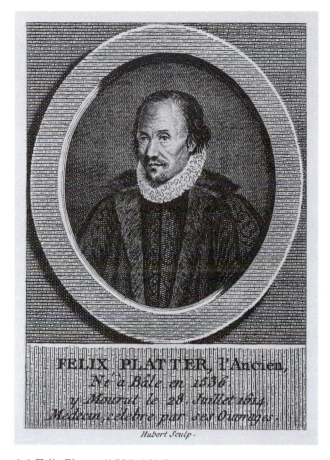

FELIX PLATTER, l'Ancien,
Né à Bâle en 1536
y Mourut le 28 Juillet 1614
Médecin, célèbre par ses Ouvrages.

Hubert Sculp.

4.4 Felix Platter (1536–1614)

are relatively sparse. Most of the journal is filled with his friends, their outings and pleasures, political events, and the executions of heretics and criminals.

Lectures dominated the curriculum and Felix "[attended] two or three lectures in the morning, and as many more in the afternoon." He recorded the names of his professors, who were not always treated with respect. "We breakfasted during Schyronius's period, for he was very old," Platter remembered, "and one day he filled his breeches in his professorial chair," much to the amusement of his youthful listeners, one assumes. Nonetheless, it seems that despite a soupçon of high jinks, Platter worked hard. His father implored him "to be honest, pious, and studious, and . . . to apply myself especially to surgery, [because] the number of doctors in Basel was great, and I should never be able to make my mark there if I did not show more than the usual ability."

And Felix was assiduous. Besides attending lectures, he frequented anatomical dissections of humans and animals. He "never miss[ed] the dissections...that took place in the College." Apparently dissatisfied with being a mere observer, he "also took part in the secret autopsy of corpses." Despite an initial repulsion, he "put [his] own hand to the scalpel." Felix and a group of his friends had taken up the offer of a rich bachelor of medicine

to join him in nocturnal expeditions outside the town, to dig up bodies freshly buried in the cloister cemetery, and [carry]...them to his house for dissection. We had spies to tell us of burials and to lead us by night to the graves.

His efforts paid off and on May 16, 1556 he sat for his bachelor's degree. The examination lasted from six until nine in the morning, during which time the "doctors of the university" argued against him. They must have liked what they heard because, after dressing in a red robe, thanking them in Latin verse, and paying eleven francs and three sols, Felix received his diploma "duly sealed." He did not immediately take the doctorate, but postponed it until he returned to Basel. Although he admitted that "it would be no small matter to pass my doctorate...considering that I was yet scarcely twenty years old, and beardless," he also expressed no particular trepidation "as I had some practice in medical discussion...and had made distinct progress in every department of medicine, *in praxi*, *chirurgia*, [and] *theoria*." The result justified his confidence. Once settled back home in Basel, he enjoyed a brilliant career. He became the city's principal physician, a professor at the university, and one of its rectors. He married well, built a sumptuous house, maintained a fine collection of natural curiosities, and educated his half-brother, Thomas, as a physician as well.

A second medical student, Daniel Bernoulli (1700–82), who lived some two hundred years later, exemplifies another, later course of study. After completing his studies at Basel's *gymnasium*, Bernoulli matriculated at the university and attained a *magister artium*. Although he demonstrated the same great talent for mathematics that his father and brother possessed, his parents intended him to become a merchant. He and his father eventually compromised on medicine, which he first studied in Basel and then in Strasbourg and Heidelberg. He finally obtained his doctorate at Basel in 1721 with a dissertation on respiration. He later became professor of anatomy and botany in his hometown.[47]

---

[47] Friedrich Huber, *Daniel Bernoulli (1700–1782) als Physiologe und Statistiker* (Basel and Stuttgart, 1959), 12–16.

The road to becoming a physician could be a more circuitous, varied, and lengthy one. Richard Kay was the son of Robert Kay, who had built a flourishing medical and surgical practice in rural Lancashire. Richard helped his father in his practice and first learned his medicine as an apprentice. Although the younger Kay often visited and treated patients, he could not make up his mind whether he wanted to become a physician or enter the ministry. Finally, in 1743 and already twenty-seven years old, he decided to go to London to train. A physician cousin paid his fees at Guy's Hospital, where on August 1 he was "entered pupil to Mr. Steade Apothecary to Guy's Hospital for a year." Richard's diary richly describes his education at Guy's which he considered "the Fountain Head for Improvement." While in London, virtually every entry in his diary begins with the phrase: "This Day I attended the Hospitals." Mixed in with his jottings about cases, such as on the amputation of a leg, was sincere religious commentary: "Lord, Let my Improvement for the Welfare and Happiness both of Soul and Body thrive and come on apace." (September 18, 1743). Over a period of about nine days in 1743, "Mr. Sharp lectur'd to us upon a dead Corpse" and Mr. Girle expounded "on a Leg that he took off Yesterday." Another lecture by Sharp addressed "the Coats and Humors of the Eye" while Girle spoke "upon the Cranium." The general feeling conveyed in the diary is that instruction revolved around single cases in the hospital, the attending physicians and surgeons, and their specific interests. Mr. Sharp, for instance, often took up matters involving vision and the eyes. In his second year, Kay heard a series of lectures by Smellie on midwifery. But we find little evidence here of a practical education and hardly any sense that he actually treated patients while a student. After leaving London in September 1744, he returned home where he shared a medical practice with his father until his own relatively early death in 1751.[48]

Not all early modern physicians found their professional feet as quickly as did Platter and Kay, who enjoyed extensive local connections. For most, especially those lacking influential friends or family ties, long, hard years of perseverance and penury awaited them before they became established. A medical degree alone did not suffice. In the last quarter of the eighteenth century, Dr. Ernst Heim (1737–1834) was more than thirty years old before he commanded an income sufficient to support himself and his family. Even then only the timely help of a friend made it possible for him to get on in the medical world. Returning to the locality from which one came was typical and smoothed the road to a settled career. The vast majority of doctors in the Kingdom of Naples, for instance,

---

[48] W. Brockbank and F. Kenworthy, eds., *The Diary of Richard Kay, a Lancashire Doctor 1716–51* (Manchester, 1968), 1–4, 66–89.

followed just this path. The timely intercession of mentors, old comrades, or family and acquaintances was often vital. For instance, a young doctor in the small town of Schöppenstedt in northern Germany was helped along by his father, the pastor there. When his son returned from studying medicine, the father circulated a note to all his clerical colleagues and to the local schoolmasters recommending the young physician to them and asking them to endorse him to their congregations and their pupils' families.[49] For many of these men, attaining an official post – such as town doctor or *physicus* (roughly, an officer of health) – was essential to their occupational and economic survival.

Medical theory and medical education developed in virtual lockstep for the academically trained physicians and surgeons of early modern Europe. This observation does not mean, however, that all physicians balanced their knowledge and practice on the cutting edge of medical thinking; far from it. A vast number of physicians still accepted Galenic principles, despite having been educated at universities that had long since rejected Galenism. Professors had their favored students and these, and not necessarily all students, benefitted from innovations such as clinical teaching. The argument runs the other way as well. Surgeons, apothecaries, and midwives, even if trained exclusively (or almost so) in an apprentice-like system, rarely lacked theoretical knowledge. Moreover, we should remember that many physicians, too, learned much of their craft as apprentices and benefitted from family relationships, often having fathers or other relatives in the profession, as was the case with Richard Kay and myriad others. As always, experience counted as a worthy mentor and virtually no one dismissed it entirely or regarded the practical, hands-on knowledge of nonlearned healers, and even women, as worthless, irrelevant, or possibly dangerous. If medical education became everywhere more formalized by the end of the eighteenth century, experience was tightly woven into its fabric.

[49] Gentilcore, *Healers and Healing*, 68–71; Lindemann, *Health and Healing*, 81.

5   Hospitals and asylums

In Tuscany, in keeping with long-standing local tradition for religious piety, wonderful hospitals are to be found, built at vast expense . . .[1]

Of rapacity and brutality, and all that is shocking to human feelings, a mad-house, that premature coffin of mind, body, and estate, is to an imputed lunatic, the concentration.[2]

Hospitals are a measure of civilization.[3]

The history of early modern medical "institutions" is extremely broad and properly treats institutions *with walls*, such as hospitals, asylums, and poorhouses, as well as the many equally important institutions *without walls*. This chapter discusses hospitals, asylums for the disturbed in mind, and patients. Chapter 6 shifts our attention to health in society and takes up the wide range of institutions without walls.

Hospitals and their histories

Hospitals – of whatever shape and description – have attracted an immense amount of historical interest.[4] Much of this work has been teleological in nature; historians have tried to trace the roots of the "modern" hospital and, in doing so, have created a number of "grand narratives"

---

[1] Leon Battista Alberti, quoted in John Henderson, *The Renaissance Hospital: Healing the Body and Healing the Soul* (New Haven, 2006), xxv.

[2] William Belcher, *Address to Humanity: Containing, a Letter to Dr. Thomas Monro; A Receipt to make a Lunatic, and seize his Estate, and a Sketch of a True Smiling Hyena* (1796), quoted in Allan Ingram, ed., *Voices of the Mad: Four Pamphlets, 1683–1796* (Gloucester, 1997), 132.

[3] Jacques Tenon (1788), *Memoirs on Paris Hospitals*, ed. with an introduction, notes, and appendices by Dora Weiner (Canton, Mass., 1996), 43.

[4] See the intelligent discussion of the historiography of hospitals in "Introduction. The World of the Hospital: Comparisons and Continuities," in John Henderson, Peregrine Horden, and Alessandro Pastore, eds., *The Impact of Hospitals, 300–2000* (Bern, 2007), 15–56. The organization of this chapter follows closely the program proposed in that introduction.

of hospital history that account for long-term developments and particularly, although not invariably, carry out a search for progress. There is certainly nothing wrong in seeking the roots of our world in the past. Indeed, such a study can help us understand better the strengths and weaknesses of modern hospitals. "Grand narratives" of whatever sort, however, invariably partition the history of hospitals into stages or phases. This approach has much to recommend it, but it bears with it the decided disadvantage of reducing the complexity of hospital and hospital systems across time, place, and cultures. It also tends to privilege modern western biomedicine as the inevitable result of progress or divides hospitals into those that were medicalized – primarily involved in medical care – and those that were not. Still, while grand narratives are all inherently flawed, they have the advantage of creating a framework for the neophyte scholar which she or he can then modify with the acquisition of more information. What follows here is a compromise: it first addresses the general outlines of hospital historiography and then examines early modern hospitals.

Generations of hospital writing tended to paint a very dark picture of medieval and early modern hospitals. According to this view, hospitals served as little more than refuges for the outcast and impoverished; medical treatment assumed a decidedly secondary role, if any role at all. Historians stressed the noxiousness of early modern hospitals, branding them "gateways" or "antechambers" to death or holding them at least partly culpable for the high mortality of early modern times. These histories accepted uncritically the rhetoric of reformers, such as the eighteenth-century philanthropist John Howard (1726–90), whose numerous publications catalogued in graphic and horrific detail the failings of "unimproved" early modern hospitals. Accordingly, the humanitarian and enlightened reform movements of the late eighteenth century set into motion improvements in construction of buildings, in nursing care, and in medical teaching, all of which combined to rework hospitals into institutions of medical teaching, medical care, and cure. This story follows one grand narrative; that of *medicalization*. The major steps in its evolution are generally identified as the introduction of bedside teaching in the eighteenth century and the rise of a clinical medicine based on morbid anatomy and pathology in the 1790s.

Many histories assumed a decidedly "triumphalist" tone, casting physicians as movers and shakers and as those largely responsible for transforming hospitals into institutions primarily devoted to medical care: "machines of cure" (*machine à guérir*). Their admirers portray these men as stalwart champions who fought the collective entrenched opposition of nonmedical administrators, nurses, patients, and a wider unenlightened

public. Not all grand narratives necessarily subscribe to such a celebratory viewpoint. An eminent historian of hospitals, Guenter Risse, has
suggested another scheme for understanding how hospitals evolved. The
hospital was in its original incarnation a "house of mercy," then a "house
of segregation" (middle ages), and subsequently a "house of rehabili-
tation" (Renaissance), a "house of care" (in the eighteenth century), a
"house of surgery" (since the late nineteenth century), and, in the twentieth century, it became a "house of science."[5]

Even more radically opposed to the triumphalist school is the interpretation the influential French philosopher Michel Foucault voiced in
The Birth of the Clinic (1963). Foucault sharply criticized western social
institutions and, rather than paying tribute to a progressive series of
improvements in hospitals, postulated something very different. Instead
of a smooth curve of improvements, Foucault located a profound break:
a sudden "rupture" in the 1790s. From that point onward, the patient's
place in hospital medicine was "objectified": he or she was opened up
to the unobstructed gaze of physicians and became the target of increasingly intrusive medical inspection and regulation. Second, whereas in
the triumphalist version, the ascendancy of medical science and the clinical method counted as an (almost) unreservedly positive phenomenon,
Foucault reversed these polarities: they betokened a defeat for patients
by solidifying the power of doctors over them. The development of hospital medicine, like the parallel development of the insane asylum, was,
therefore, altogether a bad thing for the freedom of the individual.

Both versions have had a profound impact on the writing of hospital history. "The problem ... [is] that the particular historiographical
schemes that hospitals have attracted are all skewed towards a modernity
defined by medicalisation."[6] The medicalization model has had a long
run and continues to shape much hospital history. Because it has been
so influential, it deserves at least a brief treatment here. Simply put, the
medicalization thesis argues that medieval (and even early modern) hospitals offered little medical care, or, at the very least, that was not their
primary function or chief goal. Then, over the course of a few hundred
years, and roughly by the end of the eighteenth century, hospitals gradually medicalized; they came more and more under the control of doctors
and shed their nonmedical functions; this was a Good Thing. The gradual medicalization of hospitals also proceeded in a series of steps or stages
titled "reforms" or "improvements."

---

[5] Guenter B. Risse, *Mending Bodies, Saving Souls: A History of Hospitals* (Cambridge, 1999).
[6] Henderson et al., *Impact of Hospitals*, 32.

Historians working in the medicalization framework have generally concluded that the main function of medieval and even early modern hospitals was care not cure. Bed rest, clean linen, shelter from the elements and a good meal provided the real "treatments" available. A close study of one hospital's expenditures lists outlays for fuel, food, linen, and candles, but only rarely for medicines. If these institutions were not "gateways to death," they certainly were not *machines à guérir*. The staff connected with hospitals were seen as principally caretakers – and often ones who took very good care of their charges – but medical treatment was mostly lacking. This situation generally pertained until major reforms were set into motion in the late seventeenth and, more rapidly, in the eighteenth century. The reforms thus undertaken eventually turned custodial institutions into modern hospitals where cure not care became the principal objective.

Certainly, eighteenth-century reformers found much to condemn in early modern hospitals. For example, according to one crusader writing about the Hamburg Pesthof, first established in the early seventeenth century for plague patients:

Most of the patients are incurables who either pass away soon [after being admitted] or draw out their lives with no attempt being made to treat their afflictions, or [they] are released on the slightest show of improvement . . . Not a small portion of the patients are insane . . . the quiet ones are kept in the wards . . . idiots wander about as they please . . . [and] the raving are chained to their beds.[7]

Such exposés laid the basis for the "gateways to death" critique directed at older hospitals. These attacks constituted a goodly portion of the Enlightenment's commentary on health. The French *encyclopédist* Jacques Tenon (1724–1816) took firm aim at the Paris Hôtel-Dieu, reputedly first founded in the seventh century by St. Landry. Tenon found

no hospital so badly located, so cramped, so unreasonably overcrowded, so dangerous, so filled with causes of ill-health and death as the Hôtel-Dieu. Nowhere in the whole universe is there a hospital building that combines such an important purpose with results so deadly to society.[8]

Another Frenchman, Louis-Sébastien Mercier (1740–1814), chronicled horrifying conditions in the Bicêtre: that "terrible ulcer on the body politic." Likewise, John Howard found the hospital for women at Malta so malodorous that "the governess [who] attended me through every ward . . . was constantly using her smelling bottle; in which she judged

[7] Johann Jakob Rambach, *Versuch einer physisch-medizinischen Beschreibung von Hamburg* (Hamburg, 1801), 411–12, 416–17.
[8] Tenon, *Memoirs*, 299.

very properly, for a more offensive and dirty hospital for women I have never visited."[9]

According to the medicalization model, the reform movement began early in the eighteenth century and eventually led to the "modern hospital," or, in Foucauldian terms, "the birth of the clinic." The trend toward a professionalization and regularization of medical staff in hospitals accelerated and, by midcentury, hospitals commonly contracted with a physician to visit at stated intervals, engaged full-time surgeons, hired pharmacists, and sometimes even provided in-house education for candidate physicians, surgeons, and apothecaries.

One of the first principles to which all (or almost all) these reformers adhered was the idea of medical exclusivity: hospitals were no longer to be all-purpose institutions nor principally houses of poor relief; they were to be reconstituted as centers of medical care. John Aiken (1732–1801), an early critic, insisted on the necessity of creating totally new hospitals called "infirmaries" to distinguish them from almshouses and old-fashioned "spitals." Hospitals henceforth were to be places to heal the sick and should admit only the curably ill. "I would wish to enforce as much as possible," Aiken said, "the idea of a hospital being a place designated for the *cure of the sick.*"[10] Eighteenth-century reformers sharply asserted that existing institutions were totally unsuitable for the practice of medicine and frustrated the purposeful treatment of patients. Others forcefully argued that hospitals in fact engendered diseases, such as typhus and similar distempers. Some reformers went so far as to advocate the dismantling of hospitals altogether and maintained that care outside hospitals would prove more beneficial and more cost effective (see Chapter 6). In pursuit of these aims, hospital reformers sought to exclude from their new-style hospitals the incurably or chronically ill, fever cases, pregnant women, and the venereally diseased.

Thus, the argument continues, medicalization proceeded as important alterations in hospital building and administration slowly accumulated. The characteristics generally linked to the genesis of clinical teaching in the 1790s – bedside teaching, medical experimentation, clinical observation, and statistical evaluation – were becoming common, at least in their rudiments, even earlier. Some hospitals quickly institutionalized teaching. The Quaker merchant John Bellers (1654–1725), in a 1714

---

[9] Laurence Brockliss and Colin Jones, *The Medical World of Early Modern France* (Oxford, 1997), 717–25; John Howard, *An Account of the Principal Lazarettos in Europe* (2nd edn., London, 1791), 60.

[10] John Aiken, *Thoughts on Hospitals* (1771), quoted in Roy Porter, "The Gift Relation: Philanthropy and Provincial Hospitals in Eighteenth-Century England," in Lindsay Granshaw and Roy Porter, eds., *The Hospital in History* (London, 1987), 150.

essay promoting the foundation of "new hospitals," based his appeal on the hope that "these hospitals will breed up some of the best physicians and chirurgeons [surgeons] because they may see as much there in one year as in seven anywhere else."[11]

The sea-change, however, in the medicalization movement came with the French Revolution and concomitant shifts in medical education (see Chapter 4). The revolutionary governments championed a range of social initiatives that had as far-reaching implications for hospitals as they did for medical education. The great medical historian Erwin H. Ackerknecht contended more than forty years ago that only the Revolution made implementation of the new instructional methods possible. In 1790, the French National Assembly empowered a Committee on Poverty (*Comité de mendicité*) to review that nation's sprawling array of charitable institutions. Its members assembled a massive factual base concerning hospitals in Paris and, less comprehensively, those in the provinces. After evaluating the information gained and visiting many hospitals in person, committee members proposed sweeping changes. Above all, they wished to limit admission to the curably ill and to secularize the hitherto religious direction of hospitals. The hostility of some physicians on the one hand and, perhaps even more palpably, the exigencies of war on the other, hampered or delayed many recommended innovations. But, in the end, the model of the clinic prevailed and became the modern hospital.[12] This, then, is the general outline of the medicalization argument in respect to hospital development.

As the medicalization model began to solidify and came to dominate much of the writing of hospital history, historians also began to modify it in two major ways. Historians raised doubts about the timing of medicalization and its teleological characteristics and they began to question the validity of reformers' characterizations of medieval and early modern hospitals. Many scholars did not jettison the medicalization argument entirely, but began to revise it piecemeal. Although they still implicitly accepted many of its tenets, they pushed the birth of the modern hospital further back in time.

We now realize how many characteristics that seem to flow from the Paris clinic of the 1790s were already in place earlier. If the medicalization process took quite some time to unfold, it had nevertheless already begun in the late middle ages. Long before the eighteenth century, therefore, many hospitals offered significant medical care. For example,

---

[11] Quoted in Risse, *Hospital Life*, 18.
[12] Erwin H. Ackerknecht, *Medicine at the Paris Hospital, 1794–1848* (Baltimore, 1967); Caroline Hannaway and Ann La Berge, eds., *Constructing Paris Medicine* (Amsterdam, 1998).

the number of staff in late medieval and early modern hospitals was often quite large. Besides what may be loosely classified as "medical personnel," hospitals employed many others equally important to the successful running of the institution. These included cooks, cleaners, clerks, administrators, and, if the hospital owned land (as many did), those who labored on it. In many respects, therefore, the hospital formed an economy unto itself. Medical personnel was equally varied, although we should be careful not to draw lines too clearly between the tasks of caring and curing or between medical and domestic duties. Most hospitals maintained an in-house apothecary whose duties consisted of preparing medicines for the sick. Hospital apothecaries stocked an extensive selection of simple and compound medicines and often produced large numbers of these themselves, even creating specialized drugs for particular ailments.

Nursing was, of course, critical and perhaps as responsible as anything else for successful cures. Especially in Catholic areas, but hardly only there, nursing became a calling with strong religious and social connections, especially for women. Nurses often belonged to lay female religious groups that dedicated themselves to the care of the sick as a religious duty. Their members did not take the same vows or submit to the same discipline as nuns; moreover, they were not enclosed. Yet they lived as part of a religious community within the hospital. In the seventeenth century, Counter-Reformation piety inspired the creation of new nursing orders of nuns. Path-breakers here were the Daughters of Charity founded by Vincent de Paul (1581–1660) and Louise de Marillac (1591–1660) in 1633. These communities ran hospitals throughout France and included the Sisters of Saint-Agnès in Arras, the Sisters of Charity of Nevers, and especially the Augustinian sisters at the Hôtel-Dieu in Paris. Some patients eventually became members of staff or also worked for the hospital. In contrast to the situation in modern hospitals where clear hierarchical structures pertain, in earlier hospitals "the distinctions between patient, nurse, and resident were far from clear-cut."[13] Equally fluid and complex were their identities as medical and religious figures.

Thus, the historical difference of opinion over when medical care first began to characterize hospitals misses the mark because it fails to recognize that early modern hospitals (at least until almost the end of our period) were not primarily medical institutions. Instead, they were as much religious as secular foundations. But, it is also true that even very early, substantial medical care made up an important part of hospital routines. At the hospital of San Giovanni in Turin, for instance, a

---

[13] Henderson, *Renaissance Hospital*, 188.

physician or surgeon had been visiting patients twice a day since the sixteenth century and three apprentice, or student, surgeons, known as "dressers," resided and worked in the hospital there; by 1730, there were thirteen. Finally, university reforms enacted in Italy between 1720 and 1739 mandated attendance on the wards for all students of medicine and surgery. From very early in its history (it first opened its doors in 1729), the Royal Infirmary of Edinburgh undertook clinical instruction and housed students. Since 1743, ledgers and admission books recorded cases with some meticulousness and publications drew on the experience garnered by students and professors walking the wards. William Cullen inaugurated clinical lectures in the early 1770s. It was thus possible to "see" thousands of cases and to draw lessons from them for the advancement of medical knowledge. Similar trends are observable in the Berlin Charité. Around 1730, the attending physician Johann Theodor Eller (1689–1760) published a series of clinical cases selected from daily practice there.[14]

Part of the reason it took so long for scholars to accept the gradual, but nonetheless very real, long-term evolution of hospital medicine is because the reformers of the late eighteenth century very successfully projected an image of what even twentieth-century historians were inclined to refer to as "the grim reality of the public hospital."[15] Reformers, as we have seen, presented grisly tales of enormous mortality rates, physical abuse, and mental suffering. Few simply lied. Rather, each critic picked his material carefully with an eye to convincing the public of the pressing need for change. And there were certainly wrongs to be righted. But rhetoric is not necessarily reality and the "black legend" of hospital care needs "substantial modification and nuancing."[16] We will pursue this subject at greater length in the section below on patients, but suffice it here to say that enormous difference existed in mortality rates and rarely was the die-off as fearsome as polemicists charged.

The most recent hospital histories have tended to question the medicalization model, even in its modified forms, as an organizing scheme while stressing the multiple functions hospitals fulfilled and their embeddedness in, and interaction with, larger social institutions, especially religious ones. Such scholars have devoted much time to analyzing the complex

[14] Johann Theodor Eller, *Nützliche und auserlesene medicinische und chirugische Anmerckungen so wohl von innerlichen, als auch äusserlichen Kranckheiten, und bey selbigen zum Theil verrichteten Operationen, welche bishero in den von Sr. Königl. Majestät in Preussen gestiffteten grossen Lazareth der Charité zu Berlin vorgefallen* (Berlin, 1730?).

[15] Dora Weiner, *The Citizen–Patient in Revolutionary and Imperial Paris* (Baltimore, 1993), 45–76.

[16] Brockliss and Jones, *Medical World*, 717–25.

social, economic, and cultural forces that converged in the building and administration of hospitals, recognizing, for example, along with Bernard Mandeville (1670–1730) that "Pride and Vanity . . . built more Hospitals than all the other Virtues together," but so, too, did religion, humanitarianism, and utilitarianism. Hospital administrators were often urban or provincial bigwigs and hospital financing often flowed overwhelmingly from local benefactors. Moreover, whereas previous hospital history tended to concentrate on the heroic struggles of physicians or reformers to improve hospitals and fight bigotry and ignorance, it is now usual to discuss how a miscellany of actors, including nurses, lay and ecclesiastical administrators, apothecaries, surgeons, and patients together shaped hospitals and hospital life.

The last of these, the patient, was always sadly missing from triumphalist accounts because she or he was unimportant to the success of medical science except as a kind of raw material. One virtue of the Foucauldian model was that Foucault reoriented historical inquiry toward the patient. For Foucault, the patient became victim or object and thus, he, too, ignored the ways in which patients played active roles. New hospital historians have re-centered the patient and, while not disregarding issues of mortality, have also turned to investigating how patients determined the care they received and manipulated or cooperated with staff and administrators to their own advantage. If the story of hospital patients is still not well developed – and the problems of sources are considerable – it no longer toddles around in its infancy.

The following discussion eschews a strictly chronological approach in favor of discussing the various functions hospitals fulfilled. It highlights several themes: the role of the hospital in "saving souls"; the multifariousness of "hospitals"; the interaction of hospitals with larger society; the staffing of hospitals; and, last but not least, patients. The closing sections discuss special institutions, such as military hospitals, "madhouses," and asylums.

"Mending bodies, saving souls"[17]

Someone new to hospital history might be excused for finding the names and categories historians use to designate and define hospitals perplexing, repetitive, or even incomprehensible. Of course, scholars create and employ these categories – isolation hospitals, general hospitals, leprosaria, quarantine hospitals, voluntary hospitals – to organize hospital history

---

[17] I have taken the title of this section from Guenter Risse's book, *Mending Bodies, Saving Souls*.

and build heuristically useful models. Nonetheless, one should remember that "[t]he generic hospital is an abstraction. In reality, there are only particular hospitals."[18] Yet it is difficult to do without generalizations in trying to make sense of complex and long-term developments. This section briefly reviews hospitals before the early modern period, partly, or rather principally, because many characteristics and connections established in late antiquity of the medical world shaped hospitals and their histories not only in the early modern period but today as well.

The search for the recognizable roots of early modern hospitals in the ancient world has produced only meager results. Archeologists and historians have identified some pre-Christian institutions such as ancient Greek healing temples (*Asclepieia*) or Roman *valetudinaria* for soldiers and slaves, but the real beginnings of hospital development are closely associated with early Christianity and especially with contemporary social, economic, political, and ecclesiastical conditions. Indeed, "[t]he hospital was, in origin and conception, a distinctively Christian institution, rooted in Christian concepts of charity and philanthropy." By the third century CE, the Christian church had become the chief patron of charitable works; enormously influential was the urban episcopate in Byzantium that set up houses called *xenodocheia* to provide protection for the poor and spiritual succor. Like later monastic infirmaries, the xenodocheion was "clearly identified as a religious space," the main purpose of which was to reaffirm Christian faith. The personnel comprised clerics, deacons, deaconesses, and lay volunteers. It is impossible to understand the hospitals of late antiquity and their successors without fully appreciating the indissolubility of the bond between church and hospital, lay and clerical participation.[19]

Medieval hospitals evolved in lockstep with the western form of monasticism and, like later Renaissance hospitals, preserved intact the close ties between spiritual healing (*medico spirituale*) and physical medicine (*medico fisico*). The almost ubiquitous image of *Christus medicus* (Figure 5.1) joined spiritual and physical cures, divine and secular physicians. Likewise, the frequency with which hospitals were named for saints demonstrates the same ties, as do more general names for hospitals, such as the Spanish *templos de piedad* (temples of piety and compassion). These hospitals drew on strong religious traditions and their architecture reflected monastic structures; all had chapels, cloisters, refectories, and, of course,

---

[18]   Risse, *Mending Bodies, Saving Souls*, 4.
[19]   Gary B. Ferngren, *Medicine and Health Care in Early Christianity* (Baltimore, 2009), 124–30; and two articles ("How Medicalised were Byzantine Hospitals?" and "The Confraternities of Byzantium") in Peregrine Horden, *Hospitals and Healing from Antiquity to the Later Middle Ages* (Aldershot, 2008).

Dum mœns ægrum prope Mors circumuolat alis,   O ΘΕΟΣ .   Tum me promißis beat et domus omnis adorat,
(Funestamŋ aciem iam fera iamŋ parat.   Tum vocat immensum me reuerata DEVM

5.1 *Christus medicus* – The Physician as Christ

an altar where the Mass could be celebrated.[20] Indeed, in some ways it is
artificial to separate monasteries from hospitals. In the early ninth century, for instance, a plan for a model cloister at St. Gallen (in today's
Switzerland) included the following: (1) an "infirmarium" for monks;
(2) a "hospitale pauperum" for the poor and for pilgrims who "came
on foot"; (3) a house for guests who "came mounted"; (4) a leprosar-
ium; and, finally, (5) a hospital for novices, converts, and lay brothers.
A Russian church statute of 996 erected sanctuaries for "unfortunates,"
a broad category of the ill, insane, possessed, and even criminal, who
were confined in monasteries where monks cared for them. Other western monastic orders, but especially the Cistercians, established cloister
infirmaries on a similar design.

An understanding of medieval and Renaissance hospitals is critical to
the history of early modern hospitals, if for no other reason than most
did not simply disappear to be replaced by markedly different institutions

---

[20] Henderson, *Renaissance Hospital*, 69.

after 1500. Many early modern hospitals were the very same institutions at least in name and often in physical structure. In addition, and even under the changed circumstances following the religious reformations of the sixteenth century, they retained their religious mission of "saving souls" as well as "mending bodies." These hospitals resembled each other fairly closely. Generally, hospital grounds included an enclosed area divided from the rest of the city by walls and gates; they were often placed along a main road in and out of the town. The central building was usually rectangular or cruciform. Altars and chapels formed essential features and literally concretized the religious mission of the institution. Beds, often large enough to accommodate more than one individual, were arrayed in rows down the length of the hall, allowing for participation in a central religious activity, the Mass or other church services.

The impact of the religious reformations of the sixteenth century had radical consequences for poor relief and medical care. In the countries that sheered away from Catholicism – in many German states and cities, in Denmark and Sweden, and in England – the disestablishment of the church was paired with a dissolution of monastic and ecclesiastical institutions, including hospitals. The impact proved most severe in England where Henry VIII (r.1509–47) and his vicar-general, Thomas Cromwell (c.1485–1540), broke up cloisters, religious foundations, and charitable establishments, and sold their lands. Few medieval hospitals survived this assault, even if they were not thrown down. St. Bartholomew's hospital, for instance, which had been founded in 1123, was not closed, but its income was confiscated. In 1546, Henry VIII refounded it by granting it to the City of London and giving it properties to sustain it. Other hospitals in the capital that had suffered a similarly catastrophic fate were eventually reestablished but as secular institutions (which does not mean, however, that either their associated religious mission or religious elements disappeared): St. Thomas's (1551) and St. Mary's Bethlehem (1557), for example. In any case, the effects of this pruning were drastic in the short run. Hordes of the impoverished and homeless quickly overran cities. London's poor relief mechanisms collapsed almost entirely under the pressure. Such conditions stimulated first a wave of private charitable foundations that were small but useful and which did something to fill the gap. The situation outside London was bleaker. A few hospitals survived as almshouses or cottage hospitals, but not until the eighteenth century was a new group of provincial hospitals founded.

The general trend during the Reformation was either to take over the larger urban monasteries and convert them into hospitals for the sick-poor or to merge several smaller institutions into larger ones. In Stockholm before the introduction of the Lutheran Reformation there were six hospitals concerned with poor relief and medical care. In its wake, the Crown transferred the main hospital to the old Franciscan monastery at Grämunkelholm and later, in 1555, to Danviken. Fewer hospitals existed in Finland (which was, at the time, a province of Sweden). During the Reformation, the old hospital for lepers at Åbo and the Hospital of the Holy Spirit merged. Thereafter two centralized hospitals served all Finland: the one in Åbo and another in Viborg. Helsinki had its own modest hospital. A combination of religious and charitable sentiments founded a series of small hospitals; these were often established through individual efforts. St. Anne in Aahus (Denmark) was endowed by Claus Denne (fl. 1520s) in 1525; it provided gratis care for fifty patients. The hospital of Kruunukylä (Finland) set up in 1632 had twenty-five beds. Its staff consisted of an administrator and a chaplain and the local minister superintended the whole.[21]

In southern Europe, war and politico-religious unrest, rather than centrally organized dissolutions or mergers, disrupted sixteenth- and seventeenth-century hospital life. Hospitals in the suburbs of Montpellier, for instance, were razed during a siege in 1562 and the chronic battling among French, Imperial, Papal, and Italian troops severely upset the running of hospitals especially in northern Italy. The sixteenth-century religious strife in central Europe interfered less with hospitals than did the more sweeping dislocations of the Thirty Years War (1618–48).

Catholicism underwent its own vigorous reformation (institutionalized in the decisions of the Council of Trent, 1545–63) that only partly represented a response to the Protestant challenge. Tridentine religious revivalism and the regained nerve of Catholic princes and prelates led to the foundation of numerous hospitals that, despite often being founded by secular rulers, retained strong religious elements: the Hospital of San Maurizio e Lazzaro in Turin (1575); the Juliusspital in Würzburg (1576); the Ospedale di Carità in Turin (1629); the Albergo dei Poveri in Genoa (1635); and the Great Poorhouse (*Großes Armenhaus*) in Vienna (1693). Antwerp's St. Elisabeth Hospital specified as eligible for admission "all sick residents of Antwerp who were destitute."[22] Although hospital endowment in this period was not uniquely Catholic, the number of Catholic foundations greatly exceeded the number of Protestant ones.

---

[21] E. J. Kouri, "Health Care and Poor Relief in Sweden and Finland," in Ole Peter Grell and Andrew Cunningham, eds., *Health Care and Poor Relief in Protestant Europe 1500–1700* (London and New York, 1997), 165–69, 185; Thomas Riis, "Poor Relief and Health Care Provision in Sixteenth-Century Denmark," in *ibid.* 133.

[22] Hugo Soly, "Continuity and Change: Attitudes Toward Poor Relief and Health Care in Early Modern Antwerp," in Grell and Cunningham, eds., *Health Care*, 91.

As we have seen, one question that has excited a great deal of historical investigation is just how much medical and surgical care did these institutions provide? This may be a poorly posed question, because medical care *per se* was never a hospital's *raison d'être*. Endowing a hospital was an act of piety that also manifested the wealth, position, and power of sponsors. William the Conqueror (c.1027–87) donated many churches and hospitals (in, for instance, Cherbourg, Bayeux, Caen, and Rouen) in expressions of personal devotion. Similar religious motivations impelled Nicolas Rolin (1376–1462), chancellor to the duke of Burgundy, to endow one of the most famous, opulent, and beautiful Renaissance institutions: the Hôtel-Dieu in Beaune in 1443 (Figure 5.2). Princes of the Catholic Church were also active founders. The most powerful, and perhaps also the wealthiest, prelate in Castile, Juan Pardo de Tavera (1472–1545), established the hospital of San Juan Baptista in Toledo in 1542.[23]

Hospitals in context

Hospital historians currently emphasize the necessity of understanding and placing hospitals within wider religious, social, cultural, economic, and political contexts. How, when, where, and why governments and individuals founded hospitals had much to do with these larger frameworks. Desires to fulfill many imperatives explain why so many disparate institutions cluster together under the general grouping of "hospital." In the late middle ages, for instance, strong commercial, economic, and demographic growth characterized western Europe. Municipalities grew fat on the profits of domestic exchange, international commerce, and craft production. Around 1300, cities, their wealthy inhabitants, religious fraternities, and guilds expressed their piety, but also their social standing and civic commitment, in the founding of hospitals. Dynamic commercial centers, such as Venice, Pisa, Florence, and Genoa in northern Italy, Augsburg in the prosperous German southwest, and the affluent Hansa cities of the north, all raised their own hospitals. The buildings of a particularly fine one, the Holy Ghost Hospital (*Heilig-Geist-Spital*), still stand in Lübeck.

Medieval hospitals and their early modern successors extended other services which may strike us as surprising, but which demonstrate the centrality of hospitals in their communities. Hospitals played major roles as property-owners, employers, and even banks. For instance, after 1464, the largest hospital in Florence, San Maria Nuova, acted much like an investment bank, offering a return of 5 percent for any capital placed

---

23 Catherine Wilkinson-Zerner, *The Hospital of Cardinal Tavera in Toledo* (New York, 1977).

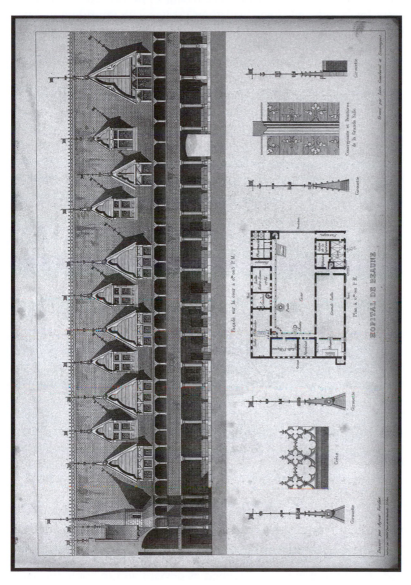

5.2 Architectural details, Hôtel-Dieu Beaune, France

in its trust. The hospital of San Giovanni in Turin worked in a similar fashion and one in medieval Cambridge lent money to "men of substance" embarrassed by their debts. Hospitals often relied on extensive property for income and managed their estates with considerable business acumen. Such institutions (like monasteries) could become major employers in an area. Of course, within the hospital itself, an almost invisibly fine line divided the patient or inmate from the employee.

Hospitals had always functioned as refuges for the poor and as a means of social control; this second function became most apparent in the development of what came to be known as *hôpitaux généraux*. A simple translation of this term as "general hospitals," however, is anachronistic and inadequate, because these institutions did not resemble what we today would understand as a general hospital, that is, a major health care facility for its region with provisions for emergency and intensive care, as well as specialized wards for children, obstetrics, surgery, and so on. The hôpitaux généraux arose in the seventeenth century to meet certain social needs or perceived ones. In 1676, Louis XIV of France ordered that each city of a certain size must build and maintain a hôpital général. The nominal aim of all the hôpitaux généraux was to immure the disorderly poor. Within their confines, administrators were to apply strictly regulated patterns of working and living to root out evil, profane, or merely unsocial behaviors and to habituate the poor to lives of thrift, diligence, and proper belief. Similar (if not quite identical) institutions existed in other European countries: in England, the *workhouses*; in German-speaking areas, the *Zuchthäuser*; in the United Provinces, the *tuchthuizen*; in Italy the *ospedali di carità*; in Spain, the *hospicios*; and in Russia, the *smiritel'nye doma*. The wonderfully baroque name of the Pforzheim institution in southwest Germany (established 1714) – "the house for the orphaned, the mad, the sick, the criminal, and the poor" (*Waisen-, Toll-, Kranken-, Zucht-, und Armenhaus*) – reflects its many missions. Such institutions could swell to gargantuan size. The Paris *hôpital général*, opened in 1656, had several buildings: among them, the Bicêtre for men, the Salpêtrière for women, and the Pitié for children. The Ospedale di Carità in Turin held almost 2,300 inmates in 1737 and the Hamburg Pesthof housed between 850 and 1,000 in its labyrinth of buildings and annexes.

According to Foucault, this kind of hospital functioned as the prime instrument of "the great confinement": the coordinated endeavor to incarcerate all those in society defined as deviant and to apply the same remedies to all of them. But scholars have subsequently discovered that, despite the stated goals of the hôpitaux généraux, they never acted as effective forms of control. In the Turin Ospedale di Carità, for instance, "the violent repression of begging via arrest and punishment seems . . . to be of marginal significance in the hospital's overall activities, and was resorted to only in moments of acute crisis."[24] Apparently, control of undesirables was neither usefully centralized nor even really envisioned by those who administered the institutions. Localities funded and ran most hôpitaux généraux in France and elsewhere. By the middle of the eighteenth century the hôpitaux généraux had largely shed whatever policing functions they once possessed and became more fully committed to care and cure. Furthermore, it is by no means certain that the efforts of the French government to close down thousands of smaller institutions in the name of greater efficiency were ever fully implemented. Vigorous opposition at the local level arose from those involved in traditional charitable undertakings or those excited by the message of the Catholic Reformation, as well as from the women of religious congregations and nursing orders and from provincial elites who sought to preserve control over "their" charities.[25]

The early eighteenth century witnessed renewed activity in the founding of hospitals that can be attributed both to new ideologies and to broader social, economic, and religious currents. The interest in increasing the size of populations and preserving their health (*populationism*) that developed in the late seventeenth century strongly affected plans to revise social welfare methods, including those connected with hospitals. Mercantilist concerns with economic advancement, especially in central Europe, Scandinavia, and Russia, complemented cameralist ones for improvements in administration and fiscal planning; the idea that state action could promote the general prosperity and well-being of the nation stimulated both. In the realm of health, these initiatives took the form of what Germans called *medical police*. Although the name was German (*medizinische Polizey*), the concept was European-wide. Johann Peter Frank (1745–1821) was its most prominent proponent. His *System einer vollständigen medizinischen Polizey* (A System of Complete Medical Police, 1779–1825) detailed projects for state intervention into virtually all areas of health. Frank viewed hospitals as integral components of a comprehensive medical police and wrote extensively on them. Another medical author, tellingly, compared hospitals to military defenses: "If a soldier may design fortresses which cost millions in order to protect

---

[24] Sandra Cavallo, "Charity, Power, and Patronage in Eighteenth-Century Italian Hospitals: The Case of Turin," in Granshaw and Porter, eds., *Hospital in History*, 97.

[25] Daniel Hickey, *Local Hospitals in Ancien Régime France: Rationalization, Resistance, Renewal, 1530–1789* (Montreal, 1997).

countries; why should not a physician be permitted to propose a hospital in order to save people from devastating diseases?"[26]

Principles of rational organization and purposeful charity dovetailed neatly with the Enlightenment's program of improvement and its faith in social engineering. Not only the state acted in pursuit of those goals, however. The wealth and prosperity of the European middle and upper classes had grown dramatically as domestic productivity, trade, and international commerce (including slaving) burgeoned. Those factors motivated actions or made them financially feasible. The creation of *voluntary hospitals* in Britain in the eighteenth century provides an excellent concrete example of this concatenation of forces. The term "voluntary hospital" refers to hospitals founded by individuals and groups, rather than by local or territorial governments.[27] Wealth, and the secular philanthropy that it nurtured, combined with rational religion to foster an array of projects designed to advance the "glory of God by promoting the usefulness of man."[28] The founding of hospitals using private funds proved a marvelously apt solution to the charitable quandary of the eighteenth century: how to deal with increasing poverty without providing handouts to the deceitful and comfort to the unworthy. It also expressed the religiously motivated charitable impulses that remained strong throughout the century and, for that matter, well into the next. Not only in Britain did such ideas find fertile ground in which to germinate: similar institutions cropped up almost everywhere in Europe.

The first voluntary hospital in Britain, the Westminster Infirmary (London), began admitting patients in 1720. By the end of the century, several others graced England's grandest city (St. George's founded in 1733, the London Hospital in 1740, and the Middlesex Hospital in 1745) and thirty in the provinces of which perhaps the best known rose in Edinburgh (1729), Winchester (1736), Bristol (1737), York (1740), and Liverpool (1749). Private individuals endowed two other hospitals in these years: Addenbrooke's in Cambridge (1719) and Guy's Hospital in London (1721). Sir Thomas Guy (1644/45–1725), a wealthy

---

[26] Johann Peter Frank, *A System of Complete Medical Police: Selections from Johann Peter Frank*, ed. by Erna Lesky (Baltimore, 1975), 407; George Rosen, "Cameralism and the Concept of Medical Police" and "The Fate of the Concept of Medical Police, 1780–1890," both in Rosen, *From Medical Police to Social Medicine: Essays on the History of Health Care* (New York, 1974), 120–58.

[27] John Woodward, *To do the Sick no Harm: A Study of the British Voluntary Hospital Movement to 1875* (London, 1974); Anne Borsay, "Cash and Conscience: Financing the General Hospital at Bath c.1738–1750," *Social History of Medicine* 4 (1991): 207–29.

[28] Risse, *Hospital Life in Enlightenment Scotland*, 17.

bookseller, designated the truly magnanimous sum of £219,499 for his hospital. Dr. John Addenbrooke (1680–1719), a physician, left considerably less, some £4,000, but enough to open a hospital for the poor. Philanthropic organizations established others on what Roy Porter termed a "joint stock principle"[29] Groups of charitably and practically minded men and women collaborated in drafting plans and collecting money. The milieu of the developing public sphere fostered such engagement. Informal exchange of ideas in reading groups, coffeehouses, and gentlemen's clubs paved the way. The plan for the Westminster Infirmary, for instance, first saw the light of day in a Fleet Street coffeehouse.

In England, the landed gentry, the mercantile middle classes, and a savoring of parsons contributed their time, energy, connections, organizing abilities, and money to the cause. Elsewhere in Europe, respectable laypeople (including many professionals and academics) and clergy, but also often government bureaucrats, took the lead. In France, reform initiatives likewise sprang from private individuals and groups. In Paris, for instance, several small projects marked the 1770s and 1780s. One can point to the *hospice de perfectionnement* set up by the Academy of Surgery for surgical or trauma cases of a difficult or peculiar nature; the Necker Hospital organized by Suzanne Necker (1737–94), wife of the French Controller-General and wealthy Swiss financier, Jacques Necker, for the parishes of St. Sulpice and du Gros Caillou; or the parish hospital supported by the *curé* Jacques-Denis Cohin (1726–83) out of his own pocket; and the one the banker Nicolas Beaujon (1718–86) endowed for Roule. These "neighborhood houses" were small and well staffed. They provided a preferred solution to the dual problems of poverty and illness during the closing years of the French Old Regime.

The Italian pattern – like the German and Russian ones – combined private initiatives and state actions. In a twenty-year period around the middle of the eighteenth century, several new institutions were endowed in Turin, such as a ward for contagious diseases at the Ospedale di Carità in 1733 and a shelter for "fallen women" in 1747. Private initiatives also proved critical in Hamburg, Lübeck, and Kiel, three cities where commercial interests dominated and where the Enlightenment in its German and Danish manifestations flourished.

Patrons and benefactors founded and sustained hospitals either by giving lump sums or paying regular subscription fees; care cost patients nothing. Those who donated large amounts tended to become members of the hospital's managing board, but even those who enrolled only the minimum subscription frequently enjoyed the right to distribute

---

[29] Porter, "Gift Relation," 149–78.

patronage by "nominating" a sufferer to a bed. Thus, subscribing to a hospital was a rational form of philanthropy that fitted well into the mercantile world and conformed just as neatly to middle-class social and religious mindsets.[30]

Typical of the solicitation among friends and colleagues that could facilitate entry into such hospitals was the mediation the novelist (and surgeon) Tobias Smollett (1721–71) undertook on behalf of an acquaintance. In 1750 he wrote to William Hunter about the son of one Mr. Louttit, an apothecary:

Mr. Professor,
Louttit was with me Saturday last, earnestly solliciting my Interest with Dr. Pitcairn in behalf of his Boy, who is (it seems) afflicted with scrobuti, lep'rous, or scrophulous ulcers, for which he desires the child should be admitted in Bartholomew's Hospital . . .

Louttit has been advised to have Recourse to the Doctor by a Gentleman belonging to the Hospital, who assures him that the Boy will be admitted, should our Friend [Dr. Pitcairn] make a Point of it, tho' otherwise, objections might be made to his Reception on account of the circumstances of the Disease. In the name of God, use your Influence with the Doctor; for Louttit is very clamorous and importunate, and will consider the favor as an indelible obligation.[31]

Patients and staff

One of the most vexed questions about patients in hospitals concerns mortality rates. Most eighteenth-century reformers cited horrifying mortality rates, often as high or higher than one quarter or one third of those admitted. Historical research over the last two decades has, however, presented an appreciably different picture, or rather replaced a single portrait of horror with a chiaroscuro of brighter and darker images. Hospitals differed in patient experiences and mortality rates. John Henderson's recent comprehensive study of Renaissance hospitals notes that, at Florentine hospitals (like most other Italian ones), there was a "rapid turnover [in patients], concentration on minor acute diseases . . . and relatively low mortality rates *pace* the traditional prejudices of historians." Yet as much as one should not generalize from the portrait painted by Howard and earlier scholars, one should also not take Florence's hospitals as typical of all contemporary ones. The hospital of Santa Creu in fifteenth-century Barcelona had much higher mortality (c. 26 percent) and the mortality at the Hôtel Dieu in Paris indeed hovered around one

---

[30] *Ibid.*; Bronwyn Croxson, "The Public and Private Faces of Eighteenth-Century London Dispensary Charity," *Medical History* 41 (1997): 127–49.
[31] *The Letters of Tobias Smollett*, ed. by Lewis M. Knapp (Oxford, 1970), 16.

third. These divergences, however, do not so much indicate better or worse care, or more or less medical attention, but rather reflect admission criteria. Spanish hospitals continued to follow a traditional pattern of caring for the aged thus elevating their mortality rates. Other hospitals refused to accept the chronically or seriously ill and their rates were therefore lower.[32] By the mid eighteenth century, and in the best-run hospitals, those frightening statistics – if ever accurate – had dropped to under 10 percent. In the teaching wards of the Royal Infirmary at Edinburgh, for example, mortality ranged from a low of 4.7 percent to a high of 10.5 percent. At the Bristol Infirmary, 86.5 percent of patients left as "cured," and a further 2.6 percent as "relieved." Death rates at the San Juan de Dios Hospital in Murcia, Spain, at midcentury, were 19.5 percent and, by the 1790s, 18.6 percent.[33]

The demographic make-up of patient populations also changed over the course of time, although perhaps not as dramatically as historians once believed. One can document, to be sure, a slow shift from admitting the poor and sick to admitting only the acutely ill, but the function of the hospital as a refuge never died out completely. Many institutions, such as Hamburg's Pesthof, continued to afford safety from the elements for the homeless, food for the needy, and rest and warmth for the ill, and one should not underestimate the worth of such aid. Early modern hospitals frequently served as way stations for the poor, who migrated through them seasonally, staying for longer or shorter periods of time. Not surprisingly, the size of the hospital population rose in winter and not only because some ailments, like those of the chest, occurred more often in cold and damp weather. Many inmates moved in and out of these institutions rather more freely than one might first expect: leaving at dawn to go to work, beg, or attend church, and returning at night for a bowl of hot soup and a safe place to sleep. Some became servants or caretakers, earning their keep by helping other "patients." Even quite late in the eighteenth century, the poor might well have viewed refuge and sustenance as a hospital's real benefit. An Edinburgh medical student in writing up the case of "a poor indigent man without house or family" noted that "what he seemed most to want was shelter and protection during the severe winter months."[34]

With little doubt, however, the sick-poor remained the most frequent inmates of early modern hospitals. Nonetheless, that generalization

[32] Henderson, *Renaissance Hospital*, 281.

[33] Risse, *Hospital Life*, 264; Mary E. Fissell, *Patients, Power, and the Poor in Eighteenth-Century Bristol* (Cambridge, 1991), 107–08; José J. Garcia Hourcade, *Beneficencia y sanidad en el s. XVIII: el Hospital de S. Juan de Dios de Murcia* (Murcia, 1996), 160–61.

[34] Quoted in Risse, *Hospital Life*, 8.

requires significant modification in light of recent work on particular hospitals. First, "the poor" does not necessarily mean the destitute. Investigations of poor relief and poor relief policies in early modern cities have revealed that a large group of the laboring poor (those who could normally make their way in life, but who fell into destitution during crises, whether personal, such as illness, or societal, such as an economic depression) often used hospitals to tide them over until better times returned. The population of many hospitals was quite diverse. The large hospital of Santa Maria Nuova in the first half of the sixteenth century drew patients from a wide range of social positions and occupations, including administrative and professional ones and well-off artisans as well as larger percentages of laborers, textile workers, and those in religious orders.[35]

Yet, it is also undeniable that in the seventeenth and eighteenth centuries, the character of hospitals slowly altered. As cities and territories began to erect more institutions for special groups and single purposes, such as poorhouses, workhouses, and orphanages, hospitals could more easily avoid admitting the merely destitute, elderly, homeless, or incurable. As hospital administrators and physicians became ever more painfully aware of the prevalence of "hospital distempers" (that is, diseases which crowded conditions and the "want of fresh air and cleanliness" bred), they sought to exclude contagious cases – those suffering from smallpox, fevers, or syphilis – or, if they did admit them, took care to isolate them or confine them to special wards or buildings. In addition, a series of specialized hospitals for incurables or "pox" sufferers cared for those not considered suitable to be housed in the more general patient population. Hospitals likewise excluded pregnant women. Those perceived as curably ill henceforth formed the principal, but never the sole, objects of hospital care.

While there is still not a great deal of material available on patients in early modern hospitals, numbers from the Bristol Infirmary, the Royal Infirmary in Edinburgh, and the hospital of San Paolo in Florence indicate that the majority of those admitted suffered from acute illnesses thought to be curable or at least amenable (see Tables 5.1, 5.2, and 5.3). They also demonstrate, however, that the exclusion of "fever" patients was never fully accomplished; indeed, the majority of male patients at San Paolo in this two-year sample (1567–68) was diagnosed with fevers. Political or economic reasons could cause exceptions to be made, as well. For instance, the Royal Infirmary in Edinburgh struck a bargain with the army and navy to treat military patients; these appeared regularly on the

---

[35] Henderson, *Renaissance Hospital*, 270–71.

Table 5.1. *Diagnostic categories – Bristol Infirmary (eighteenth century)*

Diagnostic category	Percentage
Fever	16.6
Respiratory	15.1
Trauma	13.9
Abscess, ulcer	13.2
Rheumatism, muscular	7.6
Skin problems	7.6
Digestive	5.7
Reproductive	3.8
Venereal	2.5
Operative conditions	2.4
Dropsy, etc.	1.5
Miscellaneous	10.1

Source: Mary E. Fissell, *Patients, Power, and the Poor in Eighteenth-Century Bristol* (Cambridge, 1991), 107.

Table 5.2. *Diagnostic categories – Royal Infirmary, Edinburgh (1770–1800)*

Diagnostic category	Percentage
Venereal	14.67
Fever	12.20
Pectoral	4.56
Rheumatism	4.56
Stomach	3.93
Ulcers	2.72
Sores on legs	2.39
Ague, intermittent fever	1.90

Source: Guenter B. Risse, *Hospital Life in Enlightenment Scotland: Care and Teaching at the Royal Infirmary of Edinburgh* (Cambridge, 1986), 120–21.

hospital's ledgers after the suppression of the 1745 Scottish "rising." The number of soldier-patients remained high for the rest of the century. In the 1760s they made up about one third of all patients; thereafter, the figure stood between 11 and 25 percent. Sailors, too, comprised a significant percentage of inpatients in the Infirmary in the 1760s. Military

Table 5.3. *Diagnostic categories – Hospital of San Paolo, Florence, male patients, 1567–68*

Diagnostic category	Percentage
Fevers	60.6
Skin diseases	12.7
Boils, ulcers, abscesses	4.4
French Disease	4.1
Pains	3.3
Constitutional illness	2.2
Accidents	6.3
For laxatives	1.7
Miscellaneous	4.7

Source: John Henderson, *The Renaissance Hospital: Healing the Body and Healing the Soul* (New Haven, Conn., 2006), 266.

personnel suffered the injuries and wounds characteristic of their callings, but also had frequently contracted venereal infections. The recovery rate of soldiers was the highest in the hospital at 81 percent and that of the sailors, the lowest, although still about 60 percent. By the middle of the eighteenth century, the Spanish army had made a similar contract with the hospital of San Juan de Dios in Murcia, although the numbers of soldiers admitted remained relatively small throughout the century: never more than fifteen or sixteen a year.[36]

The older picture of interminable stays in hospitals with death as the only release also needs revision. In general, patients did not linger for months or even weeks in hospitals. At the Edinburgh Infirmary, for instance, the average stay did not exceed thirty-one days. Those who had undergone major surgery, such as amputations, or who were being treated for particularly obdurate complaints, like leg ulcers, tarried longer – anywhere from forty to more than fifty-five days. Over 70 percent of patients at Santa Maria Nuova stayed fewer than thirty days; 38.3 percent ten days or less. A noticeable difference between length of stay for male and female patients suggests that the hospital was more willing to extend long-term charity to elderly or chronically ill women than to men. At the San Juan de Dios hospital, too, the duration of stay in the middle to late eighteenth century was significantly greater

[36] Fissell, *Patients*, 107; Risse, *Hospital Life*, 120–21; Henderson, *Renaissance Hospital*, 266.

for women than men: 45.2 days in 1740 for women, 18.3 days for men; in 1790, it was 41.7 and 23.3 days respectively.[37]

Some scholars have argued that as hospitals became more medical in their mission, that shift deleteriously affected patients. New conditions supposedly silenced patients' own voices and subjected them to stricter regulations imposed by physicians and surgeons and that were also gauged to meet the staff's needs and not necessarily those of the patient. Medical men supposedly "disparaged or dismissed patients' own accounts of illness and replaced them with signs and symptoms unavailable to the patient, but meaningful within an emergent profession."[38] Purportedly, patients became increasingly vulnerable to medical experimentation. At the same time, nonmedical or nonsurgical staff, such as nursing sisters, was thought to have experienced a sharp decline in their authority and in their ability to dictate daily routines: patients thus became objects and staff automatons. Likewise, as the administration of charity became more complex in the late eighteenth and early nineteenth centuries, lay governors and subscribers supposedly became more distanced from the everyday life of the hospital, abdicating control increasingly to medical men, surgeons, and paid administrative personnel.

Patients and staff were, however, never mere wax in the hands of medical men. Lay administrators maintained control of hospitals well into the nineteenth century; they did, after all, control the purse strings and thus could continue to dictate the rhythms of hospital life. In many cases, this meant the retention of strong religious and pious elements. Staff, too, was never easily elbowed aside. The quality of staffing and its numbers had always had a significant impact on hospital life and, especially, on mortality rates. Especially in Catholic countries, the nursing orders – in France, the Daughters of Charity, the Sisters of Saint Thomas of Villeneuve, and the Brothers of Charity – never really lost their ability to determine hospital routines. Sisters supervised the wards, ran hospital pharmacies, and even performed minor surgical operations. Not until the eighteenth century were physicians and surgeons able to undermine their authority and they were rarely able to dominate them entirely. The nursing orders brought a regimen of cleanliness and order to the hospitals and probably bore a good measure of the responsibility for improvements in hospital environment and mortality rates. Sisters

---

[37] Risse, *Hospital Life*, 173–74; Henderson, *Renaissance Hospital*, 262–63; Katherine Park, "Healing the Poor: Hospitals and Medical Assistance in Renaissance Florence," in Jonathan Barry and Colin Jones, eds., *Medicine and Charity Before the Welfare State* (London and New York, 1991), 36; Hourcade, *Beneficencia y sanidad*, 220.
[38] Fissell, *Patients, Power, and the Poor*, 162.

quite masterfully held their own on the wards and in matters of daily patient care, while alliances of staff and lay administrators could thwart the medical wishes of physicians and surgeons.[39]

If physicians were, by the late eighteenth century, coming to see patients as the legitimate objects of medical experimentation, that experimentation remained limited. Careful clinical trials were by no means the rule in eighteenth-century medicine. Local benefactors, for example, were extremely chary about having "their patients" delivered up to the whimsy of wild-eyed physicians and knife-crazed surgeons. Governors of hospitals remained quite sensitive to patients' complaints about brutal, humiliating, or embarrassing handling. Physicians, therefore, practiced what has been labeled "safe science" on their hospital patients and sought "to balance appropriate conservatism in practice – one does *not* experiment on patients – with a properly innovative spirit – one *does* experiment judiciously on patients – or else how would medicine advance?"[40]

Patients and their families, too, were scarcely powerless. Patients could, and frequently did, leave hospitals on their own, but they (or their friends and relatives) also vigorously resisted what they viewed as inappropriate, unproductive, or intrusive treatments. These complaints were rarely dismissed out of hand, although chronically disobedient patients were often expelled.

Special hospitals: leprosaria, incurabili, poxhouses, lock-hospitals, and lying-in wards

The first leper houses in the Latin West date from sixth-century Gaul. "Houses of St. Lazar," or *lazarettos,* soon dotted the western European landscape. By the twelfth and thirteenth centuries, many had assumed an almost monastery-like form and size. In addition, the rituals of religion and the rhythms of monastic life, with strict rules, requirements for admission, and an emphasis on celibacy, characterized them. As leprosy waned as a health problem, the lazarettos assumed new roles. Venice built its Lazaretto Vecchio in 1423 to quarantine travelers, not to incarcerate lepers. Other cities founded similar institutions to isolate, detain, and

---

[39] Colin Jones, *The Charitable Imperative: Hospitals and Nursing in Ancien Régime and Revolutionary France* (London, 1989).

[40] Andreas-Holger Maehle, *Drugs on Trial: Pharmacology and Therapeutic Innovation in the Eighteenth Century* (Amsterdam, 1999); Susan Lederer, "The Ethics of Experimentation on Human Subjects," in *The Cambridge World History of Medical Ethics,* ed. by Robert B. Baker and Laurence B. McCullough (Cambridge, 2009): 558–65; Susan Lawrence, *Charitable Knowledge: Hospital Pupils and Practitioners in Eighteenth-Century London* (Cambridge, 1996), 21.

care for plague victims: Mantua in 1450, Florence in 1463, Münster in 1475, Milan in 1488, and Frankfurt in 1494. No matter how they functioned and no matter what their target population, virtually all were (like the original leper houses) situated just outside town limits, embodied the dual medieval ideals of sheltering the sick and caring for the needy, and employed a small medical staff (often monk infirmarers).[41]

Pest or plague houses, that is, hospitals devoted specifically to those suffering from pestilences, accompanied the recognition that such patients should not be admitted to existing hospitals. In the fifteenth century, Florence's premier hospital, Santa Maria Nuova, formed an integral part in plans for combating plague. Repeated instances of plague, however, demonstrated the folly of this solution. By the end of the century, therefore, a special lazaretto, San Bastiano, was caring for plague victims, although isolation hospitals were not set up until the 1520s. In France as well, although somewhat later, hospitals gradually began to exclude plague cases as well as those ill with other infectious diseases.[42]

The creation of *incurabili* hospitals for sufferers of the Great Pox followed a similar pattern. As the disease rapidly spread in the late 1490s and early 1500s, most hospitals turned away its victims. Pressing needs, however, resulted in the development of special hospitals for these "incurabili." In Italy, where the disease first struck, a number of such institutions appeared early: San Giacomo in Rome, Santi Trinita in Florence. The impetus behind these foundations came from religiously minded laymen and women who belonged to confraternities dedicated to this purpose, known as the Companies of Divine Love. The wealthy Catalan noblewoman Maria Lorenza Longo (1463–1542) beneficed the Ospedal degli Incurabili in Naples in 1519. Similar hospitals, albeit in smaller numbers, appeared in French cities (in Strasbourg and Paris, for instance) and in larger numbers in the Germanies. Jakob Fugger, known as "the Rich,"(1459–1525), famously endowed a housing estate for the Catholic poor of Augsburg, the Fuggerei. In 1523–24, he rebuilt three of these houses as a pox hospital known as the Wood House (*Holzhaus*) because guaiacum wood was used for treatment. Over the course of some sixty years, the Holzhaus treated 3,420 patients who were subsequently discharged as "cured and healthy."[43]

As the occurrence of venereal diseases resurged in the eighteenth century and as the military became increasingly worried about the

[41] Risse, *Mending Bodies, Saving Souls*, 179, 202–03.
[42] Henderson, *Renaissance Hospital*, 93–97; Brockliss and Jones, *Medical World*, 250–51.
[43] Claudia Stein, *Negotiating the French Pox in Early Modern Germany* (Farnham, Surrey, 2009), 91–99, 172–73.

depredations the pox wrought on their soldiers and sailors, new hospitals, often charitably funded or privately run, like the London Lock Hospital (established 1746), met this greater demand. A perceived need for moral reformation led to the establishment of a Lock Asylum for prostitutes and other "immoral" women in 1787; its purpose was disciplinary as well as curative. This more sinister image characterized nineteenth-century lock-hospitals and eventually led to a strong feminist protest.[44]

Lying-in hospitals or wards might also be considered specialized institutions because they catered only to a certain segment of the population: pregnant women, often, but not invariably, indigent ones. Among those people usually excluded from hospitals were parturient women. The story of lying-in hospitals belongs as much to the history of charity and medical education (as part of clinical teaching, for instance[45]) as it does to the story of hospitals (see Chapters 4 and 6). Of course, the vast majority of women delivered their babies at home, assisted by a midwife, family members, friends, and relatives. Beginning in the late seventeenth century, populationist thinking drove the erection of small private hospitals or wards in public hospitals for women in childbirth. Here it was possible for poor pregnant women to have their children delivered by midwives or, increasingly in the eighteenth century, by men and male medical students. Considerable debate revolves around the actual nature of such wards and hospitals. Were they coercive and cruel places where women surrendered themselves up to the gaze of men, submitted themselves to strict bureaucratic regimes, and bowed to harsh discipline? Or were they, at least in their early years, a place where, as Lisa Cody has suggested, mothers experienced "the ideal of birth as a communal, female-centered, and largely natural experience among women of the urban working poor"?[46]

Special hospitals: military hospitals

Many historians still tend to undervalue military medicine and military hospitals dramatically. Anyone familiar with the tales of Florence Nightingale (1820–1910) at the Scutari Hospital during the Crimean War (1853–56) might find it difficult to accept that military hospitals

---

[44] Donna Andrew, "Two Medical Charities in Eighteenth-Century London: The Lock Hospital and the Lying-In Charity for Married Women," in Barry and Jones, eds., *Medicine and Charity*, 91–94; Henderson, *Renaissance Hospital*, 97–101; Stein, *Negotiating*.

[45] Jürgen Schlumbohm, "The Practice of Practical Education: Male Students and Female Apprentices in the Lying-In Hospital of Göttingen University, 1792–1815," *Medical History* 51 (2007): 3–36.

[46] Lisa Forman Cody, "Living and Dying in Georgian London's Lying-In Hospitals," *Bulletin of the History of Medicine* 78 (2004): 348.

often stood out as exemplars of good management, order, competency, and care in the seventeenth and eighteenth centuries.[47] But they did.

The rise of army and navy hospitals was intimately connected to the fortunes of war in early modern Europe and to the presence of standing armies. Equally germane to the history of military hospitals was the centralization and consolidation of government activities that began in the sixteenth century and gathered steam thereafter. The states that first founded military hospitals tended to be those that first organized standing armies; indeed, the two developments marched shoulder-to-shoulder. Among the earliest to arrange regular medical care for their troops were France, Spain, and some German territories. Countries that centralized governmental tasks more belatedly, and introduced standing armies only relatively late, England and the United Provinces for instance, also lagged behind in setting up efficient systems of military medicine. In Russia, this happened only in the eighteenth century, driven on by the often heavy-handed zeal of Peter the Great (r. 1682–1725) and Catherine the Great.[48]

Throughout the middle ages, neither armies nor navies possessed any orderly form of medical care for combatants. When Henry V invaded France in 1415, for instance, only one "medicus," Thomas Morest-ede, and a group of surgeons who ranked with the commonest soldiers, accompanied him. Wounded or sick soldiers and sailors were expected to help themselves, or solicit the aid of comrades-in-arms, relatives, or sympathetic bystanders. Often they were required to pay for that assistance and, while convalescent, generally forfeited part or all of their wages. Lucky ones benefitted from the largesse of officers, rulers, or nobles. Toward the end of the middle ages, governments and commanders-in-chief occasionally arranged to have soldiers and sailors admitted to civilian hospitals. But medical care for combatants remained poor. Notorious was the neglect of wounded sailors who fought against the Armada and who languished without succor in English ports. Equally badly treated were English troops during Elizabeth I's (r. 1558–1603) campaign in Ireland from 1598–1603.

During the Spanish assault on Granada at the end of the fifteenth century, Their Catholic Majesties, Ferdinand and Isabella, created the

---

[47] The interpretation presented here relies heavily on that advanced by Brockliss and Jones, *Medical World*, 689–700.

[48] Wolfram Kock, "Militärmedicinska pionjärer I Sevrige under 1700-talet," *Nordisk medcinhistorisk årsbok* (1985): 83–97; Heinz E. Müller-Dietz, *Der rüssische Militärarzt im 18. Jahrhundert* (Berlin, 1970); Christopher Storrs, "Health, Sickness and Medical Services in Spain's Armed Forces c. 1665–1700," *Medical History* 50 (2006): 325–50; Jakob Büchi, *Die Arzneiversorgung und der Sanitätsdienst der schweizerischen Truppen von 15.–18. Jahrhundert* (Stuttgart, 1981); Eric Gruber von Arni, *Hospital Care and the British Standing Army, 1660–1714* (Aldershot, 2006).

earliest recorded camp field hospital. The titanic struggle between the Habsburgs of Austria and Spain and the Valois of France in the sixteenth and seventeenth centuries saw the establishment of a permanent military hospital in Spain in 1570 and a large hospital (with 330 beds) at Malines in what is today Belgium. The English civil wars also provoked new thought to be given for soldiers and, in 1642, Parliament accepted responsibility for sick soldiers and set up a "Committee for Sick and Maimed Soldiers."[49] The first major military hospital in France opened in 1629. Large-scale conflicts almost always provoked a flurry of hospital foundings.

Care for veterans dates from a slightly later date and was measurably advanced when Louis XIV (r. 1643–1715) built the Hôtel des Invalides in Paris in 1670. Like other French hôpitaux généraux, the Invalides formed part of a royal campaign to control vagrancy and dissolute conduct. Strict house orders reflected the attitude of government administrators towards its inmates.

France had an extensive system of military hospitals in place by the middle of the eighteenth century and a set of naval hospitals at the strategically important French bases of Brest, Rochefort, and Toulon. Other countries followed not far behind and sometimes actually forged ahead with individual foundations, although the French system as a whole seems to have been the best in Europe. Berlin boasted the great Charité which had been established in 1725. During the Seven Years War (1756–63), Frederick II, often called "the Great" (r. 1740–86), founded permanent military hospitals in six garrison towns and set up field hospitals. In Spain, the first permanent army hospital was established in Pamplona in 1579. Spain's preparations for the Armada (1587–88) included organizing a medical staff of over eighty surgeons and fitting out two complete hospital ships. Austria did not have a permanent military hospital until the reign of Joseph II (1765–90).

Equally critical to good military medicine were attempts to boost the status of the medical corps. During the War of the Mantuan Succession (1628–31), French army surgeons received the title of *chirurgiens-majors des camps et des armées*; in 1731 Prussian military surgeons came to enjoy the rank of *Unterofficier* (noncommissioned officer); and, after 1742, Spanish surgeons were allowed the genteel title of *don*. The creation of autonomous hierarchies of command within the medical services freed physicians and surgeons (theoretically, at least) from the interference of

---

[49] Eric Gruber von Arni, "'Tempora mutantur et nos mutamur in illis': The Experience of Sick and Wounded Soldiers During the English Civil Wars and Interregnum, 1642–60," in Henderson *et al.*, *Impact of Hospitals*, 320.

nonmedical staff in medical and sanitary affairs. Control over the fine French system passed to medical *inspecteurs-généraux* in 1708 and supervision over all surgeons in the Prussian army to a surgeon-general in 1716. Governments also sought to better the lot of military medical men by granting them fixed salaries more consonant with what gentleman-officers earned.

Status and standing, of course, frequently depended on education. By the eighteenth century, almost every European country required its military physicians and surgeons to be qualified and often expected them to pass an examination expressly focused on military medicine. Governments nurtured new generations of surgeons and physicians in special schools. In 1775, the French royal government drew up guidelines specifying the training of army medical personnel in the military schools at Metz, Lille, and Strasbourg. In Prussia, the *theatrum anatomicum* created in 1713 grew into a *collegium medico-chirurgicum* for the instruction of military physicians and surgeons while bedside teaching took place in the recently refurbished Charité hospital. Seventy years later, the Pépinère was founded in Berlin as a college for military and civilian surgeons. Spain opened its Royal College of Surgery for naval surgeons in 1747, one for military surgeons at Barcelona in 1760, and a school for military doctors by 1760. On the other side of the Iberian peninsula, Portugal moved more slowly and had no schools for training military surgeons until 1825. In 1786, the Austrian medical–surgical institute that had been training surgeons and physicians for the army since 1782 was advanced to the level of an academy and renamed the Josephinum after the reigning Holy Roman Emperor, Joseph II. The same trends were found in Russia. In the wake of the military disasters during the initial stages of the Great Northern War (1700–21) with Sweden, Peter the Great charged the Dutch physician Nicolaas Bidloo (1673–1735) with planning a medical school and hospital in Moscow. The Moscow General Infantry Hospital opened in 1707. Also founded during Peter's reign were the Petersburg Admiralty and Infantry Hospital and the Kronstadt Naval Hospital which added formal medical and surgical schools in 1733.

The two countries that trailed behind in centralizing government and in instituting standing armies – England and the United Provinces – also lagged in developing orderly military medical services. In England, standing armies were of little consequence until the second half of the seventeenth century. Even during the titanic struggle with Revolutionary and Napoleonic France from 1792–1815, armies remained relatively small and the military medical system embryonic. Yet, already in the sixteenth century England was moving toward maritime greatness and it is therefore not surprising that more and earlier initiatives occurred in naval medicine. In the fourteenth century, Edward II (1284–1327?) endowed St. Bartholomew's Hospital in Sandwich "fyrst ordened for maryners desesed [diseased] and hurt." Most care for soldiers and sailors, however, was achieved through a contracting system: brokers arranged for sailors to be carried to private lodgings when the few available hospital beds were full. This system proved open to corruption and was, moreover, inefficient. Though some thought was given to sending physicians and surgeons to sea during times of war (surgeons were even conscripted during Elizabeth's reign) and the wounded and invalid were sometimes assigned to civilian hospitals on the coast, the general level of care remained wretched. Drawing on his own experiences, the novelist Tobias Smollett vividly portrayed very bad conditions on board ship as seen through the eyes of his fictional creation Roderick Random:

[As I] observed the situation of the patients, I was much less surprised that people should die on board, than that any sick person should recover. – Here [in the sick bay] I saw about fifty miserable distempered wretches, suspended in rows, so huddled one upon another, that not more than fourteen inches space was allotted for each with his bed and bedding; and deprived of the light of day, as well as of fresh air; breathing nothing but a noisome atmosphere of the morbid steams exhaling from their own excrements and diseased bodies, devoured with vermin hatched in the filth that surrounded them, and destitute of every convenience necessary for people in that helpless condition.[50]

Only two permanent institutions existed in England before the end of the seventeenth century for the injured and the invalid: the Chelsea hospital for soldiers (1682) and the Greenwich hospital for naval veterans (1696).

Special hospitals: "madhouses"

For most of the early modern period, care of those judged "mad" was a matter thought best left to the discretion of family and friends. Traditional care for the mad had usually been ad hoc; the nonviolent frequently wandered about more or less freely and only the raving and the dangerous were locked away. Noble and well-to-do persons maintained their deranged relatives at home or paid others to mind them. Members of less prosperous groups, too, might tend their own mad but, if this were not possible, other options existed. Even in the middle ages, some institutions, such as St. Mary Bethlehem (or Bethlem Hospital) in London, famous as Bedlam, sheltered the mad. In early modern Europe, monasteries, too, from the coast of the Atlantic to as far east as Moscow, took care of the mentally disturbed. Cities sometimes designated towers or

---

[50] Tobias Smollett, *The Adventures of Roderick Random* (2 vols.; London, 1794), I: 188.

parts of thick walls, known as "mad-towers" or "mad-boxes," for the purpose of incarcerating the insane, or confined them in special cells in existing hospitals, alms- and workhouses, or prisons.

Madness was not always viewed as incurable. Indeed, the number of patients who flocked to Richard Napier's practice with mental problems and emotional distress testifies to a general perception that the mad could be helped. Treatment for the mad could assume many shapes. It could be physical in the form of purges, emetics, and bleeding to counteract what many believed were the physical causes of madness. Or one might try exorcism to drive out evil spirits. The seventeenth century may actually have grown less confident about the ability to treat the mad than the sixteenth as the notion that madness was "associated with irrationality and the improper sense of the will" gained ascendancy and with it the willingness to lock up the mad with the other rowdy elements in society.[51]

In the eighteenth century, however, the pendulum swung back again, fostered by a sense that cures were possible and that the mad were not savages. Numerous writers, including physicians, pastors, and the laity, addressed how the insane should be handled; many advocated *moral treatment*, a mixture of decency and compassion with psychological (rather than physical) methods to alleviate what was now more commonly regarded as a mental rather than a physical disorder. Some impulses came from the humanitarianism associated with the Enlightenment, but just as many sprang from religious sentiments. In 1758, for instance, William Battie (1704–76) insisted that "management did much more than medicines" and refused to administer harsh drugs to his mad patients or to allow them to be beaten. In Florence, Vincenzo Chiarugi (1759–1820) developed a series of "soft" restraints made of leather and cloth. He avoided the use of chains and straitjackets. His rules ordered patients to be treated "with respect." Moreover, "no physical pain [is] to be inflicted under any circumstance."[52] The Brothers of Charity at the Chareton in Paris tenderly nursed the insane men entrusted to their care, neither stinting them on food nor denying them adequate shelter. In Germany, too, while asylum attendants were rarely specially trained, neither were they hardened brutes or sadists.

Simultaneously, efforts were made to separate the mad from other patients or recipients of poor relief as part of a more general tendency to

[51] Brockliss and Jones, *Medical World*, 443; Christine Vanja, "Madhouses, Children's Wards, and Clinics: The Development of Insane Asylums in Germany," in Norbert Finzsch and Robert Jütte, eds., *Institutions of Confinement: Hospitals, Asylums, and Prisons in Western Europe and North American, 1500–1950* (New York, 1996), 117–32.
[52] Vincenzo Chiarugi, *Regolamento dei Regi Spedali di Santa Maria Nuova e di Bonifazio* (Florence, 1789).

substitute specialized for catch-all institutions. If building special purpose institutions for the mad was not always feasible (or appeared too expensive), several halfway solutions existed. In Württemberg, for instance, Duke Karl Eugen created a madhouse (*Tollhaus*) in 1746 "for the melancholic and idiotic, the *maniaci* and *furiosi*" as a special building within the combined prison–workhouse he had erected ten years earlier.

Most important and innovative were the private charitable and private commercial institutions for the insane that shot up like so many mushrooms in the eighteenth century. Some were undoubtedly dreadful but others were demonstrably excellent. Private madhouses date from the seventeenth century. Keeping such a facility required little initial outlay; a couple of specially fitted rooms sufficed. Mad-minding became a money-making proposition and keepers advertised their services, as did James Newton for his business in Clerkenwell Close (London). His bill read:

[there] liveth one who by the blessing of God cures all Lunatick, distracted, or mad people; he seldom exceeds three months in the cure of the Maddest person that comes in his house; several have been cured in a fortnight and some in less time; he has cured several from Bedlam, and other mad-houses in and about the city, and has conveniency for people of what quality soever. No cure – no money.[53]

If the number of for-profit madhouses was probably greatest in England, England was hardly unique in having them. The French capital contained at least eighteen toward the end of the seventeenth century. All of these were quite small but competently and humanely managed. In England, where private madhouses were most abundant, the catalog of abuses was the longest. Violations of individual liberty, as well as physical maltreatment and inhuman conditions, formed the most frequent complaints. Not until Parliament passed the Act for Regulating Private Madhouses in 1774 did those adjudged mad receive protection from extreme cruelty or wrongful incarceration. Before then, a person could be carried off and confined on the sole authority of two justices of the peace and often for petty reasons: to curb a wife's extravagance, to prevent an unsuitable love-match, or to forestall a lawsuit. People caged arbitrarily often suffered gross indignities and even physical brutality. Samuel Brucksaw (who may or may not have been mad; and it does not matter here) was held for 284 days in a private asylum near Yorkshire by a keeper named Wilson:

[53] Quoted in Dale Peterson, ed., *A Mad People's History of Madness* (Pittsburgh, 1982), 40–41.

When Wilson shewed me to bed, he carried me up into a dark and dirty garet, there stripped me, and carried my cloathes out of the room, which I saw no more, for upwards of a month, but lay chained to this bad bed, all that time . . . they gave me bad victuals, short allowance, with sour beer, oftener water, and sometimes not that; no attendance, but what was contradictory and provoking as they could possibly invent, and frequently the most barbarous stripes [beatings].[54]

Still, one should not take negative examples as typical. Some private madhouses existed at the beneficent end of the spectrum of good and evil care. Moreover, some of the greatest innovations in moral treatment occurred in privately run institutions. The Retreat in York, proposed by William Tuke (1732–1822) and which the Quaker community opened in 1792, institutionalized the moral treatment of the insane. The Retreat provided a home-like setting and emphasized a range of nonmedical remedies. Gentleness and authority worked hand in hand to obliterate whatever mistaken notions had lodged in the patient's mind and which had caused his or her derangement. Patients lived in a pleasant brick building situated in a park, associated with other Friends (Quakers), and enjoyed plenty of opportunity to work in the asylum's gardens and wander about outside, although under supervision.[55]

Such moral treatment had became common by the end of the eighteenth century and not only in private institutions. Vincenzo Chiarugi, the physician-director of the new Bonifacio Hospital in Florence, combined medical treatments (mostly moderate blood-letting, blistering, sedatives, and stimulants) with gentleness and persuasion, his "talking cures." In addition, for some patients, especially those with suicidal inclinations, he advised religious counseling. The emblematic moment of moral treatment, however, is generally taken to be the "freeing of the insane from their chains." The French physician and hospital director Philippe Pinel (1745–1826), who struck the manacles off woman lunatics at the Salpêtrière in 1800, generally gets the credit for being the first to do so. In fact, others had done virtually the same thing before him: the superintendent of the Bicêtre, the nonphysician Jean-Baptiste Pussin (1746–1811), and the Genevan asylum director Abraham Joly (1748–1812).

Thus, even though the story of the mental asylum, like that of hospitals more generally, has often been set within the framework of a medicalization narrative, it is obvious that innovations in mental health care were often not medical but moral or religious in tone. Additionally, many

---

[54] *Ibid.*, 60.
[55] Anne Digby, *Madness, Morality, and Medicine: A Study of the York Retreat, 1796–1914* (Cambridge, 1985).

institutions even at the very end of the eighteenth century provided little more than custodial care, some of it bad, some of it excellent. It would be as wrong to accept the York Retreat as the model as to believe that abuse and inhumanity characterized all care for the mad in early modern times.

As this survey suggests, recent scholarly analyses have raised significant questions about older interpretations of hospital history. Archival evidence makes it increasingly difficult for scholars to accept a linear story of medical progress as the best grand narrative for understanding hospitals and their development in the early modern world. Hospitals and asylums were locations where a wide variety of medical, social, cultural, religious, economic, and political forces converged; unique combinations of these influences determined what a hospital did. Even if we are able to sketch out general trends, as has been done here, these provide only rough patterns into which individual hospitals fit well or poorly.

[P]ublic health is perhaps the most important of all subjects. If men are poor, the sovereign protects only the wretched; if they are sickly, he conserves only the ill.[1]

The pestilential Diseases that have of late Years walked their Rounds in Germany, Poland, Prussia, Pomerania, Hungary, Hamburgh, and some Parts of France, made us all very apprehensive for the public Health of our own Country.[2]

Medical Police, like all police science, is an art of defense, a model of protection of people and their animal helpers against the deleterious consequences of dwelling together in large numbers, but especially of promoting their physical well-being so that people will succumb as late as possible to their eventual fate from the many physical illnesses to which they are subject.[3]

Today we accept as axiomatic the idea that health forms a major concern of every community. This awareness, however, has not always characterized western civilization. The present-day sense that health requires concentrated public action is an understanding that has slowly matured since the middle ages. Indeed, "public health" as a fully articulated program first took shape in the late eighteenth century. The term itself only became current in the next century, although an early mention occurred in 1617 as a call to "appoint chiefe men to the office of providing for the publike health."[4] Still, public health serves as a convenient phrase that most historians deploy even while they recognize that it is anachronistic for the early modern period. Part of the story of health in society

---

[1] Denis Diderot, "Plan d'une université par le gouvernement de Russie ou d'une éducation publique dans toutes les sciences," quoted in Laurence Brockliss and Colin Jones, *The Medical World of Early Modern France* (Oxford, 1997), 378.

[2] Benjamin Grosvenor, *Health: An Essay on its Nature, Value, Uncertainty, Preservation, and Best Improvement* (London, 1716), i.

[3] Johann Peter Frank, *A System of Complete Medical Police: Selections from Johann Peter Frank*, ed. by Erna Lesky (Baltimore, 1975), 12–13.

[4] *OED*.

engages the history of a variety of state-sponsored actions; for instance, in maintaining the cleanliness of towns and ordering quarantines, but also in setting building codes, preventing the adulteration of food and water, and organizing firefighting.

Yet the story of health in society remains woefully incomplete if we think merely in terms of the state. Private and corporate endeavors (the latter involving, for instance, guilds and societies of physicians, surgeons, and apothecaries) proved equally decisive. Thus, any investigation of public health must embrace an array of "institutions without walls" by focusing on multiple instances, among them demography, vital statistics, medical corporations, and charitable enterprises.

If the story of public health cannot be told merely from the perspective of state action, neither is it solely the story of secular interests pursuing secular goals. Private and philanthropic efforts, often stimulated by religious and spiritual motivations, pioneered many innovations. Yet, this seemingly logical division into private and public (or state) itself proves highly artificial. Early modern people did not, as a rule, distinguish rigorously between the two spheres of activity or at least not until quite late in the period. Crucially important throughout were what we might term private/public combinations, that is, institutions private individuals organized but which had public benefits, such as the foundling home the sea captain and merchant Thomas Coram endowed in London in 1739.

The history of health in society has also been closely linked to the European experience of infectious diseases. A major study of medicine in early modern France, for instance, divides the period from 1500 to 1800 into a time "beneath the shadow of the plague" (that is, before the last major incident of plague in Marseilles in 1720) and "beyond the shadow of the plague."[5] To be sure, epidemics often catalyzed health measures, yet to write the history of public health as merely "epidemic-driven" fails to grasp the multiple dynamics involved. Fighting off incursions of disease was an essentially defensive act. Over time, however, proactive measures in the form of more coordinated attempts to prevent or avoid diseases, rather than respond to them, gained steam.

The health of the population

Chapter 1 discussed sickness and health as they affected individuals during their life-cycle and Chapter 2 looked at the broader European experience of pestilence. This section addresses themes relevant to the health of populations. Because it deals with aggregates rather than individuals

[5] Brockliss and Jones, *Medical World.*

or even single groups, we must first turn our attention to demographic profiles and vital statistics.

Demographers and epidemiologists remain unable to determine conclusively what killed our ancestors; how rapidly, when, and with what efficiency. Even thornier has been the task of assessing morbidity (sickness). The impact of death and disease differed depending on age, sex, occupation, and location. Once-accepted verities, such as that people in "the past" inevitably succumbed to ever-present disease and that lifespans were invariably short and disease-ridden, have now fallen to more sophisticated demographic analyses. We tend to believe that people in early modern Europe always ailed, but James Riley warns us that we must distinguish between the risk of *falling* sick (high) and the risk of *being* sick (low). Most prevalent diseases were acute and rapidly progressing; people got them and either recovered or died quickly. Childhood proved by far the most dangerous period of life. Once persons reached adulthood, they possessed at last some resistance to certain diseases. One cannot, therefore, conclude that "ill health prevailed among the people that survived"; rather, the opposite probably pertained, although they never, of course, developed full immunity from many infectious diseases, and especially plague and influenza.[6]

Infectious diseases waxed and waned in their intensity, and mortality in Europe did not decline in a smooth unbroken curve. Mortality dropped from the end of the sixteenth century through about 1800, then rose significantly and, in the first half of the nineteenth century, actually came to exceed the peaks of the sixteenth and seventeenth centuries. Thereafter, mortality rates fell again and have continued to decline.

The modern rise of population occurred either because killing diseases, like smallpox for example, diminished in virulence, occurred less frequently, or more people avoided them. Quarantines and travel restrictions probably successfully contained some outbreaks, and other initiatives (not always directly related to health concerns), like the draining of marshes to create more farmland, reduced the dangers from insect-borne maladies (for instance, malaria) while attempts to provide clean water slowed the propagation of many water-borne diseases such as typhoid fever and bacillary dysentery (see Table 6.1, p. 234.)

Pestilential legacies

Generations of scholars writing on the history of public health generally agreed with Carlo Cipolla that "it all started with the great pandemic

---

[6] James C. Riley, *Sickness, Recovery, and Death* (Iowa City, 1989), 62–101.

of 1347–51."[7] Accordingly, the fear and reality of plague prompted the development of boards of health as the first administrative mechanisms for addressing the health of society. Yet Cipolla's axiom is also too simple. He has a point, of course; many cities in the grip of plague first empaneled boards of health (albeit temporary ones) in the fourteenth and fifteenth centuries, placed quarantines, organized *cordons sanitaires*, and the like. But the process proceeded by no means as linearly thenceforth as his easy formulation makes it appear.

All societies develop rules on matters of sanitation and hygiene. People living in the first sedentary civilizations designated places for dumping waste and performing excretory functions and often surrounded these necessities with religious taboos about pollution. Such precepts did not produce results that satisfy twenty-first-century fastidiousness, but our ancestors were less fussy about noxious odors and offensive sights and about personal and public hygiene than we are today (although we should not overestimate the dissimilarities). Cities constrained by walls swarmed with hazards and reeked with smells. Rural areas were equally malodorous and filthy. Manure piled high along house and barn walls, unpaved streets filled with animal waste, cottages roofed with thatch that housed rats, mice, and body lice, and the close proximity of domestic animals typified living conditions in the countryside.

It was, however, the cities where the buildup of debris excited the most commentary. A report from Pisa in 1612 lamented:

None of the houses has a privy with its own underground cesspit but they shit between the houses where there are gaps between the walls...and there are hundreds of turds to be removed which, as well as stinking horribly, present an extremely disgusting sight to those who pass by in the street.[8]

Growing urban congestion exacerbated the problem and made closer regulation of basic environmental conditions desirable.

Four things combined to initiate public investment in urban improvements: economic prosperity, guild development, population aggregation, and government expansion. Economic growth generated the wealth necessary for investments in improvements financed by private individuals, the municipality, and religious foundations alike. The rise of a rudimentary administrative science and a corps of what may be called "city managers" trained in law and finance played a significant part. These men

[7] Carlo Cipolla, *Public Health and the Medical Profession in the Renaissance* (Cambridge, 1976), 11.

[8] Quoted in Carlo Cipolla, *Miasmas and Disease: Public Health and the Environment in the Pre-Industrial Age* (New Haven, Conn., 1992), 16.

took actions that eventually ameliorated the urban environment aestheti-
cally and biologically. Medieval cities began paving streets (Paris in 1185,
Prague in 1331, Nuremberg in 1368, Basel in 1387, and Augsburg in
1416); introduced canalization for better drainage; supplied fresh water;
prohibited the dumping of garbage and offal onto streets or into rivers;
erected municipal slaughterhouses; and banished noxious or dangerous
trades (tanning and slaughtering) to city suburbs.

The groundwork medieval cities laid greatly facilitated later expan-
sions and improvements. By the fourteenth century, for example, Milan
had already appointed officials to supervise street cleaning and markets.
In Amiens, councilors (or *échevins*) monitored the baking of bread, the
sale of fish, and the vending of meat. Aldermen in English towns and
Ratsherren in German cities assumed identical tasks. Admittedly, much
regulation had to do with economics, such as setting fair prices and assuring precise weights and measures, but officials also kept a keen eye on
the quality of foodstuffs and the cleanliness of market stalls.

Undoubtedly, the catastrophic mortality of the mid fourteenth century
and the subsequent incursions of plague quickened the pace of health
policies. Precautions in these centuries focused on preventing pestilential
incursions. Yet if plague was the menace that accelerated public health initiatives, it was hardly the only factor, and public health did not suddenly
pop into existence in the fourteenth century. Moreover, only the repeated
experience of several epidemics generated coordinated and permanent
programs of public health and made sanitation and medical care seem
legitimate communal and governmental concerns. Factors other than
disease, including changing attitudes toward the poor, social deviants,
and strangers, appear equally decisive. Those responsible for formulat-
ing policies also had to balance the demands of plague prophylaxis with
the larger financial, economic, and social needs of a community.[9]

When plague appeared in the middle of the fourteenth century, cities
were by no means totally unprepared. Some public health procedures
already existed and, more important, many cities had robust and well-
developed governments and experienced magistrates that responded with
energy, courage, and imagination. Cities had dealt with disasters before –
wars, famines, and fires, for example – and were not simply thrown for a

---

[9] Ann G. Carmichael, *Plague and the Poor in Renaissance Florence* (Cambridge, 1986); Brian
Pullan, "Plague and Perceptions of the Poor in Early Modern Italy," in Terence Ranger
and Paul Slack, eds., *Epidemics and Ideas: Essays in the Historical Perception of Pestilence*
(Cambridge, 1992), 101–23; Alexandra Parma Cook and Noble David Cook, *The Plague
Files: Crisis Management in Sixteenth-Century Seville* (Baton Rouge, 2009), 149–56, 190–
99, 246–51; A. Lloyd Moote and Dorothy C. Moote, *The Great Plague: The Story of
London's Most Deadly Year* (Baltimore and London, 2004).

loss or shocked into impotence. If the institutionalization of public health took time, the lag was not because civic leaders were so paralyzed with fear that they could not think.

In the late 1340s, plague first struck areas around the Mediterranean: Sicily, Sardinia, Corsica, Spain, and the north Italian city-states. While no one model fits all places and explains all circumstances, in general, the story runs thus. Cities quickly appointed officials to deal with the emergency and simultaneously implemented religious measures, organizing processions, setting aside days of prayer, calling on the healing powers of saints, and cracking down on blasphemous and ungodly behaviors. The severe conflict often postulated between "faith and reason," that is, between secular and religious (or superstitious) reactions, simply did not exist in the form that many modern observers would have us accept. Health officials enjoyed broad emergency powers and could often punish, or have punished, those who refused to observe regulations. These posts and these councils frequently disappeared as the incursion, and the fear it evoked, subsided. Only repeated instances of plague prompted the establishment of standing boards of health. Once such administrative units became semi-permanent or even permanent features of government, they acquired more extensive powers and slowly began to draft long-term plans to forestall new attacks of disease rather than merely react to an imminent threat or an existing emergency. Characteristically, laypeople, either members of the ruling elite or bureaucrats the city employed, staffed early boards of health; physicians were not necessarily members.

In Venice, as early as March 1348, the Large Council (*Consiglio Maggiore*) selected three of its own members (all, by definition, noblemen or patricians) "to consider diligently all possible ways to preserve public health and avoid the corruption of the environment." When the danger died down, this commission dissolved, only to be revived when plague recurred in 1410. By the 1480s, urban officials realized that averting epidemics was a long-term, full-time occupation that demanded the attention of the Consiglio in the same ways foreign policy and justice did. As a result, and beginning in 1486, the Consiglio annually chose three men to serve as commissioners of public health (*provveditori di sanità*) who hired paid subordinates. The latter created administrative continuity. Although medical personnel were often consulted about matters of isolation or treatment, the surveillance of public health was viewed then, and for a long time thereafter, as a bureaucratic responsibility rather than a medical one. Venice also created local boards in its mainland territories (the *terraferma*) and satellite cities.[10]

---

[10]   Cipolla, *Public Health and the Medical Profession*, 11–12.

The unfolding of public health in Florence followed much the same trajectory, although the city on the Arno developed its mechanisms somewhat more slowly. Not until 1448 did its Consiglio Maggiore delegate authority to combat the plague to an already existing body, the *Otto di Custodia*, and then only for three months. Eighty years later the city installed a group of five men to deal with a range of public health issues on a more durable basis. Like the Venetians, the Florentines organized local boards in subject cities: in Pisa, Pistoia, and Livorno. Yet neither Venice nor Florence could claim pride of place. Milan, under its capable and forceful Sforza dukes, had set up a permanent board of health in the early fifteenth century.

While historians generally accept that the Italian cities moved at the forefront of public health, other places followed close behind. Ordinances concerning plague appeared in French cities in the early sixteenth century: in Troyes in 1517, Reims in 1522, and Paris in 1531. Large states faced a more arduous task, but by the mid-to-late sixteenth century numerous territories attempted to isolate areas beset by plague by erecting cordons sanitaires. Not until the next century was the battle truly joined. In the seventeenth century, the trickle of plague ordinances for territories (like the "Plague Orders" promulgated in England in 1543) swelled to a flood. In times of widespread outbreaks, fighting pestilence could form the principal business of government, assuming a salience and urgency equaling that of impeding invasion by hostile forces.

Combating plague, or any other pestilence for that matter, depended on how people understood its cause (etiology) and how it spread (transmission). As discussed in Chapter 2, interpretations varied and contemporaries mixed religious or providential explanations with other factors. Explanations based on occult (secret or unseen) forces and natural causes happily coexisted in one and the same person. The tendency to separate them is a modern one. Chief among the natural causes counted miasmas, whose presence was revealed by stench. If, however, cleaning up the environment served as a major defense against plague, most people (and that includes governmental figures) also believed that plague passed insidiously and directly from person to person. Isolation, cordons sanitaires, and quarantines thus stocked every plague-fighting armory.

The 1599 plague ordinance (*Pestordonnantie*) for the Dutch city of Hoorn nicely illustrates this multifaceted approach. The opening paragraph referred to the plague as the "fiery rod" of God and underscored the necessity of establishing "a good order" in the city. Eighteen subsequent points explicated the usual rules of plague prophylaxis and established fines and punishments for noncompliance. Houses harboring plague patients were to be marked with "a straw bundle about one-half ell long and as thick as a [man's] arm or with a straw wreath of the same dimensions." No fewer than twenty-four hours were to elapse before burying those who died from plague (to prevent them being buried alive), but all bodies were to be underground within *twenty-eight* hours. The ordinance prohibited inhabitants of plague houses from freely circulating among "the good people [of the town, or] in the markets, churches, or any other places" until six weeks after the last plague patient in their homes had recovered or succumbed. They must never handle foods displayed for sale. The city ordered householders to burn infected bedding, taking great care, however, not to let the fire spread out of control. Citizens should keep indoors or chain up dogs "large and small." Carcasses, offal from slaughtered animals, or guts from cleaned fish were not to be thrown onto "streets, dikes, or in any canals or streams within the city." Another clause forbade barber-surgeons to spill human blood onto the streets or pour it into the waterways. The Pestordonnantie tightened up other measures of municipal housekeeping, doubling firefighting precautions, ordering the immediate repair of drains and gutters, and banishing the practically ubiquitous pigs outside the walls. The actions taken in Hoorn differ little from those found in cities elsewhere throughout Europe. In London, for instance, in 1636, *Certain Necessary Directions* outlined similar plague precautions (Figure 6.1). "Crisis management" in Seville, too, combined processions, prayers, clean-up campaigns, isolation, and emergency care.[11]

Measures against plague frequently included the naming of extraordinary medical personnel – plague-physicians, plague-surgeons, and plague-midwives – in addition to lay "searchers" and "watchers" (called *visitators* in the Low Countries), grave-diggers, and carters. Already in the late fifteenth century, special *physici epidemie*, as they were known in Italy (the Dutch and Flemish called them *pestmeesters* and the Germans *Pest-chirurgien* or *Pest-medici*), cared for plague sufferers; their letters of appointment specifically forbade them to treat other patients.

Plague-fighting tactics combined attempts to secure spiritual assistance (prayers, processions, charms, and amulets) with measures to purify the atmosphere (by lighting fires, shooting off cannon to agitate the air, burning aromatic herbs, and sprinkling vinegar everywhere) and with those

---

[11] "Pestordonnantie" (1599) for Hoorn, reprinted in J. Steendijk-Kuypers, *Volksgezond-heidszorg in de 16e en 17e eeuw te Hoorn: een bijdrage tot de beeldvorming van sociaalge-neeskundige structuren in een stedelijke samenleving* (Rotterdam, 1994), 374–76; *Certain Necessary Directions, as well for the Cure of the Plague, as for Preuenting the Infection; With many easie Medicines of small Charge, very Profitable to his Maiesties Subiects; Set downe by the College of Physicians by the Kings MAIESTIES speciall command* (London, 1636); Cook and Cook, *Plague Files*.

6.1 *Certain Necessary Directions as well for the Cure of the Plague* (1665 edition)

that strove to reduce contacts with plague sufferers or contaminated goods. Despite recognizing the seriousness of a plague emergency, governments never lost sight of the fact that disease prevention formed only part of their responsibilities and tried to balance, for example, control of the movement of people and goods to prevent the spread of plague with allowing the circulation of sufficient traffic to sustain the economy. Health passes facilitated both goals. Obviously, towns with walls found it easier (if by no means simple!) to control travel than did rulers of territories with extended and porous borders.

For individuals, the time-tested advice, passed down from antiquity, prescribed "flee early, go far, return late." It was sound counsel and many took it to heart. In the middle of the fourteenth century, more elaborate recommendations on how to preserve onself from plague or how to cure it began to appear and soon made up a significant part of public health initiatives. *Plague tracts* combined medical disquisitions on cause and propagation with guidance on prevention and treatment. The advent of printing resulted in a vast proliferation of such advice. Learned works in Latin, such as *De preservatione a peste* (On the Preservation from Plague) written by Giovanni di Michele Savonarola (1386?–1466?) or Fracastoro's classic *De contagione* (On Contagion, 1546) reached a smaller audience than did the cheaply printed vernacular handbooks that flooded off the presses in the sixteenth and seventeenth centuries. Authors characteristically proffered advice in the form of a dialogue or in a question-and-answer format like a religious catechism. Popular treatises, such as the "friendly conversation" between "Polylogum Curiosulum" and "Orthhophilum Medicum" produced in 1681 or the astrologically inspired "Promptvarium" of 1576 written to inform "each and every healthy and sick person, old or young . . . man or woman," followed these conventions. The city physician in Ulm, Germany, Heinrich Steinhöwel produced a *Büchlein der Ordnung der Pestilenz* (Little Book of Rules for Plague, 1473). His rules reflected the typical measures discussed above, including advice for effective public health measures and on how individuals should conduct themselves in times of plague.[12]

Steinhöwel also fretted about the presence of "wandering folk" (*fahrendes Volk*) during times of pestilence and his apprehension was not unique. The plague in fact played a major role in molding new forms of poor relief in early modern Europe. The *Certain Necessary Directions* mentioned above reflected these more obdurate attitudes toward beggars and vagabonds. Once regarded as "the poor of God," they were now coming to be viewed with suspicion, dislike, and even fear: "Nothing is more to complain on, than the multitude of Rogues and wandering Beggars, that swarme in euery place about the City, being a great cause of the spreading of the infection." To drive the point home, the printers of the *Certain Necessary Directions* appended a "Proclamation for quickning the Lawes made for the reliefe of the poor, and suppressing, punishing and setling of the sturdy Rogues and Vagabonds."[13]

The connections between mendicancy and disease forged in the great waves of pestilence that flooded over Europe in the mid fourteenth century held on tenaciously. The North Sea city of Hamburg, like many

---

[12] Karl Sudhoff, *Der Ulmer Stadtarzt Dr. Heinrich Steinhöwel (1429–1482) als Pestauthor* (Munich, 1926), 197–204.
[13] *Certain Necessary Directions*.

ports, suffered several severe bouts of plague. Physicians and city fathers linked poverty and epidemic disease, having, they argued, "learned from experience . . . that such contagions spring from the poor and are spread by wandering rabble." In 1596, the city physician, Johannes Böckel, warned against beggars who carried the "plague seed" with them in their bodies or on their rags and transmitted it to those who charitably gave them alms or sheltered them in their homes. The progress of the 1712–14 epidemic in Hamburg produced additional damning evidence; the most impoverished areas of the city succumbed first. A cruel combination of economic disruption, harsh weather, and endemic warfare drove thousands to Hamburg. Poor relief soon became the most pressing affair of the city's newly reconstituted board of health. Terror of the poor replaced sympathy for them and remained alive well into the nineteenth century; it reappeared with the cholera epidemics of the late nineteenth and early twentieth centuries.[14]

One may ask: were any of these measures effective? Certainly, from the perspective of the early twenty-first century, we might be inclined to condemn the efforts of our ancestors as foolish and misinformed. Obviously, contemporaries had no inkling of the pathogens responsible or the vectors involved in the transmission of diseases. They frequently attributed contagions to divine wrath, stench, natural disasters (like earthquakes), meteorology, and cosmic events like comets. Yet it is well to bear in mind that the responses of early modern people to incursions of disease were also rational and carefully gauged; some actions, it seems, had positive effects. A light diet, sufficient water, rest, and cleanliness did no harm and good nursing care saved lives. Shutting up houses kept sick people off the streets, although it also immured the healthy with the infected and with the fleas and rats that spread the disease. Killing off dogs and cats probably allowed the rat population to grow, but the fleas of domestic animals have not yet been totally exonerated from some role in the spread of plague. Obviously, many measures authorities condoned and implemented did little or nothing to halt or check the plague. Quarantines and cordons sanitaires, however, may have been different matters altogether.

Evidence is mounting that the efforts of governments to close cities and seal territorial borders, to interdict the movement of people, and to disallow communications with infected areas may have considerably reduced the speed at which plague propagated. More rapid and reliable forms of transportation and communication facilitated a prompt awareness

---

[14] Adolf Wohlwill, *Hamburg während der Pestjahre, 1712–1714* (Hamburg, 1893); Richard Evans, *Death in Hamburg: Society and Politics in the Cholera Years 1830–1910* (Oxford, 1987).

of new threats, but at the same time accelerated the transmission of disease. One thing is sure: plague epidemics began to decline in frequency and ferocity after about the middle of the seventeenth century (although London experienced its "Great Plague" in 1665) before they vanished from western Europe after 1721. States, however, did not immediately dismantle their anti-plague mechanisms and, throughout the eighteenth century, plague outbreaks in eastern Europe sent shivers down the collective western European spine and revived strong preventive measures. When plague ravaged Moscow in 1771, the French observer Charles de Mertens (1737–88) commented that "to a country situated like ours, histories of this terrible disorder occurring in the northern parts of Europe are more particularly interesting, by holding up to our view a picture of what it probably would be, whenever it should visit it again." Fortunately for France, Mertens proved a poor prophet.[15]

While epidemics play a major historical role, it is easy to overestimate their impact. The rich documentation they have generated draws historians like bees to the hive and has resulted in a somewhat skewed perspective on health and disease in the past. Epidemics were – are – important, but not exclusively so. A fuller treatment of communal health must engage a series of other topics and trace their developments from the late middle ages through the end of the eighteenth century: the appearance of a network of town and state physicians; more vigorous attempts to regulate medical practice; the entwining of medicine and charity; and, finally, the rise of a new environmentalism in the late seventeenth and eighteenth centuries.

Town and state physicians

Medical historiography has traditionally connected the appearance of the medical officer of health with the evolution of public health. Any such administrative innovation, however, needs to be firmly situated within broader historical changes of several kinds. As we have seen, the growth of cities and the increasing administrative capabilities of states shaped the mechanisms of communal health as powerfully as did theories of medicine and the exigencies of epidemic diseases.

The term "medical officer of health" is, moreover, not really an appropriate designation. What the English call the "medical officer of health" developed (mostly) in the nineteenth century and thus is anachronistic

---

[15] Charles de Mertens, *An Account of the Plague which Raged at Moscow in 1771* (trans. from French, London, 1799; reprinted and annotated with an introduction and bibliography by John Alexander, Newtonville, Mass., 1977), iii.

when applied to early modern times. Moreover, it is an imperfect English translation for a variety of words and phrases – most common were Latinate titles such as *physicus* or *medicus civilis* – that referred to men accorded special administrative and medical functions within a particular political area. The earliest town and state physicians did not always even possess specifically defined public health or administrative duties, but were hired to provide medical care to a community otherwise lacking it.

The town physician (*medicus civili*) can be traced back to the late middle ages. They initially appeared in northern Italy. By the fifteenth and early sixteenth centuries, numerous municipalities throughout Europe regularly engaged them. To ensure the presence of a physician, city governments contracted with men who then became known as civic doctors (*medici condotti* in Italian or *Stadtärzte* in German). The scarcity of medical practitioners gave rise, therefore, to the *medico condotto*. The custom of hiring civic doctors faded, however, as cities grew and began to attract more academically trained practitioners. Exactly when this level was attained varied considerably: earlier in Italy, later in northern and western Europe, and even more belatedly in central and eastern Europe. Nonetheless, the process was roughly comparable everywhere. Two specific examples illustrate the rise and fall of the civic doctor: one comes from Italy and the other from Holland.

Many historians consider Ugo Borgognoni of Lucca (?–1252/58) the first prominent example of a *medico condotto*. In 1214, he concluded an agreement with Bologna "to provide free treatment for the army, and for all injured residents of the city and for those of the countryside who have been brought to the city, save for those with abdominal hernia."[16] By the fourteenth century, many Italian cities had one or more such medici condotti on their payrolls. As the number of trained physicians in a locality increased, however, the office of medico condotto withered away, so that by the sixteenth century larger Italian towns no longer felt it necessary to hire them. Venice had regularly employed between seven and ten in the 1300s; none remained in the sixteenth century. In the small towns that always encountered difficulties attracting physicians, the practice continued and even expanded over the next 200 years. Surgeons and midwives were often retained on similar terms.

Virtually the same sequence of events pertained in other places, although the timing often differed. In the Dutch city of Hoorn, for

[16] Quoted in Vivian Nutton, "Continuity or Rediscovery? The City Physician in Classical Antiquity and Mediaeval Italy," in Andrew Russell, ed., *The Town and State Physician in Europe from the Middle Ages to the Enlightenment* (Wolfenbüttel, 1981), 26.

example, the burgomasters lured a physician named Albert Dircxzoon to the city by offering him a salary, citizenship, and tax relief. By about 1600, Hoorn employed three *stadsdoctors*. In the middle of the seventeenth century, however, only two remained and their salaries were much reduced. The decline of the stadsdoctor must partly be attributed to the mid-1600s economic malaise that enervated Hoorn, but it was also true that more physicians then resided there.

This discussion has tried to discriminate scrupulously between civic doctors and what were later called medical officers of health or *physici* (on the continent). The distinction itself is by no means so clear-cut; one flowed into the other and hybrids were common. Moreover, not everyone obeys these niceties of language and one finds the term physicus used fairly indiscriminately, sometimes indicating an administrative function, sometimes meaning nothing more than "doctor."[17] Sixteenth-century cities often appointed physicians with designated administrative duties, but the establishment of networks of them that covered a territory and provided medical care for a rural population did not develop until the eighteenth century

A series of concurrent developments – in towns, in territories, and in rural areas – demonstrate the slow coalescence of a more elaborate health grid, at least partly activated by state initiatives. Because developments across Europe differed, sometimes fairly drastically, these examples are not models; rather they illustrate the heterogenous ways in which systems of public health arose.

One set of examples comes from the German-speaking areas. Two of the earliest documented Stadärzte were Hermann "Medicus" selected by Wismar in 1281 and Master Berchtoldus by Munich in 1312. During the fourteenth century, the number of such posts proliferated: Cologne in 1371; Strasbourg in 1383; and Frankfurt am Main in 1384. In 1431, the Emperor Sigismund mandated that "each imperial city should have a physician." Zurich's records list town physicians from the fifteenth century onwards and one can locate similar initiatives in other Swiss towns, such as Geneva, Bern, and Basel from about the same time. In Hungary, a like process occurred, although 200 years later than in western Europe; not until after 1735.[18]

The duties of these early modern physici were many and expectations for them expanded over time. Comprehensive medical ordinances first

---

[17] For Hungary, Norbert Duka Zólyomi suggested a way to categorize the many types although his schema does not exhaust the possibilities. "The Development of the District Medical Officer in Hungary," in Russell, ed., *Town and State Physician*, 133.

[18] Alfons Fischer, *Geschichte des deutschen Gesundheitswesens* (2 vols.; Berlin, 1933), I: 58–102.

began to appear in cities in the sixteenth century (in 1502 in Würzburg, for instance). These documents generally charged the physicus with caring for the sick-poor; with conducting forensic examinations (doing postmortems, viewing wounds, judging victims of sodomy, while midwives assumed the delicate tasks of determining virginity or establishing rape); with advising political authorities in all matters of health; with supervising sanitary conditions (testing wells, patrolling markets, investigating animal diseases, and so on); and with instructing, examining, and superintending all subordinate medical personnel. This catalog demonstrates a typical mixture of administrative and medical duties; over time, the former came to dominate. Physici received regular salaries. Sometimes, the form of payment was exclusively cash, but most places provided physici with compensation in benefits in kind as well: freedom from taxes; free schooling for his children; wood for fuel; or a fixed measure of city wine or beer. More intangible, but especially meaningful in a world concerned with display and status, counted grants of citizenship and marks of special distinction, such as invitations to city festivities or the allotment of a place of honor in city processions.[19]

Medical conditions outside of towns tended to be more haphazardly ordered and supervised, although one must guard against the tendency to regard towns as beacons of progress and rural areas as invariably mired in dirt, disease, and ignorance. Still, before the middle of the eighteenth century, provincial medical officers or physici were few and were generally appointed to cope with emergencies like plague or the "bloody flux" in humans or rinderpest in cattle. Rural areas close to cities might benefit from an extension of urban arrangements. Florence, for example, dispatched help to the village of Monte Lupo during the plague epidemic of 1631.[20] Creating a more comprehensive network of resident medical officers in the countryside took longer.

In France the organization of rural health remained a work in progress. Ad hoc occurrences and sudden initiatives fostered by particular individuals or groups drove many improvements. The first nationwide effort to centralize or coordinate medical care came quite late, with the founding of the *Société royale de médicine* in 1776. The Société, however, did not act as a national board of health but rather functioned as a corresponding society, linking physicians throughout France in an effort to gather accurate information. Earlier in the century, other pieces of the public health

[19] Mary Lindemann, *Health and Healing in Eighteenth-Century Germany* (Baltimore, 1996), 72–143.

[20] Carlo Cipolla, *Faith, Reason, and the Plague in Seventeenth-Century Tuscany* (New York, 1979).

puzzle had fallen into place. Some had nothing to do with medicine directly. The French system of *intendants* delegated to each province enhanced the state's ability to cope with medical emergencies swiftly or at least to know when and where actions were required. Improvements in transportation and communication likewise facilitated the collection of information. In response to the Marseilles plague of 1720, the royal government quickly dispatched physicians and surgeons to assist and the overall effect was excellent.[21]

These efforts became more frequent and better coordinated as the European Old Regime drew to a close. In various parts of France after 1750, intendants commissioned physicians and surgeons to act during outbreaks of disease. As in Italy and Germany, towns often contracted with local medical practitioners, offering them a supplementary payment in return for providing medical care in areas that might not otherwise attract physicians. Not only towns initiated such measures. Provincial estates, the churches, or "even socially aware local notables" might also employ physicians for the common good. In Biarritz in southwestern France, some 253 families paid out 2 francs each to contract the services of a surgeon. The Fürstenberg porcelain manufactory in northwestern Germany, for example, organized medical care for its workers on a subscription basis. Another of the French government's sustained efforts was the distribution of boxes of remedies (*boîtes des remèdes*) that began in the late seventeenth century. None of this, however, added up to an extensive or fully coordinated system of health care. Yet, whereas once it was accepted that "public medicine at the end of the Old Regime remained essentially an emergency measure designed to supplement other kinds of charity during a crisis such as an epidemic," more recently historians have judged the efforts of governments to create at least a rudimentary framework of public health on a national or territorial basis as more effective.[22]

And some places had moved more rapidly down the road to coordinated medical provision and supervision, even if the system thus created remained patchy and not always tremendously efficient. German territories may have gone furthest in building up networks of state-appointed and state-salaried physicians. The Austrian physician Johann Peter Frank advocated a wide range of government-sponsored programs in public health and his influence was greatest in the Germanies, the Habsburg territories, and northern Italy. The deliberate construction of a web of physici can be followed in developments in several German territories.

[21] Brockliss and Jones, *Medical World*, 347–56.

[22] Toby Gelfand, "Public Medicine and Medical Careers in France During the Reign of Louis XV," in Russell, ed., *Town and State Physician*, 101–03, 116.

The plague years of the late sixteenth and early seventeenth centuries, especially the widespread outbreaks in the late 1500s and early 1600s, occasioned new public health ordinances. After the Thirty Years War (post-1648), renewed threats of plague and dysentery advanced the regulation of health to a more constant concern of government. In the larger cities and towns, the office of physicus became at least semi-permanent and was rarely allowed to remain vacant for more than a few months at a time. The appointment of physici remained a jealously guarded local prerogative – a patronage plum – controlled by urban magistrates. When more comprehensive medical ordinances were passed, physici usually received salaries directly from the central government. These physici differed, however, from the old medici condotti in that they neither worked solely for the state nor were they supposed to function as physicians to the entire populace residing in their district. The physici were not primarily physicians-to-the-poor, although most contracts required them to treat the destitute for which they were reimbursed from local poor relief funds. No physicus enjoyed a monopoly of practice in his area and, judging by the frequency of quarrels between physici and other academically trained physicians, he was usually not the sole "real" physician. How successful and accepted he became in a community depended on a variety of factors, many of them nonmedical: his position as a property-owner, as debtor or creditor, his propriety, his comportment, his piety, his manners, and even his dress.

Building out a territory-wide network of physici was not the only initiative launched or solution proposed. Seventeenth- and eighteenth-century reformers took special interest in preserving the health of productive members of society, especially peasants. They had grown increasingly sensitive to the problems of the countryside more generally. One might, of course, promise all sorts of incentives (tax relief, for instance) to encourage physicians to move to rural areas. Other, more ingenious, solutions took shape and offered the added benefit of costing less. Reformers in several countries advocated creating a corps of *routiniers* or auxiliary medical practitioners who received less training than physicians but who were also neither surgeons nor apothecaries. In 1751, the Swedish botanist Carolus Linnaeus (1707–78) sketched out a plan for involving rural clergymen in medical care. The idea was not entirely new in the mid eighteenth century. Basic medicine had formed part of theological curricula in Lutheran Denmark since the seventeenth century. The priest- or pastor-doctor solution gained favor in several places, if usually only in draft form. Even in Sweden, no pastor-doctors ever took to the field. Of course, many priests and pastors distributed medical advice or mediated medical care for their parishioners even if they were not officially trained to do so.

Revolutionary France trod a different path. The new republican government had abolished older medical educational and regulatory structures (such as guilds and colleges of physicians and surgeons). Early in the nineteenth century, however, the Napoleonic government stepped in to reestablish both. As a stop-gap measure, Fourcroy's Law of 1803 mandated the instruction and placement of "practitioners of a lower degree." These men, called *officiers de santé*, learned medicine in an apprentice system; they were to be deployed in times of war and in rural areas. Officiers de santé continued to practice in France until the end of the nineteenth century, despite the growing opposition of academically trained physicians.[23]

Health in the countryside was not only a matter of human medicine. Curiously, until recently few historians have spent much energy investigating the importance of epizootics or the development of veterinary medicine in early modern Europe. This neglect is particularly strange considering that about 80–95 percent of the western European population lived on the land and from agriculture. Animals were significant economic and military assets. The trades of war and peace alike required horses; and the treatment of equine diseases, as well as attempts to breed better animals, was serious business. By the eighteenth century, while the concern for horses did not disappear, interest in other domestic animals, especially cattle and sheep, grew dramatically. These concerns paired with initiatives to improve agriculture (in France, this was known as *physiocracy*). Several waves of rinderpest (cattle plague) had an enormous impact. Rinderpest apparently first appeared in northern Italy in 1711 and then swept like wildfire over Europe in two great waves: once in the 1740s and 1750s and then again thirty years later. The disease decimated cattle populations and caused enormous economic losses. Attempts to halt its spread included quarantines, the isolation of herds, large-scale slaughtering of animals, and experiments with bovine inoculation. These measures taken together may have eventually slowed its progress. This shocking experience motivated the founding of schools for veterinary medicine that appeared in several European countries during the course of the eighteenth century. Once again, France took the lead, establishing colleges in Lyon (1762) and in Alfort near Paris (1766).[24]

If historians have only slowly given their attention to the health of animals, they have been even less attentive to plant health. Even if, as Mary

[23]   Robert Heller, "'Priest-Doctors' as a Rural Health Service in the Age of Enlightenment," *Medical History* 19 (1975): 361–83.
[24]   Lise Wilkinson, *Animals and Disease: An Introduction to the History of Comparative Medicine* (Cambridge, 1992); Caroline Hannaway, "Veterinary Medicine and Rural Health Care in Pre-Revolutionary France," *Bulletin of the History of Medicine* 51 (1977): 431–47.

Matossian observes, "it may seem irregular to use plant health . . . as an index of human health," they are closely related. Diseases of plants, such as ergot (resulting from a form of mold on rye), could sicken humans. Ergot poisoning produces a series of more or less alarming symptoms, including cardiac arrest, gangrene of the extremities, convulsions, and psychoses, and may be an abortifacient for humans and other animals.[25] Diseases of plants had other far-reaching effects, as they could destroy crops thus triggering famines, precipitating nutritional decline, and causing severe economic losses. In addition to pestiferous vermin of all kinds (rats, mice, and insects), various "blights," caused by fungi, bacteria, worms, protozoa, and parasitic plants, repeatedly wreaked havoc on food supplies: barley fell prey to smuts and rusts; rye to halo spot and powdery mildew; and wheat to crazy top and kernel smudge. When major food crops failed, dearth, famine, and malnutrition were not far behind.

Regulating medical practice

The regulation of medical practice always had multiple objectives: the maintenance of standards, the limitation of competition, and the preservation of traditional educational methods. These goals were concretely expressed in the development of medical licensing and semi-judicial forms of medical regulation. No single agency succeeded in monopolizing all these functions. Medical corporations (or guilds), government organizations, and universities shared in the regulation of medical practice and their interests did not always neatly coincide.

The regulation of medical practice began early in human history. Although several ancient law codes provided compensation for victims of what we might term malpractice (most famously in Hammurabi's code of the seventeenth century BCE), none evolved a systematic form of licensing. Roger of Sicily (r. 1130–54) and his grandson, the Emperor Frederick II (r. 1220–50), drafted rules governing medical practice and required all those who wished to practice to obtain a license. Ecclesiastical authorities, not secular governors, however, issued the credentials.

Guilds embodied a more comprehensive concept of licensing (at least in a sense) and something like "quality control." Guilds were often known as corporations; thus much of the medical structure of early modern Europe was essentially corporate in nature. For example, by 1293, Florence had a guild that incorporated medici, apothecaries, and

---

[25] See Mary Kilbourne Matossian's flawed but provocative book on molds: *Poisons of the Past: Molds, Epidemics, and History* (New Haven, 1989), quote 155.

grocers, while a College of Physicians for university-trained doctors existed in Venice by 1316. In France, the surgeons' and barber-surgeons' corporations in Montpellier (1252) and in Paris (1268; the Collège de Saint Côme) were the earliest recorded ones and enjoyed the greatest prestige. A similar college of physicians did not appear in England until almost three centuries later, in 1518.

Corporations attempted to restrict or even monopolize medical practice. Some were quite successful, others appreciably less so. Corporations that combined practitioners of different types, surgeons and physicians, for example, often became embroiled in bitter internecine feuds over rights and authority. When established in the mid thirteenth century, the Collège de Saint Côme included two levels: the clerical barber-surgeons "of the long robe" and the lay barbers "of the short robe." The former were empowered to examine and certify the latter. Not surprisingly, conflicts arose. Battles over supremacy and authority became especially intense at those moments when the more academically trained surgeons sought to distance themselves from their artisan brethren. Guilds and corporations were essentially exclusionary organizations. All had rules specifying who might become a member and whom or which groups were excluded. Illegitimate birth disqualified one from many guilds; patricians or nobles were only eligible for membership in others; and women were almost always denied admittance.

The movement to bar women became pronounced in the later middle ages and continued to grow in early modern times. Previously, some women had belonged to guilds or even occasionally had enjoyed academic training, although they always made up a small minority. The widows of surgeons, barber-surgeons, apothecaries, and bathmasters might be allowed to continue their spouse's occupation for a time or with the aid of a journeyman. Midwifery, while not in fact guilded, often had a sort of semi-guilded structure, particularly in the realm of education.[26]

Corporatism remained the preferred form of medical organization until near the end of the early modern period, when the corporate structure in medicine, as in other realms of life, began to decay. Notable regional differences, however, always pertained. Medical corporatism never grew as strong in England as, for example, in France. Corporatism in France also produced what Brockliss and Jones have termed a "differentiated medical community," that is, a community divided into several occupations, each with its characteristic rights and privileges, distinct fields of action, and

---

[26] See the several essays in Hilary Marland, ed., *The Art of Midwifery* (London and New York, 1993).

proper means of defending its "territory" against the encroachment or trespass of others.[27]

But it would be wrong to think that the French system pertained everywhere. In Italy and Spain, for example, the tendency to separate physicians from surgeons in different corporations that characterized the rest of western Europe was never strong, at least not until well into the sixteenth century. In Renaissance Venice and even later, physicians and other medical practitioners belonged to the same guild. In Florence, however, the old Guild of Physicians and Apothecaries dissolved when the grand-duke established a Florentine medical college in 1560. Farther down the boot of Italy, in Naples, the situation was similar but not identical: two medical colleges existed distinct from the guild of barber-surgeons and apothecaries.[28]

The history of corporations tells part, but only part, of the story of medical regulation and practice in early modern Europe. In France, for example, corporate life was not firmly planted even in the sixteenth century and corporations demonstrated significant variations. For instance, although theoretical training and university education generally set physicians off from surgeons, many physicians, just like surgeons, had learned their craft as apprentices. During the course of the sixteenth and seventeenth centuries, the pace of incorporation quickened due to the desire of the monarchy to foster it. Estimates suggest that by the end of the seventeenth century, France had between thirty-six and forty-three colleges of physicians or medical faculties, three hundred corporations of surgeons, and about the same number for the apothecaries.[29] Yet, as the following chapter shows, regular members of medical corporations by no means monopolized, or even dominated, the medical marketplace. Literally thousands of noncorporate medical practitioners thrived as well.

During the eighteenth century in France, three developments sapped the vigor of the once-powerful corporations. First, university faculties became less relevant for medical education. As Chapter 4 discussed, private medical training (especially in the fields of surgery and obstetrics) provided strong competition. Second, and simultaneously, corporations became more elitist in their orientation, seeking to define ever more narrowly their proper membership. Third, the numbers of medical practitioners of all stripes, including those who belonged to no corporation,

[27] Brockliss and Jones, *Medical World*, 20–31.
[28] David Gentilcore, *Healers and Healing in Early Modern Italy* (Manchester, 1998), 60–62.
[29] Brockliss and Jones, *Medical World*, 186–87.

rose dramatically. Thus, by the closing decades of the eighteenth century, the corporate medical world – and not only in France – was in disarray, even crisis. The French revolutionary government administered the *coup de grâce*, democratically abolishing the corporations along with all other "privileged bodies."

The history of medical corporatism in England and Germany followed different paths than in France, despite some similarities. By 1550, three corporations controlled medical practice in London: the Society of Apothecaries, the Barber-Surgeons Company, and the College of Physicians (later the Royal College of Physicians). The first two had existed since the middle ages. The College of Physicians was much younger: Henry VIII chartered it in 1518 in response to the supplications of court and academic physicians under the leadership of the humanist physician Thomas Linacre (c.1460–1524). In theory, but not always in practice, the two older corporate bodies bowed to the superior authority of the College of Physicians.

The College of Physicians was many things at once: a learned society, a club for academically trained physicians, and a sanctioning agency. Full membership as fellows became possible only for men who had achieved the degree of MD at one of the country's two universities (Cambridge or Oxford). In addition, the applicant had to sit an examination conducted in Latin and based on his knowledge of Galenic and Hippocratic texts. Examiners charged fees; in 1684, the not inconsiderable sum of £20. Practical experience was neither considered relevant, nor tested.

By the middle of the seventeenth century, the College had significantly expanded its membership by granting licenses to men with baser academic qualifications. These *licentiates* were, however, not necessarily or even typically men of lesser accomplishment or skill. Thomas Sydenham, the "English Hippocrates," was one of the College's most celebrated licentiates. On the whole, however, the members of the College represented an academically trained medical elite that exercised its right to try cases of malpractice and to proceed against what it designated illicit practice. Of course, the College's authority was limited to London and it exerted no control over practitioners outside the capital. Moreover, one could receive authorization to practice in other ways. In 1512, for example, Parliament endowed bishops with the right to grant medical licenses within their dioceses and thus the sway of the College remained imperfect even in the capital.[30]

---

[30] On the history of the (Royal) College of Physicians in these years, see Harold J. Cook, *The Decline of the Medical Old Regime in Stuart London* (Ithaca, N.Y., 1986) and George C. Clark, *A History of the Royal College of Physicians of London* (2 vols.; Oxford, 1964–66).

Medical corporatism in England never exhibited the resilience it did in France and the "medical Old Regime" declined earlier and faster in England. The College of Physicians suffered a massive blow to its authority in 1704 in a famous case involving the apothecary William Rose, in which the House of Lords resolved that apothecaries, too, possessed the right to practice medicine. By the early eighteenth century, several developments combined to sap the power of the College. As in France, the medical marketplace had greatly expanded and physicians as a group became more fragmented in methods, origins, and aspirations. Fresh currents in medical thought ate away at the conceptual supports of academicism that had once held together the community of physicians and endowed it with a common identity. English physicians who planned to set up a Society of Chemical Physicians in 1665, for instance, privileged experience and experimentation over the text-oriented medicine of the College's members. By the final third of the seventeenth century, moreover, the College could no longer count on the unequivocal backing of the court. The Glorious Revolution of 1688 had weakened monarchical power in general. Simultaneously, many aristocrats and courtiers had become fans of the new science and found the textualism of collegial orthodoxy stale and unappealing. Thus, the intellectual, social, and political worlds of early eighteenth-century England were no longer congenial to the closed corporatism of the College or to its brand of medicine. The Rose decision only made reality manifest.[31]

The German situation defies easy characterization and was not directly comparable to either the French or English models, although similarities pertained. "Germany" (like "Italy," for that matter) simply did not exist until the late nineteenth century except as a geographic designation; there were many "Germanies." State power, even within the territories that had undergone a process of centralization since the sixteenth century, was always more diffuse than in France, for example. Throughout the Germanies, corporate life was not overwhelmingly important and German physicians (unlike those in parts of Italy) never organized in guilds.

Some other German practitioners are easier to characterize and to fit into a corporate model. Surgeons, barber-surgeons, apothecaries, and bathmasters had been guilded since the fourteenth and fifteenth centuries. Jurisdictional disputes over specific rights and practices were intra- and inter-guild, although not until the seventeenth century did real clefts open up. Especially bitter wrangling took place in the protracted battles between surgeons and barber-surgeons and between barber-surgeons and bathmasters. In the duchy of Braunschweig-Wolfenbüttel, for example, a legal quarrel over the division of rights ignited in the middle of the

---

[31] Cook, *Decline.*

sixteenth century, smoldered for decades, flared up repeatedly, and finally burned itself out in the imperial courts between 1635 and 1738. At issue was the attempt of the surgeons to peel away from the barber-surgeons and to confine the latter to clipping hair, setting cups, and applying leeches. That goal was achieved by the end of the eighteenth century but not without a great deal of controversy in the interim.

By the late seventeenth and early eighteenth centuries, moreover, the task of licensing in German territories had mostly devolved on newly founded collegia medica. Typically, all physicians were supposed to submit their credentials for approval to the local collegium before settling down to practice. In general, however, the collegium did not test candidates' competence; instead they "checked their papers." Later, collegia medica often held *viva voce* (in Latin) as prerequisites for entering practice. Once a candidate passed the examination, however, he did not become a member of the collegium; only the privy council or the ruler himself appointed members.

Peoples and places

To a great extent, the history of health in early modern society remains a story of the relationship of peoples to places. Since antiquity, people have been aware that health somehow hinges on location. Even when ideas of contagion dominated, contemporaries deemed environmental influences significant and often determinant. Although the bacteriological age (beginning no earlier than the middle of the nineteenth century) helped push concerns about place into the background, this change may itself only represent a temporary or partial hiatus in an age-old tradition. Certainly today we have lost our complacency about the ability of "magic bullets," like sulfa drugs or antibiotics, to conquer all diseases and have become acutely sensitive to illnesses caused by environmental pollutants, such as asbestos, lead, and dioxins, as well as to the more general ways in which our health depends on the health of the environment.

"Contagion" and "miasma" were the terms most often employed to explain how disease spread. Roughly speaking, contagion means that diseases are passed from person to person, either directly or through water, air, or inanimate objects, while miasma suggests that some condition of the atmosphere bears the principal responsibility. These words never carried exclusively medical connotations. Ideas about contagion, for instance, "are inseparable from notions of individual morality, social responsibility, and collective action."[32] Early modern people deemed some diseases contagious and others due to an "putrefaction" or

---

[32] Margaret Pelling, "Contagion/Germ Theory/Specificity," in W. F. Bynum and Roy Porter, eds., *Companion Encyclopedia of the History of Medicine* (London, 1993), 310.

"degeneration" of the air or joined them to especially insalubrious places, like swamps. It makes an important difference in how people formulate public health policies whether one thinks that diseases pass principally from person to person or diffuse through the subtle mechanism of the air.

Ever since the Greeks, people have connected diseases to physical surroundings. The Hippocratic works – principally *Airs, Waters, and Places*, *Epidemics I*, and *Epidemics III* – contrasted the healthiness and unwholesomeness of locations. The authors of these texts argued that numerous factors affected the environment and the humans who lived in it: prevailing winds, native waters, soil, seasons and their alterations, sudden meteorological shifts, and terrestrial upheavals, especially earthquakes and volcanic eruptions. This mode of explanation persisted well into the eighteenth and even nineteenth centuries. When, for example, Professor Gottfried Beireis investigated the causes of an "alarming mortality" in the small northwest German town of Schöppenstedt in 1766, he identified the culprit as a persistent damp which

weakens the mechanism of breathing, hinders the preparation of the blood in the lungs, and abruptly stops up the perspiration. [These] are the causes of the almost always fatal chest diseases, which continue unchecked throughout the year there, of the irregular intermittent fevers . . . [and] of the preponderance of tumors and of dropsy, the last [of which] is almost endemic in Schöppenstedt and the cause of most adult deaths.[33]

Several decades earlier, the English physician John Arbuthnot (1667–1735), in observing an epidemic of catarrhal fever, emphasized the effects of the previous year's drought because such dry spells

exert their Effects after the Surface of the Earth is again opened by Moisture; and the Perspirations of the Ground, which was long suppress'd, is suddenly restor'd. It is probably that the Earth then emits several new Effluvia hurtful to Human Bodies.

Such "Effluvia" had global effects. Arbuthnot noted how "a previous ill Constitution of the Air" had earlier attacked animals and provoked a "Madness among Dogs." Moreover, "the Horses were seiz'd with the Catarrh before Mankind; and a Gentelman averr'd to me, that some Birds, especially the Sparrows, left the Place where he was during the Sickness."[34] Neither analysis would have seemed the least bit odd to contemporaries. All affirmed an intimacy between the environment and the action of the humors within living bodies, animal and human alike.

---

[33] Quoted in Lindemann, *Health and Healing*, 283–84.
[34] Quoted in James C. Riley, *The Eighteenth-Century Campaign to Avoid Disease* (New York, 1987), 25.

The concept of corrupted air, therefore, dominated much thinking on how disease originated and spread. Generally thought capable of contaminating the air were rotting vegetation, decaying corpses, discarded entrails, and fetid excrement. People who were sick breathed out transpirations that fouled the atmosphere. Mother Earth herself was not innocent. Natural history taught that exhalations from craters and gaps in the earth occasioned by tremors, for instance, endangered health. How corrupted air worked on the individual or on his or her humors stimulated fierce debate, but it was widely believed that even a small quantity of tainted air could be dangerous and could sully the atmosphere, much as a particle of dye in water colored its entire volume. These ideas motivated the many measures taken during outbreaks of disease to purify air, to keep it moving (stagnant air was harmful and more prone to corruption), and to clean up anything that emitted bad smells.

The strong identification of places as either healthy or not equally influenced thinking about colonies. As Europeans discovered "new" worlds, they encountered climates significantly different from their own basically temperate one. While by no means all explorations or colonial ventures carried Europeans into non-temperate regions, many did. Explorers and settlers in the Caribbean, the southern parts of North America, in India, Africa, and the East Indies, all feared the effects of "hot climates" and their reports dwelt on the dangers such places posed. This "fear of hot climates" lay rooted in early modern beliefs about the internal workings of the body and its intimate relationship with the environment. Everyone acknowledged that "the human constitution was responsive to and shaped by climate, air, and diet."[35] Thus, Europeans were unfitted for tropical or subtropical climates and required a period of seasoning to adapt. Rapid transposition from one place to another, even from one temperate zone to another, was fraught with danger as humans (and their animals as well) had to accommodate themselves to different foods, other waters, and altered seasonal patterns. The ability of climatic factors to operate on humors and influence individual constitutions formed an almost reflexive part of early modern understandings of health; the colonial experience did much to reinforce that basic belief.

Even a portrait of the new American colonies as a "Garden of Eden" or a "Land of Milk and Honey" preserved intact the relationship between health and environment albeit in a more beneficent version; people conceived more children, lived longer, while animals grew bigger, produced

---

[35] Karen Ordahl Kupperman, "Fear of Hot Climates in the Anglo-American Colonial Experience," *The William and Mary Quarterly*, 3rd. Ser. 42, no. 2 (April 1984), 213.

more offspring, and gave more milk. Decisions about where to found colonies were often predicated on these ideas although greed frequently trumped caution as the colonies considered the most dangerous, such as the West Indies (especially after the importation of yellow fever in the late eighteenth century), were also where Europeans acquired riches most rapidly. Likewise, perceptions of relative risk or safety determined whether or not to send women to the colonies, to plant settlements, or to take native, or later African, concubines as better suited to harsh and inhospitable environs.

As critical as place was in the thinking of early modern people about disease, not only specific or filthy localities made one ill: other people, and especially diseased ones, did as well. Despite the lack of an explicitly articulated idea of contagion, most people fully accepted that many diseases, and especially pestilences, were catching. This ancient and deep-seated belief shaped public responses that sought to prevent the ill from coming into contact with the well. Not all diseases, and not even all pestilences, counted as equally communicable. Smallpox existed at the high end of the contagiousness continuum; diseases like malaria at the opposite. Syphilis, a "new" disease in the sixteenth century, had, as we have seen, a strong impact on European society and bolstered the logic of contagionism.

The Veronese physician Girolamo Fracastoro introduced the term *fomes* or *fomites* to designate "inert carriers" of disease. This "discovery" has frequently earned Fracastoro a place in the pantheon of sixteenth-century scientific precursors that includes the Flemish anatomist Andreas Vesalius and the Polish astronomer Nicolaus Copernicus (1473–1543). The eminent American historian of public health George Rosen, writing in 1958, referred to Fracastoro's book as "one of the great landmarks in the evolution of a scientific theory of communicable disease." Yet Fracastoro did not perceive "the categorical distinctions between contagion, infection, and noncontagious disease which are so important from the modern point of view."[36] Thus, it is ahistorical to transform Fracastoro into an early bacteriological guru.

In truth, throughout the early modern period, the dual strands of miasmatic and contagious interpretations coexisted and combined in myriad ways to explain the cause of disease in a convincing manner. Few, if any, public health measures rested solely on one or the other, as any quick perusal of plague ordinances adequately demonstrates. Both ideas were always present, but in the late seventeenth and early eighteenth centuries the emphasis on miasmatic interpretations grew and the thread

---

[36] Pelling, "Contagion/Germ Theory/Specificity," 319.

of environmentalism, or what has been called a new Hippocratism, was thickening.[37]

By the beginning of the eighteenth century, many people were persuaded that disease could be avoided, even if it could not be cured. This faith in the ability to manipulate one's surroundings was a novelty. The Greek view of the environment had been an essentially fatalistic one: physicians could treat individual patients but nothing could be done to prevent epidemics. Eighteenth-century environmentalists thought otherwise and launched a "campaign to avoid disease." A first step was to assemble precise information on physical phenomena. They then sought to uncover patterns hidden in that data. Once these patterns were exposed, they argued, it should be possible to learn what to avoid and what to alter in their surroundings, as well as how. It proved, of course, not so easy to do either but the attempt was noteworthy and by no means totally without value.

Improved methods of studying the atmosphere and weather patterns made the projects of the environmentalists seem feasible. New and more accurate instruments (barometers and thermometers) facilitated the measurement of air pressure, temperature, rainfall, and wind velocity. From about the 1660s onward, those interested in the weather began to keep daily records of meteorological occurrences, diligently tracking them for years. This pursuit expanded into a studied attempt to correlate weather and other environmental conditions with disease outbreaks. The star of this new Hippocratism guided the writing of a new natural history genre: *medical topography*. These works typically reviewed climatic and environmental factors, patterns of illness, and the unique situations of certain localities.

The Italian physician Bernardino Ramazzini (1633–1714) penned one of the earliest medical topographies. Several others followed the model account of Modena he published in 1685. Friedrich Hoffmann studied epidemics in Halle, while Johann Philipp Burggrave (1673–1746) and Johann Adolph Behrends (1740–1811) authored works on Frankfurt am Main. As Europeans stretched their influence out over the globe and settled in climates they found strange and biologically perilous, they composed medical topographies in order to comprehend and perhaps even exert control over these newfound lands. James Lind's (1716–94) *An Essay on Diseases Incidental to Europeans in Hot Climates* (1768) and

---

[37] The discussion in the next pages of the "new environmentalism" or the "new Hippocratism" of the eighteenth century relies heavily on the work of Riley, *Campaign*. See also Caroline Hannaway, "Environment and Miasmata," in Bynum and Porter, eds., *Companion Encyclopedia*, 292–308.

Lionel Chalmers's (c.1715–77) account of South Carolina in 1776 were the classics, but there were literally thousands of others. The most expansive of these efforts was that written by the man often known as the father of *medical geography*, Leonhard Ludwig Finke (1747–1837). Finke's three-volume *Versuch einer allgemeinen medicinisch-praktischen Geographie* (Medical-Practical Geography, 1792–95) became the standard for subsequent generations.

Yet, the medical topographers of the eighteenth century proved far more successful in collecting information than in transforming that knowledge into useful practices. Part of the problem lay in the overwhelming size of samples, but another part in the lack of consensus on how to observe. Did one, for instance, record temperatures indoors or out? At 6 a.m. or 6 p.m.? Using which of several competing scales? Scientific instruments had improved greatly by the middle of the eighteenth century, but were nonetheless liable to lose their accuracy with time, temperature changes, and use. The absolute babel of terms used to describe diseases greatly exacerbated an already difficult situation. Efforts to quantify data and to develop what has been called an "applied environmental mathematics" remained crude; prediction was impossible. Nonetheless, these trials substantially differed from an older, qualitative emphasis on "airs, waters, and places" and pointed toward a medicine based on the science of large numbers. Even the imperfect data thus gathered suggested to eighteenth-century observers that improvements in the environment would reduce mortality and morbidity.

The historian James Riley describes these initiatives as attempts to "avoid disease" and divides them into four groups: (1) draining; (2) lavation or the cleaning of streets, gutters, and other public facilities such as privies; (3) ventilation; and, finally (4) new burial practices. While the eighteenth century invented none of these, it pursued them with uncommon fervor and on a larger scale than previously.[38]

Reformers deemed the noisome exhalations from swamps and bogs especially harmful and even in the seventeenth century had set into motion projects to drain them. Equally rank were the closer environments of cities and towns. Urban streets often gave off virtually overpowering stenches, and rivers like the Thames and the Tiber were little more than open sewers. In the sixteenth and seventeenth centuries, cleaning streets remained the responsibility of residents. In England, for instance, towns required houseowners to sweep the streets outside their homes at least once a week and they fined delinquents. Minor criminal offenders might be sentenced to remove the accumulated mess from thoroughfares and

---

[38] Riley, *Campaign*, 89–102.

haul night soil away. Rather than hiring their own corps of street cleaners, municipalities contracted with private individuals to perform these tasks. These arrangements, however, often proved less effective and more costly than anticipated. Larger cities began to flush streets regularly, opening sluices and water gates to allow fresh water to flood down the streets, and laid simple, open storm sewers to carry off the filth thus dislodged from surfaces. In the nineteenth century, sanitary engineers, as they came to be known, accomplished massive public works projects literally raising the streets of cities the size of Chicago and sinking public water pipes.

Providing adequate quantities of potable water remained a major task. Frequently, the nearest and most convenient water supplies were the very rivers that conveyed away a city's muck. Paris, for instance, had two major sources of drinking water: the Seine River and an aqueduct. The Seine provided little safe water and the flow from the aqueduct dribbled unreliably. Medieval London relied on wells and three rivers: the Thames, the Fleet, and the Walbrook. In 1613, Sir Hugh Myddleton, a goldsmith, formed the New River Company to bring water to London. While Myddleton's intention was primarily entrepreneurial, others undertook similar projects for civic or philanthropic reasons. The latter grew quickly in the eighteenth century. Systems of water filtration, although proposed in the seventeenth century, waited until the nineteenth century to be introduced.[39]

The picture was not altogether bleak. Even the "great wen" of London had been much improved by the early eighteenth century through the efforts of private persons and local authorities. In 1767, for instance, Dr. Thomas Short (1690?–1772) wrote approvingly that

many of its [London's] streets have been widened, made straight, raised, paved with easy Descents to carry off the Water; besides Wells in most public Yards; and Pipes for conveying Plenty of fresh Water to keep them clean and sweet.[40]

Because contemporaries firmly held that "air corrupted by putrefaction is the most fatal of all causes of illness,"[41] the atmosphere, too, required purification. Motion was considered the best way to cleanse air of impurities. When experiments revealed that several gases comprised air and that many particles floated in its "materia," air's role in thinking

---

[39] Jean-Pierre Goubert, *The Conquest of Water: The Advent of Health in the Industrial Age* (Cambridge, 1989); F. W. Robbins, *The Story of Water Supply* (Oxford, 1946).

[40] Quoted in Roy Porter, "Cleaning up the Great Wen: Public Health in Eighteenth-Century London," in W. F. Bynum and Roy Porter, eds., *Living and Dying in London* (London, 1991), 68.

[41] Quoted in Riley, *Campaign*, 97.

about disease causation grew. Novel ideas about ventilating buildings where many people resided, such as jails, orphanages, workhouses, and hospitals, rested on just these principles. Reformers at the end of the eighteenth century valued good aeration in hospitals as the *sine qua non* of a healthful construction, but they recognized that need as equally vital for maintaining the well-being of any crowded population, whether on land or at sea. Inventors devised mechanical fans to supplement simple techniques of opening doors and windows, shaking out and sunning bedding, and letting light and air into the dark and musty corners of old buildings. When, for instance, the high mortality in Newgate prison alarmed the London aldermen responsible for its oversight, they consulted Dr. John Pringle (1707–82), an expert on the prevention of disease in the armed forces, and Stephen Hales (1677–1761), a clergyman and avid experimenter with ventilators. Pringle and Hales recommended the installation of new devices in the building which did the trick. The Pringle–Hales team demonstrates the characteristic mix of medical expertise and philanthropic concern in eighteenth-century public health ventures.

Perhaps the most intriguing part of the four-pronged attack on environmental nuisances involved the disposal of the dead. For centuries, Christian corpses had been immured in church walls, buried under flagstones, and sunk in ever more crowded churchyards. Sepulchers and graves regularly had to be opened and the remains of ancestors removed to make way for their descendants. The stench arising from beneath church floors (especially in hot weather) and the juices oozing into the earth greatly troubled eighteenth-century sanitarians. Around the middle of the century, horrifying reports of multiple deaths resulting from the opening of church crypts sensationalized the matter. Very quickly a call arose to halt the practice of burials within churches and to relocate cemeteries in the suburbs. Reinterment campaigns gained momentum throughout western Europe. Significantly, the first to be buried outside city walls were the poor and executed criminals. The initial advocates of cremation appeared about the same time, although it was not until the twentieth century that "fire burials" (as they were called) became respectable.[42]

The moment of death fascinated early modern peoples. In the middle ages, *ars moriendi* books instructed Christians on dying the "good death" by resisting despair and giving one's soul willingly up to God. By the late seventeenth and early eighteenth centuries, the focus had shifted. A series of humanitarian projects arose to prevent burial alive and to restore to life

---

[42] Brian Parsons, *Committed to the Cleansing Flame: The Development of Cremation in Nineteenth-Century England* (Reading, 2005).

the perhaps still-living victims of drowning or those struck by lightning.[43] Life-saving institutes cropped up first in towns with many waterways and canals, such as Hamburg, Amsterdam, and Haarlem. Deep-seated prejudices about touching the "almost dead" often frustrated attempts to revive them by the use of measures such as tobacco enemas, brisk rubbing of limbs, and suspending them by their feet. These campaigns could offend the religious sensibilities and funerary rituals of Christians and non-Christians alike. Physicians advised, for instance, that one should wait at least twenty hours, and up to three days before burial, to ensure that a person was truly dead and had not merely slipped into a trance or coma. Attempts to legislate these recommendations, however, flew against Jewish burial customs that mandated that the deceased be under earth within a single day.

Did these initiatives have, in the end, any constructive impact on health in early modern Europe? Did they contribute to any appreciable decline in mortality and morbidity? These questions are virtually impossible to answer, mostly because we are unable to correlate improvements in environmental conditions with statistical declines in either sickness or death. Local studies have traced both positive and negative results. A correlation in time between the rise of the medicine of the environment and the global decline of mortality in western Europe certainly exists. Coincidence, however, is not the same as cause and effect. The variables involved are multiple and thus hard to evaluate. It seems logical, and even probable, that the clean-up campaigns banished some pathogens from the environment. Of course, contemporaries saw themselves as combating something else: miasmas, feculent air, and noxious odors. It may also be, as historians have long suggested, that "useful measures were taken for the wrong reasons."[44]

"The bookkeeping of the state"[45]

The passage of a few hundred years has allowed modern demographers to build up a much different picture of diseases in early modern times than contemporaries possessed. But early modern people

---

[43] Patrick Mouchet, "Une préoccupation nouvelle du XVIIIe siècle: La lutte contre les enterrements précipiés," *Annales de la société belge de histoire des hôpitaux et de la santé publique* 28 (1993): 35–49. Jan Bondeson, *Buried Alive: The Terrifying History of Our Most Primal Fear* (New York, 2001) offers a popular, albeit somewhat sensationalist, account.

[44] Riley draws a similar conclusion in *Campaign*, 151–54.

[45] "The bookkeeping of the state" is the phrase George Rosen applied to "political arithmetic" in Rosen, *A History of Public Health* (New York, 1956), 87.

certainly "knew" what killed them, their friends, and their relatives. Their perceptions, not ours, of course, conditioned responses both as individuals and as a collectivity and some of this knowledge built on numbers. Governments started counting to assess the impact of disease on their subjects rather early. Only in the seventeenth century, however, did these attempts become systematic, regular parts of governing. Raw data for the quantitative analysis of population and its state of health first began to be generated in the sixteenth century. Even before mid-century, Protestant parishes started to keep information on births and deaths, or rather on christenings and burials, as well as weddings. The Council of Trent (1545–63) required Catholic parishes to record christenings and marriages and, by the beginning of the seventeenth century, burials as well. One purpose of these registrations was religious; they documented legitimate marriages and births within different Christian communities. But governments quickly seized on the practical and political advantages accurate record-keeping promised for taxation and military purposes.

Even before parish registers became standard elements of the western European historical record, another document arose that offers scholars insights into the health and demographic stability of a given population: *Bills of Mortality* (Figure 6.2). Milan first recorded deaths from plague in 1452; other early bills date from 1496 in Mantua, 1504 in Venice, and 1554 in Modena. In England, the first ones appeared in 1538 and noted only plague deaths. Causes of death other than plague began to be registered in 1625. France collected similar numbers after 1667; Sweden began in 1686. Elsewhere in Europe the process of data collection on a large scale, to say nothing of collation or analysis, lagged. Some German and Italian states moved faster than others, but the political fragmentation of both areas frustrated the accumulation of "national" statistics.

Private individuals, rather than governments, took the initial steps toward purposeful analyses of data. William Petty (1623–87) was first of the so-called political arithmeticians and coined the term *political arithmetic*. Petty assembled an immense number of facts about England's commerce, population, and economic resources. His friend, John Graunt (1620–74), then correlated deaths with age in his *Natural and Political Observations on the Bills of Mortality* (1662). Graunt figured that by age six, one third of all human mortality had already occurred; thereafter, the chances of dying in any subsequent decade up to the age of seventy six was roughly equal. Like other great political arithmeticians of the day, such as Edmund Halley (c. 1656–1742) of comet fame and Johann Süssmilch (1707–67) in his *Die göttliche Ordnung in den Veränderungen des menschlichen Geschlechts* (The Godly Order in Human Affairs, 1756),

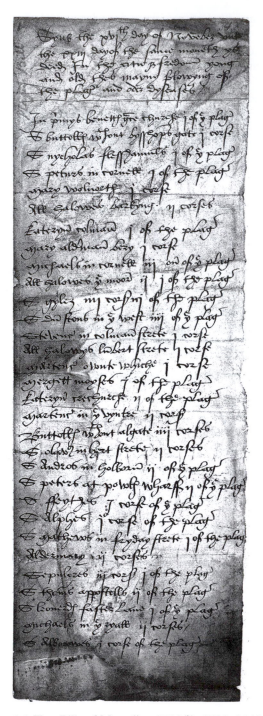

6.2 Two Bills of Mortality, 1512(?)–1532, 1665

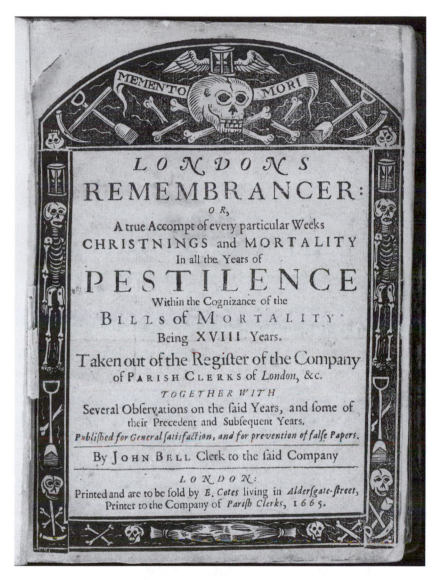

6.2 *(cont.)*

Graunt sought to illustrate the "grim regularity" of mortality statistics. Of course, no such simple uniformity exists and Graunt and others "as much invented as discovered" what Süssmilch admired as "a constant, general, great, complete, and beautiful order."[46]

[46] Lorraine Daston, *Classical Probability in the Enlightenment* (Princeton, 1988), 127–30.

Why did the search for patterns of mortality consume these men? Continued faith in the regularity of divine providence surely played a central role for some, but most were equally intrigued by the possibility of answering questions in political economy. Mercantilism, for instance, taught that the wealth of nations depended not only on their stores of precious metals, but also on the size, industriousness, and health of their human capital. The proper collection and analysis of vital statistics promised to allow for rational planning by determining, for example, whether there would be enough recruits of a proper age for the military available in any given year.

Other uses for vital statistics existed, of course. Many political arithmeticans wanted to create more accurate actuarial tables so that insurance schemes and annuities could be properly calculated and paid out without bankrupting the funds. A rash of financial failures involving early pension plans resulted from faulty conjectures about length of life and the chances of dying at any given age. Halley's famous "life table" (1693) took an important step in the direction of rational planning. The term for all this cataloguing and surveying came from the German: the word *statistic* is derived from the German word *Staat*.

The most famous, or notorious, demographic analysis of these years flowed from the pen of the Reverend Thomas Malthus (1766–1834). His *Essay on the Principle of Population* (1798) first conjured up the frightening specter of *over*population. Malthus argued that population growth, if unchecked, would soon outrun food supplies resulting in widespread distress, famine, and death. Malthus lived at the very end of our period and represents a significant shift away from the perspectives of other early modern political arithmeticians, political economists, and government authorities. These men had always worried about the unpropitious decline of population and hoped to use statistics to develop plans to increase its size. Malthus reversed the equation dramatically. To be sure, the political arithmeticians knew that overpopulation could engender misery and they never foolishly believed in the maxim of "the more the merrier." Frank expressed what many others understood: "if the increase in the number of people were left to the free play of the instincts of the sexes, we would soon attain a number that could cause mankind to suffocate itself."[47] While the vision of Frank and the mercantilists led in general to a vigorous expansion of public poor relief and medical care, Malthus provided opponents of charity with powerful ammunition for their case. According to him, charity all too often undermined industriousness, encouraged idleness, and led inevitably to greater wretchedness.

[47] Frank, *System*, 24.

The charitable impulse

The bonds among medical care, charity, and religion have always been tight. Judeo-Christian teachings encouraged beneficence to the less fortunate and especially to their coreligionists. Indeed, some scholars have persuasively argued that not only was the "philanthropic motive of the church . . . essential to its early success," but also that in the "development and extension of that role lies Christianity's chief contribution to healthy care."[48] Admittedly, feelings toward the poor were not always kindly or sympathetic. Still, nothing dried up the wellsprings of charity entirely. Chapter 5 demonstrated how frequently individuals and groups initiated the founding of hospitals. The realm of charity did not stop there, however. Aid to the suffering sick characterized many nursing and religious orders as well as the individual activities of laymen and women, while in late seventeenth and eighteenth centuries medical charities became a favored form for expressing a utilitarian type of benevolence. In exploring the relation between medicine and charity, we are once again confronted with complex bonds between religious and secular initiatives and between private and public activities. All private medical charities fulfilled civic desiderata and offered social benefits.

Virtually no early modern commentator on poor relief failed to count the ill among the fitting beneficiaries of charity. The sixteenth-century Englishman William Harrison (1534–93) numbered among the worthy poor: "the aged, blind, and lame," the "diseased person that is judged to be incurable," "the wounded soldier," and "the sick persone visited with grieuous . . . diseases," all of whom he separated from the thriftless and improvident who, in his opinion, merited no support.[49] In this, Catholic and Protestant attitudes differed hardly at all. The Swiss reformer Huldrych Zwingli (1484–1531) referred to the deserving poor and the ill as the "living images of God."

Many changes in poor relief and social welfare once facilely labeled "reformed" can be found in the policies of medieval cities and in the writings of fifteenth-century humanists. Natalie Zemon Davis for instance, has shown that in Lyon poor relief reform "cut across religious boundaries" and resulted from urban growth, economic expansion, the combined interests of professional men, city governors, and humanist

---

[48] Gary B. Ferngren, *Medicine and Health Care in Early Christianity* (Baltimore, 2009), 139.

[49] Quoted in Robert Jütte, *Poverty and Deviance in Early Modern Europe* (Cambridge, 1994), 11.

reformers. Moreover, "Protestants and Catholics worked together...
[thus showing] the extent to which it [poor relief] rested on values and
insights common to both."[50]

More recent historical research, however, has to some extent reinstated
the differences between Protestant and Catholic versions of poor relief.
Perhaps the greatest contribution of the Protestant Reformation was to
ally poor relief closely with religious reform. By binding charity more
tightly to existing governmental structures, the Reformers sought to erect
a Christian Commonwealth which "had an obligation to look after its
destitute members with the aim of helping them once more to become
valuable members of society."[51]

Both humanist and reformed writers on poor relief sharpened the distinction between the deserving and the undeserving poor: the medically
indigent, however, remained safely among the former. With the Reformation (although not solely because of the Reformation), medical care
became a central ingredient of poor relief at least in cities. Poor relief and
medical care entwined ever more closely with parish life.[52] Church officers (often known as deacons and elders) managed these programs. They
decided on an applicant's "worthiness." Assistance might involve arrang-
ing for a person to be admitted to a hospital, or for free medical care
from physicians, surgeons, apothecaries, or midwives who either contributed their services or were compensated through the common chest.
In Amsterdam during the 1630s, the well-known anatomist Nicolaes
Tulp (1593–1674), a physician, burgomaster, and elder of the Reformed
Church, drafted a plan to employ physicians, a surgeon, and an apothecary to care for the city's poor. Similarly crafted schemes were found
in Groningen and in the three Lutheran cities of Bremen, Hamburg,
and Lübeck. Such alternatives to institutional care reached a far larger
number of the poor in a community than could be admitted to hospitals.

Territorial states, like Denmark, Sweden, and England, likewise began
extending medical care to people who were not hospital inmates. The
spread of a Protestant ideology can account for much of this similarity
of thought and simultaneity of action, but the movement of people –
religious refugees, for instance – explains much as well. The influence
of Dutch non-Catholics who fled the Low Countries for England, or

---

[50] Natalie Zemon Davis, "Poor Relief, Humanism, and Heresy," in N. Z. Davis, *Society and Culture in Early Modern France: Eight Essays* (Stanford, 1965), 17–64, quote 59–60.
[51] Ole Peter Grell, "The Protestant Imperative of Christian Care and Neighbourly Love," in Grell and Andrew Cunningham, eds., *Health Care and Poor Relief in Protestant Europe, 1500–1700* (London, 1997), 58.
[52] Grell and Cunningham, eds., *Health Care*; and Grell and Cunningham, with Jon Arriza-balaga, eds., *Health Care and Poor Relief in Counter-Reformation Europe* (London, 1999).

Catholic areas for Protestant ones, was crucial. While in exile they endowed small hospitals and arranged home visiting care for members of their own community. They carried these ideas back with them when they returned to their homelands, but also left lasting impressions on their English hosts.[53]

The availability of health care for the indigent continued to expand, even when economic crises depressed the level of charitable giving. The definition of medical need widened in the centuries subsequent to the Reformation. While charitable medical assistance had never been restricted to the incurably ill, the invalid, and the elderly, by the seventeenth century medical relief more often sought to succor those Jean-Pierre Gutton once called the *potential poor* (*paupérisable*) or what others have referred to as the *laboring poor*. These people did not require relief as long as they remained healthy and able to work. Once they fell ill or lost their employment, however, they tumbled from the ranks of laborers into indigence. The eighteenth century witnessed a growing interest among medical men and the medical laity alike in experimenting with newer forms of medical charity, such as *dispensaries*, for just this category of the contingent poor.

Medical care for the poor was never value-free. Suspicion lingered that some medical conditions directly resulted from improvidence and vice. Moreover, while medical and charitable reformers spoke by no means hypocritically of the "reduction of human suffering" as their principal goal, they never lost sight of the need to "preserve the lives of the [laboring] poor [who] . . . are the hardest workers and thus the most valuable to the state." Christoph Wilhelm Hufeland (1762–1836) insisted that "only the sick man lacks all resources." Considerations of "capital" and "returns on investments" were frequently employed metaphors and informed a great deal of thinking about medical relief.

As criticisms of the "evils" of existing hospitals grew, plans for *domiciliary care* gained in popularity. These programs provided home-care by physicians who either donated their time or received payment from public funds. Such schemes had the apparent virtue of offering more economical forms of relief than hospitals. Not everyone agreed, however. Throughout Europe, the debate over the best form of medical care for the poor raged. Academic societies, such as the Göttingen Academy of Sciences, announced prize essays on the topic. An expansive and successful scheme opened in Hamburg in 1779, where a combination

---

[53] "The Reformation," in Grell and Cunningham, eds., *Health Care*, 34–35; Jonathan Israel, "Dutch Influence on Urban Planning, Health Care and Poor Relief: The North Sea and Baltic Regions of Europe, 1567–1720," in *ibid.*, 66–83.

of enlightened reformers, pastors, and physicians crafted a plan to provide medicines and medical care to the poor. From 1779 to 1781, this medical institute for the sick-poor attended about 3,500 patients; it treated another 90,000–100,000 cases from 1788–1815. Significantly, a large portion of these were not registered recipients of poor relief but members of the working classes who received medical care only. Physicians in eighteenth-century Barcelona advocated and staffed a similarly organized program of domiciliary assistance. Many English dispensaries, too, provided at-home care.[54]

These innovators largely accepted structural definitions of poverty in believing that economic dislocations caused most impoverishment. Nonetheless, Hamburg was not alone in assuring its financial supporters that it did not treat diseases arising from "criminal dissipations," from imprudence, or from lack of restraint, such as venereal diseases, alcoholism, and the pregnancies of unwed mothers. In point of fact, poor relief officers just as often helped "guilty" as well as "innocent" victims. Other forms of medical charity had slightly different roots and took somewhat different forms. Concurrent transformations in medical education, such as the founding of the Baldinger clinic in Göttingen in 1773, included the treatment of outpatients as well as serving as a school for ongoing medical students. Student doctors sometimes visited very ill patients in their homes.

Philanthropic impulses underlay a wide variety of specialized medical benefactions that became positive fads among the well-to-do. Between 1740 and 1770, for instance, Londoners founded at least two dozen medical charities. The Philanthropic Society in Paris (est. 1780) offered aid to artisans and shopkeepers struck by illness in order to forestall eventual destitution. Friendly societies in Barcelona did so as well. Provincial towns had charities, too, even if in smaller numbers than in capital cities.

Dispensaries, therefore, catered to a wide range of the working poor by distributing medical care and medicines. While historians have studied the rise of the dispensary movement most extensively in England, other countries also participated. Subscriptions underwrote dispensaries and drew funds from the affluent, but the influence of medical men was also central. Théophraste Renaudot organized one of the earliest dispensaries in Paris in 1630. His *bureau d'adresse* functioned both as a labor

[54] Mary Lindemann, "Urban Growth and Medical Charity: Hamburg, 1788–1815," in Jonathan Barry and Colin Jones, eds., *Medicine and Charity before the Welfare State* (London, 1991), 113–32; Alfons Zarzoso, "Poor Relief and Health Care in 18th and 19th Century Catalonia and Barcelona," in Ole Peter Grell, Andrew Cunningham, and Bernd Roeck, eds., *Health Care and Poor Relief in 18th and 19th Century Southern Europe* (Aldershot, 2005), 128; Browyn Croxson, "The Public and Private Faces of Eighteenth-Century London Dispensary Charity," *Medical History* 41 (1997): 128.

exchange and a facility for treating the sick-poor. The College of Physicians in London established a number of such institutions in the late seventeenth century and funded them until about 1725. In 1769, Dr. George Armstrong (1719–89) set up the first English dispensary for "the infant poor" in Red Lion Square, London. Armstrong's project died with its founder, but more dispensaries soon cropped up in London and then in provincial cities such as Bristol, Doncaster, Liverpool, Newcastle, and Birmingham. All acknowledged the same purpose of "administer[ing] medicine and advice to the poor, not only at the Dispensary, but also at their own habitations."[55]

Lying-in charities, too, neatly fused the goals of populationism with the wish to limit aid solely to the worthy poor. The London Lying-In Charity for Delivering Poor Married Women in Their Own Habitations (1758) bore "open testimony" in favor of marriage "on which not only the comfort, but the very support of human life so greatly depends; [and] which is the foundation of families and governments." The Society for Maternal Charity (*Société de charité maternelle*, 1788) served "a class of poor for whom there are neither hospitals nor foundations at Paris – namely the legitimate infants of the poor." Other organizations did not discriminate so rigorously between the married and unmarried. The Hamburg poor relief, for instance, paid midwives, surgeons, and accoucheurs to attend both married and unmarried women in childbirth. Perhaps most famously, Johann Peter Frank explicitly advocated care for all mothers: "The condition of pregnancy in unwed mothers is as estimable as in married women; both carry a citizen and a creature of God's making under their hearts."[56]

This longish history of health in society argues that initiatives in public health emerged from several sources. While the state in whatever form was never a trivial player, it is too simple – and wrong – to regard public health as exclusively the product of state initiatives. In all European countries, private endeavors and religious motivations powerfully

---

[55] Kathleen Wellman, *Making Science Social: The Conferences of Théophraste Renaudot, 1633–1642* (Norman, Okla., 2003), 38–47; J. C. Lettsom, *Medical Memoirs of the General Dispensary in London* (London, 1774), 19. On the history of the dispensary movement in England, see Irvine S. Loudon, "The Origins and Growth of the Dispensary Movement in England," *Bulletin of the History of Medicine* 55 (1981): 322–42; Croxson, "The Public and Private Faces," 127–30.

[56] Donna T. Andrew, "Two Medical Charities in Eighteenth-Century London: The Lock Hospital and the Lying-In Charity for Married Women," in Barry and Jones, eds., *Medicine and Charity*, 85; Stuart Woolf, "The Société de charité maternelle, 1788–1815," in *ibid.*, 100; Frank quoted in Mary Lindemann, "Maternal Politics: The Principles and Practices of Maternity Care in Eighteenth-Century Hamburg," *Journal of Family History* 9 (1984): 45.

Table 6.1. *Modern population rise,*
western Europe, 1500–1900 (ten selected
countries: Ireland, England, Norway,
Sweden, Netherlands, France, Germany,
Russia, Italy, Spain)

Year	Total inhabitants/millions
1500	84
1550	97
1600	111
1650	112
1700	125
1750	146
1800	195
1850	288
1900	422

Source: Massimo Livi Bacci, *The Population of*
Europe: A History, trans. by Cynthia De Nardi
Ipsen and Carl Ipsen (Oxford, 2000), 8.

affected public health if for no other reason than they provided the money
for charitable projects. If the relative abundance or scarcity of such undertakings varied from place to place, broader historical factors best explain
their presence or absence and the range of their activities. In the end we
must conclude that early modern society never regarded the health of its
people apathetically.

7 Healing

O *Thou Afflicted*, and under Distemper, Go to *Physicians* in *Obedience* to God, who has commanded the *Use of Means*. But place thy *Dependence* on God alone to Direct and Prosper them.[1]

So that the Physician, as a great Commander, hath as subordinate to him cooks for Diet, the surgeons for manual Operation, the Apothecaries for confecting and preparing medicine. You see how good and ample patrimony Physick hath . . .[2]

Take the sick person's . . . belt and bind it round his naked body as usual. When it is later removed, hang it on a nail, while saying these words: I pray to God, [and] to the three holy virgins, Margarita, Mary Magdalene, and Ursula, that you give this person a sign to let him know if he is suffering from a demon's work or not.[3]

Millions of people practiced medicine in early modern Europe. Few had academic qualifications and most were women. Healers came in many sizes, shapes, and descriptions, and offered an exceedingly wide array of services and medicines to the European population. Cooperation and coexistence characterized the relationships among these practitioners (and between them and their patients) as much as did competition and conflict. This chapter considers that range of early modern healers in all its richness.

It once seemed very simple for scholars to construct two medical worlds that faced each other as antagonists or stood for two totally

---

[1] Cotton Mather, "The Angel of Bethesda," quoted in James H. Smylie, "The Reformed Tradition," in Ronald L. Numbers and Darrel W. Amundsen, eds., *Caring and Curing: Health and Medicine in the Western Religious Tradition* (New York, 1986), 313.

[2] The seventeenth-century physician Francis Herring, quoted in Lucinda McCray Beier, *Sufferers and Healers: The Experience of Illness in Seventeenth-Century England* (London, 1987), 10.

[3] Description of a folk remedy by the sixteenth-century physician, Johannes Weyer, quoted in Robert Jütte, *Ärzte, Heiler und Patienten: Medizinischer Alltag in der frühen Neuzeit* (Munich, 1991), 152.

opposed approaches to medicine: that of the "quacks" and that of the few bonafide healers whose legitimation depended on their education, licenses, or membership in a guild. The latter group included physicians, surgeons (and barber-surgeons), apothecaries, bathmasters, and midwives and represented progress and "right-thinking." Beginning in the 1960s, however, social historians entering the field of medical history in greater numbers began to think in different ways about those two groups. Increasingly, they emphasized not knowledge and ignorance, but economic and cultural conflicts between "elite" and "popular" medicines. At first, scholars tended to view the two types or groups as isolated from, and hostile to, each other. In the succeeding decades, however, historians began to recognize the multiplicity of healers and the heterogeneity of healing practices, noting, for instance, the prominent role of apothecaries as "general practitioners"; the importance of surgeons and barber-surgeons; the functions of magic and astrology in healing; the centrality of religion; and indeed the vast if often ill-defined area of what was called "popular medicine." In addition, attention turned more to a consideration of the multiple roles of the patient: sufferer, patron, client, and also (self-)healer.

This work led historians to realize that "the frontiers between orthodox and unorthodox medicine have [always] been flexible . . . So mobile have become their boundaries, that one age's quackery has often become another's orthodoxy."[4] Thus, the therapeutic practices and even, to a large extent, the medical theories of the village quack, the sufferer seeking her or his own cure, the surgeon, the apothecary, and the university-trained physician rarely differed all that much. Moreover, newer work in medical history, and especially in gender history, has suggested fruitful ways of reconceptualizing "medicine" that allow virtually invisible healers, that is, those often absent or poorly represented in written records or whose presence was only noted by their opponents, to emerge from obscurity. Katherine Brown and Mary Fissell have recently argued that healing should be situated within a larger framework they term "bodywork" that "investigate[s] the relationship between the work we consider medicine and the broader category of attending to the human body." Those who labored in the field of bodywork thus included, for example, searchers (mostly women) for plague, barbers, wet-nurses, and, for that matter, executioners. This wider definition allows us to understand the ways in which bodyworkers practiced medicine and also directs us to

---

[4] W. F. Bynum and Roy Porter, "Introduction," to Bynum and Porter, eds., *Medical Fringe and Medical Orthodoxy, 1750–1850* (London, 1987), 1.

include care as well as cure within our conception of what medicine "did."[5]

While historians of medicine have often been interested in discussing the professionalization process, seeking its roots in early modern times, for example, and searching for the beginnings of a purported medicalization, these issues concerned sufferers rarely, if at all. Certainly, by 1500 a university education had become for the physician a way to separate himself from artisanal healers, to situate himself among the intellectual elite, and also to attain social prominence. Once the academic study of medicine had been institutionalized in the medieval universities, the status of the physician often derived from his reputation as a *litterateur*. The Dutch physician and philologist Gisbert Longolius (1507–43) provides a good example of the phenomenon. A body-physician to the archbishop of Cologne, he was also a well-respected teacher and translator of Greek.

Whether or not people placed much faith in the capacity of such intellectuals to heal or chose them as their doctors are other matters altogether. Not until the nineteenth century, and probably not much before the end of that century, were Europeans successfully medicalized to the extent that physicians became their clear first choice as healers. Shifting patterns of medical licensing and more vigorous state intervention into medical practice and public health spurred that evolution. Before then, people generally did not perceive academically trained physicians as especially or uniquely qualified to heal. Physicians, in short, by no means monopolized and controlled, or even dominated, the medical marketplace. Rather, physicians competed on equal or even disadvantageous terms with a wide range of healers for the medical trade of the day.

Sufferers and healers

The patient–practitioner relationship is an important one for the history of medicine, but it has proved somewhat difficult to open up to historical scrutiny. In the 1940s, the eminent American sociologist Talcott Parsons addressed the reciprocity inherent in the interaction between doctors and patients. When ill, the patient assumes what Parsons called "the sick-role." The sick person is, on the one hand, excused his or her social

[5] Mary Fissell, "Introduction: Women, Health, and Healing in Early Modern Europe," *Bulletin of the History of Medicine* [Special edition on "Women, Health, and Healing in Early Modern Europe] 82 (2008): 10–14; Margaret Pelling, "Nurses and Nursekeepers: Problems of Identification in the Early Modern Period," in Margaret Pelling, *The Common Lot: Sickness, Medical Occupations, and the Urban Poor in Early Modern England, Essays* (London, 1998), 179–202.

responsibilities, but, on the other, is expected to desire a return to health and to comply unquestioningly with the directives of medical experts in order to achieve this goal.[6] Unfortunately, this model works only very imperfectly for early modern times.

More historically relevant is the interpretation the sociologist Nicholas Jewson advanced on the historical evolution of the patient's role. In two frequently cited articles, Jewson documents a shift from what he calls "bedside medicine" – in which the patient controlled the medical consultation – to "hospital medicine" – in which the patient was increasingly subordinated to the voice of a medical authority, especially that of the physician. (A third step in this process, toward "laboratory medicine," occurred in the late nineteenth and early twentieth centuries and further accelerated the alienation of the patient from his or her own perceptions of illness.)[7]

In early modern times, therefore, patients largely determined the dynamics of the medical encounter as well as having a good deal to say about the course of treatment. The patient functioned as a patron, who called the physician to the bedside. Because most people who consulted physicians, according to Jewson's model, were wealthy or at least prosperous, the patient's status frequently exceeded that of the attending doctor. Patients quickly dismissed practitioners whose medicines did not work, whose cures they disliked, or whom they found personally distasteful, unpleasant, or discourteous. The early modern medical consultation, Jewson argues, depended heavily on the patient's reporting her or his own case-history: the *patient narrative*. Reliance on the patient narrative reversed the roles we have come to expect: the patient, not the practitioner, played the active partner in the consultation or medical encounter. Not until about 1800, with the rise of hospital medicine and the clinico-anatomical method (see Chapter 3), did control migrate away from the patient. Physicians then moved to center stage in the drama of medical practice. The patient's own story was subordinated to the physician's special knowledge gained from increasingly meticulous and intrusive physical examinations and clinical studies informed by morbid anatomy and pathology.

Jewson's paradigm has greatly influenced historians studying the dynamics of medical practice. While his version neatly links transformations

---

[6] Talcott Parsons, "Definitions of Health and Illness in the Light of American Values and Social Structure," in E. Gartly Jaco, ed., *Patients, Physicians, and Illness: Sourcebook in Behavioral Science and Medicine* (New York, 1958), 165–87.

[7] N. D. Jewson, "Medical Knowledge and the Patronage System in 18th Century England," *Sociology* 8 (1974), 369–85; Jewson, "The Disappearance of the Sick-Man from Medical Cosmology, 1770–1870," *Sociology* 10 (1976), 225–44.

in social and cultural authority with developments in medical knowledge and with institutional change, it fails to catch the complexities of early modern medical encounters, and it does not really address the most frequent of these: those between sufferers and nonphysician healers, where power and status relationships differed substantially from those between wealthy patients and physicians. Many factors influenced interactions between healers and sufferers and the relationship was neither exclusively that of patient/practitioner nor that of patron/client.

Historians have also been interested in assessing the availability of healers. Throughout our period, rural/urban differences remained significant. Writing in 1974, Jean-Pierre Goubert spoke of late eighteenth-century France as a *désert médical*. Goubert's striking phrase, however, has been much misinterpreted.[8] By it, he indicated the dearth of university-trained physicians, and not of other practitioners, who, he recognized, were plentiful in both country and city. Historians writing on early modern medical practice tend to accept the position Margaret Pelling and Charles Webster charted out. They defined a medical practitioner as "any individual whose occupation is basically concerned with the care of the sick." That occupation need not be, and seldom was, a full-time job and often did not supply a majority or even a goodly portion of a person's income.[9] Dr. Daniël van Buren, who lived in Amsterdam in the first half of the eighteenth century, had trained at the university of Leiden. He served as physician to the city's *gasthuis* (a combined hospital and almshouse) and on the board of the municipality's *collegium* medici. But he also owned a fleet of boats and barges and was a merchant contractor heavily engaged in the inland water trade from which he drew most of his considerable income. Likewise, in the 1620s and 1630s, the Reformed pastor, Henricus Alutarius, resident in Woerden and then Rotterdam, combined a clerical career with that of *medicus*.

Thus, the answer to the question of "how many practitioners" varies depending on the definition. Some examples, however, illustrate contemporary realities. Groningen, a provincial center in the north of the Dutch Republic with a population of about 20,000, had fourteen physicians in the sixteenth century, fifty-three in the seventeenth century, and thirty in the eighteenth. Nonphysician practitioners present between 1553 and 1594 included thirty-seven barber-surgeons. The guild of master surgeons registered 171 members from 1597 to 1730. In about the same period (1578–1730) some sixty-five itinerants (*reizende meesters*) – a group

---

[8] Jean-Pierre Goubert, *Malades et médecins en Bretagne, 1770–1790* (Paris, 1974).
[9] Margaret Pelling and Charles Webster, "Medical Practitioners," in Webster, ed., *Health, Medicine and Mortality in the Sixteenth Century* (Cambridge, 1979), 166.

including dentists, corn-parers, cutters for bladder stones (*lithotomists*), and oculists who specialized in treating cataracts – applied to the city government for permission to practice; several peripatetics were female. Rural provinces, such as Veluwe and Overijssel, had about one practitioner for every 1,400–1,700 inhabitants, while the more urbanized areas of North Holland had one for every 500. Late sixteenth-century Norwich (England) had about one practitioner for every 200 town residents. Roughly 50 physicians, 100 surgeons, the same number of apothecaries, and 250 "other" practitioners resided in sixteenth- and seventeenth-century London. During the same centuries in France, only large towns like Paris, Montpellier, Lyon, and Marseilles supported many graduate practitioners. And the numbers fluctuated. Best-guess estimates suggest that there were about 400 such physicians in France in 1520, and 1,750 in the middle of the seventeenth century, but perhaps only 1,300 by 1700. Surgeons were more plentiful: about 2,000 in the 1530s and 1540s; more than 3,000 a half-century later; 8,400 in the 1650s; and 6,350 in the 1690s. This state of affairs changed dramatically in the eighteenth century. In France, as elsewhere in western and central Europe, the total number of practitioners shot up as did the number of physicians. Paris, for instance, with a population of 660,000, had 153 physicians, 192 surgeons, and 135 apothecaries, while Orléans, a city of 48,500, was proportionately as well-endowed with 10 physicians, 16 surgeons, and 14 apothecaries.[10]

Yet, despite this overwhelming evidence to the contrary, the myth of medical insufficiency persists. In fact, the range and actual number of healers in early modern times were always great and "someone who fell ill . . . found a profusion of health care providers eager for his or her custom." Matthew Ramsey points out that "it now appears that by the end of the Old Regime the majority of Frenchmen may have been in a position to consult an authorized healer."[11] Even in rural areas, by the 1700s the number of university-trained physicians was growing and the increase occurred fastest in places like many of the German states, parts of Scandinavia, and some Italian states, where governments had erected networks of health officers and paid them salaries.

---

[10] Laurence Brockliss and Colin Jones, *The Medical World of Early Modern France* (Oxford, 1997), 198–207; Frank Huisman, *Stadsbelang en standsbesef: gezondheidszorg en medisch beroep in Groningen 1500–1730* (Rotterdam, 1992), 57, 95–96, 103–06; Margaret Pelling, "Occupational Diversity: Barber-Surgeons and Other Trades, 1550–1640," in Pelling, *The Common Lot*, 203–29.

[11] Mary E. Fissell, *Patients, Power, and the Poor in Eighteenth-Century Bristol* (Cambridge, 1991), 37; Matthew Ramsey, *Professional and Popular Medicine in France, 1770–1830: The Social World of Medical Practice* (Cambridge, 1988), 62.

The proportion of physicians to all other practitioners remained low, of course. The number of licensed surgeons, barber-surgeons, apothecaries, midwives, bathmasters, and even itinerant *operators*, always far exceeded the number of academically trained physicians. But multitudinous others practiced medicine, too. Among them we find cunning-folk, astrological healers, Catholic priests, Protestant clergymen, gentlefolk, executioners, and nobles, to list just some. By 1800, almost all governments had regulations in place to define legitimate practice and practitioners. Still, these ordinances by no means reflect the reality of medical practice. Moreover, the constraints governments set on practice did not coincide with popular understanding of "proper" or "appropriate" healers.

The selection of a healer turned on many variables: the perception of ability counted, of course, but so, too, did the healer's position in a community, personal habits, and fees. Scholars have often evoked this last factor – expense – to explain why few people consulted physicians: they were too dear. Such a calculation goes wrong in two ways. First, many physicians took on a good deal of what might be termed *pro bono* work. Moreover, many physicians received payments from government agencies, like parishes, to treat those unable to afford their services. Second, and more important, medical decision making was a complex process. People frequently paid what might objectively seem exorbitant sums for medicines and advice. Thus, a simple correlation comparing, for example, the amount of a day's wage to the cost of a drug or a fee misses the point.

Above all, medical promiscuity characterized early modern people. They often, perhaps even usually, consulted several practitioners serially or concurrently. That behavior was by no means limited to the lower reaches of society; a monarch, a lord, or a wealthy patrician just as readily sought advice from a range of practitioners as did an artisan, cowherd, or goose-girl. It is simply not true that the well-to-do patronized "legitimate" practitioners, and especially physicians, while the less well-off frequented the lower ranks of medical practitioners or sought out "quacks."

Medical practice for virtually everyone, however, began at home. Self-help, of course, quickly shaded over into guidance sought from friends, neighbors, and family and the lines separating the "family" from the "household" from the "outside" should not be too firmly drawn; the boundaries were in fact extremely fluid. Every household treasured its own assortment of time-tested remedies for everyday ills. Recipe collections and commonplace books, which ranged from meticulously written, laboriously compiled, and beautifully bound tomes to scraps of paper stuffed into folders almost haphazardly, abounded in the early modern world. Not surprisingly, women assembled many of them.[12]

Most people had a sense of what they required to remain well, even if these ideas might seem today rather odd or even counterproductive. They felt confidence in their own decisions about medicines. Correspondence between physicians and patients (albeit obviously literate and mostly wealthy or noble ones) indicates that physicians, too, allowed patients considerable latitude in their choices, offering suggestions rather than giving orders.[13] Daily habits depended heavily on individual differences, but usually reflected deep-seated Galenic principles. In other words, what was considered good for one person might prove harmful or even deadly to another. Joan Lane, in a review of the diaries and letters of the eighteenth-century English, refers to a man who blamed his bodily discomfort to eating "unwisely." He seldom found himself ill if he consumed only "plain foods," while "made dishes and sauces" always upset his digestion. A sixteenth-century German refrained from cheese and anything containing it because it caused physical discomfort.[14]

These examples indicate how indistinct was the boundary between preventive and therapeutic care. Regimens to preserve health usually rested explicitly or implicitly on the medical doctrine of the six nonnaturals and stressed moderation in eating, drinking, and sexual intercourse, and regularity in evacuations and exercise. With the advent of printing, regimen books and self-help manuals began to pour off the presses. These recommended ways to assure a long life (what later became known as *prolongevity*). Particularly popular, and often reprinted, were Thomas Elyot's (1490?–1546) *Castel of Helth* (1539); Luigi Cornaro's *Discorsi della vita sobria* (Sure and Certain Methods of Attaining a Long and Healthy Life, which appeared in twelve editions and in several languages from 1558–1724); George Cheyne's (1673–1743) *An Essay on Health and Long Life* (1724); and, finally, Christoph Hufeland's best-selling *Die Kunst des menschlichen Lebens zu verlängern* (The Art of Prolonging Life, in eight editions from 1776 to 1860).

Guides to a long life were not the sole form of medical self-help literature available. Manuals also addressed sexuality, reproduction,

---

[12] Linda A. Pollock, *With Faith and Physic: The Life of a Tudor Gentlewoman, Lady Grace Mildmay, 1552–1620* (London, 1993); Elaine Leong, "Making Medicines in the Early Modern Household," *Bulletin of the History of Medicine* 82 (2008): 145–68.

[13] Alisha Rankin, "Duchess, Heal Thyself: Elisabeth of Rochlitz and the Patient's Perspective in Early Modern Germany," *Bulletin of the History of Medicine* 82 (2008): 125.

[14] Joan Lane, "'The Doctor Scolds Me': The Diaries and Correspondence of Patients in Eighteenth Century England," in Roy Porter, ed., *Patients and Practitioners: Lay Perceptions of Medicine in Pre-Industrial Society* (Cambridge, 1985), 241; Jütte, *Ärzte, Heiler und Patienten*, 43.

child-bearing and child-rearing. In the middle of the seventeenth century, Nicholas Culpeper (1616–54) produced a number of popular guides to health including one that appeared in 1651 with the subtitle: *A Guide for Women, in their Conception, Bearing, and Suckling their Children.* Jean-Charles Desessartz (1729–1811) wrote a *Traité de l'education corporelle des enfans en bas âge* (Treatise on the Physical Education of Very Young Children, 1760) that railed against the custom of sending children out to wet-nurses. But nothing was as nearly so influential as Jean-Jacques Rousseau's (1712–78) novel, *Émile, ou de l'Éducation* (1762). There were also manuals for old age, such as John Floyer's *Medicina Gerocomica or, the Galenic Art of Preserving Old Men's Healths, Explain'd in Twenty Chapters* (1724) and, for those who lived a sedentary lifestyle, such as Samuel Tissot's *Avis, au gens des lettres et aux personnes sédentaires sur leur santé* (Advice to Men of Letters and Sedentary Persons on their Health, 1767). The Swiss Tissot was a publishing phenomenon who churned out a widely disseminated and frequently translated general guide to health, as well as penning an anti-masturbation jeremiad.

Choices

What did people do when they "recognize[d] some pain, discomfort, or other signs of organic malfunctioning"? In other words, to use the term medical sociologists often apply, what was their "illness behavior"?[15] Whom did they consult? When did they go beyond self-help or move outside the circle of family, friends, neighbors, and relatives? How far afield did they range in searching for healers? In 1978, Øvind Larsen proposed an "onion model" of morbidity that postulated a fairly regular progression from "feeling sick," to seeking the assistance of a physician, to entering a hospital. This model is, of course, too inflexible to catch the many permutations of medical choices that early modern people made; people did not necessarily start at home and move progressively outward. Medical choice always has an idiosyncratic character to it. Thus, no single example can typify early modern medical decision making.

Still, much medical care took place in the home and this meant that the first practitioners of choice were frequently family members, and often women. A recent analysis of women's role in healing is unequiv-ocal: "Women . . . were central to health and healing before 1800."[16] At every level of society, this held true. Noblewomen, like Anna of Saxony, for instance, not only treated their household members but frequently

---

[15] Edward A. Suchman, "Stages of Illness and Medical Care," in Jaco, ed., *Patients*, 145.
[16] Fissell, "Introduction," 1.

involved themselves in medicine more widely.[17] At the same time, illness within the family created disorder, discomfort, and anxiety shared to a greater or lesser extent by all. Families often decided on treatments and on when to move outside the family for assistance and whom to consult. "Family medicine" could include paid assistance in the form of servants or specially hired helpers. The ability to employ outsiders, of course, depended on a level of wealth but it was hardly unusual for servants to be involved in household medical care. When ill they, too, were usually nursed at home. In addition, outsiders could become influential in family decisions and not only about medicines. The presence of a physician, surgeon, or midwife could complicate the process of medical decision making within the family by creating alliances or factions.[18]

Evidence on medical choice comes from numerous and disparate sources: diaries, chronicles, correspondence, and legal cases. The sixteenth-century Cologne city councilor Hermann Weinsberg (1518– 97) filled more than 4,000 manuscript pages with his autobiographical "notes."[19] Weinsberg recorded 153 bouts of illness or afflictions affecting his family. In thirty-four cases he consulted a "Medicus"; in twenty-five cases, a surgeon; and in six cases an "Empiriker" or a wise woman. Otherwise, Weinsberg did nothing or applied home remedies. When his nephew suffered from "fever and chills," Weinsberg advised "good beer and bread and some wine and herbs mixed with sugar." Weinsberg possessed a herbal for reference and used vegetable remedies, either self-concocted or purchased from an apothecary or a root-wife. Knowledge of common plants and their prophylactic and curative powers was virtually universal. Herbs like fennel, broom, rhubarb, mustard, and valerian, that grew almost everywhere, could be used to treat myriad ailments.

Because regularity of evacuations counted as one of the golden rules of regimen, many people believed health demanded a periodic internal "cleansing." Purges and blood-letting made up part of the treatment that Weinsberg's wife received when she fell seriously ill in 1557. First, she had blood let. Her urine was examined (by a physician?). Weinsberg then called in two or three "medici" and solicited the advice of a wise woman.

---

[17] Alisha Michelle Rankin, "Medicine for the Uncommon Woman: Experience, Experiment, and Exchange in Early Modern Germany" (diss., Harvard University, 2005).

[18] Robert Jütte, "'Wo kein Weib ist, da seufzet der Kranke'– Familie und Krankheit im 16. Jahrhundert," *Jahrbuch des Instituts für Geschichte der Medizin der Robert Bosch Stiftung* 7 (1988): 7–24; Lisa W. Smith, "Reassessing the Role of the Family: Women's Medical Care in Eighteenth-Century England," *Social History of Medicine* 16 (2003): 327–42.

[19] Material on Hermann Weinsberg is taken from Jütte, *Ärzte, Heiler und Patienten*, 12, 77, 82, 97.

Another physician recommended a purge. All for naught; less than two weeks after falling ill, she died.

Samuel Pepys, surely the most famous of English diarists, commented almost obsessively on health and illness, especially his own.[20] When Pepys commenced his diary in 1660, he was twenty-six years old. He had already survived a serious illness and undergone a major surgical intervention; four years earlier he had been successfully "cut for the stone." Urological complaints, however, recurred throughout the years his diary covered (1660–69) and eventually led to his death in 1703. Like many contemporaries, he worried about chills and especially their effect on his "yard and stones" (penis and testicles). In 1666, he recorded being "in some pain of the collique [colic or belly ache] – hav[ing] of late taken too much cold by washing my feet and going in a thin silk waistcoat, without any other coat over it, and open-breasted." Pepys's normal precautions for preserving his health involved not "ketching cold."

Pepys's regimen was hardly unique; it was not even unusual. Besides avoiding damp and drafts, he had blood let at irregular intervals. On Sunday, May 4, 1662, he called upon the surgeon Mr. Holliard to "let me blood, about 16 ounces" as he felt "exceedingly full of blood." Later, he turned to phlebotomy for therapeutic reasons and in summer 1668 wrote that he "was let blood, and did bleed about 14 ounces, toward curing my eyes." Regimens could be preventive or therapeutic and the advice friends gave him in 1664 to "cure" his childlessness included widely accepted notions:

1. Do not hug my wife too hard nor too much.
2. Eat no late suppers.
3. Drink juyce of sage.
4. Tent [a Spanish wine] and toast.
5. Wear cool holland-drawers [loose undergarments].
6. Keep stomach warm and back cool.
7. Upon my query whether it was best to do at night or morn, they answered me neither one nor other, but when we have most mind to it.
8. Wife not to go too straitlaced.
9. Myself to drink mum [an herbal ale] and sugar.
10. Mrs. Ward did give me to change my plat [diet].

In 1667, his eyes began to trouble him greatly and diary entries from 1668 and 1669 record repeated bouts of eyestrain and his fears of going blind. In June 1668, he consulted the celebrated eye specialist Dawbigney Turberville (1612–96) who recommended a laxative and "also a glass

---

[20] The standard edition is *The Diary of Samuel Pepys: A New and Complete Transcription*, ed. by Robert Latham and William Matthews (11 vols., London, 1970–83).

of something to drop into my eyes." In spring 1669, on going to his haberdasher to pick up a belt "the colour of my new suit," he learned that "the mistress of the house, an oldish woman in a hat, hath some water for the eyes, she did dress me, making my eyes smart most horribly," and yet he hoped "it will do me good." Despite these efforts his vision deteriorated, leading him to abandon writing his journal a month later. Pepys did not, however, go blind. His eyes improved, but fear of losing his sight made him dictate his journal to clerks thereafter.

Liselotte von der Pflaz (1652–1722), the sister-in-law of Louis XIV, regarded doctors skeptically.[21] When Liselotte first arrived at court in 1671, Madame de Sévigné noted that

she has no use for doctors and even less for medicines . . . When her doctor was presented to her, she said that she did not need him, that she had never been purged or bled, and that when she is not feeling well she goes for a walk and cures herself by exercise.

Although she did submit, reluctantly, to the ministrations of physicians and surgeons on occasion, she continued to believe that the best ways of preserving and recovering her health were to exercise regularly, drink lots of water, and to use only a few simple remedies such as an egg beaten with boiling water, sugar, and cinnamon for a cough or warm baked bread applied to an aching ear. In 1683, on the death of the queen, she castigated the royal physicians whose "ignorance . . . killed her as surely as if they had thrust a dagger into her heart." Moreover, she insisted that "no child is safe [at court], for the doctors here have already helped five of the Queen's to the other world." Other court healers fared little better with her. In 1697, she fractured her arm in a hunting accident. A country-barber set it and "it would have healed in two weeks if the court barbers had not practiced their art on me afterward, which, I believe, will cripple me for good." While Liselotte's disdain for doctors may have been more pronounced than typical for seventeenth-century nobles, many agreed with her. Liselotte's generally robust health and her attitude toward preserving it was echoed by the experience of another princess: Catherine the Great of Russia. Like Liselotte, Catherine eschewed the treatments her physicians prescribed in favor of relaxation, bed rest, moderate diet, and mild exercise.

The journal of the Reverend Ralph Josselin offers a picture of what a family of the middling sort might do when faced with illness or

---

[21] Here I rely on the excellent work of Elborg Forster, trans., *A Woman's Life in the Court of the Sun King: Letters of Liselotte von der Pflaz, 1652–1722* (Baltimore, 1984) and her "From the Patient's Point of View: Illness and Health in the Letters of Liselotte von der Pflaz (1652–1722)," *Bulletin of the History of Medicine* 60 (1986): 297–320.

accidents.[22] Josselin mentions illness 762 times, but only in 79 of these instances did he record treatments and in only 21 cases does he indicate consulting a healer outside the family circle. He and his wife, Jane, diagnosed and handled most familial ills, dosing themselves, their children, and their servants. While they relied heavily on herbal remedies (like many other women, Jane brewed common medicines such as hyssop syrup herself), they occasionally obtained preparations from an apothecary or used proprietary medicines such as Daffy's Elixir and Tabor's Pills. The couple also sought assistance from others: a nearby gentlewoman, several neighbors, and two local bonesetters (both women). The Josselins rarely called upon a physician: once for Ralph, during an attack of ague, once to the bed of a dying child, and twice for Ralph in his final illness.[23]

The Josselin diary highlights several important points. First, the family did not distinguish clearly between trifling ailments which could be safely relegated to home remedies and more serious ones for which they felt it imperative to call on a physician or surgeon. Second, children were not neglected. Parents frequently consulted a physician or surgeon for their offspring and certain maladies or accidents, such as fractured limbs, genital deformities, or eye conditions that threatened loss of sight, were reasons to confer with a physician or surgeon. Miquel Parets in seventeenth-century Spain, for example, recorded that his ten-year-old son had "died [in 1651] of a disease of a bone in his arm following five years of illness which cost me a great many ducats, and during the last year and a half surgeons came daily to look after him."[24] Finally, the Josselin family had its own identity and unique characteristics. Their behavior did not typify families of a middling sort. The Josselins, perhaps more than others, believed that "the best preventive medicine was a sinless life," but that precept was so widely accepted that it does not portend exceptional religious feeling (despite Ralph's profession as a pastor). Many God-fearing people, such as the Reverend Cotton Mather, whose quote begins this chapter, fully believed in availing themselves of a physician's assistance. Other families and other individuals, of course, made different choices in similar circumstances.

[22] *The Diary of Ralph Josselin, 1616–1683*, ed. by Alan Macfarlane (London, 1976).
[23] Lucinda McCray Beier, "In Sickness and in Health: A Seventeenth Century Family's Experience," in Porter, ed., *Patients and Practitioners*, 101–28.
[24] James S. Amelang, trans. and ed., *A Journal of the Plague Year: The Diary of the Barcelona Tanner Miquel Parets 1651* (New York, 1991), 60; Margaret Pelling, "Child Health as a Social Value in Early Modern England," in Pelling, *The Common Lot*, 105–33.

Diaries, journals, correspondence, and autobiographies are articulate witnesses, but also unusual sources. While we possess some similar documents for artisans and peasants, we usually must look elsewhere to discover the medical practices of the great majority of early modern people who were illiterate, kept no journals, or never wrote letters. Fortunately, some sources allow us to peer into their lives. Beginning in the sixteenth century, the European lettered elite became curious about popular culture, if often only to deplore its errors and vulgarity. Laurent Joubert (1529–83) meticulously recorded *Erreurs populaires au fait de la médecine et régime de santé* (Popular Errors in Regard to Medicine and the Regimen of Health, 1578). We should not, however, accept his perceptions as accurate reflections of reality; they perhaps tell us more about Joubert and his social group than about "the people" he observed. Governments, too, assembled huge caches of information that illuminate the process of medical choice in the early modern world. Most famous of these was the *enquête* the *Société royale de médecine* initiated toward the end of the eighteenth century. It uncovered surprisingly deep reservoirs of "superstitious practices." Other documents, however, present a different and more nuanced picture. Notions labeled "errors" or "superstitions" were often deeply entwined with religious beliefs as well as with naturalistic concepts of cure. For example, if we look at the ways ordinary people made their medical choices in the late seventeenth and eighteenth centuries, we observe how varied were the possibilities and how mixed, but not irrational, was the logic behind them.

One way to do this is to examine some individual practitioners. The seventeenth-century London surgeon Joseph Binns (d. 1664) had an extensive practice. Most frequently he treated venereal diseases, but he also tended many cases of wounds, fractures, tumors, and fistulas. His patients came from virtually all social classes, but a plurality from the "middling" groups. He treated more men than woman, by about a ratio of 3:1, and visited most of his patients more than five times.[25] In the early decades of the eighteenth century, Dr. Johann Barthold maintained an extensive medical practice in the smaller town of Braunschweig in northwestern Germany. (While it seems that "Dr." Barthold had never acquired a doctorate in medicine, he had studied at the University of Helmstedt.) Similarly, people from almost every social group called upon his services. Barthold had established a contract with the Tailors' Guild and treated a large number of them, their family members, and their servants. During an eighteen-month period in 1712–14, he saw 329 patients: 211 were adults (67.2 percent) and 103 were

---

[25] Beier, *Sufferers and Healers*, 51–96.

children under fourteen (31.3 percent); 162 were male (49.2 percent) and 112 were female (34.0 percent). Thus, although he saw about two adults for every child and somewhat more men than women, neither women nor children nor the elderly, for that matter, were unrepresented. He did not have an extensive gynecological practice, treating just an occasional case of the "vapors" (fainting or hysteria), for instance. Patients most often came to him with fevers (which made up 39.2 percent of all cases); "ardent or burning fever" formed his most frequent diagnosis. Ninety-one patients (27.7 percent) sought his help for chest ailments ranging from consumption and pleurisy to "suffocation" and "tightness"; twelve (3.65 percent) saw him for dysentery; and seven (2.1 percent) for head colds. The remaining quarter of his business included scattered cases of epilepsy, rheumatism, arthritis, vertigo, jaundice, dropsy, "hectic," stroke, apoplexy, indigestion, and palpitations (this last only among women). The few surgical interventions (sixteen) included treatments for stones, hernias, cataracts; his practice was far more medical than surgical in nature by a ratio of at least 20:1.[26]

More people lived in rural areas than cities and towns, but we tend to know less about them. Still, the countryside is by no means a complete *terra incognita*. In the small market town of Hehlen in northwestern Germany (with 673 inhabitants in 1793), the pastor, Johann Uphoff, faithfully recorded causes of death and incidences of illness from 1751 to 1760. He listed a total of eighty-one "ill." Although many villagers saw no one for their problems, just as many, it seems, saw several practitioners. No physician dwelt in Hehlen, but thirteen people went to physicians elsewhere, traveling several miles down the Weser River to the town of Hameln. Eight persons procured medicines and advice from apothecaries in the nearby towns of Bodenwerder and Heyen. Three relied exclusively on home remedies; two purchased medicines from an unspecified "elsewhere"; and two swore by "the remedies of a man by the name of Meßing in Halle," another small town not far away. Ten turned to a local military surgeon or the regimental surgeon stationed in Hameln. Another person saw a surgeon whose name she failed to recall, one woman consulted an executioner, and four persons called on a man named Flentje, who was identified as a shepherd. In forty-three instances the name of the healer was listed as "unknown," or Uphoff remarked that the patient had seen "no doctor" or "used no medicine."[27]

---

[26] Robert Jütte, "A Seventeenth-Century German Barber-Surgeon and His Patients," *Medical History* 33 (1989): 184–98; Mary Lindemann, *Health and Healing in Eighteenth-Century Germany* (Baltimore, 1996), 324–25.

[27] Lindemann, *Health and Healing*, 252–57.

As these accounts suggest, people often moved from one healer to another in long-term quests for cure, even for ailments they perceived as neither particularly dangerous nor life-threatening. In thinking about this process of selecting a healer, we should bear four points in mind. First, serial and simultaneous consultations were the rule. People rarely satisfied themselves with the advice of a single healer and conferred with a number of people at the same time; they felt thereby little disquietude or embarrassment. Second, a wide range of healers was at hand. Third, little sense existed that particular ailments or afflictions belonged exclusively to the territory of a certain practitioner, although specialists – bone-setters, lithotomists, oculists, and tooth-drawers – abounded. Finally, people rarely seem to have distinguished rigorously between minor and major ailments. The first might quickly become the second as scabies or "the itch" could turn inward and cause a more perilous "corruption." Likewise, most people linked the external and internal domains of the body, as well as body and soul. Lay and learned medical knowledge assumed that external ailments could become internal ones, that external ailments might need internal treatments, or that an external sign indicated an internal condition. Similarly, seeking physical help did not rule out providential cures as well.

Decisions were never totally predictable and individuals behaved with little regard to historians' wishes to discover patterns. Many people struck by grave illness or who were suffering from serious wounds or terrible accidents never consulted anyone outside their families. Some feared or disdained physicians and surgeons. Some simply saw no sense in external aid and trusted their own remedies as more efficacious. Geographical isolation, too, might prevent a person from seeing a healer, but considering the vast profusion of choices, as well as the frequency of consultation by correspondence and intermediaries, that probably was not a frequent explanation. And it was a strange village indeed that was not home to some sort of local healer, whether bathmaster, root-wife, cunning-man or woman, or just a neighbor known for his or her skills in, for instance, setting bones.

We must be careful as well not to pigeonhole early modern medical practitioners into tidy categories of "amateur" and "professional" or "learned" and "lay" by applying historical terms out of context. "Charlatan" is a good example. In early modern Italy, charlatans were licensed practitioners whose practice was not regarded in any way as wrong or bad and who received licenses to peddle medicine legally. Other excellent examples of how worlds met and overlapped can be easily found. The Elizabethan gentlewoman Lady Grace Mildmay treated ailments that ranged from epilepsy to hemorrhage, syphilis to fright, and flatulence to gout. She used herbs, but also Galenic medicines, and she distilled chemical ones as well. She was conversant with the works of both Galen and Paracelsus. Her practice was, in short, "extensive, systematic and at the forefront of contemporary medical knowledge." Likewise, Anna of Saxony was not only involved in healing but also in experimentation.[28]

Religion, magic, and healing

In the early modern world, people from all walks of life put great trust in magical and astrological healers and cures. It is, however, exceedingly difficult to draw a clean line between "magic" and "religion." Anthropologists have pointed out that the modern western secular attitude often assumes that what "we" do is religion, while what "others" do is magic. To an appreciable extent, early modern religious and magical practices rested on a similar supposition: that supernatural or occult (that is, hidden) forces could affect nature. This held true whether one chanted a magical incantation or spoke a humble prayer.

Astrology rests on the assumption that the celestial bodies can affect terrestrial affairs including health and personality. In the early modern world, astrology was a reputable intellectual pursuit with a large scholarly and elite following. While astrological healing by the eighteenth century was by no means as widespread or reputable as it once had been, it formed an important part of the medical and healing landscape in the sixteenth and seventeenth centuries. Thanks largely to work on Richard Napier, we possess an excellent study of the practice of a man who was at once healer, *magus*, and cleric.[29] Over a period of almost four decades, between 1597 and 1634, thousands found their way to the small town of Great Linford, Buckinghamshire, to consult him; hundreds more sent letters. Like others influenced by Renaissance neoplatonism, Napier's medical practice blended religion, astrology, and natural philosophy.

So what did Napier do when approached by sufferers seeking help? After jotting down vital data on each visitor – place of birth, present location, and reason for consultation – he noted the precise time of the meeting. He then mapped the heavens, recorded the person's description of his or her problems, and then compared the two, selecting treatments indicated by the stars and current medical thinking. He generally

[28] David Gentilcore, *Medical Charlatanism in Early Modern Italy* (Oxford, 2006); Pollock, *With Faith and Physic*, 108; Rankin, "Medicine for the Uncommon Woman."

[29] Michael MacDonald, *Mystical Bedlam: Madness, Anxiety, and Healing in Seventeenth-Century England* (Cambridge, 1981); Ronald Sawyer, "Patients, Healers, and Disease in the Southeast Midlands, 1597–1634" (diss., University of Wisconsin, 1986).

prescribed standard therapies, for example, bleeding or purging. He rarely turned to the use of amulets or exorcism. By the end of the seventeenth century, however, his method of curing was becoming unfashionable but not because people found it ineffective but because the "traditional fusion of natural and supernatural beliefs . . . was discredited." Thus, despite his popularity as a healer "his arts declined; in time, he was forgot."[30]

Magical healing is more difficult to pinpoint and describe for several reasons. First, while astrological healing formed part of the Great Tradition of European intellectualism, other forms of magic were much less theoretical and far more varied in their practice and possibilities. Moreover, with a growing assault on popular culture and on superstitions dating from at least the mid sixteenth century and that tied into a religious reformism stressing a more rigorous and orthodox approach to belief, magical practices became less respectable and were even, at times, proscribed. Still, there is no indication that attempts at suppression were fully or immediately effective and a wide range of magical practices continued, as they do today. Because they were so prolix, all one can do is suggest some of the ways magic, religion, and healing entwined in early modern times. One should always remember that healers who used magic to heal also commonly used physical methods. Nor, for that matter, did all licensed or academic physicians eschew magic; often, for instance, advising the wearing of amulets in specific cases, such as to alleviate the problems associated with teething in young children.

Nonetheless, and despite the frequency with which people might call on magic to assist them in illness, at times and in places, for instance, where the Counter-Reformation Inquisition pressed its campaign against heresy, those who cured magically could also be suspected of harming magically. The Holy Office in Venice, for instance, in 1590 investigated one Lucia Nicetta who used oils to cure babies. She saw her practice as mediating God's will through the use of holy oils; the Inquisition saw it as possibly diabolical. She believed herself a healer; her judges saw a *strega*, a witch.[31]

Christianity has always been connected with healing. Because most Christians ultimately regarded illness as the wages of sin, evidence of divine displeasure, or a testing of faith, they ultimately turned to God for assistance. Still, early Christians did not eschew natural means of

---

[30] MacDonald, *Mystical Bedlam*, 231.
[31] Guido Ruggiero, "The Strange Death of Margarita Marcellini: *Male*, Signs, and the Everyday World of Pre-Modern Medicine," *American Historical Review* 106 (2001): 1148–50.

healing and their medical knowledge, too, derived from the precepts of the (pagan) ancients.[32] On many points, little distinguished the various Christian denominations from each other and only late in our period did the general belief in the supernatural origins of disease fade. Thomas Becon (1512–67), much like his medieval predecessors, believed that "sickness and adversity are sent . . . unto the children of men for their great profit and singular commodity." He consoled "all faithful christians" to behave "patientlie and thankfulie" when afflicted with disease and to "prepare themselves gladlie and godlie to die."[33] Christian thought and practice affiliated saving souls and healing bodies. The most immediate and useful remedy for the soul – prayer – was also the most certain relief for the body. The English "Great Litany" of 1544 petitioned God for "pity upon us miserable sinners, that are now visited with great sickness and mortality, that like as thou didst command thy angel to cease from punishing, so it may now please thee to withdraw from us this plague and grievous sickness."[34]

If Christians accepted that in the final analysis illness came from God, that acceptance did not, however, prevent people from seeking, and being advised to seek, natural cures. By 1500, the Roman Catholic Church had long since come to terms with secular medicine. Thus, while clergy of all stripes emphasized that prayer and penitence alone assured the success of any cure, they also counseled Christians not to disdain the aid of physicians nor to spurn the medicines God had put in this world for human benefit.

Although prayer remained the preferred and most frequent religious panacea for illness, early modern Europeans engaged in a wide variety of other religious practices. Besides praying, one could invoke the aid of Christ, the Virgin Mary, or saints. Although the Roman Catholic Church never taught that saints could cure, nonetheless the cult of the saints provided additional recourse in illness. People entreated saints to intervene and associated certain ones with particular diseases or afflictions: Sts. Roch and Sebastian with plague; St. Anthony with plague and also with the skin inflammation known as St. Anthony's Fire; St. Hubert with mental illness; and St. Laurent with burns. Women in labor would cry out to St. Anne for assistance, while epileptics journeyed to the shrine

---

[32] Gary B. Ferngren, *Medicine and Health Care in Early Christianity* (Baltimore, 2009).
[33] Thomas Becon, *The Sicke Mans Salve* (London, 1587).
[34] Quoted in John Booty, "The Anglican Tradition," in Numbers and Amundsen, eds., *Caring and Curing*, 249; Andrew Wear, "Religious Belief and Medicine in Early Modern England," in Hilary Marland and Margaret Pelling, eds., *The Task of Healing: Medicine, Religion and Gender in England and the Netherlands, 1450–1800* (Rotterdam, 1996), 147–52.

of St. Cornelius near Cologne or to that of St. Willibrod in Echternach (today's Luxemburg). Other popular sites were Canterbury for the help of St. Thomas à Becket, St. Sebastian's in Rome for protection from plague, or the Marian site in Kevelaer in the Rhineland. Pilgrims often signified their gratitude and attested their recovery by leaving an *ex-voto* (a symbolic object) at the shrine. The lame would leave their crutches, for instance.

Individuals turned to prayers, pilgrimages, and supplications to recover their health or that of relatives and friends. Epidemics, however, called forth more structured, large-scale religious responses. Masses and processions counted among the commonest communal reactions to disease outbreaks. Processions drew in the entire society or at least its representatives. Images of saints or crucifixes formed the focal point of processions that wound their way through an entire city, stopping at, or passing through, all places of religious or civic relevance. In 1651, the Spanish tanner Miquel Parets related how

The city of Barcelona, seeing that Our Lord was so angered with us and that the plague kept spreading ... decided to hold a procession and carry the relic of glorious Saint Severus along the entire Corpus route. This procession took place with great devotion on April 30 ... and was attended by the lord councilors and the governor ... and the wool weavers, who marched with torches and dressed as pilgrims, as they always do whenever the relic of the glorious saint is brought out. A great crowd came to this procession.[35]

Processions and communal days of fasting and repentance remained part of mainstream religious and communal life in both Catholic and Protestant areas. If Protestants no longer turned to what they called "graven images" or sought the intervention of saints or the Virgin Mary, they had not abandoned the habit of public prayer and penance during crises. Nor did they hesitate to thank God for their deliverance.

Clergy, of course, played a prominent role in medicine. Throughout the middle ages, and well into the early modern period, clergymen practiced medicine. Medieval monasteries long served as repositories of medical knowledge and care. Religion and healing coexisted not only intellectually but also physically in the body of the priest-, monk-, or nun-infirmarer. The attempt to separate medicine and religion or lay and religious practitioners proceeded slowly and was conditioned by ideological, theological, and socioeconomic forces rather than by strictly medical ones. One can trace three major steps in the process. The Roman Catholic Church took the first one in the late middle ages. The second came with the

---

[35] Amelang, *Journal of the Plague Year*, 47.

religious reformations of the sixteenth century. And the third arose from the increasing skepticism and secularization of the mid-to-late seventeenth century. The separation was never complete, but the gradual trend was to define two spheres of activity and to hold them apart from each other: the care of souls and the cure of body. Yet, as we have seen, hospitals always retained many religious elements; indeed, they can be best thought of as religious and medical amalgams.

As early as the twelfth and thirteenth centuries, the Roman Catholic Church began to limit the clerical practice of medicine. Mounting disquietude among the upper ranks of the clergy with the healing activities of monks, nuns, and priests partially drove the shift, but the timing also coincided with the rise of the universities and urban growth. Church councils pared away at the medical practice of clergy, first banning them from doing surgery and then forbidding regular clergy (the cloistered clergy who lived according to a rule, *de regula*) the practice of medicine unless they had also attained a medical degree. The Second Lateran Council (1139) ordered that "monks and canons regular are not to study jurisprudence and medicine for the sake of temporal gain."

If clergy were slowly being pushed out of medical practice as physicians or surgeons, they nonetheless remained crucially important as healers in other ways. Most people continued to believe that many illnesses, especially those characterized by bizarre or intemperate speech (or, conversely, inability to speak), convulsions, or spasmodic and wild bodily motions, resulted from possession or bewitchment. For these, the spiritual healer remained the practitioner of choice. Priests performed exorcisms and attempted to lift spells, as did cunning-folk whose white magic seemed an effective response to malevolent forces. The Catholic priest Johann Joseph Gassner (1727–79) was celebrated for his ability to "cast out devils" even during the Enlightenment.[36]

The sixteenth-century Reformation had transformed the relationships between magic, religion, and healing. Martin Luther, as we have seen (Chapter 3), had a powerful impact on Paracelsus and may have influenced the course of anatomy as well. Like most people of his day, Luther believed that God was the ultimate cause of healing and that physicians were but God's tools. Moreover, he felt that a person was "wretched" who relied solely on terrestrial physicians. But Luther's and the general Protestant attack on the special character of the clergy proved more decisive. The Protestants denied the ability of priests to "work miracles" (especially to transform bread and wine into the body and blood of Christ),

---

[36] H. C. Erik Midelfort, *Exorcism and the Enlightenment: Johann Joseph Gassner and the Demons of Eighteenth-Century Germany* (New Haven, 2005).

and that skepticism extended to healing. Protestants decried the whole range of what they termed "superstitious practices": the use of the sacraments or sacramental objects such as communion wafers or holy oil to work wonders; the veneration of saints and the Virgin Mary; pilgrimages; and exorcisms. Of course, Protestants never denied the power of God to heal, but emphasized that prayer and repentance were the only proper spiritual recourse for the ill.

More practically, Protestants stressed the worth of pastoral counseling in illness. The Dutch Reformed Church, for instance, appointed "comforters of the sick" (*ziekentroosters*) who visited the ill, prayed with them, and helped them make sense of pain and suffering; they also gave medical advice.[37] Protestant clergymen crafted special prayers for the occasion of sickness and placed them in prayer books. Both Catholics and Protestants believed that only a good man – one of conscience and right belief – made a good physician. Protestant theologians, too, strengthened the claims of learned physicians by advising the sick to employ medicines and consult physicians in illness. Luther, despite his reservations about relying entirely on the aid of physicians, taught that "God created medicine and provided us with intelligence to guard and take care of the body so that we can live in good health."[38] Likewise, the reformers' teachings tended to undercut beliefs in the nonnatural origins of disease. One famous opponent of witchcraft persecutions was the Dutch Protestant physician Johannes Weyer who insisted that diseases supposedly caused by witches could be traced to natural origins. Still, this tendency hardly prevented witchcraft persecutions and witch hunts from occurring in Protestant lands as frequently as in Catholic places (or even more frequently).

The Catholic Church in the sixteenth century underwent its own reformation and revitalization, called the Catholic Reformation or the Counter-Reformation. From the mid sixteenth century onward, the church accelerated its retreat from claiming special healing powers for its clergy. In 1626, for instance, the Congregation for the Propagation of the Faith (the part of the church in charge of missionary activities) forbade priests in Bulgaria to dispense medicines to the sick, "whether they be of the Faith or not."[39] Exorcism, too, was no longer accepted as the unquestioned prerogative of the clergy and the Catholic Church discouraged, but did not prohibit, its use. In the decades after the Council of Trent, which formalized reformed Catholicism, some clergy used

---

[37] Johan de Niet, *Ziekentroosters op de pastorale markt 1550–1880* (Rotterdam, 2006).

[38] Quoted in Carter Lindberg, "The Lutheran Tradition," in Numbers and Amundsen, eds., *Caring and Curing*, 178; Wear, "Religious Belief," 161.

[39] Quoted in Marvin O'Connell, "The Roman Catholic Tradition Since 1545," in Numbers and Amundsen, eds., *Caring and Curing*, 120.

exorcism and spiritual healing to retain believers for Mother Church or to convince strays to return to her bosom. Missionary orders in other parts of the world combined winning souls with curing bodies. The Jesuits were deeply involved in exorcisms and their reliance on such practices accounts, in part, for their success as missionaries. While introducing Christianity in the North American southwest, the Franciscans adroitly manipulated the magic of Pueblo Indians to their own, and their church's, benefit.[40] Jesuits in Naples actively encouraged belief in miracle cures and the French *dévots* (members of the laity dedicated to ideals of the Catholic Reformation) pushed programs of reform that included medicine. Everywhere in Europe, there was great pressure on clerics to engage in healing.

Protestantism and Catholicism also changed over the course of time. Both were profoundly affected by broader intellectual, social, and economic currents as well as by internal forms of religious revivalism. Jansenism first developed in the Low Countries but became most influential in seventeenth- and early eighteenth-century France. Its teachings diverged from orthodox Catholicism on free will, exhibited a strong strand of mysticism, and promoted spiritual healing. Protestantism in the late seventeenth and eighteenth centuries experienced similar waves of revivalism, in the forms of Pietism in Germany (a mystical and inner-directed religious movement within Lutheranism) and Methodism in England. Both elevated the role of religion in healing. At the Pietist-influenced university in Halle (Prussia), the university clinic educated theological students to minister to the sick. The university established a pharmaceutical industry and dispatched boxes of medications throughout the world. Missionaries educated in Halle, like Batholomaeus Zigenbalg (1683–1719) who went to India and Henry Melchior Muhlenburg (Heinrich Melchior Mühlenberg, 1711–87) who missionized in America, practiced medicine along with their theology.[41] John Wesley (1703–91), an early leader of the Methodist movement, criticized the standard medical practices of his day and developed his own "physick." Wesley believed in forestalling disease by healthy living. He inveighed against expensive medicines and recommended time-tested inexpensive remedies. Still, and while he believed in spiritual healing, he held medicine and religion separate.[42]

---

[40] Ramón A. Gutierrez, *When Jesus Came, the Corn Mothers Went Away: Marriage, Sexuality, and Power in New Mexico, 1500–1846* (Stanford, Calif., 1991).

[41] Renate Wilson, *Pious Traders in Medicine: A German Pharmaceutical Network in Eighteenth-Century North America* (University Park, Pa., 2000).

[42] Deborah Madden, *A Cheap, Safe and Natural Medicine: Religion, Medicine and Culture in John Wesley's Primitive Physic* (Amsterdam, 2007), 268.

But the vast majority of religious healers were not members of the clergy, nor were they sanctioned by any established church or secular authorities. They remained very popular even well into the nineteenth century. In mid-eighteenth-century France, people celebrated an erstwhile shepherd named Pierre Richard as the "saint of Savières." In 1767, when already in his fifties, he began curing with holy water and at the height of his popularity reportedly treated hundreds each day. It is important not to dismiss him as a mere "quack" or regard him as a fraud; there is no reason to believe that his objective was merely to deceive.[43] Throughout early modern times, we can trace the activities of literally hordes of healers whose methods combined religion and magic. They prayed, recited bits and pieces of liturgy, signed the cross, used amulets, and provided charms. In the Italian archbishopric of Brindisi, in the mid sixteenth century, for instance, a Franciscan friar sang a *cantilena* (a lyrical melody) to relieve skin infections and one Don Giuseppe Memo said Paternosters and Ave Marias to cure blisters on cows' tongues. As late as the 1780s, Don Pietro de Laurentiis, "famous for his heavy drinking and healing," recited the *orazione di Sant'Onofrio* over children to remove their worms.[44]

To sum up: in the early middle ages, religion, magic, and healing coexisted rather comfortably within the framework of Christianity. By the thirteenth century, however, the Catholic Church was well on the way to disengaging religion from healing without abandoning the latter altogether. The various religious reformations of the sixteenth century produced churches that focused more single-mindedly on the care of souls than on the cure of body, but the former never supplanted the latter. By the middle of the seventeenth century, and with a few exceptions, most clergy attached to the established churches were reluctant to attempt supernatural cures. Still, neither religious nor magical healing disappeared. Clearly in many regions religious and magical healing held on longer than in other places. Yet it is far too simple to accept that country people, the lower orders, or those living on the "fringes of civilization" clung most fiercely to practices that the more civilized inhabitants of towns and cities, or the higher social groups, had long since abandoned under the influence of the secularizing tendencies and the new science of the seventeenth century or the Enlightenment of the eighteenth.

---

[43] Matthew Ramsey, *Professional and Popular Medicine in France, 1770–1830: The Social World of Medical Practice* (Cambridge, 1988), 199–200; for the nineteenth century, see Judith Devlin, *The Superstitious Mind: French Peasants and the Supernatural in the Nineteenth Century* (New Haven, Conn., 1987).

[44] All of these examples are taken from David Gentilcore, *From Bishop to Witch: The System of the Sacred in Early Modern Terra d'Otranto* (Manchester, 1992), 103–04, 132.

Cures that relied on religion and magic were, however, not the only options. The breadth of other choices was enormous: local healers of many kinds, midwives, traveling practitioners, surgeons, apothecaries, and physicians.

Local healers

Early modern Europe supported a wide range of practitioners who met the medical needs of their communities. The medical providers treated in this section as "local practitioners" resided more or less permanently in one locality but were neither surgeons nor physicians to whom special sections are devoted. The division is clearly artificial, but it catches, I believe, the significance of connections, networks, and place that characterized early modern medical practices. It also separates these practitioners from the many itinerants. Local healers were by no means exclusively secular, of course, and many healers who relied on magic, for example, were entrenched in their communities. While the density and assortment of practitioners varied, most areas no matter how small boasted several resident healers who drew at least part of their living from medicine. Some people, of course, practiced only in the spirit of good neighborliness. The category of local practitioners as handled here also included people who tended to be more frequently designated "irregulars" by secular and religious authorities. These included cunning-folk, executioners, root-wives, and bonesetters.

Cunning-folk drew on a store of magical cures for countering the effects of evil magic. But while they called upon supernatural aid, they also possessed intimate knowledge of local plants and concocted salves, lotions, and elixirs taken internally or smeared on blisters, sores, aching gums, and bruises. They might set bones or bind wounds. Cunning-folk, root-wives, and herbalists overlapped in their activities, and a root-wife, for instance, might have nothing at all to do with magical healing. Bonesetters specialized in reducing fractures and resetting dislocated joints. They often learned their trade secrets from a relative or friend; bonesetting frequently ran in families. Some bonesetters viewed their abilities as a God-given gift rather than an acquired skill.

Executioners were a special instance. Small settlements rarely needed to employ their own executioner and most executioners worked in larger towns. Executioners in some parts of Europe, and especially in central Europe, were regarded as dishonorable people and contact with them was seen as polluting. Still, because they mediated between the realms of life and death, people valued them as healers. Executioners served double-duty as torturers and often treated the injuries torture inflicted.

Thus, they might come to possess good techniques for healing burns, cuts, and dislocations. The executioner frequently sold things of medical value. As he was often the city's knacker, he marketed the fat of dogs and horses as well as *Menschenfett* (human fat). He might sell body parts from executed criminals, although authorities explicitly forbade this practice. Some human parts were thought to possess inherent curative powers. Stroking a withered limb with a dead man's hand supposedly would restore it to use; a thumb corrected male sexual incapacity; and hair from a corpse's head was thought a sure cure for baldness.

People consulted these healers regularly. Few believed they were some-how less valuable medically than those who possessed licenses and academic training. Two variables in particular deeply conditioned medical choices: first, the economic niche they occupied within their village or neighborhood, and, second, their social and communal relations with their colleagues, competitors, and clients. To understand early modern medical practice properly, it is essential to remember that medical decisions turned on many factors, not all (or perhaps not even most) of which were strictly medical. Doctrinal orthodoxy and church member-ship could count, and so, too, did one's standing in the community. A "good woman" or a "good man" made for a good practitioner and merit hinged upon a general feeling that such people fulfilled the community's social, moral, and economic expectations, or at the very least did not flagrantly violate them. Villagers proved reluctant to patronize healers who drank to excess, blasphemed, chased women, or ran up debts. It also helped, of course, to be tightly coupled to a local hierar-chy by ties of blood, marriage, or debtor–creditor relationships. Their qualities as house-father or -mother, husbandman, debtors, creditors, and churchgoers were likewise essential parts of their identities as med-ical providers. Not surprisingly, most rarely lived from medical practice alone.

The urban environment generally offered a greater range of medical choices than the countryside. More physicians, surgeons, and barber-surgeons lived in towns. Moreover, there were probably more practition-ers on the ground in the eighteenth than in the seventeenth century. Yet, no rule holds true everywhere. Groningen in the northern part of the Dutch Republic actually had more physicians in the seventeenth than in the eighteenth century. More prosperous areas supported a larger number of healers as well. Spas like Bath in England and Spa in the Spanish/Austrian Netherlands, for instance, attracted a disproportionate number.

By the middle of the eighteenth century, and perhaps even earlier, other changes had shifted how medicine would be practiced. A consumer society had taken root by the early 1700s. Medicines counted among the most widely advertised and distributed consumer products and, in fact, medical advertising took the vanguard in this new market surge. Newspaper columns bulged with come-ons for proprietary medicines, including many sure cures for embarrassing or obdurate ailments such as venereal diseases. Perhaps the most famous and successful of the mail-order medicine vendors was the French entrepreneur Jean Ailhaud. Ailhaud advertised his purgative powders (*poudres d'Ailhaud*) extensively. He and his son constructed distribution networks that spread over France and reached into the Germanies, commissioning agents and establishing depots in strategic places, such as Strasbourg. Not only irregulars and market specialists like Ailhaud exploited advertising techniques. The darling of the French court, the Dutch physician Jean-Adrien Helvétius, puffed his own remedies in print and, by the 1720s, was manufacturing over 100,000 doses a year.[45]

Mail-order and long-distance marketing on a national or international scale, however, only became common by 1750, although long before then medicine peddlers were to be found busily hawking their wares across vast distances. Some peddlers and mountebanks – the oil-peddlers (*Ölitatenkramer*) of central and eastern Europe or the *orviétan* sellers in France, for example – specialized in specifics, offering theriac or oil of turpentine, as well as an assortment of tinctures. Other colporteurs carried a wider selection of goods and sold distillates, lotions, pills, and powders along with household items such as ribbons, string, cloth, knives, combs, pots, pans, and sieves.

Itinerants

Reference to the traveling medicine peddlers brings us to a consideration of the many itinerant practitioners that plied the highways and byways of early modern Europe. There is a tendency to classify peripatetic practitioners as charlatans and quacks. Some were, but many were quite learned and just as many functioned as mediators between the worlds of learned and popular healing, accelerating the flow of information in both directions. Moreover, many itinerants were highly skilled, much in demand, and offered important services. One primary reason for their mobility was specialization. Oculists, lithotomists, and dentists, for instance, could be found as sedentary practitioners in larger cities; others had to take to the road. All three were by no means snake-oil salesmen, although their abilities and their attainments varied, of course.

---

[45] Brockliss and Jones, *Medical World*, 652–56; Lindemann, *Health and Healing*, 172–73.

Moreover, most peripatetics required a license to practice in a particular territory or town and receiving a license usually meant that they had to be examined by a university faculty, a medical *collegium*, or city physician. The itinerant practitioners moved as well in the forefront of medical advertising (Figure 7.1), producing flyers and pamphlets that lauded their skills and appended testimonials of their cures.

Oculists often exhibited great dexterity in treating cataracts and good evidence suggests that their operations could restore sight, despite the danger of infection. A skilled practitioner like Jochimb Schmidt, who restored vision to the seventy-four-year-old Duke of Braunschweig-Wolfenbüttel in 1653, was just one of these.[46] Most famous perhaps was John Taylor (1703–72), known as the "Chevalier," who made a triumphant progress around France, curing blindness and bragging about it in numerous flyers and pamphlets. But Taylor was not only a successful eye-specialist, he had earlier qualified as a physician. Not all oculists took to the road, of course, and one of the most famous of them, the surgeon Jacques Daviel, who developed a new method of treating cataracts, worked mostly in Marseilles; although he, too, occasionally moved about. Oculists also vended eye-ointments and eyewashes.

Dentists, too, traveled. Like the oculists, their skills varied from the exquisite to the nonexistent. Bad teeth were a curse of the early modern world, although it is possible that matters actually worsened in the nineteenth century when sugar came to be consumed in larger quantities. In addition to pulling decayed teeth, dentists sold tooth-powders and mouthwash and provided custom-made or ready-to-wear false teeth. The eighteenth-century Amsterdam diarist Jacob Bicker-Raye praised the master-carpenter *qua* dentist Hermannus Mulder who was "a great artist in his ability to set teeth in the human mouth and even created entire sets of upper and lower [ones]" which he affixed with leather bands.[47]

Apothecaries, barber-surgeons, and surgeons

Apothecaries, barber-surgeons, and surgeons provided a large percentage of all medical care in early modern Europe. The city of Lyon, for instance, with a population of approximately 58,000 in 1545, had 8 physicians but 20 surgeons and 45 apothecaries. Reims in France was half that size yet

---

[46] Jill Kohl [Bepler] and Mary Lindemann, "Augustus in tenebris," in Martin Bircher, Jörg-Ulrich Fechner, and Gerd Hillen, eds., *Barocker Lust-Spiegel: Studien zur Literatur des Barock* (Amsterdam, 1984), 187–204.

[47] Jacob Bicker-Raye, *Dagboek Bicker-Raye*, entry from November 11, 1772, in Stadsarchief Amsterdam.

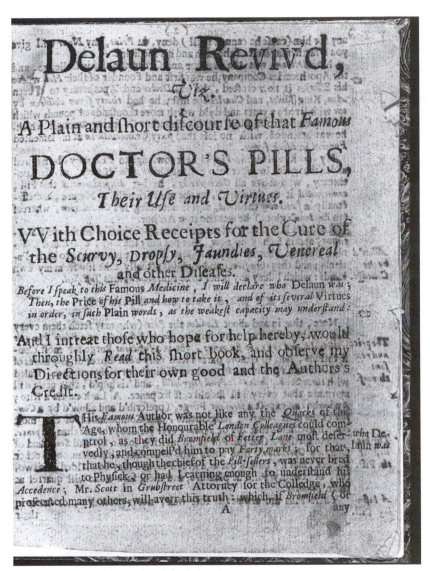

7.1 Medical advertising, c.1680

6 physicians, 20 surgeons, and 6 apothecaries resided there.[48] As many as 25,000 barber-surgeons may have been practicing in France toward the end of the eighteenth century. Thus, early modern people would have

[48] Brockliss and Jones, *Medical World*, 204.

been quite familiar with practitioners who were not physicians and often turned to them for medical assistance.

In some ways, the apothecary was the quintessential sedentary practitioner because his usual place of business was the apothecary shop. One found apothecaries in all cities, most towns, and even many villages. Like many practitioners, however, their livelihood did not necessarily derive solely from supplying medicines. Many functioned as general practitioners or involved themselves in producing medicines wholesale, selling liquors and spirits, or producing/distilling chemicals for use as medicines (such as Glauber and Epsom salts) or in manufacturing. Others became deeply involved in the new science of the sixteenth and seventeenth centuries, participating actively in the "Republic of Letters" and collaborating with famous natural historians. The Amsterdam apothecary and sugar refiner Pieter Geerit and his relative in London, James Garret, assisted the renowned scientific horticulturist Carolus Clusius (1526–1709) in assembling a collection of American plants, for example.[49]

Apothecaries, of course, prepared, stored, and sold medicines: simple, compounded, herbal, and chemical. Simples, as the name implies, were single ingredient medicines. Composita were compounds mixed up in advance or on the spot. These were sometimes intimidatingly complex. For example, a sixteenth-century receipt for "a most precious and excellent balm" called for, among other things, sixty-eight herbs, twenty types of gum, six laxatives, and twenty-four different roots chopped fine.[50] Early modern pharmacopoeias (lists of medicinals) contained a range of arcane ingredients, such as powdered unicorn's horn. Many of these remedies, as well as the perfectly respectable ones of theriac and mithradium (used to treat plague), disappeared or were expunged from official lists by reforms introduced in the eighteenth century. Apothecary ordinances designated what apothecaries were to stock. They were, for instance, permitted to keep only small quantities of notorious poisons and enjoined to distribute only tiny quantities of them. The 1763 "Instruction" for apothecaries in the Dutch town of Delft forbade them to mix and sell antiquated remedies, or those which had over the course of time come to be regarded as useless; for instance, "mithradatium, theriaca, diascordium, philonium Romanam, and acqua vitae Mattioli." The same rules required Delft apothecaries to have always on hand some thirty-one specific remedies including a wide range of spirits, salts, and oils.

---

[49] "The Knowledgeable Apothecary" was the subject of a symposium at the Wellcome Trust Centre for the History of Medicine at UCL on June 13, 2008. See also the discussion of James Garret in Deborah E. Harkness, *The Jewel House: Elizabethan London and the Scientific Revolution* (New Haven, Conn., 2007), 15–19.

[50] Pollock, *With Faith and Physic*, 103.

Urban, territorial, and national governments regulated the trade and, in most places, specifically denied apothecaries the practice of medicine. Nor were they permitted to prescribe except on the express order of a physician. Typical, for instance, were the provisions laid down in the Amsterdam medical ordinance of 1519 which prohibited anyone, apothecaries not excepted, to dispense medicines except when ordered by a physician.

What happened in daily life often differed, sometimes substantially, from what the rules prescribed. In London, after a bitter fight with the physicians, apothecaries gained the right to dispense on their own, literally becoming general practitioners. Moreover, if this *de jure* system pertained only in a handful of places, *de facto* it was common. Almost everywhere apothecaries not only compounded and sold drugs that physicians ordered, they also did so on their own, proffered medical advice, and even visited patients. Throughout early modern Europe, therefore, the competition among apothecaries, physicians, and surgeons for customers could be quite fierce. Yet little actually differentiated the type of medicine the apothecaries provided from that of others. They used the same pills and potions physicians did and they followed the same intellectual concepts, such as Galenism and Paracelsianism, as their academically trained colleagues and competitors.

The apothecary's social and economic position in the community conditioned his practice. The shop and its contents were considerable economic assets. When the Staffordshire apothecary Henry Fogg died in 1750, his shop goods totaled a substantial £51 10s and consisted of "Drugs simples spirits vials Bottles Gallipots counter drawers shelves weights & scales brass & copper pans mortars and pestles pewter measures bleeding cups pair of Screws & all the Shop utensils." He also possessed a "case of lancets" which suggests that he let blood. Another apothecary purchased Fogg's thirty-three books, mostly on medicine.[51] The taxes the apothecary Dirck Outgaertzs Cluyt paid in Delft in the sixteenth century ranked him among its most affluent citizens. The English surgeon-apothecary William Elmhirst enjoyed rents from his estates, although his medical practice provided a heftier part of his income.

Not all apothecaries, of course, were affluent. In small towns and villages, apothecaries seldom belonged to a guild, might lack formal training entirely, and be left pretty much on their own, escaping the gaze of the authorities. These apothecaries could be very poor and poorly run. Some

---

[51] Joan Lane and Anne Tarver, "Henry Fogg (1707–1750) and His Patients: The Practice of an Eighteenth-Century Staffordshire Apothecary," *Medical History* 37 (1993): 189–91.

stocked a pathetically meager quantity of drugs; some were simultaneously grocers and tavern-keepers. Shops often passed from one generation to the next, creating dynasties of apothecaries, such as the Boulducs in seventeenth- and eighteenth-century Paris. Widows of apothecaries, too, sometimes continued their husband's practice, although usually only if they employed a competent (male) journeyman.

Today we have a rather jaundiced view of early modern surgery, one which the facts do not bear out. Certainly, almost all surgery was painful and brought with it the real perils of life-threatening infections and tetanus. Probably only a quarter of patients survived the initial shock and subsequent dangers of amputating a major limb. For these reasons, most surgeons acted with caution. They almost never invaded the cavities of the chest or abdomen and rarely took on major operations, such as amputations or mastectomies, unless deemed absolutely necessary. Yet, despite these grim survival rates and the many harrowing first-person accounts of surgical "torture," surgery was a success story. Many surgeons had acquired enviable skills through years of hands-on training as well as commanding a high degree of theoretical knowledge.[52] Some had studied medicine. The Dutchman Petrus Camper (1722–89) obtained his medical degree from Leiden, but specialized in surgery and midwifery. His practice revolved around the treatment of hernias, bladder stones, prolapsed anuses, fistulas, lameness, and facial disfigurements, especially those of the nose.[53]

Radical surgery remained rare. Military and naval surgeons performed the overwhelming majority of amputations. The best study we have of everyday surgical practices establishes that surgeons were far from being "knife-crazy." Richard Wiseman (1622?–76) in his *A Treatise of Wounds* (1672) noted that

In small and superficial wounds . . . Nature of her own accord is wont to effect the cure, without the help of any Medicament; from us only is required that the lips of the wound be brought close together by bandage, that neither hair, nor dust, nor any other things fall between them.[54]

In critical cases, surgeons vastly preferred to work closely with colleagues, partly to add experience and partly to spread the blame if things went

---

[52] Sabine Sander, *Handwerkschirurgen: Sozialgeschichte einer verdrängten Berufsgruppe* (Göttingen, 1989); Toby Gelfand, *Professionalizing Modern Medicine: Paris Surgeons and Medical Science and Institutions in the 18th Century* (Westport, Conn., 1980).

[53] Cornelis J. Doets, *De heelkunde van Petrus Camper, 1722–1789* (Leiden, 1948).

[54] Quoted in Stephen Jacyna, "Physiological Principles in the Surgical Writings of John Hunter," in Christopher Lawrence, ed., *Medical Theory, Surgical Practice: Studies in the History of Surgery* (London and New York, 1992), 142.

awry. Most surgical practices probably revolved around lancing boils, setting broken limbs, binding wounds, treating contusions, rectifying dislocations and the like.

Surgeons were not all alike, however. Three types of surgeons practiced in early modern Europe: surgeons (or master-surgeons), barber-surgeons, and military surgeons. In addition, bathmasters performed minor surgical tasks. Visiting a bathhouse was often a communal activity. Sixteenth-century prints, for instance, depict whole families strolling down the street on the way to the bathhouse, clad only in shirts and petticoats. Bathhouses existed in large numbers in the sixteenth century, especially in the German territories, the northern Italian states, and Scandinavian countries. The spread of the Great Pox in the 1500s, however, undercut their popularity and bathhouses quickly fell into disrepute and many closed. Bathmasters usually rented a house from the commune for a fee and provided a variety of services: they administered warm and cold baths, cut hair, pared corns, cupped, and set leeches. Cupping, like leeching, was a mild form of blood-letting.

As the name suggests, barber-surgeons were generally licensed to cut hair in addition to performing minor surgical operations, such as cupping, leeching, lancing boils, binding wounds, and pulling teeth. Many barber-surgeons also let blood. Although definitions of what barber-surgeons were legally permitted to do varied throughout Europe, they frequently came into conflict with the bathmasters over cupping and leeching and with the surgeons over various operations. Much depended on the definition of "minor" surgery. Barber-surgeons repeatedly infringed on the province of the surgeons by letting blood or performing complicated operations. This sort of poaching also worked in the other direction: barber-surgeons constantly complained that surgeons interfered with their livelihood by cutting hair.

These conflicts were ubiquitous and in fact determined much of the daily life and even the identity of surgeons. Surgeons sought to define themselves as separate and distinct from barber-surgeons and bathmasters even when they were gathered in the same guild structure. Military surgeons also involved themselves in territorial squabbling. Technically, military surgeons only treated soldiers and were forbidden civilian practice. While on furlough and reduced pay, however, they treated civilians, drawing howls of protest from their nonmilitary colleagues.

Navies and the merchant marine employed shipboard surgeons. These men confronted not only the injuries of battles, but the manifold health hazards that accompanied long, slow voyages, demanding work conditions, and the deleterious consequences of close confinement, monotonous and inadequate diets, the lack of sufficient drinking water, and poor hygienic conditions. An insufficiency of vitamin C caused scurvy, an ailment that commonly afflicted sailors. Usual, too, were ruptures and hernias as well as the inevitable falls and other injuries typical of the trade. Syphilis, verminous infestations, and typhus filled out a catalog of major and minor ills to which seafaring flesh was prone. Indeed, typhus often went under the name "ship-fever" (or "jail-fever") because it spread so rapidly in confined populations.

Midwives

Throughout the early modern period, virtually every person entered the world through a midwife's hands (Figure 7.2). With some exceptions, that remained true well into the nineteenth century and, in places, even into the twentieth. Historical writing about midwifery, however, has tended to concentrate on the disappearance of the midwife from the birthing chamber and her replacement by man-midwives, surgeon-midwives, or accoucheurs. Moreover, some scholars have analyzed early modern childbirth as a "bonding experience" and a female world of ritual and support that vanished when men took over. The short version of the story runs that man-midwives, with the cooperation of state authorities, professional organizations, and educational institutions, gradually pushed the midwife into the background and simultaneously turned the natural process of childbirth into a pathological state needing treatment. Feminist historians first argued that, by defining childbirth as a medical event, it more easily became the province of male physicians and surgeons. The majority of births even in the early modern period (one historian, working with British data, estimates over 90 percent) were uneventful whether attended by a physician, a midwife, or a stork. Still, some births (perhaps as many as 3 percent) caused difficulties and an ability to turn the child *in utero* could spell the difference between a live birth or a tragedy for mother or child or both. Likewise forceps, despite the dangers of introducing infection, tearing the membranes of the birth canal or labia, or injuring the child, could result in the live birth of an otherwise undeliverable child. Thus, the answer to the old question of whether man-midwives or midwives were the better birth attendants is not simple. Some midwives were indeed dirty, ignorant, and dangerous; some man-midwives saved lives with their forceps; and some births were doomed to disaster.

The most obvious – and important – of the midwife's tasks was, of course, birthing children. Generally, a pregnant woman would make arrangements in advance with the local midwife and then call her when the labor pains began. Even before then, however, the midwife might advise a pregnant woman on how to prevent miscarriages, applying

7.2 Jane Sharp, *The Compleat Midwife's Companion* (1724)

poultices, recommending other measures such as bed rest, blood-letting, warm baths, and boiling up herbal infusions and barley water. The midwife was supposed to hurry to the laboring woman's side when called, assess the progress of labor, and, if delivery seemed reasonably near, not depart until the birth was accomplished. The woman's family and friends plied the midwife with food and drink (preferably not intoxicating) while she was on duty. Midwives did physical examinations, using their hands and fingers to ascertain the state of cervical dilation, straighten twisted limbs, and lubricate the birth canal with oils or fats to ease the child's passage. They might administer soothing or bracing drinks. The midwife was also expected to offer moral and emotional succor. Madame du Coudray instructed her pupils to

console [the woman] as affectionately as possible . . . but you must do it with an air of gaiety that gives her no fear of danger. Avoid all whisperings [in the ears of others], which can only make her nervous and make her worry about bad things. You must speak to her of God, and engage her in thanking him for putting her out of peril. Avoid letting her do anything that will depress her.[55]

After the child was born, the midwife tied off and severed the umbilical cord, cleaned the newborn (making sure membranes and blood had been removed from nose and mouth), and administered tonics if the child or its mother seemed weak. In many places, she performed immediate "emergency baptisms" on feeble children. The midwife then delivered the afterbirth, checking it to make sure it had been completely expelled and no part remained in the mother's womb. Retained afterbirths were a fairly common complication and the Spanish midwife Luisa Rosado used a gentle technique and, "without any instrument other than her hands placed on the belly, nor more violence in her movements than that produced by her almost imperceptible touch," succeeded in resolving most cases quickly and safely.[56] If hemorrhage ensued, the midwife massaged the abdomen to halt the bleeding. Midwives were allowed to administer bracing cordials and strengthening teas, but were to refrain from using other drugs. Midwives dressed wounds to the vagina and surrounding tissues and would sometimes stitch lacerations with a needle and thread.

In the days following the birth, the midwife returned to check on the progress of the woman and the newborn child. Although childbed (puerperal) fever occurred less often before births in hospitals and with instruments became more routine, it was not unknown. It was frequently mortal. There was nothing a midwife (or anyone else) could do to halt its fearsome progress. Such fatal complications usually accompanied traumatic and exhausting births, but midwives with soiled hands or whose clumsiness caused more tearing than necessary certainly contributed.

Postnatal care of mothers was another task. Midwives assisted women (especially those bearing their first children) in beginning breastfeeding

---

[55] Quoted in Nina R. Gelbart, *The King's Midwife: The History and Mystery of Madame du Coudray* (Berkeley and Los Angeles, 1998), 45, 69.

[56] Quoted in Teresa Ortiz, "From Hegemony to Subordination: Midwives in Early Modern Spain," in Hilary Marland, ed., *The Art of Midwifery: Early Modern Midwives in Europe* (London, 1993), 106.

and treated sore breasts with hot compresses or lotions. They applied other mixtures to "toughen" nipples. If a woman suffered from post-partum constipation, the midwife administered an enema. The midwife might also launder soiled linen, cook for the household, and generally help out around the house. The eighteenth-century Maine (USA) mid-wife Martha Ballard (1734/35–1812) took on all these chores, although often, one suspects, impelled by a sense of Christian charity as much as by duty or for pay.[57]

For their assistance at births, midwives received payment sometimes set by fee-tables, but habitually determined by custom. Wealthier clients paid more than less well-do-do, while parishes footed the bills for poor women or families on relief. In addition, midwives enjoyed additional fees for supplementary duties. Affluent couples might give a midwife quite substantial gratuities and presents, whereas rural women offered chickens, bread, grain, and garden produce in lieu of cash. In addition, the midwife usually carried the child to the church to be christened, for which she received "christening money." Prosperous or socially prominent parents and godparents presented midwives with gifts at the ceremony. In the end, however, few midwives lived from midwifery alone; the majority were midwives only occasionally and their earnings from midwifery constituted merely a portion of their total income.

Historians have frequently asserted that the social status of midwives was low. If we look at what most women earned from midwifery alone, then most would have hovered on the brink of destitution. Because mid-wifery, however, only comprised part of their income, the economic status of midwives is hard to determine and probably diverged rather widely. Many were mouse-poor. In fact, appointing a woman as midwife to a village helped keep some off poor relief. Many midwives were wed to artisans or substantial farmers, and their fees supplemented the family income. Moreover, and with some exceptions, midwifery was not a "career choice." One can, of course, point to famous midwives who served royalty such as Louise Bourgeois and Justine Siegemund. Most midwives were middle-aged or older. Some midwifery ordinances, as well as common practice, stipulated that midwives had to be beyond childbearing age and have already borne children. While many midwives fit the picture of age and indigence, others were younger women and more financially secure. Some, like Madame du Coudray and Justine Siegemund, never married or gave birth. The percentage of older, widowed, and poorer midwives probably pertained more in rural than urban

---

[57] Laura Thatcher Ulrich, *A Midwife's Tale: The Life of Martha Ballard Based on Her Diary, 1785–1812* (New York, 1990).

areas. In towns and cities, especially by the mid eighteenth century, many more women received extensive theoretical and practical training and chose midwifery as an occupation. While it is difficult to determine what most midwives thought of their trade and their skills, it is clear that the elite among them took justifiable pride in their accomplishments and regarded themselves as skilled and knowledgeable practitioners. Madame du Coudray, for instance, situated herself firmly in modern medical and scientific practice and had little patience for the ignorance of other woman practicing the craft. Even Luisa Rosado, who insisted that her knowledge was empirical, not scientific, and always deferred to surgeons and physicians, nonetheless valued her own attainments and skills.[58]

Physicians

The final healer this chapter addresses is the physician. This prioritization may first seem strange, but it reflects the reality of medical practice in early modern Europe. Most people did not, as a matter of course, turn to physicians or use them exclusively when ailing. One hastens to qualify this statement, however. First, the availability of physicians was not the same everywhere. In cities, where most physicians resided, where there were more hospitals, and where parish and municipal forms of poor relief existed, a wide segment of the population (even among the poor) had some contact with university-trained practitioners. As we saw in the previous chapter, cities often appointed a physician whose titles included that of physician-to-the-poor. Guilds, too, contracted with physicians (as well as with other practitioners) to serve their members.

Second, it is simply not true that early modern people shunned physicians and harbored a deep-seated antipathy to them. Some, of course, expressed skepticism and even enmity. Contemporary prints and the works of many novelists, playwrights, and satirists, such as Molière in *The Imaginary Invalid*, frequently targeted physicians.[59] One must wonder, however, if the mistrust of physicians was not more a fashionable phenomenon among some elites or a trenchant literary and pictorial trope than a deeply rooted and widespread conviction. In places where

---

[58] Wendy Perkins, *Midwifery and Medicine in Early Modern France: Louis Bourgeois* (Exeter, 1996); "Volume Editor's Introduction," to Justine Siegemund, *The Court Midwife*, ed. and trans. by Lynne Tatlock (Chicago, 2005); Gelbart, *King's Midwife*; Ortiz, "From Hegemony to Subordination."

[59] For an excellent discussion of Molière as a medical commentator, see Brockliss and Jones, *Medical World*, 336–44.

physicians resided, the evidence strongly indicates that patients consulted them as part of a typical range of practitioners they thought suitable, even if they did not prefer physicians to all other healers.

Third, the number of physicians tended to increase throughout Europe over time and especially rapidly in the eighteenth century. By late century, many spoke of a glut, rather than a scarcity, of physicians (at least in towns and cities) as part of a more general superfluity of those aspiring to the learned professions. As more and more physicians settled outside major population centers, as once small towns grew, and as states began to appoint officers of health, the physician became an ever more familiar face. In addition, many medical consultations proceeded by correspondence, thus increasing the number of patients a single physician might "see" and treat. Finally, many physicians were not full-time medical practitioners, but like other healers, pursued other occupations.

Why, then, would a person choose a physician over another healer? This question is easy to pose and almost impossible to resolve. Surely part of the answer lies in individual preferences. Status differences played a role, although, as we have seen, a neat formula that equates the use of physicians with a European elite and relegates the rest of the population to other less-skilled practitioners fails to catch reality. Fashion might explain the popularity one physician enjoyed over another, or over nonphysician competitors (although it also explains enthusiasm for faddish cures, such as balaneotherapy, electrotherapy, and mesmerism). Broader intellectual or religious inclinations, such as Protestantism, could attract a patient to one practitioner over another.

When people did not consult physicians, it was not (necessarily) because they feared the expense or felt culturally alienated from such learned men, but perhaps because they perceived that physicians were good for some things, yet not for others. Parents rarely called in a physician (or any other healer for that matter) when their offspring fell ill with smallpox, for instance; not because they considered their children unimportant or replaceable, but because they quite rightly discerned that a physician offered little hope. The same reasoning often applied during widespread disease outbreaks, such as of dysentery, where the disease progressed swiftly. Still, many people consulted physicians for assorted "fevers" (especially recurring fevers), for myriad chronic or slow-progressing diseases like dropsy, tumors, vision problems, and gynecological complaints.

What did physicians do when called? How early modern physicians examined patients might seem strange to us today. First, physicians generally went to see the patient, rather than the other way around.

Second, the standard parts of the physical examination we have come to expect – listening to heart and lungs with a stethoscope; taking the temperature with a thermometer; palpating the abdomen; percussing the thorax; doing a digital rectal examination; monitoring blood pressure with a sphygmomanometer; testing blood, urine, and stool – were all absent, as were numerical calibrations of normal and abnormal. An early modern physician might view the patient's urine, spittle, or stools, examine a furred tongue, or feel the pulse, but he observed qualitative signs rather than obtaining basically quantitative measures. The idea of evaluating deviations from a set norm as "disease" was alien to him and his patients both. Descriptions of physical phenomena differed and the early modern physician drew other meanings from them. Take the pulse, for example. Few doctors counted beats per minute, rather they noted the qualities of the pulse: it was rapid, weak, pounding, feeble, or tremulous. A pleurisy patient's pulse might be "rapid and full but not particularly hard" while a fever patient's "fluttered."

For the early modern physician, as for his patients, the complexion and temperament presented reliable guides to health and illness that could be perceived on the bodily exterior and, especially, in the face. A seventeenth-century practitioner read death in a countenance where "the Nose is sharp, the Eyes hollow, the Temples fallen, the Ears cold and drawn in." The physical examination, therefore, depended on correctly deciphering external signs. William Brownrigg, who practiced in Cumberland in the eighteenth century, recorded the appearance of his patients carefully. Mrs. James Milham, who suffered from "inflammation of the intestines," was "[a] pretty young woman of 18 with a beautiful complexion and a dainty figure." Brownrigg was not merely admiring her shapely form: her complexion and delicate frame reliably indicated her predisposition to certain afflictions and her receptivity to particular treatments.[60]

Physicians used their five senses unassisted and unamplified by instruments. Only in the nineteenth century did the stethoscope and the clinical thermometer ("fever-stick") come into use. An early modern physician gauged fever by touching the brow or feeling the chest; he evaluated stools and urine by sight, smell, and occasionally by taste (the urine of a diabetic patient is sweet). He might indeed palpate a hernia, feel a lump or fibrous growth, but seldom did he probe orifices (especially female ones) with an invasive finger. He listened to the patient's heart and

---

[60] Quoted in Fissell, *Patients, Power, and the Poor*, 32; *The Medical Casebook of William Brownrigg, M.D., F.R.S. (1712–1800) of the Town of Whitehaven in Cumberland*, ed. and trans. by Jean E. Ward and Joan Yell (London, 1993), 61, 100.

breathing, but far more often he paid close attention to what the patient had to say.

The patient's narrative formed the centerpiece of the early modern examination. A physician used the details related by the patient to make diagnoses, determine treatments, and shape prognoses. The physician's ears were as important as his eyes and hands. Patients emphasized what they felt and observed going on within their own bodies. The language of their narratives often corresponded to the words a physician himself used (although few patients employed Latin terms). The early eighteenth-century German physician Johann Storch shared a vocabulary with his female patients: they spoke of the body as a vessel of fluids, for instance.

Because of the overwhelming significance of the patient narrative and, of course, because distance separated many patients from their physician of choice, consultation by correspondence was common and become more frequent in the eighteenth century with the spread of literacy, the growth of advertising, and the improvement of postal and transporta-tion networks. Patients, family members, or friends wrote to physicians and physicians communicated with their colleagues about intractable or unusual cases. Patients often provided extremely detailed accounts. George Cheyne was a popular physician to the social elite and a pio-neer in vegetarianism. For ten years, he conducted a social and medical correspondence with Selina, Countess of Huntingdon (1707–91), which can serve as an illustration of consultation by letter but also of the way in which a medical practice in the early eighteenth century could be conducted. The tone throughout is that of a friend and counselor. He suggests, he does not order, and he never scolds, but he is also not def-erential. While the countess was pregnant in 1732–33, Cheyne sent her many letters recommending moderate blood-letting, purging, and vom-its to correct "the sharp scorbutic humour" of her blood, but particularly advocating a diet for a "childing lady."

Ripe fruit you may deal in as much as you please. Salad use with a little oil and vinegar if it agrees. Chicken, partridge, a little white fish, lobster, cray fish, lambstons [testicles], veal feet, jellies, especially fruit ones, at dinner only. Milk and milk meats, butter, new cheese, light pudding, rice, sago, and the like for supper are good.[61]

We also tend to believe that early modern cures were inevitably harsh, unpleasant, and dangerous (as well as useless). Some certainly were,

---

[61] *The Letters of George Cheyne to the Countess of Huntingdon*, ed. with an introd. by Charles F. Mullett (San Marino, Calif., 1940), 16, 39; see also Steven Shapin, "Trusting George Cheyne: Scientific Expertise, Common Sense, and Moral Authority in Early Eighteenth-Century Dietetic Medicine," *Bulletin of the History of Medicine* 77 (2003): 263–97.

but many relied heavily on nature or cautious wait-and-see tactics. The final illness of the Holy Roman Emperor, Charles V (r.1519–56, d.1558) suggests how his two body-physicians went about treating him. One is struck here by their restraint. Over the course of several weeks, they administered very little physic, only twice giving him a "strong dose of rhubarb in three pills" to relieve his constipation. He was also bled – mildly – three times. To make him more comfortable and alleviate his thirst, he drank barley water and sugar. As soon as it became apparent that his illness was mortal, they merely tried to make him comfortable. Yet the medical moderation Charles's physicians practiced cannot be taken as typical.[62] His son, Philip II of Spain (r.1556–98), suffered agonies under the hands of his doctors as he lay dying.

The advice and care of physicians was often mixed with that of other healers and different systems competed. When the court decided that the madness (or imbecility) of Duke Albrecht Friedrich (1553–1618) of Prussia required treatment, they first approached the celebrated Paracelsian Leonhard Thurneisser (1530–96), sending him Albrecht Friedrich's urine in 1574. Thurneisser diagnosed his problem and prescribed treatment without seeing the disturbed duke; nor did he (or anyone else) think a closer physical examination necessary. According to Thurneisser, the urine revealed that Albrecht Friedrich suffered from "internal fear and horror together with bitter bad temper and deep contemplation," and that he was melancholic. The prince's blood, he opined, had become "overcooked" and was thick, black, and choleric. He advised that Albrecht Friedrich follow a disciplined regimen of food, drink, sleep, and exercise. But he also recommended that "the spirit and mind must be cured with medicines just as much as the body." The Galenists at court, however, countered and overturned his advice. At virtually the same moment, court officials consulted another healer (not a physician) who prescribed a wide variety of herbal remedies.[63]

What might be called the "medical encounter" could take place in a variety of ways, as these examples demonstrate. When describing their own experience of the encounter, people told stories that fit into the normal rhythms of their lives. Hearsay, rumor, accident, and reputation, as much as purpose, drew people to a particular healer or range of healers. Near 1800, a man in a small town in northwestern Germany was suffering

---

[62] William Stirling-Maxwell, *The Cloister Life of Charles V* (4th edn., London, 1891), 333–58.

[63] H. C. Erik Midelfort, *The Mad Princes of Renaissance Germany* (Charlottesville, Va., 1994), 80–81.

from what he described as a "stitch" in his side. He sent his sister-in-law with a flask of his urine to the nearest large town to obtain medicines for him. As she entered the town, with which she was unfamiliar, she approached an unknown man and asked him "where a clever healer could be found." He recommended that she go to a soldier named Lange "who had already accomplished many important cures." Lange viewed the urine and diagnosed a chest inflammation for which he sold her some medicines. Not everyone picked their healers in this way, but neither is this story bizarre or extraordinary.[64]

Colonial practice and practices

As the Europeans dispersed across the globe, not only to the New World but also to Asia, Africa, and the Great South Sea, they came in contact with indigenous peoples whose medical practices the Europeans often transformed. Exotic remedies, however, significantly affected European medicine at home and in their colonies. We have already seen how New World and Asiatic plants entered the European pharmacopeia and how Europeans adopted some practices, such as moxibustion, tobacco smoking, and chocolate drinking. Likewise, Africans were inoculating long before the Europeans had any inkling of the procedure. One source of Cotton Mather's knowledge about inoculation was a slave from Africa and the West Indies.

In the early days of colonization medical practitioners were thin on the ground and many communities did without, relying exclusively on self-help and home-care. Many missionaries, such as the Pietists and Quakers, brought their own medicines with them or were supplied with instructions and drugs from Europe. Gradually, of course, as settlements grew, the number of practitioners expanded. Colonial medicine slowly began to take on many characteristics of the European system although, as we have seen, the granting of medical degrees in North America did not begin until quite late. Until then, most doctors learned their craft in an apprentice or preceptorship system.

Europeans also came into contact with different peoples and different systems of healing. While some plants proved useful commodities that quickly entered into trade, native medical systems tended to be less influential. And yet, the medical systems and healing practices of the indigenous African, American, and Asian populations frequently resembled European ones. Conceptions of disease in India, including

---

[64] Lindemann, *Health and Healing*, 353, 356.

the ancient Indian science of *ayurveda* medicine, linked health and the environment and relied on humoral interpretations. Africans and Americans used herbal remedies that varied in their content – using licorice and okra, for instance – but not in their application. Moreover, all accepted the ultimate divine origins of disease, but the multiple gods of African and American societies, as well as some of their practices such as human sacrifice, were anathema to Europeans. For these reasons, the Spanish sought to suppress Aztec healing. In response, the majority of Indians, mestizos, and blacks turned to an underground medical practice called *curanderismo* that emerged in the wake of the conquest.

African and indigenous American societies tended to see illness as relational, caused by a disturbance or enmity within the larger society. While this belief also held in early modern Europe, it had waned with the assault on popular culture that came with the Reformations of the sixteenth century and with the Enlightenment. Yet, the strange and unknown, or barely known, had its own allure in what the anthropologist Michael Taussig refers to as "the healing power of wildness." Many newcomers sought out and used native healers. In the Putumayo foothills of the Andes between Brazil and Colombia, for example, in 1668 the Bishop Alonso de la Peña Montenegro seriously worried about the Indians' heretical influence on whites who used indigenous healers.[65]

Slavery and medical practice, too, interacted in multiple ways. Between 1500 and 1870, some 9 million Africans were shipped to the New World as slaves. They brought with them their own medicine, but at the same time became the objects of "white" medicine. Because slavery was a "total institution," slaves rarely fully controlled the medical care they received. While they might dose themselves for minor problems, masters and overseers took over in more serious illnesses and applied many standard European remedies: bleeding, sweating, vomiting and the like. Because two prevalent beliefs about Africans dominated European and colonial thinking – that they were more animals than human and that they possessed stronger constitutions than whites – drugs were given in larger, harsher doses or more blood was drawn. Slaves hated and feared these treatments, sometimes believing that their white masters sought to kill them. Because they accepted that hatred and ill will could cause disease, slaves often turned to conjuring medicine (similar, of course, to that

---

[65] Michael Taussig, *Shamanism, Colonialism, the Wild Man: A Study in Terror and Healing* (Chicago, 1987), 219.

used by European cunning-folk) for help. Like magical practitioners in Europe, conjuring magic – called Obeah in the Caribbean – worked best in treating sudden or inexplicable diseases, including paralysis, stroke, or epilepsy.[66]

On the other hand, slaves could also be practitioners, as well as being responsible for a great deal of bodywork (grooming, bathing, dressing, and delousing, for instance). In Saint Domingue, enslaved healers filled multiple roles. Enslaved women took charge of plantations hospitals or worked as aids (*infirmières*), midwives, herbalists, and practitioners of veterinary medicine. They were also *kaperlatas*; that is, diviners and purveyors of talismans. In that last capacity, colonists often feared them as poisoners. The medicine of enslaved healers combined African heritages with Caribbean and western medicines to create "medical systems more closely attuned to the health needs of a population that struggled under the physical and psychological burdens of slavery."[67]

In concluding this chapter on practice and practitioners, we may want to ask ourselves: what did patients really expect from the healers they consulted? Perhaps this seems a foolish question: surely all people sought an end to their ills. But did they? Early modern medicine had few cures and could provide little relief for most illnesses and ailments. Opiates could deaden pain, but the side effects were considerable and the chance of accidental death or addiction great. Surgeons alleviated some excruciating, dangerous, and debilitating conditions by extracting bladder stones, couching cataracts, lancing boils, and amputating smashed limbs, but the dangers of infection and gangrene remained high, and most surgical interventions caused agony. Yet few people abandoned medicine and healers or resigned themselves to illness, suffering, and death. The accounts presented in this chapter demonstrate how vigorously people pursued health. Few abandoned the quest entirely. They might, of course, turn to spiritual physic as well as medicines or physicians for assistance, or seek out cunning-folk, but they rarely forsook the possibility of cure.

Some historians, however, have suggested a rather different interpretation: that early modern people did not go to healers with the same goals in mind that we hold today. A magisterial treatment of medicine in early modern France concluded that

---

[66] Richard B. Sheridan, *Doctors and Slaves, a Medical and Demographic History of Slavery in the British West Indies, 1680–1834* (Cambridge, 1985); S. M. Fett, *Working Cures: Healing, Health, and Power on Southern Slave Plantations* (Chapel Hill, N.C., 2002).

[67] Karol K. Weaver, *Medical Revolutionaries: The Enslaved Healers of Eighteenth-Century Saint Domingue* (Urbana and Chicago, 2006), quote 2.

the majority [of French men and women] were . . . fatalists and stoics. They might crave release from their ills, but they also recognized that the length of their days was measured by God. It made little sense to change physicians repeatedly in a vain attempt to defeat divine nemesis. It was irrational as well as unseemly.[68]

Illness and suffering could be interpreted positively, as marks of God's favor, for instance. Today most of us view health as a good to be attained and preserved and pain as an evil to be feared and avoided. According to those who draw sharp distinctions between us and our ancestors, no such expectations existed in the early modern period. People were accustomed to experiencing a succession of minor and major ailments, as well as intermittent or constant pain, throughout their lives, which were often "poore, nasty, brutish, and short." When they approached practitioners, they might have sought psychological support rather than physical aid. Thus, they went to healers to have their own diagnoses confirmed and to gain a sense of their prognosis: was the illness deadly? Temporary? Incapacitating? Or nothing to worry about?

It is indeed difficult to decide which of these two accounts comes closer to being correct. The truth probably lies somewhere in the middle. Early modern people held different expectations of healers than we do, certainly, but they also had their own ideas of what health should be and desired it greatly. Although it seems fairly clear to us that early modern medicine was powerless to cure most ailments, it was not completely impotent. Laudanum, hot compresses, some herbal remedies, and surgery were effective in relieving symptoms. Good nursing care, cleanliness, and proper and sufficient food must have often made the difference between those who survived an attack of influenza, for instance, and those who did not. Finally, the sense of "doing something" was an excellent psychological prop and that alone might have justified "going to the doctor" for many people. In that, surely, our early modern ancestors were much like us.

[68] Brockliss and Jones, *Medical World*, 305.

Conclusion

The history of medicine can be written in many ways. One can decide to relate a compelling tale of progress, dwell on the titillating details of quaint or gruesome practices, or, as I have done here, stress the affinities between the history of medicine and the historical mainstream, between medicine and society. Some scholars (by now a dying breed) still regard medicine in early modern Europe as something best forgotten. Those were the "bad old days" of ignorance, misery, error, and unrelieved suffering. Religion and superstition stood against "science" and the struggle between "faith and reason" had not yet been decided in favor of the latter. In this dark age, it is true, there glimmered here and there a hopeful development. An occasional isolated genius stood out, preternaturally endowed with an unerring sense of the "right path" forward. This handful of intrepid men, scientists before science was born, were Prometheans who kindled the fire of knowledge and passed it down through the ages to us, their true descendants. Yet even while acknowledging these many points of light, the gloom-and-doom school regarded the vast majority of medical providers as worse than useless or as "quacks" and "charlatans" who knowingly deceived their patients for the sake of gain. Theory was, moreover, sterile and utterly divorced from practice, wrongheaded because it did not worship the twin gods of modern science: observation and experimentation.

This book has rejected that perspective and has emphasized the richness of the medical worlds we have lost and are still rediscovering. In presenting a historiographical perspective, I have tried to represent debates fairly but also have endeavored to inform readers about "new approaches" to the vast subject of medical history. I hope I have done so without suggesting that any of these interpretations is final or "right." Indeed, the whole volume is in many ways merely an assessment of the "state of play" in medical history at the beginning of the twenty-first century. I have, however, highlighted certain points and interpretations that I would like to recapitulate briefly.

My version of medicine and society avoids teleological ways of writing medical history whether the end goal or interpretative scheme is either that of progress or medicalization. I have attempted to discuss continuities as well as changes. Several parts have pointed out the fallacies inherent in writing early modern medical history into the progressive story of the "rise of science." The ideas of a universal form of science and a generally agreed upon way of doing science were not born with the Scientific Revolution of the seventeenth century. Scholars have collected much evidence that questions the very existence of such a revolution as historians once spoke of it and I have accepted that point of view as the currently best substantiated one. No sharp rupture characterized what happened over some three hundred years and men like William Harvey, Andreas Vesalius, and Isaac Newton were as much heirs of an older world as founders of a new one. Likewise, the often postulated breakthrough toward clinical and scientific medicine that purportedly happened in the late eighteenth century with the "birth of the clinic" was not a sudden rupture (as Foucault suggested) but the result of multifarious conditions and forces, some of which can easily be traced to medieval precedents. Lines of continuity stretched back into the medieval and ancient worlds as well as forward into the nineteenth and twentieth centuries. Nonetheless, the period from 1500 to 1800 was not an undifferentiated whole, and, as we have seen, change could be slow and easily assimilated or rapid and unsettling.

Context has dominated this account. Medicine is embedded in the larger frameworks of life and history; it cannot be divorced from them. Demographic growth and decline, religious turmoil, sectarian squabbling, the European discoveries of the world, the forging of great colonial and trading empires, wars, natural disasters, social and economic changes, urbanization, and the rise of a consumer society; all these, and more, deeply affected the shape medicine took.

Perhaps more than other historical fields, the history of medicine has been plagued by a tendency to think in presentist terms by judging our ancestors according to our standards not theirs and by a desire to know what diseases or illnesses "really" were. Was the pestilence of the 1340s really bubonic plague? What was the sweating sickness of the sixteenth century? This book has tried to avoid, as much as possible, thinking in terms of an "us" and "them" dichotomy, drawing simple conclusions about issues of great complexity, or accepting monocausal explanations. For instance, the continued importance of religion characterized medicine and medical care throughout the period. While one might speak of a growing secularization, that grand historical narrative is not necessarily the best way to approach an understanding of responses to illness.

Moreover, while it is important to recognize that early modern peoples did not think or act in "modern" ways, one must also be careful not to overstate the variance. It is not that they were "wrong" and we are "right," or that they were "ignorant" and we are "knowledgeable." Historical dynamics affect us as much as they did our ancestors and our early twenty-first-century perceptions and understandings are just as liable to revision as previous ones. Neither we nor they, however, are the hapless dupes of larger forces that we barely perceive and cannot control. Rather, our ancestors' actions proceeded from their often shrewd assessments of the world about them and it is our job as students of the past to seek to understand and esteem their solutions and not merely judge them.

Further reading

[This list focuses principally on English-language publications. Additional references, including those in other languages, can be gleaned from the footnotes to each chapter.]

MAJOR JOURNALS IN THE HISTORY OF MEDICINE

Bulletin of the History of Medicine
Isis
Journal of the History of Medicine and Allied Sciences
Medical History
Social History of Medicine

GENERAL WORKS, BROAD SURVEYS, TEXTBOOKS, AND REFERENCE

Blécourt, Willem de and Cornelia Usborne, eds. *Cultural Approaches to the History of Medicine: Mediating Medicine in Early Modern and Modern Europe*. New York, 2004.

Brockliss, Laurence and Colin Jones. *The Medical World of Early Modern France*. Oxford, 1997.

Bynum, W. F. and Roy Porter, eds. *Companion Encyclopedia of the History of Medicine*. 2 vols. London, 1993.

The Cambridge History of Science. Vol. 3: Early Modern Science. Ed. Katherine Park and Lorraine Daston. Cambridge, 2006; Vol. 4: *Eighteenth-Century Science*. Ed. Roy Porter. Cambridge, 2003.

The Cambridge World History of Human Disease. Ed. Kenneth F. Kiple. Cambridge, 1993.

The Cambridge World History of Medical Ethics. Eds. Robert B. Baker and Laurence B. McCullogh. Cambridge, 2009.

Conrad, Lawrence, Michael Neve, Vivian Nutton, Roy Porter, and Andrew Wear. *The Western Medical Tradition, 800 BC to AD 1800*. Cambridge, 1995.

Cooter, Roger. "After Death/After-'Life': The Social History of Medicine in Post-Modernity," *Social History of Medicine* 20 (2007): 441–64.

Corsi, Pietro and Paul Weindling, eds. *Information Sources in the History of Medicine and Science*. London, 1983.

Elmer, Peter, ed. *The Healing Arts: Health, Disease and Society in Europe, 1500–1800*. Manchester, 2004.

Elmer, Peter and Ole Peter Grell, eds. *Health, Disease and Society in Europe, 1500–1800: A Source Book*. Manchester, 2004.

Fissell, Mary E., ed. "Women, Health, and Healing in Early Modern Europe." Special Issue of the *Bulletin of the History of Medicine* 82, no. 1 (Spring 2008).

Foucault, Michel. *The Birth of the Clinic: An Archaeology of Medical Perception*. Cambridge, 1989.

Herzlich, Claudine and Janine Pierret. *Illness and Self in Society*. Trans. Elborg Forster. Baltimore, 1987.

Jones, Colin and Roy Porter, eds. *Reassessing Foucault: Power, Medicine, and the Body*. London, 1994.

Lachmund, Jens and Gunnar Stolberg, eds. *The Social Construction of Illness: Historical, Sociological, and Anthropological Perspectives*. Stuttgart, 1992.

Leavitt, Judith Walzer. "Medicine in Context: A Review Essay of the History of Medicine." *American Historical Review* 95 (1990): 1471–84.

McGowan, Randall. "Identifying Themes in the Social History of Medicine." *Journal of Modern History* 63 (1991): 81–90.

McKeown, Thomas. *The Role of Medicine: Dream, Mirage, or Nemesis?* Princeton, N.J., 1979.

Nutton, Vivian, ed. *Medicine at the Courts of Europe, 1500–1837*. London, 1990.

Pelling, Margaret. *The Common Lot: Sickness, Medical Occupations and the Urban Poor in Early Modern England*. London and New York, 1998.

Porter, Roy. *The Greatest Benefit to Mankind: A Medical History of Humanity from Antiquity to the Present*. London, 1997.

"The Patient's View: Doing Medical History from Below." *Theory and Society* 14 (1985): 178–98.

Porter, Roy and Andrew Wear, eds. *Problems and Methods in the History of Medicine*. London, 1987.

Shapin, Steven. *The Scientific Revolution*. Chicago and London, 1996.

Sheils, William, ed. *The Church and Healing*. Oxford, 1982.

Wear, Andrew, ed. *Medicine in Society: Historical Essays*. Cambridge, 1992.

Webster, Charles, ed. *Health, Medicine and Mortality in the Sixteenth Century*. Cambridge, 1979.

ANCIENT AND MEDIEVAL BACKGROUND

Amundsen, Darrel W. *Medicine, Society, and Faith in the Ancient and Medieval Worlds*. Baltimore, 1996.

Ferngren, Gary B. *Medicine and Health Care in Early Christianity*. Baltimore, 2009.

French, Roger. *Medicine Before Science: The Rational and Learned Doctor from the Middle Ages to the Enlightenment*. Cambridge, 2003.

Gracia-Ballester, Luis, Roger French, Jon Arrizabalaga, and Andrew Cunningham, eds. *Practical Medicine from Salerno to the Black Death*. Cambridge, 1993.

Green, Monica H. *Making Women's Medicine Masculine: The Rise of Male Authority in Pre-Modern Gynaecology.* Oxford, 2008.

McVaugh, Michael. *Medicine Before the Plague: Practitioners and Their Patients in the Crown of Aragon.* Cambridge, 1993.

McVaugh, Michael and Nancy Siraisi, eds. *Renaissance Medical Learning: Evolution of a Tradition.* Philadelphia, 1990.

Nutton, Vivian. *Ancient Medicine.* London, 2004.

Siraisi, Nancy. *Medieval and Early Renaissance Medicine: An Introduction to Knowledge and Practice.* Chicago, 1990.

1 SICKNESS AND HEALTH

Bynum, W. F. and Vivian Nutton, eds. *Theories of Fever from Antiquity to the Enlightenment.* London, 1981.

Bynum, W. F. and Roy Porter, eds. *Living and Dying in London.* London, 1991.

Conrad, Lawrence I. and Dominik Wujastyk, eds. *Contagion: Perspectives from Pre-Modern Societies.* Aldershot, 2000.

Duden, Barbara. *The Woman Beneath the Skin: A Doctor's Patients in Eighteenth-Century Germany.* Trans. By Thomas Dunlap. Cambridge, Mass., 1991.

Fissell, Mary E. *Patients, Power, and the Poor in Seventeenth-Century Bristol.* Cambridge, 1991.

Jewson, N. D. "The Disappearance of the Sick-Man from the Medical Cosmology." *Sociology* 10 (1976): 225–44.

"Medical Knowledge and the Patronage System in Eighteenth-Century England." *Sociology* 8 (1974): 369–85.

MacDonald, Michael. *Mystical Bedlam: Madness, Anxiety, and Healing in Seventeenth-Century England.* Cambridge, 1981.

Macfarlane, Alan. *The Family Life of Ralph Josselin, a Seventeenth-Century Clergyman: An Essay in Historical Anthropology.* Cambridge, 1970.

Midelfort, H. C. Erik. *A History of Madness in Sixteenth-Century Germany.* Stanford, 1999.

Porter, Roy, W. F. Bynum, and M. Shepherd, eds. *The Anatomy of Madness.* vol. 1: *People and Ideas.* London, 1985.

Riley, James C. *Sickness, Recovery and Death: A History and Forecast of Ill Health.* Iowa City, 1989.

Rosenberg, Charles and Janet Golden, eds. *Framing Disease: Studies in Cultural History.* New Brunswick, N.J., 1992.

2 PLAGUES AND PEOPLES

Alchon, Suzanne Austin. *A Pest in the Land: New World Epidemics in a Global Perspective.* Albuquerque, 2003.

Alexander, John. *Bubonic Plague in Early Modern Russia: Public Health and Urban Disaster.* Baltimore, 1980.

Amelang, James S., trans. and ed. *A Journal of the Plague Year: The Diary of the Barcelona Tanner Miquel Parets 1651*. New York, 1991.

Arrizabalaga, Jon, John Henderson, and Roger French. *The Great Pox: The French Disease in Renaissance Europe*. New Haven, Conn. and London, 1997.

Benedictow, Ole J. *The Black Death, 1346–1353: The Complete History*. Woodbridge, 2004.

Biraben, Jean-Noel. *Les Hommes et la peste en France et dans les pays européens et méditerranéens*. 2 vols. Paris, 1975–76.

Calvi, Giulia. *Histories of a Plague Year: The Social and the Imaginary in Baroque Florence*. Berkeley and Los Angeles, 1989.

Carmichael, Ann G. *Plague and the Poor in Renaissance Florence*. Cambridge, 1986.

Cohn, Samuel K., Jr. *The Black Death Transformed: Disease and Culture in Early Renaissance Europe*. Oxford, 2002.

Cook, Alexandra Parma and Noble David Cook. *The Plague Files: Crisis Management in Sixteenth-Century Seville*. Baton Rouge, 2009.

Cook, Noble David. *Born to Die, Disease and New World Conquest, 1492–1650*. Cambridge, 1998.

Crosby, Alfred W., Jr. *The Columbian Exchange: Biological and Cultural Consequences of 1492*. Westport, Conn., 1972.

Cunningham, Andrew and Ole Peter Grell. *The Four Horsemen of the Apocalypse: Religion, War, Famine and Death in Reformation Europe*. Cambridge, 2000.

Demaitre, Luke. *Leprosy in Premodern Medicine: A Malady of the Whole Body*. Baltimore, 2007.

Dols, Michael. *The Black Death in the Middle East*. Princeton, N.J., 1977.

Fenn, Elizabeth A. *Pox Americana: The Great Smallpox Epidemic of 1775–82*. New York, 2001.

Healy, Margaret. *Fictions of Disease in Early Modern England: Bodies, Plagues, and Politics*. New York, 2001.

Herlihy, David. *The Black Death and the Transformation of the West*. Ed. Samuel K. Cohn, Jr. Cambridge, Mass., 1997.

Hopkins, Donald R. *The Greatest Killer: Smallpox in History*. Chicago, 2002 [2nd edn. of *Princes and Peasants*. Chicago, 1983].

McNeill, William H. *Plagues and Peoples*. New York, 1976.

Miller, Geneviève. *The Adoption of Inoculation for Smallpox in England and France*. Philadelphia, 1957.

Mormando, Franco and Thomas Worcester, eds. *Piety and Plague: From Byzantium to the Baroque*. Kirksville, M., 2007.

Nutton, Vivian, ed. *Pestilential Complexities: Understanding Medieval Plague*. London, 2008.

Quétel, Claude. *History of Syphilis*. Trans. by Judith Braddock and Brian Pike. Baltimore, 1990.

Ranger, Terence and Paul Slack, eds. *Epidemics and Ideas: Essays on the Historical Perception of Pestilence*. Cambridge, 1992.

Razzell, Peter. *The Conquest of Smallpox: The Impact of Inoculation on Smallpox Mortality in Eighteenth-Century Britain*. Sussex, 1977.

Slack, Paul. *The Impact of Plague in Tudor and Stuart England*. London, 1984.

Stein, Claudia. *Negotiating the French Pox in Early Modern Germany*. Aldershot, 2009.

Twigg, Graham. *The Black Death: A Reappraisal*. London, 1984.

3 LEARNED MEDICINE

Ackerknecht, Erwin H. *Medicine at the Paris Hospital, 1794–1848*. Baltimore, 1967.

Broman, Thomas H. *The Transformation of German Academic Medicine, 1750–1820*. Cambridge, 1996.

Bynum, W. F. and Roy Porter, eds. *William Hunter and the Eighteenth-Century Medical World*. Cambridge, 1985.

Cunningham, Andrew. *The Anatomical Renaissance: The Resurrection of the Anatomical Projects of the Ancients*. Aldershot, 1997.

Cunningham, Andrew and Roger French, eds. *The Medical Enlightenment of the Eighteenth Century*. Cambridge, 1990.

Debus, Alan G. *The Chemical Philosophy: Paracelsian Science and Medicine in the Sixteenth and Seventeenth Centuries*. 2 vols. New York, 1977.

French, Roger. *Dissection and Vivisection in the European Renaissance*. Aldershot, 1999.

   Medicine before Science: The Rational and Learned Doctor from the Middle Ages to the Enlightenment. Cambridge, 2003.

French, Roger and Andrew Wear, eds. *The Medical Revolution of the Seventeenth Century*. Cambridge, 1989.

French, Roger, Jon Arrizabalaga, Andrew Cunningham, and Luis García-Ballester, eds. *Medicine from the Black Death to the French Disease*. Aldershot, 1998.

Fuchs, Thomas. *Mechanization of the Heart: Harvey and Descartes*. Rochester, N.Y., 2001 [1992].

Furdell, Elizabeth Lane. *Publishing and Medicine in Early Modern England*. Rochester, N.Y., 2002.

   The Royal Doctors, 1485–1714: Medical Personnel at the Tudor and Stuart Courts. Rochester, N.Y., 2001.

García-Ballester, Luis. *Galen and Galenism: Theory and Medical Practice from Antiquity to the European Renaissance*. Aldershot, 2002.

Grell, Ole Peter, ed., *Paracelsus: The Man and His Reputation, His Ideas, and Their Transformation*. Leiden, 1998.

Grell, Ole Peter and Andrew Cunningham, eds. *Medicine and Religion in Enlightenment Europe*. Aldershot, 2007.

   eds. *Medicine and the Reformation*. Cambridge, 1993.

Hunter, Lynette and Sarah Hutton, eds. *Women, Science and Medicine, 1500–1700: Mothers and Sisters of the Royal Society*. Stroud, 1997.

King, Lester S. *Medical Thinking: A Historical Preface*. Princeton, N.J., 1982.

   The Philosophy of Medicine: The Early Eighteenth Century. Princeton, N.J., 1982.

Knoeff, Rina. *Herman Boerhaave (1668–1738): Calvinist Chemist and Physician*. Amsterdam, 2002.

Larson, Magali Sarfatti. *The Rise of Professionalism: A Sociological Analysis*. Berkeley and Los Angeles, 1977.

Maclean, Ian. *Logic, Signs and Nature in the Renaisssance: The Case of Learned Medicine*. Cambridge, 2002.

Moran, Bruce T. *Distilling Knowledge: Alchemy, Chemistry, and the Scientific Revolution*. Cambridge, Mass., 2005.

Park, Katherine. *Doctors and Medicine in Early Renaissance Florence*. Princeton, N.J., 1985.

Porter, Roy, ed. *Medicine in the Enlightenment*. Amsterdam and Atlanta, 1995.

Temin, Owsei. *Galenism: Rise and Decline of a Medical Philosophy*. Ithaca, N.Y., 1973.

Webster, Charles. *Paracelsus: Medicine, Magic, and Mission at the End of Time*. New Haven, 2008.

Wellman, Kathleen. *La Mettrie: Medicine, Philosophy, and Enlightenment*. Durham, N.C., 1992.

4 LEARNING TO HEAL

Beumers, Harm and J. Moll, eds. *Clinical Teaching, Past and Present*. Special issue of *Clio Medica*. Amsterdam, 1989.

Brockliss, Laurence and Colin Jones. *The Medical World of Early Modern France*. Oxford, 1997.

Broomhill, Susan. *Women's Medical World in Early Modern France*. Manchester, 2004.

Cook, Harold J. *The Decline of the Old Medical Regime in Stuart London*. Ithaca, N.Y., 1986.

Gelbart, Nina Rattner. *The King's Midwife: A History and Mystery of Madame du Coudray*. Berkeley, 1998.

Gelfand, Toby. *Professionalizing Modern Medicine: Paris Surgeons and Medical Science and Institutions in the Eighteenth Century*. Westport, Conn., 1980.

Gentilcore, David. *Healers and Healing in Early Modern Italy*. Manchester, 1998.

Hannaway, Caroline and Ann La Berge, eds. *Constructing Paris Medicine*. Amsterdam, 1998.

Lawrence, Christopher, ed. *Medical Theory, Surgical Practice: Studies in the History of Surgery*. London, 1992.

Lawrence, Susan C. *Charitable Knowledge: Hospital Pupils and Practitioners in Eighteenth-Century London*. Cambridge, 1996.

Le Roy Ladurie, Emanuel. *The Beggar and the Professor: A Sixteenth-Century Family Saga*. Trans. Arthur Goldhammer. Chicago, 1997.

Marland, Hilary, ed. *The Art of Midwifery*. London and New York, 1993.

Mooij, Annet. *Doctors of Amsterdam: Patient Care, Medical Training and Research (1659–2000)*. Amsterdam, 2002.

Nutton, Vivian and Roy Porter, eds. *The History of Medical Education in Britain*. Amsterdam and Atlanta, 1995.

O'Boyle, Cornelius. *The Art of Medicine: Medical Teaching at the University of Paris, 1250–1400*. Leiden, 1998.

Perkins, Wendy. *Midwifery and Medicine in Early Modern France*. Exeter, 1996.

Rosner, Lisa. *Medical Education in the Age of Improvement: Edinburgh Students and Apprentices, 1760–1826.* Edinburgh, 1991.

Sander, Sabine. *Handwerkschirurgen: Sozialgeschichte einer verdrängten Berufsgruppe.* Göttingen, 1989.

Waddington, Keir. *Medical Education at St. Bartholomew's Hospital, 1123–1995.* Woodbridge, 2003.

Wilson, Adrian. *The Making of Man-Midwifery: Childbirth in England, 1660–1770.* Cambridge, Mass., 1995.

5 HOSPITALS AND ASYLUMS

Andrews, Jonathan and Andrew Scull. *Customers and Patrons of the Mad-Trade: The Management of Lunacy in Eighteenth-Century London, with the Complete Text of John Monro's 1766 Case Book.* Berkeley and Los Angeles, 2002.

Undertaker of the Mind: John Monro and Mad-Doctoring in Eighteenth-Century England. Berkeley and Los Angeles, 2001.

Borsay, Anne. *Medicine and Charity in Georgian Bath: A Social History of the General Infirmary, c. 1739–1830.* Aldershot, 1999.

Digby, Anne. *Madness, Morality, and Medicine: A Study of the York Retreat, 1796–1914.* Cambridge, 1995.

Granshaw, Lindsay and Roy Porter, eds. *The Hospital in History.* London, 1987.

Henderson, John. *The Renaissance Hospital: Healing the Body and Healing the Soul.* New Haven, Conn., 2006.

Henderson, John, Peregrine Horden, and Alessandro Pastore, eds. *The Impact of Hospitals: 300–2000.* Bern, 2007.

Horden, Peregrine. *Hospitals and Healing from Antiquity to the Later Middle Ages.* Aldershot, 2008.

Houston, R. A. *Madness and Society in Eighteenth-Century Scotland.* Oxford, 2000.

Porter, Roy, W. F. Bynum, and Michael Shepherd, eds. *The Anatomy of Madness.* 3 vols. London, 1985.

Risse, Guenter B. *Hospital Life in Enlightenment Scotland: Care and Teaching at the Royal Infirmary of Edinburgh.* Cambridge, 1986.

Mending Bodies, Saving Souls: A History of Hospitals. Oxford, 1999.

Siena, Kevin P. *Venereal Disease, Hospitals, and the Urban Poor: London's "Foul Wards."* Rochester, N.Y., 2004.

Tenon, Jacques. *Memoirs on Paris Hospitals.* Ed. with an introduction, notes, and appendices by Dora Weiner. Canton, Mass., 1996.

Wilkinson-Zerner, Catherine. *The Hospital of Cardinal Tavera in Toledo.* New York, 1977.

6 HEALTH AND SOCIETY

Cavallo, Sandra. *Charity and Power in Early Modern Italy: Benefactors and Their Motives in Turin, 1541–1789.* Cambridge, 1995.

Cipolla, Carlo. *Miasmas and Disease: Public Health and the Environment in the Pre-Industrial Age.* New Haven, Conn., 1992.

Public Health and the Medical Profession in the Renaissance. Cambridge, 1976.

Frank, Johann Peter. *A System of Complete Medical Police: Selections from Johann Peter Frank*. Ed. Erna Lesky. Baltimore, 1975.

Gentilcore, David. "'All that Pertains to Medicine': Protomedici and Protomedicati in Early Modern Italy." *Medical History* 35 (1994): 121–42.

Grell, Ole Peter and Andrew Cunningham, eds. *Health Care and Poor Relief in Protestant Europe, 1500–1700*. London, 1997.

Medicine and the Reformation. London, 1993.

Grell, Ole Peter and Andrew Cunningham, with Jon Arrizabalaga, eds. *Health Care and Poor Relief in Counter-Reformation Europe*. London, 1999.

Grell, Ole Peter, Andrew Cunningham, and Robert Jütte, eds. *Health Care and Poor Relief in 18th and 19th Century Northern Europe*. Aldershot, 2002.

Grell, Ole Peter, Andrew Cunningham, and Bernd Roeck, eds. *Health Care and Poor Relief in 18th and 19th Century Southern Europe*. Aldershot, 2005.

Hannaway, Caroline. "Veterinary Medicine and Rural Health Care in Pre-Revolutionary France." *Bulletin of the History of Medicine* 51 (1977): 431–47.

Heller, Robert. "'Priest-Doctors' as a Rural Health Service in the Age of Enlightenment." *Medical History* 19 (1975): 361–83.

Henderson, John. *Piety and Charity in Late Medieval Florence*. Oxford, 1994.

Jones, Colin and Jonathan Barry, eds. *Medicine and Charity before the Welfare State*. London, 1991.

Jütte, Robert. *Poverty and Deviance in Early Modern Europe*. Cambridge, 1994.

Martz, Linda. *Poverty and Welfare in Habsburg Spain: The Example of Toledo*. Cambridge, 1983.

Nutton, Vivian, ed. *Medicine in the Renaissance City*. Special Issue of *Renaissance Studies: Journal of the Society for Renaissance Studies*, 15, no. 2 (2001). Oxford, 2001.

Porter, Roy. *Mind-Forg'd Manacles: A History of Madness in England from the Restoration to the Regency*. Cambridge, Mass., 1987.

Riley, James C. *The Eighteenth-Century Campaign to Avoid Disease*. New York, 1987.

Rosen, George. *From Medical Police to Social Medicine: Essays on the History of Health Care*. New York, 1974.

Rusnock, Andrea. *Vital Accounts: Quantifying Health and Population in Eighteenth-Century England and France*. Cambridge, 2002.

Russell, Andrew, ed. *The Town and State Physician in Europe from the Middle Ages to the Enlightenment*. Wolfenbüttel, 1981.

Weiner, Dora. *The Citizen–Patient in Revolutionary and Imperial Paris*. Baltimore, 1993.

Wilkinson, Lise. *Animals and Disease: An Introduction to the History of Comparative Medicine*. Cambridge, 1992.

7 HEALING

Beier, Lucinda McCray. *Sufferers and Healers: The Experience of Illness in Seventeenth-Century England*. London, 1987.

Broomhill, Susan. *Women's Medical Work in Early Modern France*. Manchester, 2004.

Cook, Harold J. *Matters of Exchange: Commerce, Medicine, and Science in the Dutch Golden Age*. New Haven, Conn., 2007.

Evenden, Doreen. *The Midwives of Seventeenth-Century London*. Cambridge, 2000.

Gentilcore, David. *Healers and Healing in Early Modern Italy*. Manchester, 1998. *Medical Charlatanism in Early Modern Italy*. Oxford, 2006.

Gowing, Laura. *Common Bodies: Women, Touch and Power in Seventeenth-Century England*. New Haven, Conn., 2003.

Jones, Colin. "Pulling Teeth in Eighteenth-Century Paris." *Past and Present* 166 (2000): 100–45.

King, Roger. *The Making of the "Dentiste," c.1650–1760*. Aldershot, 1998.

Lemay, Edna H. "Thomas Hérrier: A Country Surgeon Outside Angoulême at the End of the Eighteenth Century." *Journal of Social History* 10 (1976/77): 524–37.

Lindemann, Mary. *Health and Healing in Eighteenth-Century Germany*. Baltimore, 1996.

Loudon, Irvine. *Medical Care and the General Practitioner, 1750–1850*. Oxford, 1986.

Marland, Hilary and Margaret Pelling, eds. *The Task of Healing: Medicine, Religion and Gender in England and the Netherlands, 1450–1800*. Rotterdam, 1996.

Nagy, Doreen Evenden. *Popular Medicine in Seventeenth-Century England*. Bowling Green, Ohio, 1988.

Numbers, Ronald L. and Darrel W. Amundsen, eds. *Caring and Curing: Health and Medicine in the Western Religious Tradition*. New York, 1986.

Ortiz de Montellano, Bernard. *Aztec Medicine, Health and Nutrition*. New Brunswick, 1990.

Pelling, Margaret. "Medical Practice in Early Modern England: Trade or Profession?" In *The Professions in Early Modern England*. Ed. Wilfrid Prest, 90–128. London, 1993.

Perkins, Wendy. *Midwifery and Medicine in Early Modern France: Louise Bourgeois*. Exeter, 1996.

Pollock, Linda A. *With Faith and Physic: The Life of a Tudor Gentlewoman, Lady Grace Mildmay*. London, 1993.

Pomata, Gianna. *Contracting a Cure: Patients, Healers, and the Law in Early Modern Bologna*. Baltimore, 1998.

Porter, Dorothy and Roy Porter. *Patient's Progress: Doctors and Doctoring in Eighteenth-Century England*. Stanford, Calif., 1989.

Porter, Roy, ed. *Patients and Practitioners: Lay Perceptions of Medicine in Pre-Industrial Society*. Cambridge, 1985.

Ramsey, Matthew. *Professional and Popular Medicine in France, 1770–1830: The Social World of Medical Practice*. Cambridge, 1988.

Savitt, Todd. *Medicine and Slavery: The Diseases and Health Care of Blacks in Antebellum Virginia*. Urbana, Ill., 1978.

Schiebinger, Londa. *Plants and Empire: Colonial Bioprospecting in the Atlantic World*. Cambridge, Mass., 2004.

Schiebinger, Londa and Claudia Swan, eds. *Colonial Botany: Science, Commerce, and Politics in the Early Modern World*. Philadelphia, 2005.

Sheridan, Richard B. *Doctors and Slaves, a Medical and Demographic History of Slavery in the British West Indies, 1680–1834.* Cambridge, 1985.

Walker, Timothy. *Doctors, Folk Medicine, and the Inquisition: The Repression of Magical Healing in Portugal during the Enlightenment.* Leiden, 2005.

Weaver, Karol K. *Medical Revolutionaries: The Enslaved Healers of Eighteenth-Century Saint Domingue.* Urbana and Chicago, 2006.

Wilson, Renate. *Pious Traders in Medicine: A German Pharmaceutical Network in Eighteenth-Century North America.* University Park, Pa., 2000.

Index

NEW APPROACHES TO EUROPEAN HISTORY